Better Homes and Gardens®

BIGGEST BOOK OF

30 MINUTE MEALS

Meredith® Books
Des Moines, Iowa

BIGGEST BOOK OF 30-MINUTE MEALS
Editor: Tricia Laning
Project Editor and Indexer: Spectrum Communication Services, Inc.
Writer: Cynthia Pearson
Contributing Designer: Joyce DeWitt
Cover Designer: Daniel Pelavin
Copy Chief: Terri Fredrickson
Publishing Operations Manager: Karen Schirm
Edit and Design Production Coordinator: Mary Lee Gavin
Editorial Assistant: Cheryl Eckert
Book Production Managers: Pam Kvitne, Marjorie J. Schenkelberg, Rick von Holdt, Mark Weaver
Contributing Copy Editor: Carol DeMasters
Contributing Proofreaders: Jane Carlson, Callie Dunbar, Karen Fraley
Test Kitchen Director: Lynn Blanchard
Test Kitchen Product Supervisor: Marilyn Cornelius
Test Kitchen Home Economists: Marilyn Cornelius; Juliana Hale, Laura Harms, R.D.; Jennifer Kalinowski, R.D.; Maryellyn Krantz;
   Jill Moberly, Dianna Nolin; Colleen Weeden; Lori Wilson; Charles Worthington

Meredith Books
Executive Director, Editorial: Gregory H. Kayko
Executive Director, Design: Matt Strelecki
Senior Editor/Group Manager: Jan Miller
Marketing Product Manager: Gina Rickert

Publisher and Editor in Chief: James D. Blume
Editorial Director: Linda Raglan Cunningham
Executive Director, Marketing: Jeffrey B. Myers
Executive Director, New Business Development: Todd M. Davis
Executive Director, Sales: Ken Zagor
Director, Operations: George A. Susral
Director, Production: Douglas M. Johnston
Business Director: Jim Leonard

Vice President and General Manager: Douglas J. Guendel

Better Homes and Gardens Magazine
Editor in Chief: Karol DeWulf Nickell
Deputy Editor, Food and Entertaining: Nancy Hopkins

Meredith Publishing Group
President: Jack Griffin
Executive Vice President: Bob Mate

Meredith Corporation
Chairman and Chief Executive Officer: William T. Kerr
President and Chief Operating Officer: Stephen M. Lacy

In Memoriam: E. T. Meredith III (1933-2003)

Our Better Homes and Gardens® Test Kitchen seal on the back cover of this book assures you that every recipe in *Biggest Book of 30-Minute Meals* has been tested in the Better Homes and Gardens® Test Kitchen. This means that each recipe is practical and reliable, and meets our high standards of taste appeal. We guarantee your satisfaction with this book for as long as you own it.

TABLE OF CONTENTS

INTRODUCTION

Speed matters. When time is short, you've got your priorities. It's more important to spend time at the table, or with family and friends, than fussing over meal preparation. With the *Biggest Book of 30-Minute Meals* at hand, you can enjoy a delicious meal prepared at home—quickly. Start to finish—30 minutes to an entrée, side dish, or dessert for your family. The recipes and timesaving techniques are tested in the Better Homes and Gardens® Test Kitchen so you know they'll work. And every recipe in the entrée pages has a menu suggestion for a quick and easy side dish and dessert, making the whole planning process even speedier.

Of course meals at home are important. Part food, part ritual, enjoying a good meal in your own home is a little piece of heaven. It's not just the food; it's the anticipation, the aromas, and the joy of being on your own for a few minutes of comfort, calm, and revival.

And if you would like to have friends over more often, but don't have the time to prepare, take a look at the Party Foods chapter. There are fabulous 30-minute (or less) recipes that will have you taking advantage of convenient shortcuts and quick-cooking ingredients.

Good food is good food! And whether you've slaved over a hot stove all afternoon or turned out mouthwatering goodness in half an hour, it's you who has had the savvy to do it, and well.

Let's get started!

> **SET THE TABLE BEFORE YOU LEAVE HOME IN THE MORNING, OR HAVE A FAMILY MEMBER DO IT. SEEING A SET TABLE WHEN YOU COME HOME AND KNOWING DINNER IS JUST 30 MINUTES OR LESS AWAY IS A WELCOME THOUGHT.**

MASTER YOUR LISTS

Part of getting a meal on the table quickly is always having what you need. Use your computer to make a master shopping list, including blank lines on which to add specialty ingredients.

• Keep shopping list copies in the kitchen and stash some in your car to help spur your memory when stopping for groceries on the way home.

• Arrange the shopping list by department or by your favorite store's layout.

• Carry copies of your favorite quick recipes with you (in your purse, PDA, or glove compartment) so you can pick up ingredients on a whim.

Shopping Savvy

• Stick with "your" grocery store. Whether you routinely shop at one or two, knowing where to find what you're after speeds the effort.

• No time to shop? Find a shopping and delivery service to bring groceries to your door. Check the phone book and Internet to find services—with many, you can order online. Your grocery store may even offer such services.

HELPFUL TIP

Turn over shopping tasks to a teenager. It's a great way for the teen to contribute to the family and develop shopping skills.

STOCK YOUR PANTRY, REFRIGERATOR, AND FREEZER

Use this list as a starter, adding or deleting items to suit your needs and preferences. Getting a feel for how fast you and your family consume various items also will help you keep your kitchen stocked.

Produce, Fruit
Tip: Slice fruits to serve with a meal, then for best appearance, toss apple or pear slices with a little lemon or lime juice diluted with water so the slices won't turn brown.
• Apples and pears
• Berries
• Grapes
• Lemons and limes
  (fresh or bottled juice)
• Oranges and grapefruit
• Peaches and Plums
• Pineapple

Produce, Vegetables
Tip: Steam fresh vegetables and serve them with a squeeze of lemon and pat of butter.
• Asparagus
• Beans
• Broccoli
• Carrots
• Cauliflower

EMBRACE CONVENIENCE

Who's not short on time? Convenience foods once had a reputation for being inferior, but grocers and food marketers eager to keep customers happy are responding with an increasing number of high-quality convenience products. Pricing is good too, especially when you consider the alternatives— dining out, food that has gone bad, and nutritious food groups missed altogether. Listed below are a number of timesaving food options; more appear every day. Invest a few minutes roaming the grocery store to find time-savers that you can use.
• Chopped fresh fruits
• Chopped fresh veggies
• Deli-prepared potatoes, macaroni and cheese, and side-salads
• Frozen meals including ethnic and vegetarian options
• Frozen meal kits ready for the slow cooker
• Frozen meal starters for a quick stir-fry
• Frozen prepared desserts —remove a few portions to thaw during dinner
• Marinated meat and poultry
• Torn salad greens

- Garlic *(fresh or bottled minced)*
- Ginger *(fresh or bottled minced)*
- Onions
- Peas
- Potatoes *(white or sweet)*
- Salad greens
- Zucchini or summer squash

Meat Department

Tip: Ask your butcher to lend a hand. Most are more than happy to remove skin from fish, or rewrap your meat, fish, and poultry purchases in the portion sizes that you need most.

Tip: While you're chatting with the butcher, ask for suggestions on quick, tasty ways to prepare your purchases. The store staff often knows quick prep methods and is happy to share.
- Chicken breasts
- Deli meats
- Ground meat *(beef, pork, or turkey, bulk or patties)*
- Hot dogs
- Meat cut for stir-fries
- Pork chops
- Salmon
- Shrimp *(cooked and peeled)*
- Tenderloins *(beef or pork)*
- Tuna steaks

Dairy
- Butter and/or margarine
- Cheeses *(chunk, sliced, or grated)*
- Eggs
- Half-and-half
- Milk
- Sour cream and yogurt

Bread, Baked Goods
- Bagels
- Bread
- English muffins
- Tortillas *(corn or flour, plain or flavored)*

Refrigerator & Freezer Case
- Frozen fruit *(berries, peaches, or rhubarb)*

- Pasta
- Piecrust *(ready to bake)*
- Pizza shells *(prebaked)*
- Vegetables

Shelf & Canned Goods
- Beans *(dried or canned)*
- Biscuit mixes
- Bouillon cubes and/or base *(beef or chicken)*
- Bread crumbs
- Broth *(chicken, beef, or vegetable)*
- Brownie or cake mixes
- Chiles
- Corn bread mix
- Couscous
- Flour
- Honey
- Mushrooms *(canned or dried)*
- Nuts *(almonds, pecans, walnuts, peanuts, or other nuts)*
- Pasta, dried *(various shapes)*
- Refried beans
- Rice *(white, brown, or wild)*
- Roasted red peppers
- Soups
- Sugar *(granulated, brown)*
- Tomatoes *(whole, diced, or stewed)*
- Tomato paste
- Tomato sauce
- Tuna *(canned or pouches, plain or seasoned)*
- Vegetables *(various kinds)*
- Water chestnuts

Oils, Condiments, & Seasonings
- Barbecue sauce
- Herbs and spices
- Horseradish
- Hot sauce
- Ketchup
- Mustard *(yellow, brown, Dijon-style, or specialty)*
- Oil *(vegetable, olive, sesame, or specialty)*
- Olives
- Pickles
- Salad dressings, bottled
- Salsa

- Seasoning blends *(Italian, taco, Cajun, lemon-pepper, or specialty)*
- Soy sauce
- Vinegar *(cider, white, wine, rice, or specialty)*
- Worcestershire sauce

IN THE KITCHEN
Your Supplies
A well-stocked kitchen serves any cook well. Take inventory of your supplies and shop sales at local discount and department stores, or online.

- Aluminum foil *(standard and heavy duty)*—line pans with foil to speed cleanup
- Bowls *(multisize sets)*
- Brown lunch bags for ripening pears and stone fruits
- Colander
- Cutting boards *(polyethylene or wood—for safety sake, reserve one exclusively for use with raw meat or poultry)*
- Grater/shredder
- Food thermometer
- Hot pads/trivets—flexible silicone varieties double as hot pads and nonskid trivets
- Kitchen shears
- Knives *(chef, paring, and serrated)*
- Liquid measuring cups *(large and small sizes)*
- Measuring cups sets
- Measuring spoon sets
- Mixing spoons
- Nonstick cooking spray
- Plastic wrap
- Refrigerator and freezer containers *(various sizes)*
- Spatulas
- Tape and markers for labeling leftovers
- Vegetable peeler
- Vegetable steamer—keep it in a saucepan on the stovetop ready to go
- Waxed paper
- Wooden spoons
- Zester for cutting citrus peels

APPLIANCE AND EQUIPMENT POINTERS

• Follow the will-it-make-a-difference rule: Are you thinking that buying washed and cut fresh vegetables is an indulgence? It's not, if having to wash and cut them yourself means that you'll skip them all together. Do you need a food processor? Not if the cleanup keeps you from using it, and you're buying prepped veggies anyway. And is that countertop grill an indulgence? If it's saving you from purchasing pricey, less healthful meals out, it's a bargain! Remember, Grandma might have loved to use these options had she the choice.

• Follow the golden dishwasher/sink rule: If you're buying a new piece of kitchen equipment, make sure that it's dishwasher safe and will fit in your machine. Similarly, if the item won't fit in your sink, skip it. You'll keep cleanup a cinch with this guideline.

• An increasing number of countertop appliances and tools are being produced with parts that are dishwasher-safe. Slow cookers, electric skillets, and grilling machines are among them. These can be great timesavers.

• Beware of oversize baking sheets and platters. Though they often hold a few more cookies or steaks, they often don't fit easily in the dishwasher or sink.

CLEAR THE CLUTTER, DOUBLE UP

Don't waste any more time rummaging through the utensil drawer looking for tongs or wrestling a pan from the tangles of a lower cupboard. Get a few transparent tubs in small, medium, and large sizes and go through your cupboards and drawers. Remove everything that you don't use often. Be ruthless. Now, send those tubs to the basement or attic—get rid of the stuff if you want to or store it for later. The point is to get it out of your way.

   Now that you can see the stuff you use, decide if you need more of what you have. No kidding. Having doubles or more of your most frequently used tools—cutting boards, liquid measures, and favorite-size saucepans—will speed your way through meal prep and cleanup.

PLUG IN!

While some electric countertop appliances are used a few times and then resigned to clutter the cupboard, others are reached for time and again, earning their keep while speeding and simplifying meal prep. The trick lies in knowing your personal preferences. Also, within each appliance type you'll find models that are compact, easy to slip in the dishwasher, and store— and others that don't have any of those qualities. Choose wisely. These appliances rate consideration but you be the final judge of whether each one will work for you:

Slow cookers do meal prep while you're away. They also can stand unattended on buffet tables for parties.

Grilling machines let you prepare meat, poultry, and seafood quickly and simply.

Electric skillets add stovetop capacity and make fast work of whipping up a meal for the gang.

Food chopper/processors shred cheese and chop veggies quickly.

Hand blenders are favored by many for pureeing soups, mashing potatoes, and preparing beverages.

IF YOU CAN, BUY A GOOD SINK & FAUCET

Meal prep and cleanup are a breeze when you're in sync with your sink—you probably won't even notice how well it serves you. But if you've ever been drenched trying to wash a big pot in a too-small sink, you understand. Low-profile faucets can make sink work awkward too. So when it's time to replace a sink or faucet—or if you're buying a new home—opt for a sink style with a small prep sink (fitted with a garbage disposal) on one side and an oversize deep bowl on the other. Also, choose a tall gooseneck-style faucet that won't get in your way as you wash large items or lift them from the sink.

WHEN TIME'S IS OF THE ESSENCE SETUP MATTERS

• Empty the dishwasher before beginning meal preparation so it's ready to fill as you work.

• Store dishes near the dishwasher for fast, easy unloading. Put them on lower shelves so a youngster can handle the task.

• Get a good-looking swing-top or foot-operated pop-top trash can in a size bigger than you think you need. A too-small trash can that is stowed behind a door fills too quickly and gets marred with spills—as do doors and door pulls nearby.

• Store pots, pans, cutting boards, and utensils within easy reach of where you cook.

• Keep hand towels and paper towels near every location in the kitchen where you'll use them.

• Stash frequently used seasonings and oils near the counter where you use them.

NOW YOU'RE COOKING! AND QUICKLY . . .

When time's short, try these quick meal ideas:

• Cut up leftover chicken, beef, pork, or seafood from last night's dinner and sprinkle it on cheese-topped tortillas to make quesadillas for tonight's meal. If you like, add chopped olives, roasted red peppers, and/or chili seasoning.

• Making French toast? Slice strawberries, peaches, or bananas and sear them in a hot skillet to serve as a juicy accompaniment.

• Leftover French toast? Cool the extra slices and slip them into zipper bags to stash in the fridge. Reheat for quick weekday breakfasts.

• Make breakfast for dinner. Scramble eggs or make an omelet. If you like, heat slices of ham or sausage links. They're quick and tasty. Add toast and fruit salad.

• Make a quiche—or two. Slices reheat quickly in the microwave and make a delicious meal with a salad or fruit.

• Stretch leftover chili or stew by ladling hot leftovers over quick-cooking couscous, baked potatoes, or corn bread.

• When you're relying on leftovers for the main dish, have dessert! Make it or buy it, but let the focus fall to this guilty pleasure.

• Stock the fridge with sandwich makings. Then use them for a meal. Make it fun and encourage creative sandwich-making. Serve a soup or dessert to round out the menu.

• Impromptu guests? Thaw some frozen raspberries to sprinkle over lemon sherbet or pool alongside a bakery brownie drizzled with chocolate sauce.

SIMPLE ACCOMPANIMENTS ARE SMART, QUICK

You'll eat better meals when you complement your quick entrées with straightforward accompaniments. Choose them to complement the flavor of your main dish. Think texture too. For appeal, foods should vary in shape and form.

Balance opposites:
Hot—Cool (temperature and seasoning)
Crunchy—Soft
Salty—Sweet
Complex—Mellow

Go-with ideas:
Apples or pears
Beans
Cheese and crackers
Chewy bread
  (sourdough, whole wheat, or specialty)
Corn bread
Cottage cheese topped with fresh sliced
  strawberries, raspberries, or blueberries
Couscous
Hard-cooked egg slices
Heat-and-eat side dishes from a supermarket
  deli counter
Melon wedges
Olives
Orange or grapefruit sections
Pasta
Peaches, plums, or nectarines
Pineapple slices
Potatoes *(whole or half, they're a quick bake
  in the microwave)*
Rice
Salads from a supermarket deli counter
  or salad bar
Steamed or grilled vegetables
Torn mixed greens tossed with bottled
  salad dressing
Vegetable dippers with purchased dip
Yogurt

MEAT

7

The onion marmalade adds a wonderful extra layer of flavor and richness to this satisfying and hearty dish.

STEAK WITH SAUTÉED ONIONS

START TO FINISH:

25 minutes

MAKES:

6 servings

MENU IDEA:

Cheese-Garlic Crescents *(see p. 328)*

Purchased New York-style cheesecake topped with sliced fresh fruit

6	beef tenderloin steaks, cut 1 inch thick (about 1½ pounds total)
¼	teaspoon salt
¼	teaspoon black pepper
2	tablespoons butter or margarine
1	small red onion, cut into 6 wedges
1	teaspoon bottled minced garlic (2 cloves)
1	teaspoon dried basil, crushed
½	teaspoon dried oregano, crushed
2	tablespoons whipping cream
6	tablespoons onion marmalade or orange marmalade

1 Sprinkle meat with salt and pepper; set aside. In a large skillet melt butter over medium heat. Add red onion and garlic. Cook and stir for 6 to 8 minutes or until onion is tender. Remove onion from skillet.

2 Increase heat to medium-high. Add steaks to skillet; cook to desired doneness, turning once. (Allow 10 to 13 minutes for medium-rare [145°F] to medium doneness [160°F].) After turning, sprinkle meat with basil and oregano.

3 Remove meat from skillet; place on serving platter. Return onion to skillet; heat through. Remove onions from skillet. Remove skillet from heat. Stir in whipping cream. Spoon cream over steaks. Top steaks with marmalade; divide cooked onion wedges among steaks.

Nutrition Facts per serving: 271 cal., 13 g total fat (6 g sat. fat), 73 mg chol., 110 mg sodium, 14 g carbo., 0 g fiber, 24 g pro.

Don't wait for company to try this recipe! These tender steaks with mushroom-wine sauce are incredibly quick to make and are great for everyday eating or special occasions.

COMPANY-STYLE STEAKS

4   beef tenderloin steaks (about 1 pound total) or 1 pound beef top sirloin, cut ¾ inch thick

1   tablespoon Dijon-style mustard or coarse-grain brown mustard

2   tablespoons olive oil

3   cups sliced fresh mushrooms

⅓   cup dry red wine, sherry, or beef or chicken broth

1   tablespoon Worcestershire sauce for chicken

2   teaspoons snipped fresh thyme

½   cup beef broth

1   teaspoon cornstarch

1 If using top sirloin, cut meat into 4 pieces. Spread mustard evenly over steaks. In a large skillet heat 1 tablespoon of the oil over medium heat. Add steaks; cook until desired doneness, turning once. (Allow 7 to 9 minutes for medium-rare [145°F] to medium doneness [160°F].) Transfer steaks to a serving platter. Keep warm.

2 Add remaining 1 tablespoon oil to skillet drippings. Add mushrooms; cook and stir for 4 minutes. Stir in wine or broth, Worcestershire sauce, and thyme. Simmer, uncovered, for 3 minutes. Combine the ½ cup broth and cornstarch. Stir into mushroom mixture. Cook and stir until thickened and bubbly. Cook and stir for 2 minutes more. Spoon over steaks.

Nutrition Facts per serving: 263 cal., 14 g total fat (4 g sat. fat), 64 mg chol., 176 mg sodium, 5 g carbo., 1 g fiber, 23 g pro.

START TO FINISH:

25 minutes

MAKES:

4 servings

MENU IDEA:

Spinach, Red Onion & Cherry Tomato Salad *(see p. 307)*

Vanilla ice cream topped with crushed purchased shortbread cookies and toasted chopped pecans

The ingredient list may be short but these steaks are long on flavor.

STEAKS WITH HORSERADISH-CREAM SAUCE

START TO FINISH:

20 minutes

MAKES:

2 to 4 servings

MENU IDEA:

Steamed broccoli
tossed with butter and
lemon-pepper

**Crunchy Pound
Cake Slices**
(see p. 343)

1	tablespoon olive oil
2	beef tenderloin steaks, cut 1½ inches thick (about 1 pound total)
	Salt
	Freshly ground black pepper
½	cup whipping cream
3	tablespoons horseradish mustard
	Cracked black pepper

1 In a large skillet heat oil over medium heat. Sprinkle both sides of each steak with salt and freshly ground pepper; add to hot skillet. Cook about 4 minutes or until browned, turning once. Transfer to a 2-quart square baking dish. Bake the steaks in a 400°F oven, uncovered, for 10 to 13 minutes or until medium-rare doneness (145°F).

2 Meanwhile, in a medium bowl beat whipping cream with an electric mixer on low speed until soft peaks form. Fold in horseradish mustard.

3 To serve, place steaks on warm dinner plates; spoon whipped cream mixture over steaks. Sprinkle with cracked pepper.

Nutrition Facts per serving: 641 cal., 47 g total fat (21 g sat. fat), 221 mg chol., 620 mg sodium, 4 g carbo., 0 g fiber, 50 g pro.

Blue cheese and walnuts are a classic taste combination that goes perfectly with beef.

BEEF TENDERLOIN WITH BLUE CHEESE & WALNUTS

4	beef tenderloin steaks, cut 1 inch thick (about 1 pound total)
½	teaspoon garlic salt
	Nonstick cooking spray
⅓	cup dairy sour cream
3	tablespoons crumbled blue cheese
3	tablespoons chopped walnuts, toasted

1 Sprinkle steaks with garlic salt. Lightly coat an unheated large skillet with cooking spray. Preheat skillet over medium-high heat. Add steaks. Reduce heat to medium. Cook until desired doneness, turning once. (Allow 10 to 13 minutes for medium-rare [145°F] to medium doneness [160°F].) Transfer steaks to a serving platter.

2 Meanwhile, in a small bowl stir together sour cream and blue cheese. Spoon mixture on top of steaks. Sprinkle with walnuts.

Nutrition Facts per serving: 264 cal., 17 g total fat (6 g sat. fat), 81 mg chol., 255 mg sodium, 2 g carbo., 0 g fiber, 26 g pro.

START TO FINISH:
20 minutes
MAKES:
4 servings

MENU IDEA:
Royal Purple Mashed Potatoes
(see p. 270)

Raspberry or pineapple sorbet served with fresh raspberries

Succulent beef tenderloin steak is the perfect partner for this elegant mushroom cream sauce.

STEAK & MUSHROOMS

START TO FINISH:

20 minutes

MAKES:

4 servings

MENU IDEA:

Seeded Dinner Rolls
(see p. 330)

Mango sorbet served
with sliced pineapple
and kiwi fruit

4   beef tenderloin steaks, cut 1 inch thick (about 1 pound total)

1   tablespoon olive oil

8   ounces fresh crimini, shiitake, baby portobello, and/or button mushrooms, sliced

¼   cup seasoned beef broth

¼   cup whipping cream

1 In a large skillet cook steaks in hot oil over medium heat until desired doneness, turning once. (Allow 7 to 9 minutes for medium-rare doneness [145°F] or 10 to 13 minutes for medium doneness [160°F].) Transfer steaks to a serving platter; keep warm.

2 In the same skillet cook and stir mushrooms for 4 to 5 minutes or until tender. Stir in broth and cream. Cook and stir over medium heat about 2 minutes or until slightly thickened. Spoon mushroom mixture over steaks.

Nutrition Facts per serving: 271 cal., 18 g total fat (7 g sat. fat), 90 mg chol., 116 mg sodium, 2 g carbo., 0 g fiber, 26 g pro.

Broiling the onions will bring out their delicious sweetness. If the capers are too pungent for your taste, simply leave them out.

STEAK WITH CREAMY ONION SAUCE

1   medium sweet onion (such as Vidalia, Maui, or Walla Walla), thinly sliced

4   beef ribeye steaks, cut 1 inch thick (about 1½ pounds total)

1   tablespoon Mediterranean seasoning blend or lemon-pepper seasoning

1   8-ounce carton dairy sour cream

2   tablespoons drained capers

1 Place onion slices on the rack of an unheated broiler pan. Broil 3 to 4 inches from heat for 5 minutes; turn onion slices. Meanwhile, sprinkle steaks with 1½ teaspoons of the seasoning blend. Place steaks on the broiler pan rack with onion slices. Broil steaks and onion slices about 5 minutes more or until onion slices are browned. Remove onion slices to a cutting board. Broil steaks until desired doneness, turning once. (Allow 7 to 9 minutes more for medium-rare doneness [145°F] or 10 to 13 minutes more for medium doneness [160°F].)

2 Meanwhile, for sauce, coarsely chop onion. In a small saucepan combine cooked onion, sour cream, capers, and remaining 1½ teaspoons seasoning blend. Cook over medium-low heat until heated through (do not boil). Transfer steaks to serving plates. Serve sauce with steaks.

Nutrition Facts per serving: 398 cal., 22 g total fat (11 g sat. fat), 106 mg chol., 472 mg sodium, 4 g carbo., 0 g fiber, 39 g pro.

PREP:
10 minutes

BROIL:
5 minutes + 5 minutes + 7 minutes

MAKES:
4 servings

MENU IDEA:

Spicy Pasta & Broccoli *(see p. 280)*

Fresh strawberries topped with whipped cream

Oh so simple to prepare but oh so satisfying. Sprinkle, sizzle, sauce—and supper is ready.
If you don't have chives on hand, use finely chopped green onions instead.

SIRLOIN STEAK WITH MUSTARD & CHIVES

PREP:
10 minutes

GRILL:
9 minutes

MAKES:
4 servings

4	boneless beef top sirloin or ribeye steaks, cut ¾ inch thick (about 1½ pounds total)
2	teaspoons garlic-pepper seasoning
½	cup dairy sour cream
2	tablespoons Dijon-style mustard
1	tablespoon snipped fresh chives

1 Sprinkle steaks with 1½ teaspoons of the seasoning. Place steaks on the rack of an uncovered grill directly over medium heat. Grill until desired doneness, turning once. (Allow 9 to 11 minutes for medium-rare doneness [145°F] or 11 to 13 minutes for medium doneness [160°F].) Transfer steaks to a serving platter.

2 Meanwhile, in a small bowl combine sour cream, mustard, chives, and remaining ½ teaspoon seasoning. Spoon sour cream mixture on top of steaks.

Nutrition Facts per serving: 277 cal., 12 g total fat (5 g sat. fat), 114 mg chol., 619 mg sodium, 2 g carbo., 0 g fiber, 37 g pro.

MENU IDEA:

Purchased refrigerated mashed potatoes, cooked and mixed with sour cream and shredded cheddar cheese

Cherry Trifles
(see p. 344)

Your family will think you have been at the stove all day when you serve this main dish.

PEPPERY STEAK WITH BORDELAISE SAUCE

1¼   cups water

1   cup sliced fresh mushrooms

1   medium onion, finely chopped

1   0.75- to 1.2-ounce package brown gravy mix

¼   cup dry red wine

2   teaspoons garlic-pepper seasoning

4   beef ribeye, top sirloin, or tenderloin steaks,
     cut ¾ inch thick (about 1½ pounds total)

2   tablespoons olive oil

1 For sauce, in a medium saucepan bring the water to boiling. Add mushrooms and onion. Reduce heat. Cover and cook for 3 minutes. Stir in dry gravy mix; stir in red wine. Cook about 3 minutes or until thickened, stirring occasionally. Cover; keep warm.

2 Sprinkle garlic-pepper seasoning evenly over steaks; rub in with your fingers. In a large heavy skillet heat oil over medium-high heat. Add steaks. Reduce heat to medium; cook until desired doneness, turning once. (Allow 7 to 12 minutes for medium-rare [145°F] to medium doneness [160°F].)

3 Serve steaks with the sauce on warmed plates.

Nutrition Facts per serving: 366 cal., 18 g total fat (5 g sat. fat), 81 mg chol., 954 mg sodium, 7 g carbo., 1 g fiber, 39 g pro.

START TO FINISH:
25 minutes
MAKES:
4 servings

MENU IDEA:

Fruit & Nut Couscous *(see p. 290)*

Purchased carrot cake topped with toasted chopped walnuts

This lively combination of curry and apple jelly creates an aromatic and enticing sauce for beef.

CURRIED BEEF WITH APPLE COUSCOUS

START TO FINISH:

30 minutes

MAKES:

4 servings

MENU IDEA:

Sesame Zucchini
(see p. 276)

Purchased brownies
drizzled with hot fudge
sauce and sprinkled
with chopped peanuts

10	ounces beef top sirloin steak, cut 1 inch thick
	Salt
	Black pepper
1	tablespoon apple jelly
$\frac{1}{2}$	teaspoon curry powder
1	teaspoon cooking oil
2	medium tart green apples, chopped
1	medium red and/or green sweet pepper, cut into thin strips
1	medium onion, coarsely chopped
1	tablespoon curry powder
2	cups apple juice, apple cider, or water
1	tablespoon instant beef bouillon granules
1	10-ounce package quick-cooking couscous
$\frac{1}{3}$	cup chopped peanuts

1 Lightly sprinkle meat with salt and black pepper. For glaze, in a small saucepan combine apple jelly and the $\frac{1}{2}$ teaspoon curry powder. Cook and stir over medium heat until jelly is melted. (Or microwave in a microwave-safe bowl on 100% power [high] about 30 seconds.) Set aside.

2 Place meat on the unheated rack of a broiler pan. Broil 3 to 4 inches from the heat until desired doneness, turning once and brushing occasionally with glaze during the last 2 to 3 minutes of broiling. (Allow 15 to 17 minutes for medium-rare doneness [145°F] or 20 to 22 minutes for medium doneness [160°F].)

3 Meanwhile, in a large skillet heat oil over medium heat. Add apples, sweet pepper, and onion; cook for 5 minutes. Stir in the 1 tablespoon curry powder. Cook and stir for 1 minute. Add apple juice and bouillon granules. Bring to boiling. Stir in couscous; remove from heat. Cover and let stand about 5 minutes or until liquid is absorbed.

4 To serve, fluff couscous with a fork. Thinly slice meat across the grain. Serve meat on top of couscous. Sprinkle with peanuts.

Nutrition Facts per serving: 506 cal., 11 g total fat (2 g sat. fat), 43 mg chol., 818 mg sodium, 74 g carbo., 8 g fiber, 29 g pro.

For variety and a rich earthiness, try a mixture of button, crimini, shiitake, and portobello mushrooms. The alcohol in the red wine is cooked off leaving just the delightful flavor.

WINE-BALSAMIC GLAZED STEAK

2	teaspoons cooking oil
1	pound beef top loin or top sirloin steak, cut ½ to ¾ inch thick
1½	teaspoons bottled minced garlic (3 cloves)
⅛	teaspoon crushed red pepper
¾	cup dry red wine
2	cups sliced fresh mushrooms
3	tablespoons balsamic vinegar
2	tablespoons soy sauce
4	teaspoons honey
2	tablespoons butter or margarine

START TO FINISH:

30 minutes

MAKES:

4 servings

1 In a large skillet heat oil over medium-high heat. Add steak. (Do not add any liquid and do not cover skillet.) Reduce heat to medium. Cook for 10 to 13 minutes or until desired doneness, turning meat occasionally. If meat browns too quickly, reduce heat to medium-low. Transfer meat to platter; keep warm.

2 Add garlic and crushed red pepper to skillet; cook for 10 seconds. Remove skillet from heat. Carefully add wine. Return to heat. Boil, uncovered, about 5 minutes or until most of the liquid is evaporated. Add mushrooms, balsamic vinegar, soy sauce, and honey; return to simmer. Cook and stir about 4 minutes or until mushrooms are tender. Stir in butter until melted. Spoon over steak.

Nutrition Facts per serving: 377 cal., 21 g total fat (9 g sat. fat), 82 mg chol., 588 mg sodium, 12 g carbo., 0 g fiber, 27 g pro.

MENU IDEA:

Broken Pasta with Italian Parsley *(see p. 281)*

Purchased plain sugar cookies spread with canned cream cheese frosting and sprinkled with flaked coconut

Snipping or crushing the rosemary releases the oils that carry the spice's distinctive aroma and flavor.

SAUCY STRIP STEAK

PREP:

15 minutes

GRILL:

14 minutes

MAKES:

4 servings

$\frac{2}{3}$ cup orange marmalade

2 tablespoons butter or margarine

1 teaspoon snipped fresh rosemary or $\frac{1}{4}$ teaspoon dried rosemary, crushed

4 beef top loin steaks, cut 1 inch thick (about 2 pounds total)

   Salt

   Black pepper

1 In a small saucepan combine marmalade, butter, and rosemary. Cook and stir over low heat until butter is melted and mixture is heated through. Set aside.

2 Sprinkle steaks with salt and pepper. Place steaks on the rack of an uncovered grill directly over medium heat. Grill to desired doneness, turning once halfway through grilling and brushing with marmalade mixture during the last 5 minutes of grilling. (Allow 14 to 18 minutes for medium-rare doneness [145°F] or 18 to 22 minutes for medium doneness [160°F].) Transfer steaks to a serving platter. Spoon any remaining marmalade mixture over steaks.

BROILER METHOD: Sprinkle steaks with salt and pepper. Place steaks on unheated rack of a broiler pan. Broil 3 to 4 inches from heat to desired doneness, turning once halfway through broiling time and brushing with marmalade mixture during the last 5 minutes of broiling. (Allow 12 to 14 minutes for medium-rare doneness [145°F] or 15 to 18 minutes for medium doneness [160°F].) Transfer steaks to a serving platter. Spoon any remaining marmalade mixture over steaks.

Nutrition Facts per serving: 464 cal., 14 g total fat (7 g sat. fat), 123 mg chol., 357 mg sodium, 35 g carbo., 0 g fiber, 49 g pro.

MENU IDEA:

Pineapple Coleslaw
(see p. 308)

Chocolate ice cream topped with canned cherry pie filling and whipped cream

Here's a quick-prep method for this traditional old world recipe. It's also a great way to get anyone to eat broccoli. Topping it with the tempting stroganoff mixture will make it impossible to resist.

STROGANOFF-STYLE BEEF WITH BROCCOLI

3	cups dried wide noodles
3	cups fresh broccoli spears (12 ounces)
½	cup light dairy sour cream
1½	teaspoons prepared horseradish
½	teaspoon snipped fresh dill
1	pound beef ribeye steak, trimmed and cut into thin bite-size strips
1	small onion, cut into ½-inch slices
½	teaspoon bottled minced garlic (1 clove)
1	tablespoon cooking oil
4	teaspoons all-purpose flour
½	teaspoon black pepper
1	14-ounce can beef broth
3	tablespoons tomato paste
1	teaspoon Worcestershire sauce

START TO FINISH:

30 minutes

MAKES:

4 servings

MENU IDEA:

Steamed sugar snap peas tossed with butter and shredded orange peel

Quick Apple Crisp *(see p. 332)*

1 Cook noodles according to package directions, adding broccoli for the last 5 minutes of cooking; drain well. Return noodle mixture to pan; cover and keep warm.

2 Meanwhile, in a small serving bowl stir together sour cream, horseradish, and dill; cover and chill until serving time.

3 In a large skillet cook half of the beef, the onion, and garlic in hot oil until beef is desired doneness and onion is tender. Remove from skillet. Add remaining beef; cook and stir until beef is desired doneness. Return all of the meat mixture to the skillet; sprinkle flour and pepper over meat. Stir to coat.

4 Stir in broth, tomato paste, and Worcestershire sauce. Cook and stir until thickened and bubbly. Cook and stir for 1 minute more. Serve beef mixture on top of noodle mixture. Pass sour cream mixture.

Nutrition Facts per serving: 368 cal., 15 g total fat (5 g sat. fat), 81 mg chol., 454 mg sodium, 32 g carbo., 4 g fiber, 29 g pro.

Sautéing is a quick and low-fat way to get supper on the table in no time. To make it even faster, buy beef that is already thinly sliced and ready for stir-fries. Kids can help by snapping off the stem ends of the asparagus.

BEEF & ASPARAGUS SAUTÉ

START TO FINISH:

25 minutes

MAKES:

4 servings

MENU IDEA:

Sourdough bread
served with
honey butter

Mango Parfait
(double the recipe)
(see p. 365)

12	ounces fresh asparagus
2	teaspoons olive oil
1	pound beef sirloin or tenderloin steak, trimmed and cut into thin bite-size strips
	Salt
	Freshly ground black pepper
½	cup coarsely shredded carrot
1	teaspoon dried herbes de Provence, crushed
½	cup dry Marsala
¼	teaspoon grated lemon peel
	Hot cooked rice

1 Cut off and discard woody bases from asparagus. If desired, scrape off scales. Bias-slice asparagus into 2-inch-long pieces; rinse and drain well.

2 In a large nonstick skillet heat 1 teaspoon of the oil over medium-high heat. Add half of the beef to hot oil. Sprinkle with salt and pepper. Cook and stir for 3 minutes. Remove meat; keep warm. Repeat with remaining beef and remaining 1 teaspoon oil. Return all of the meat to the skillet. Add asparagus, carrot, and herbes de Provence; cook and stir for 2 minutes more. Add Marsala and lemon peel; reduce heat.

3 Cook for 3 to 5 minutes more or until beef is cooked through and asparagus is crisp-tender. Serve over hot cooked rice.

Nutrition Facts per serving: 327 cal., 7 g total fat (2 g sat. fat), 69 mg chol., 209 mg sodium, 29 g carbo., 2 g fiber, 28 g pro.

The tangy Buttermilk Dressing makes the perfect counterpoint to the rich flavor of the beef, vegetables, and greens.

STEAK SALAD WITH BUTTERMILK DRESSING

8   cups torn mixed salad greens

2   medium carrots, cut into thin bite-size strips

1   medium yellow sweet pepper, cut into thin bite-size strips

1   cup cherry tomatoes or pear-shape cherry tomatoes, halved
     Nonstick cooking spray

8   ounces beef top sirloin steak, trimmed and
     cut into thin bite-size strips

¼   cup finely shredded fresh basil
     Salt
     Black pepper

1   recipe Buttermilk Dressing

1 Divide salad greens, carrots, sweet pepper, and tomatoes among 4 dinner plates. Set aside.

2 Lightly coat an unheated large skillet with cooking spray. Preheat over medium-high heat. Add meat. Cook and stir for 2 to 3 minutes or until meat is slightly pink in the center. Remove from heat. Stir in basil. Lightly sprinkle with salt and black pepper to taste.

3 To serve, spoon the warm meat mixture over greens mixture. Drizzle with Buttermilk Dressing. Serve immediately.

BUTTERMILK DRESSING: In a small bowl combine ½ cup plain low-fat yogurt, ⅓ cup buttermilk, 3 tablespoons freshly grated Parmesan cheese, 3 tablespoons finely chopped red onion, 3 tablespoons light mayonnaise dressing or salad dressing, 2 tablespoons snipped fresh parsley, 1 tablespoon white wine vinegar or lemon juice, ½ teaspoon bottled minced garlic (1 clove), ¼ teaspoon salt, and ⅛ teaspoon black pepper. Cover and chill for at least 30 minutes or until ready to serve.

Nutrition Facts per serving: 226 cal., 10 g total fat (4 g sat. fat), 32 mg chol., 387 mg sodium, 17 g carbo., 4 g fiber, 19 g pro.

START TO FINISH:
30 minutes
MAKES:
4 servings

MENU IDEA:
Focaccia wedges

Fresh Strawberry Fool *(see p. 364)*

Frozen vegetable medleys are a boon to today's busy cook. Keep a variety on hand for quick stir-fries and meals-in-minutes like this zesty and colorful dish.

QUICK ITALIAN PEPPER STEAK

START TO FINISH:

25 minutes

MAKES:

4 or 5 servings

MENU IDEA:

Purchased garlic cheese bread loaf, baked

Cannoli *(see p. 356)*

1	9-ounce package refrigerated fettuccini
12	ounces beef top sirloin steak, trimmed and cut into thin bite-size strips
1/4	teaspoon crushed red pepper
2	tablespoons olive oil
1	16-ounce package frozen pepper stir-fry vegetables (yellow, green, and red sweet peppers and onion), thawed and well drained
2	tablespoons balsamic vinegar
1	15-ounce can chunky Italian-style tomato sauce
2	tablespoons pine nuts, toasted (optional)
	Crushed red pepper (optional)

1 Cook pasta according to package directions; drain well. Return pasta to pan; cover and keep warm.

2 Meanwhile, combine steak strips and the 1/4 teaspoon crushed red pepper; set aside.

3 In a large skillet heat 1 tablespoon of the oil over medium heat; add thawed vegetables. Stir-fry for 2 to 3 minutes or until crisp-tender. Carefully add balsamic vinegar; toss to coat. Remove from skillet. Cover and keep warm.

4 Heat remaining 1 tablespoon oil in the same skillet; add beef. Stir-fry for 2 to 3 minutes or until desired doneness. Stir in tomato sauce; heat through.

5 Toss beef mixture with pasta and vegetables. If desired, sprinkle with pine nuts and pass additional crushed red pepper. Serve immediately.

Nutrition Facts per serving: 415 cal., 11 g total fat (2 g sat. fat), 87 mg chol., 648 mg sodium, 50 g carbo., 6 g fiber, 28 g pro.

Fast enough for a weekday meal and fancy enough for casual company on weekends, this combination is sensational. Tarragon adds a touch of class but the bowtie pasta keeps it fun. If asparagus isn't available use broccoli florets or baby bok choy.

PASTA WITH BEEF & ASPARAGUS

1	pound fresh asparagus
8	ounces dried bowtie pasta
1	8-ounce carton dairy sour cream
2	tablespoons all-purpose flour
⅔	cup water
1	tablespoon honey
½	teaspoon salt
¼	teaspoon black pepper
1	teaspoon cooking oil
8	ounces beef top sirloin steak, trimmed and cut into thin bite-size strips
2	tablespoons finely chopped shallot
2	teaspoons snipped fresh tarragon

START TO FINISH:
30 minutes
MAKES:
4 servings

MENU IDEA:
Purchased soft breadsticks, served with butter and grated Parmesan cheese

Gooey Brownie Cups *(see p. 339)*

1 Cut off and discard woody bases from asparagus. If desired, scrape off scales. Bias-slice asparagus into 1-inch pieces; set aside. Cook pasta according to package directions, adding asparagus for the last 3 minutes of cooking; drain well. Return pasta mixture to pan; cover and keep warm.

2 In a medium bowl stir together sour cream and flour. Stir in the water, honey, salt, and pepper. Set aside.

3 In a large nonstick skillet heat oil over medium-high heat. Add meat and shallot; cook and stir about 5 minutes or until meat is brown. Drain off fat.

4 Stir sour cream mixture into meat mixture in skillet. Cook and stir until thickened and bubbly. Cook and stir for 1 minute more. Stir in drained pasta, asparagus, and tarragon. Heat through.

Nutrition Facts per serving: 462 cal., 17 g total fat (9 g sat. fat), 113 mg chol., 358 mg sodium, 53 g carbo., 3 g fiber, 24 g pro.

TEST KITCHEN TIP: For a lower-fat pasta, substitute light dairy sour cream for the regular sour cream.

Nutrition Facts per serving: 421 cal., 11 g total fat (4 g sat. fat), 107 mg chol., 373 mg sodium, 54 g carbo., 3 g fiber, 26 g pro.

A melding of Cajun and Asian influences translates into intense flavor in this quick-to-fix dish. Who needs take-out when you can do fusion at home?

BLACKENED BEEF STIR-FRY

START TO FINISH:

25 minutes

MAKES:

4 servings

MENU IDEA:

Frozen egg rolls, prepared according to package directions and served with bottled hoisin or plum sauce

Quick Strawberry Shortcakes *(see p. 337)*

12	ounces beef top sirloin steak or top round steak, trimmed and cut into thin bite-size strips
2¼	teaspoons blackened seasoning for beef
⅔	cup water
2	tablespoons tomato paste
2	teaspoons cornstarch
½	teaspoon instant beef bouillon granules
1	tablespoon cooking oil
1	16-ounce package frozen stir-fry vegetables (any combination)
	Hot cooked rice

1 Sprinkle steak strips with 2 teaspoons of the blackened seasoning; toss to coat well.

2 For sauce, in a small bowl stir together the water, tomato paste, cornstarch, beef bouillon granules, and remaining ¼ teaspoon blackened seasoning. Set aside.

3 In a wok or large skillet heat oil over medium-high heat. (Add more oil as necessary during cooking.) Add stir-fry vegetables. Stir-fry for 2 to 3 minutes or until crisp-tender. Remove vegetables from wok. Add beef strips to hot wok. Cook and stir for 2 to 3 minutes or until desired doneness.

4 Push meat from center of wok. Stir sauce; add to center of wok. Cook and stir until thickened and bubbly. Return vegetables to wok. Stir to coat all ingredients with sauce. Heat through. Serve over rice.

Nutrition Facts per serving: 342 cal., 7 g total fat (2 g sat. fat), 40 mg chol., 367 mg sodium, 43 g carbo., 3 g fiber, 25 g pro.

Prepared pasta sauce is one of the most versatile ingredients to keep in stock in the pantry. Here it adds color and a hearty tang to the dish.

GREEK BEEF & PASTA SKILLET

8	ounces dried rotini pasta
12	ounces beef top sirloin steak or top round steak, trimmed and cut into thin bite-size strips
1	tablespoon cooking oil
1	26-ounce jar ripe olive and mushroom pasta sauce, ripe olive and green olive pasta sauce, or marinara pasta sauce
1/4	teaspoon salt
1/4	teaspoon ground cinnamon
1/2	of a 10-ounce package frozen chopped spinach, thawed and well drained
1/3	cup crumbled feta cheese

1 Cook pasta according to package directions; drain well. Return pasta to pan; cover and keep warm.

2 Meanwhile, in a large skillet cook and stir beef in hot oil for 2 to 3 minutes or until desired doneness. Add pasta sauce, salt, and cinnamon. Cook and stir until sauce is bubbly. Add cooked pasta and spinach. Cook and stir until heated through. Sprinkle individual servings with feta cheese.

Nutrition Facts per serving: 483 cal., 12 g total fat (3 g sat. fat), 63 mg chol., 1,063 mg sodium, 60 g carbo., 6 g fiber, 32 g pro.

START TO FINISH:
25 minutes

MAKES:
4 servings

MENU IDEA:

Pita bread, cut into wedges, brushed with olive oil, sprinkled with cracked black pepper, and toasted

Miniature Fruit Tarts
(see p. 348)

With its subtly sweet and fruity sauce, this main dish is nutritious and low in fat, making it a hit with busy people.

BEEF & BROCCOLI WITH PLUM SAUCE

START TO FINISH:

30 minutes

MAKES:

4 servings

MENU IDEA:

Steamed snow pea pods tossed with butter and grated fresh or ground ginger

Blueberries & Orange Cream
(see p. 365)

¾	cup water
½	cup bottled plum sauce
2	tablespoons reduced-sodium soy sauce
1	tablespoon cornstarch
1	teaspoon grated fresh ginger
1	tablespoon cooking oil
1	cup broccoli florets
1	small onion, cut into 1-inch pieces
1	teaspoon bottled minced garlic (2 cloves)
12	ounces beef top round steak, trimmed and cut into thin bite-size strips
3	cups lightly packed, coarsely chopped bok choy
2	medium plums, pitted and cut into thin wedges
	Hot cooked Chinese egg noodles, fine egg noodles, or rice

1 For sauce, in a small bowl stir together the water, plum sauce, soy sauce, cornstarch, and ginger. Set aside.

2 In a nonstick wok or large skillet heat oil over medium-high heat. (Add more oil as necessary during cooking.) Add broccoli, onion, and garlic; stir-fry for 3 minutes. Remove broccoli mixture from wok. Add beef to hot wok. Cook and stir for 2 to 3 minutes or until browned. Push beef from center of wok. Stir sauce. Add sauce to center of wok. Cook and stir until thickened and bubbly.

3 Return broccoli mixture to wok. Add bok choy and plums. Stir to coat all ingredients with sauce. Cover and cook about 2 minutes more or until heated through. Serve over hot cooked noodles or rice.

Nutrition Facts per serving: 413 cal., 10 g total fat (3 g sat. fat), 74 mg chol., 533 mg sodium, 54 g carbo., 4 g fiber, 26 g pro.

Look for Thai seasoning and unsweetened coconut milk at larger supermarkets or Asian food stores.

THAI BEEF PASTA

- 8 ounces dried angel hair pasta
- ¾ cup unsweetened coconut milk
- 1 teaspoon Thai seasoning
- 1 tablespoon cooking oil
- 12 ounces beef top round steak, trimmed and cut into thin bite-size strips
- 1 cup fresh pea pods, trimmed
- ½ cup shredded carrot
- ¼ cup chopped dry roasted peanuts

1 Cook pasta according to package directions; drain well. Return pasta to pan; cover and keep warm. For sauce, in a small bowl stir together coconut milk and Thai seasoning; set aside.

2 Meanwhile, in a wok or large skillet heat oil over medium-high heat. Stir-fry beef in hot oil for 2 to 3 minutes or until desired doneness. Remove beef from wok (drain, if necessary). Add pea pods and carrot to wok. Cook and stir for 1 minute. Push from center of wok. Stir sauce; add to center of wok. Cook and stir until bubbly. Add beef and cooked pasta to wok. Stir to coat all ingredients with sauce. Sprinkle with peanuts.

Nutrition Facts per serving: 516 cal., 22 g total fat (10 g sat. fat), 50 mg chol., 223 mg sodium, 49 g carbo., 2 g fiber, 29 g pro.

START TO FINISH:

30 minutes

MAKES:

4 servings

MENU IDEA:

Pan-Fried Baby Bok Choy *(see p. 255)*

Sliced fresh nectarines or peaches topped with half-and-half and sprinkled with ground cinnamon

An easy meal-in-one, this bowl of comfort is full of refreshing ingredients such as ginger and cilantro. Use low-sodium soy sauce for great taste with less salt.

ASIAN BEEF & NOODLE BOWL

START TO FINISH:

30 minutes

MAKES:

4 servings

....

MENU IDEA:

Sautéed green beans tossed with bottled minced garlic and soy sauce

Purchased pound cake with Apricot-Orange Sauce *(see p. 372)*

....

4	cups water
2	3-ounce packages ramen noodles (any flavor)
2	teaspoons chili oil, or 2 teaspoons cooking oil plus ⅛ teaspoon cayenne pepper
12	ounces beef flank steak or top round steak, trimmed and cut into thin bite-size strips
1	teaspoon grated fresh ginger
1	teaspoon bottled minced garlic (2 cloves)
1	cup beef broth
2	tablespoons soy sauce
2	cups torn fresh spinach
1	cup shredded carrot
¼	cup snipped fresh cilantro

1 In a large saucepan bring the water to boiling. If desired, break up noodles; drop noodles into the boiling water. (Reserve the flavor packets for another use.) Return to boiling; boil for 2 to 3 minutes or just until noodles are tender but still firm, stirring occasionally. Drain noodles; set aside.

2 Meanwhile, in a 12-inch skillet heat oil over medium-high heat. Add beef, ginger, and garlic; cook and stir for 2 to 3 minutes or until beef is desired doneness. Carefully stir beef broth and soy sauce into skillet. Bring to boiling; reduce heat.

3 Add spinach, carrot, cilantro, and cooked noodles to skillet; stir to combine. Heat through.

Nutrition Facts per serving: 381 cal., 17 g total fat (3 g sat. fat), 34 mg chol., 1,503 mg sodium, 30 g carbo., 2 g fiber, 26 g pro.

Kidney beans and a hint of cinnamon make this marinara sauce reminiscent of Cincinnati-style chili, which traditionally is served over pasta.

SPAGHETTI WITH CINCINNATI-STYLE MARINARA

12	ounces dried spaghetti
1	pound ground beef
1	large onion, chopped
1	to 2 tablespoons chili powder
¼	teaspoon ground cinnamon
1	15-ounce can red kidney beans, rinsed and drained
1	14-ounce jar marinara sauce
½	cup water
1	cup shredded cheddar cheese (4 ounces)

1 Cook spaghetti according to package directions; drain well. Return to pan; cover and keep warm.

2 Meanwhile, in a large skillet cook beef and onion until meat is brown and onion is tender. Drain off fat. Stir chili powder and cinnamon into meat mixture; cook and stir for 2 minutes. Add kidney beans, marinara sauce, and the water. Cook over medium heat until boiling, stirring occasionally.

3 Place hot cooked spaghetti in a large serving bowl. Spoon sauce over spaghetti; sprinkle with cheddar cheese.

Nutrition Facts per serving: 522 cal., 17 g total fat (7 g sat. fat), 67 mg chol., 527 mg sodium, 62 g carbo., 7 g fiber, 32 g pro.

START TO FINISH:

30 minutes

MAKES:

6 servings

MENU IDEA:

Parmesan Corn Bread Swirls
(see p. 328)

Lemon sorbet
served with purchased gingersnap cookies

You don't need a special occasion to prepare stroganoff, especially when it's this simple and all of the ingredients are at hand in the pantry or refrigerator.

HEARTY HAMBURGER STROGANOFF

START TO FINISH:

25 minutes

MAKES:

4 or 5 servings

1	pound ground beef
1	medium onion, chopped
½	teaspoon bottled minced garlic (1 clove)
8	ounces fresh mushrooms, sliced
1	10½-ounce can condensed beef broth
3	tablespoons lemon juice
1	tablespoon dry red wine (optional)
4	ounces dried angel hair pasta, broken
1	8-ounce carton dairy sour cream
	Salt
	Black pepper

MENU IDEA:

Roasted Asparagus Parmesan *(see p. 252)*

Purchased angel food cake topped with canned cherry or peach pie filling and whipped cream

1 In a 12-inch skillet cook beef, onion, and garlic until meat is brown and onion is tender. Drain off fat.

2 Stir in mushrooms; cook and stir about 5 minutes or until mushrooms are tender. Stir in broth, lemon juice, and, if desired, wine. Bring to boiling; reduce heat. Stir in uncooked pasta.

3 Cover and simmer about 5 minutes more or until pasta is tender. Stir in sour cream. Cook and stir until heated through. Season with salt and pepper.

Nutrition Facts per serving: 543 cal., 34 g total fat (15 g sat. fat), 106 mg chol., 780 mg sodium, 30 g carbo., 1 g fiber, 31 g pro.

TEST KITCHEN TIP: For a lower-fat stroganoff, substitute light dairy sour cream for the regular sour cream

Nutrition Facts per serving: 434 cal., 20 g total fat (8 g sat. fat), 90 mg chol., 943 mg sodium, 30g carbo., 1 g fiber, 33 g pro.

If you like, try this recipe with ground turkey or chicken for a great-tasting twist on an old favorite.

EASY SHEPHERD'S PIE

1	pound lean ground beef or uncooked ground turkey or chicken
1	medium onion, chopped
1	10-ounce package frozen mixed vegetables, thawed
¼	cup water
1	10¾-ounce can condensed tomato soup
1	teaspoon Worcestershire sauce
¼	teaspoon dried thyme, crushed
1	20-ounce package refrigerated mashed potatoes or 3 cups leftover mashed potatoes
½	cup shredded cheddar cheese (2 ounces)

1 In a large skillet cook ground meat and onion until meat is brown and onion is tender. Drain off fat. Stir mixed vegetables and the water into meat mixture in skillet. Bring to boiling; reduce heat. Cover and simmer about 5 minutes or until vegetables are tender.

2 Stir in tomato soup, Worcestershire sauce, and thyme. Return to boiling; reduce heat. Drop mashed potatoes in 6 mounds on top of hot mixture. Sprinkle potatoes with cheese. Cover and simmer for 10 to 15 minutes or until potatoes are heated through.

Nutrition Facts per serving: 301 cal., 12 g total fat (5 g sat. fat), 58 mg chol., 570 mg sodium, 27 g carbo., 3 g fiber, 20 g pro.

START TO FINISH:
30 minutes
MAKES:
6 servings

MENU IDEA:

Torn fresh spinach tossed with crisp-cooked bacon, croutons, and purchased balsamic vinaigrette salad dressing

Apricot-Peach Cobbler *(see p. 332)*

Chili gets a fresh update with a dab of tangy sour cream and a sprinkle of refreshing cilantro.

WHITE & GREEN CHILI

PREP:

15 minutes

COOK:

15 minutes

MAKES:

4 servings

MENU IDEA:

Crackers and/or bagel chips served with assorted cheeses

Fruit-Filled Waffle Bowls *(see p. 354)*

1	pound unseasoned meat loaf mix (⅓ pound each ground beef, pork, and veal), lean ground beef, or ground pork
1	small onion, chopped
2	15-ounce cans Great Northern beans or white beans, rinsed and drained
1	16-ounce jar green salsa
1	14-ounce can chicken broth
1½	teaspoons ground cumin
2	tablespoons snipped fresh cilantro
¼	cup dairy sour cream (optional)

1 In a 4-quart Dutch oven combine meat loaf mix or ground meat and onion. Cook over medium heat about 5 minutes or until meat is brown and onion is tender, breaking up pieces of meat with a spoon. Drain off fat. Stir beans, salsa, chicken broth, and cumin into meat mixture in Dutch oven. Bring to boiling; reduce heat. Cover and simmer for 15 minutes.

2 To serve, stir in 1 tablespoon of the cilantro. Divide among 4 serving bowls. Sprinkle with remaining 1 tablespoon cilantro. If desired, top individual servings with sour cream.

Nutrition Facts per serving: 400 cal., 11 g total fat (4 g sat. fat), 73 mg chol., 1,404 mg sodium, 41 g carbo., 13 g fiber, 31 g pro.

A bottle of beer transforms brown gravy mix into a tasty complement for mushrooms and beef. Be sure to have some rolls on the table for mopping up every bit of the savory sauce!

BEEF "STEAKS" WITH WILD MUSHROOM SAUCE

1	medium onion, cut in half
1¼	pounds ground beef
¾	teaspoon salt
	Salt
	Black pepper
8	ounces assorted fresh mushrooms (such as oyster, crimini, and shiitake), sliced
1½	cups beer (preferably honey lager) or nonalcoholic beer (12 ounces)
1	0.75- to 1.2-ounce package brown gravy mix
2	teaspoons snipped fresh thyme or ½ teaspoon dried thyme, crushed

1 Finely shred half of the onion. Thinly slice remaining onion; set aside.

2 In a large bowl combine shredded onion, ground beef, and the ¾ teaspoon salt, mixing lightly but thoroughly. Lightly shape meat mixture into four ½-inch-thick oval "steaks." Sprinkle tops with additional salt and pepper.

3 Preheat a large nonstick skillet over medium heat. Place patties in hot skillet; cook for 10 to 12 minutes or until done (160°F),* turning once. Remove from skillet; keep warm.

4 Add sliced onion, mushrooms, and ¼ cup of the beer to same skillet; cook over medium-high heat about 5 minutes or until vegetables are tender, stirring occasionally. In a small bowl stir together dry gravy mix and remaining 1¼ cups beer, mixing until smooth; stir into mushroom mixture in skillet. Add half of the thyme; simmer about 1 minute or until thickened, stirring frequently. Spoon sauce over patties; sprinkle with remaining thyme.

*NOTE: The internal color of a patty is not a reliable doneness indicator. A beef, veal, lamb, or pork patty cooked to 160°F is safe, regardless of color. To measure the doneness of a patty, insert an instant-read thermometer through the side of the patty to a depth of 2 to 3 inches.

Nutrition Facts per serving: 351 cal., 18 g total fat (7 g sat. fat), 89 mg chol., 732 mg sodium, 12 g carbo., 1 g fiber, 29 g pro.

START TO FINISH:
30 minutes
MAKES:
4 servings

MENU IDEA:

Creamy Mashed Potatoes *(see p. 269)*

Canned apple pie filling topped with vanilla ice cream and toasted sliced almonds

Talk about quick! By using bottled pasta sauce and just one skillet, this typically labor-intensive family favorite is streamlined enough that you can make and enjoy it at a moment's notice.

QUICK SKILLET LASAGNA

START TO FINISH:

30 minutes

MAKES:

6 servings

3	cups (6 ounces) dried mafalda (mini lasagna) noodles
12	ounces lean ground beef or bulk pork sausage
1	26- to 28-ounce jar red pasta sauce
1½	cups shredded mozzarella cheese (6 ounces)
¼	cup grated Parmesan cheese (1 ounce)

1 Cook pasta according to package directions; drain well.

2 Meanwhile, in a 10-inch nonstick skillet cook meat until brown. Drain off fat. Set meat aside. Wipe skillet with paper towels.

3 Spread about half of the cooked pasta in the skillet. Cover with about half of the pasta sauce. Spoon cooked meat over sauce. Sprinkle with 1 cup of the mozzarella cheese. Top with remaining pasta and remaining sauce. Sprinkle remaining ½ cup mozzarella cheese and the Parmesan cheese on top.

4 Cover and cook over medium heat for 5 to 7 minutes or until heated through and cheese melts. Remove skillet from heat. Let stand, covered, for 1 minute.

Nutrition Facts per serving: 375 cal., 17 g total fat (6 g sat. fat), 50 mg chol., 1,046 mg sodium, 30 g carbo., 2 g fiber, 25 g pro.

MENU IDEA:

Mixed greens tossed with sliced red and/or green sweet peppers and bottled creamy Italian salad dressing

Mocha Mousse Cups *(see p. 363)*

Rich and creamy Gorgonzola cheese and intensely flavored dried tomatoes give these burgers an elegant appeal. Crumbled goat cheese or feta cheese would also work well, offering a milder taste for those who don't enjoy strong cheeses.

ITALIAN-AMERICAN CHEESEBURGERS

1½	pounds lean ground beef
1	cup crumbled Gorgonzola cheese (4 ounces)
⅓	cup snipped dried oil-packed tomatoes
1	tablespoon snipped fresh thyme
2	teaspoons bottled minced garlic (4 cloves)
½	teaspoon salt
½	teaspoon coarsely ground black pepper
6	sourdough rolls, split and toasted
	Red onion slices
	Tomato slices

PREP:
15 minutes

GRILL:
14 minutes

MAKES:
6 servings

1 In a large bowl combine beef, ¾ cup of the Gorgonzola cheese, all but 1 tablespoon of the snipped dried tomatoes, the thyme, garlic, salt, and pepper. Shape into six ¾-inch-thick patties.

2 Place patties on the lightly oiled rack of an uncovered grill directly over medium heat. Grill for 14 to 18 minutes or until done (160°F),* turning once.

3 Remove burgers from grill. Top with remaining ¼ cup Gorgonzola and remaining 1 tablespoon snipped dried tomatoes. Serve on toasted sourdough rolls with sliced red onions and tomatoes.

***NOTE:** The internal color of a burger is not a reliable doneness indicator. A beef, veal, lamb, or pork patty cooked to 160°F is safe, regardless of color. To measure the doneness of a patty, insert an instant-read thermometer through the side of the patty to a depth of 2 to 3 inches.

Nutrition Facts per serving: 385 cal., 17 g total fat (8 g sat. fat), 85 mg chol., 723 mg sodium, 27 g carbo., 0 g fiber, 29 g pro.

MENU IDEA:

Summer Fruit with Sesame Dressing *(see p. 314)*

Strawberry or peach ice cream served with purchased coconut macaroon cookies

Grilled, golden slices of sourdough bread brushed with fragrant olive oil and rubbed with pungent garlic make these burgers something special.

CAESAR SALAD BEEF BURGERS

PREP:
15 minutes

GRILL:
14 minutes

MAKES:
8 servings

MENU IDEA:

Frozen potato wedges, cooked and tossed with butter and cracked black pepper

Strawberry Dip *(see p. 367)*

3	pounds ground beef
6	cloves garlic, minced
1	teaspoon salt
½	teaspoon black pepper
16	slices sourdough bread
	Olive oil
4	large cloves garlic, cut lengthwise into quarters
8	romaine leaves (optional)
½	cup shredded Parmesan cheese (2 ounces)

1 In a large bowl combine ground beef, minced garlic, salt, and pepper. Shape mixture into eight ¾-inch-thick patties, shaping patties to fit the bread.

2 Place patties on the rack of an uncovered grill directly over medium heat. Grill for 14 to 18 minutes or until done (160°F),* turning once.

3 Meanwhile, brush both sides of each bread slice with olive oil. Place bread slices around outer edge of grill. Grill a few minutes until lightly toasted, turning once; remove from grill. Rub both sides of each slice with a garlic quarter.

4 To serve, place a romaine leaf (if desired) and a burger on each of 8 bread slices. Sprinkle with Parmesan cheese. Top with remaining bread slices.

*NOTE: The internal color of a burger is not a reliable doneness indicator. A beef, veal, lamb, or pork patty cooked to 160°F is safe, regardless of color. To measure the doneness of a patty, insert an instant-read thermometer through the side of the patty to a depth of 2 to 3 inches.

BROILER METHOD: Place patties on unheated rack of a broiler pan. Broil 3 to 4 inches from heat for 12 to 14 minutes or until done (160°F), turning once.

Nutrition Facts per serving: 569 cal., 33 g total fat (12 g sat. fat), 119 mg chol., 766 mg sodium, 27 g carbo., 2 g fiber, 39 g pro.

Sealing the cheese and bacon inside the beef patties makes for a tasty surprise.
The burgers are easy to eat and the delicious toppings won't end up on the floor or in your lap.

BACON-CHEESE BURGERS

1¼	pounds lean ground beef
8	thin slices Colby Jack cheese or cheddar cheese (about 4 ounces)
4	slices bacon, crisp-cooked and crumbled
4	pepper-topped or plain hamburger buns, split and toasted
¼	cup dairy sour cream onion dip

PREP:
15 minutes

BROIL:
10 minutes + 1 minute

MAKES:
4 servings

1 Shape the ground beef into eight ¼-inch-thick patties. Place a cheese slice on top of each of 4 of the patties; sprinkle with crumbled bacon. Place remaining 4 patties on top of the bacon-and-cheese-topped patties. Seal edges well.

2 Place patties on the unheated rack of a broiler pan. Broil 3 to 4 inches from the heat for 10 to 12 minutes or until cooked through, turning once. Place remaining 4 cheese slices on top of patties. Broil for 1 minute more.

3 Meanwhile, spread cut sides of toasted buns with the onion dip. Serve burgers on prepared buns.

Nutrition Facts per serving: 635 cal., 41 g total fat (19 g sat. fat), 133 mg chol., 691 mg sodium, 25 g carbo., 1 g fiber, 37 g pro.

MENU IDEA:

Assorted
potato chips

Rocky Road Malts
(see p. 379)

The dried tomatoes and the lemon peel are bold additions that give plain ground beef some zing. Using spinach leaves instead of the usual lettuce is a great way to boost the nutrients. And who knows? Maybe the children won't even notice!

DRIED TOMATO BURGERS

PREP:

15 minutes

GRILL:

10 minutes

MAKES:

4 servings

MENU IDEA:

Assorted fresh vegetables served with purchased veggie dip

Blueberry-Lemon Tarts *(see p. 353)*

1   pound lean ground beef

2   tablespoons dried tomato-flavored light mayonnaise dressing

2   tablespoons oil-packed dried tomatoes, drained and chopped

1   teaspoon finely shredded lemon peel

4   onion hamburger buns

¼   cup dried tomato-flavored light mayonnaise dressing

2   tablespoons snipped fresh basil

1   small red onion, thinly sliced

1   cup fresh spinach leaves

1 In a medium bowl combine beef, the 2 tablespoons mayonnaise dressing, the dried tomatoes, and lemon peel. Mix lightly but thoroughly. Shape into four ½-inch-thick patties.

2 Place patties on the rack of an uncovered grill directly over medium heat. Grill for 10 to 13 minutes or until done (160°F),* turning once. For the last 1 to 2 minutes of grilling, place buns, cut sides down, on grill rack to toast.

3 Meanwhile, in a small bowl combine the ¼ cup mayonnaise dressing and the basil. Top bun bottoms with patties. Top with mayonnaise dressing mixture, onion slices, and spinach. Add bun tops.

***NOTE:** The internal color of a burger is not a reliable doneness indicator. A beef, veal, lamb, or pork patty cooked to 160°F is safe, regardless of color. To measure the doneness of a patty, insert an instant-read thermometer through the side of the patty to a depth of 2 to 3 inches.

BROILER METHOD: Place patties on unheated rack of a broiler pan. Broil 3 to 4 inches from heat for 10 to 12 minutes or until done (160°F), turning once.

Nutrition Facts per serving: 509 cal., 34 g total fat (12 g sat. fat), 100 mg chol., 496 mg sodium, 25 g carbo., 2 g fiber, 24 g pro.

Because this recipe uses nacho cheese soup, bottled salsa, and preshredded taco cheese, you'll be saying olé to these tostadas in no time at all.

SKILLET TOSTADAS

8	ounces ground beef
1	medium onion, chopped
1	15-ounce can red kidney beans, rinsed and drained
1	11-ounce can condensed nacho cheese soup
1/3	cup bottled salsa
8	tostada shells
1	cup shredded taco cheese (4 ounces)
	Shredded lettuce
	Chopped tomatoes
	Dairy sour cream or guacamole (optional)

START TO FINISH:
25 minutes

MAKES:
4 servings

1 In a 10-inch skillet cook ground beef and onion until meat is brown and onion is tender. Drain off fat. Stir kidney beans, nacho cheese soup, and salsa into beef mixture. Heat through.

2 Divide beef-salsa mixture among tostada shells. Top with cheese. Top with lettuce and tomatoes. If desired, serve with sour cream or guacamole.

Nutrition Facts per serving: 576 cal., 33 g total fat (15 g sat. fat), 81 mg chol., 1,277 mg sodium, 42 g carbo., 11 g fiber, 26 g pro.

MENU IDEA:

Purchased corn bread served with apple butter or honey and butter

Citrus Freeze *(see p. 381)*

To save you time and to get others involved in the kitchen, set out the tortillas, filling, and condiments. Everyone can assemble their own wraps.

BEEF & CABBAGE WRAPS

START TO FINISH:

20 minutes

MAKES:

4 servings

MENU IDEA:

Corn chips

**Fudge Cookies in
Chocolate Cream**
(see p. 347)

8	8-inch flour tortillas
12	ounces lean ground beef
½	cup chopped red or green onion
2	cups packaged shredded cabbage with carrot (coleslaw mix)
1	cup loose-pack frozen whole kernel corn
¼	cup bottled barbecue or hoisin sauce
1	teaspoon toasted sesame oil
	Bottled barbecue sauce or hoisin sauce (optional)

1 Stack tortillas and wrap in foil. Heat in a 350°F oven for 10 minutes to soften. Meanwhile, for filling, in a large skillet cook ground beef and onion until meat is brown and onion is tender. Drain off fat. Stir coleslaw mix and corn into meat mixture in skillet. Cover and cook about 4 minutes or until vegetables are tender, stirring once. Stir in the ¼ cup barbecue sauce or hoisin sauce and the sesame oil. Cook and stir until heated through.

2 Spoon about ½ cup of the filling below center of each tortilla. Fold bottom edge up and over filling. Fold opposite sides in, just until they meet. Roll up from bottom. If desired, serve with additional barbecue or hoisin sauce.

Nutrition Facts per serving: 388 cal., 14 g total fat (5 g sat. fat), 54 mg chol., 409 mg sodium, 44 g carbo., 4 g fiber, 21 g pro.

Hearty and satisfying, these wraps are not only delicious but go together in just 25 minutes. You can't go wrong serving this quick-to-fix meal.

BEEF & BLACK BEAN WRAPS

8	ounces lean ground beef
1	large onion, chopped
1	teaspoon bottled minced garlic (2 cloves)
1½	teaspoons ground cumin
1	teaspoon chili powder
½	teaspoon ground coriander
1	15-ounce can black beans, rinsed and drained
1	large tomato, chopped
¼	teaspoon salt
¼	teaspoon black pepper
6	8-inch whole wheat flour tortillas
1½	cups shredded lettuce
1	to 1½ cups shredded cheddar or Monterey Jack cheese (4 to 6 ounces)
	Bottled salsa (optional)

START TO FINISH:
25 minutes

MAKES:
6 servings

1 In a large skillet cook ground beef, onion, and garlic about 5 minutes or until meat is brown and onion is tender. Drain off fat. Stir cumin, chili powder, and coriander into meat mixture in skillet. Cook and stir for 1 minute. Stir in black beans, tomato, salt, and pepper. Cover and cook for 5 minutes more, stirring occasionally.

2 To serve, spoon some of the beef mixture down the center of each tortilla. Sprinkle with lettuce and cheese. Roll up. If desired, serve with salsa.

Nutrition Facts per serving: 267 cal., 10 g total fat (5 g sat. fat), 44 mg chol., 593 mg sodium, 27 g carbo., 14 g fiber, 19 g pro.

MENU IDEA:

Speedy Southwestern-Style Tomato Soup *(see p. 293)* served with corn tortilla chips

Lemon and/or lime sherbet

Any noodle will complement this dish, but consider spaetzle, which are small dumplings made with flour and eggs. Be warned though—they are very filling. Find them in the pasta section of larger supermarkets.

EASY POT ROAST

START TO FINISH:

25 minutes

MAKES:

4 servings

MENU IDEA:

Sweet Saucy Carrots & Pecans
(see p. 261)

Frozen strawberry yogurt served in waffle ice cream cones

1 17-ounce package refrigerated cooked beef pot roast with juices

1 tablespoon butter or margarine

2 tablespoons minced shallots

2 tablespoons tarragon vinegar

2 cups fresh, pitted fruit cut into wedges (such as peaches, green plums, and/or red plums)

Hot cooked spaetzle (optional)

1 teaspoon snipped fresh tarragon

1 Remove meat from package, reserving juices. In a large skillet melt butter over medium heat. Add shallots; cook for 1 minute. Add pot roast; reduce heat. Cover and simmer about 10 minutes or until pot roast is heated through.

2 In a small bowl stir together reserved meat juices and tarragon vinegar. Pour over meat. Spoon fruit on top. Cover; heat for 2 minutes more. If desired, serve with cooked spaetzle. Sprinkle with snipped tarragon.

Nutrition Facts per serving: 259 cal., 12 g total fat (6 g sat. fat), 72 mg chol., 459 mg sodium, 19 g carbo., 2 g fiber, 24 g pro.

"Caliente" means "hot to the touch" in Spanish. The fiery Tex-Mex influence is the ultimate complement to succulent beef pot roast. Avocado and sour cream offer a creamy, cooling counterpart to the picante sauce.

CALIENTE POT ROAST

1	17-ounce package refrigerated cooked beef pot roast with juices
1½	cups sliced fresh mushrooms
1	8-ounce bottle picante sauce
1	14-ounce can chicken broth
1	cup quick-cooking couscous
2	tablespoons snipped fresh cilantro
	Dairy sour cream (optional)
	Chopped fresh tomato (optional)
	Sliced avocado (optional)

1 Transfer liquid from pot roast package to a large skillet; add mushrooms and picante sauce. Cut pot roast into 1- to 1½-inch cubes; add to skillet. Bring to boiling; reduce heat. Cover and simmer for 10 minutes.

2 Meanwhile, in a medium saucepan bring broth to boiling; stir in couscous. Remove from heat. Cover and let stand for 5 minutes. Fluff with a fork; stir in cilantro.

3 To serve, spoon pot roast mixture over couscous mixture. If desired, serve with sour cream, tomato, and/or avocado.

Nutrition Facts per serving: 379 cal., 10 g total fat (4 g sat. fat), 65 mg chol., 1,314 mg sodium, 44 g carbo., 3 g fiber, 31 g pro.

START TO FINISH:

20 minutes

MAKES:

4 to 6 servings

MENU IDEA:

Old-Fashioned Corn Bread *(see p. 327)*

Purchased bakery or frozen chocolate cream pie

There is nothing more comforting on a cold day than a steaming hot, thick, and savory beef stew. The cheddar cheese soup and the sour cream add a rich creaminess.

BEEF RAGOUT

25 minutes

MAKES:

6 servings

Mixed greens salad
tossed with bottled
vinaigrette dressing

Cookies & Cream
(see p. 350)

10	ounces dried wide egg noodles
1	17-ounce package refrigerated cooked beef tips with gravy
1	10¾-ounce can condensed cheddar cheese soup
1	9-ounce package frozen Italian-style green beans
1	4½-ounce jar (drained weight) whole mushrooms, drained
½	cup water
3	tablespoons tomato paste
2	tablespoons dried minced onion
½	cup dairy sour cream

1 Cook noodles according to package directions; drain well. Return noodles to pan; cover and keep warm.

2 Meanwhile, in a 4-quart Dutch oven combine beef tips with gravy, cheddar cheese soup, green beans, mushrooms, the water, tomato paste, and dried minced onion. Bring to boiling; reduce heat. Cover and simmer for 10 to 15 minutes or until green beans are crisp-tender, stirring occasionally. Stir in sour cream; cook for 2 to 3 minutes more or until heated through. Serve over hot cooked noodles.

Nutrition Facts per serving: 378 cal., 13 g total fat (5 g sat. fat), 90 mg chol., 954 mg sodium, 49 g carbo., 4 g fiber, 22 g pro.

This is an eye-catching dish that is perfect for warm summer meals when fresh produce is at its tastiest. Just assemble and serve because no cooking is required. Make the mushroom relish the day before to give the flavors time to meld.

BEEF SALAD PLATE WITH MUSHROOM RELISH

1	cup finely chopped fresh mushrooms
1/4	cup finely chopped green onions
2	tablespoons Worcestershire sauce for chicken
1	tablespoon hazelnut oil, walnut oil, or salad oil
1/4	teaspoon freshly ground white pepper
3	cups beet greens or other leafy greens, rinsed, drained, and patted dry
1	pound thinly sliced cooked roast beef
4	red and/or yellow plum, cherry, or teardrop tomatoes, cut up
1/2	of a small red onion, thinly sliced
	Snipped fresh rosemary (optional)

1 For mushroom relish, in a small bowl stir together mushrooms, green onions, Worcestershire sauce, oil, and white pepper.

2 Divide greens among 4 chilled plates. Top greens with sliced beef, tomatoes, and onion. Spoon the mushroom relish onto plates. If desired, sprinkle tomatoes and onion with snipped fresh rosemary.

MAKE-AHEAD TIP: Prepare the mushroom relish. Cover and chill for up to 24 hours.

Nutrition Facts per serving: 296 cal., 19 g total fat (6 g sat. fat), 80 mg chol., 377 mg sodium, 6 g carbo., 2 g fiber, 28 g pro.

START TO FINISH:

20 minutes

MAKES:

4 servings

MENU IDEA:

Purchased refrigerated breadsticks, sprinkled with garlic-herb seasoning and baked

Cherry-Bananas Foster *(see p. 360)*

The ultimate in convenience, these sandwiches have a mouthwatering smokiness thanks to the chipotle peppers. They're perfect for after football practice or when you have friends over for a weekend get-together.

CHIPOTLE BRISKET SANDWICH

START TO FINISH:

15 minutes

MAKES:

6 servings

1	pound refrigerated cooked beef with barbecue sauce
1	to 2 canned chipotle peppers in adobo sauce, chopped
½	of a 16-ounce package shredded cabbage with carrot (coleslaw mix) (about 4 cups)
⅓	cup bottled coleslaw dressing
6	kaiser rolls, split and toasted

1 In a large saucepan combine beef with barbecue sauce and chipotle peppers. Cook and stir about 5 minutes or until heated through.

2 Meanwhile, in a large bowl combine coleslaw mix and coleslaw dressing.

3 To serve, spoon beef mixture onto roll bottoms. Top with coleslaw mixture and roll tops.

Nutrition Facts per serving: 406 cal., 17 g total fat (5 g sat. fat), 37 mg chol., 1,050 mg sodium, 47 g carbo., 2 g fiber, 16 g pro.

MENU IDEA:

Kettle-cooked potato chips served with purchased dairy sour cream chip dip

Banana & Caramel Cream Pies
(see p. 353)

Teaming a canned soup with additional ingredients is a quick way to boost flavor. Enhanced with golden onions, tender morsels of browned beef, and bubbling Gruyère cheese, this soup is so delicious no one will mind that it isn't homemade!

FRENCH ONION & BEEF SOUP

3	tablespoons butter or margarine
1	medium onion, thinly sliced and separated into rings
2	10½-ounce cans condensed French onion soup
2½	cups water
8	ounces cooked roast beef, cubed
4	1-inch slices French bread
½	cup shredded Gruyère or Swiss cheese (2 ounces)

START TO FINISH:

25 minutes

MAKES:

4 servings

1 In a large skillet melt butter over medium heat. Add onion; cook about 5 minutes or until very tender. Stir in French onion soup, the water, and cooked beef. Bring to boiling, stirring occasionally.

2 Meanwhile, place the bread slices on a baking sheet. Broil 4 inches from the heat about 1 minute or until toasted on one side. Top the toasted sides of bread slices with shredded cheese; broil about 1 minute more or until cheese is melted.

3 To serve, ladle soup into soup bowls. Top with bread slices, cheese sides up.

Nutrition Facts per serving: 465 cal., 21 g total fat (10 g sat. fat), 82 mg chol., 1,701 mg sodium, 40 g carbo., 3 g fiber, 28 g pro.

MENU IDEA:

Citrus Salad with Glazed Pecans
(see p. 311)

Purchased oatmeal raisin cookies, spread with canned vanilla frosting and sprinkled with ground cinnamon

If you are looking for a new way to use leftover roast beef, give this stew a try.

HURRY-UP BEEF-VEGETABLE STEW

START TO FINISH:

20 minutes

MAKES:

5 servings

MENU IDEA:

Baguette-style French bread, sliced, spread with garlic butter, and toasted

Tropical Fruit Shortcakes *(see p. 337)*

2　cups water

1　10¾-ounce can condensed golden mushroom soup

1　10¾-ounce can condensed tomato soup

½　cup dry red wine or beef broth

2　cups chopped cooked roast beef (about 10 ounces)

1　16-ounce package frozen sugar snap stir-fry vegetables or one 16-ounce package frozen cut broccoli

½　teaspoon dried thyme, crushed

1 In a 4-quart Dutch oven combine the water, golden mushroom soup, tomato soup, and wine or broth. Stir in beef, frozen vegetables, and thyme. Cook over medium heat until bubbly, stirring frequently. Cook for 4 to 5 minutes more or until vegetables are crisp-tender, stirring occasionally.

Nutrition Facts per serving: 231 cal., 4 g total fat (1 g sat. fat), 42 mg chol., 906 mg sodium, 21 g carbo., 4 g fiber, 20 g pro.

Horseradish and beef, common sandwich partners, pair up once again. Here the horseradish seasons crunchy broccoli slaw.

ROAST BEEF SANDWICHES WITH HORSERADISH SLAW

⅓	cup dairy sour cream
2	tablespoons snipped fresh chives
2	tablespoons spicy brown mustard
1	teaspoon prepared horseradish
½	teaspoon sugar
¼	teaspoon salt
1	cup packaged shredded broccoli (broccoli slaw mix)
8	ounces thinly sliced cooked roast beef
8	½-inch slices sourdough bread, toasted

1 In a medium bowl combine sour cream, chives, brown mustard, horseradish, sugar, and salt. Add shredded broccoli; toss to coat.

2 To assemble, divide roast beef among 4 of the bread slices. Top with broccoli mixture and remaining bread slices.

Nutrition Facts per serving: 312 cal., 12 g total fat (5 g sat. fat), 52 mg chol., 612 mg sodium, 29 g carbo., 2 g fiber, 21 g pro.

START TO FINISH:

15 minutes

MAKES:

4 servings

MENU IDEA:

Orange Dream Fruit Salad *(see p. 314)*

Neapolitan ice cream served with purchased chocolate-filled sugar wafer cookies

Use leftover or deli roast beef for this flavor-packed sandwich. For a heartier meal, serve it with your favorite soup.

ITALIAN STEAK & CHEESE SANDWICH

START TO FINISH:

25 minutes

MAKES:

6 sandwiches

½	cup mayonnaise or salad dressing
2	medium green sweet peppers, cut into rings
1	medium onion, sliced
¼	cup bottled zesty-style clear Italian salad dressing
12	ounces thinly sliced cooked roast beef
6	French-style rolls, split and toasted
½	cup shredded mozzarella cheese (2 ounces)

1 In a large skillet heat 2 tablespoons of the mayonnaise over medium heat. Add sweet peppers and onion; cook and stir about 5 minutes or until vegetables are crisp-tender. Remove vegetable mixture from skillet; keep warm.

2 Add remaining mayonnaise and the Italian dressing to skillet. Add meat to skillet; cook over medium heat about 5 minutes or until heated through. Fill rolls with meat and vegetable mixture. Top with cheese.

Nutrition Facts per sandwich: 444 cal., 24 g total fat (5 g sat. fat), 36 mg chol., 956 mg sodium, 37 g carbo., 2 g fiber, 19 g pro.

MENU IDEA:

Purchased vinaigrette coleslaw

Lemon Cheesecake Mousse *(see p. 363)*

You can take your choice of roast beef, ham, or turkey—or use some of each—to make this easy meal-size sandwich. Ranch-flavored sour cream dip adds a little extra pizzazz.

DELI-STYLE SUBMARINES

1	16-ounce loaf French bread
½	of an 8-ounce carton dairy sour cream ranch dip
1	large carrot, shredded
1	cup shredded lettuce
½	of a medium cucumber, seeded and shredded
8	ounces thinly sliced cooked roast beef, ham, or turkey
4	ounces thinly sliced mozzarella or provolone cheese

1 Cut French bread in half lengthwise. Spread cut sides of bread with dip. On the bottom portion of the bread, layer carrot, lettuce, cucumber, roast beef, and cheese. Cover with top portion of bread. Cut into 8 pieces. Secure pieces with decorative toothpicks.

MAKE-AHEAD DIRECTIONS: Prepare as directed, except do not cut into pieces. Wrap sandwich in plastic wrap and chill for up to 4 hours. Cut and serve as directed.

Nutrition Facts per serving: 286 cal., 10 g total fat (5 g sat. fat), 41 mg chol., 551 mg sodium, 33 g carbo., 2 g fiber, 17 g pro.

TEST KITCHEN TIP: For a lower-fat sandwich, substitute light dairy sour cream ranch dip for the regular sour cream ranch dip.

Nutrition Facts per serving: 250 cal., 6 g total fat (3 g sat. fat), 24 mg chol., 743 mg sodium, 34 g carbo., 2 g fiber, 14 g pro.

START TO FINISH:

20 minutes

MAKES:

8 servings

MENU IDEA:

Corn tortilla chips served with bottled fruit salsa

Choose-a-Flavor Shake (make the recipe 4 times) *(see p. 380)*

With the ingredients on hand and this recipe flagged and waiting, you'll always have something nourishing that's ready in a hurry.

ITALIAN MEATBALL SOUP

START TO FINISH:

25 minutes

MAKES:

4 servings

MENU IDEA:

Italian bread, sliced, spread with bottled creamy garlic salad dressing, and toasted

Banana Tostadas
(see p. 355)

1	14-ounce can beef broth
1	14½-ounce can diced tomatoes with onion and garlic, undrained
1½	cups water
½	teaspoon dried Italian seasoning, crushed
½	of a 16- to 18-ounce package frozen Italian-style cooked meatballs
½	cup small dried pasta (such as tripolini, ditalini, stellini, or orzo)
1	cup loose-pack frozen mixed vegetables
1	tablespoon finely shredded or grated Parmesan cheese

1 In a large saucepan stir together beef broth, undrained tomatoes, the water, and Italian seasoning; bring to boiling.

2 Add frozen meatballs, pasta, and frozen vegetables. Return to boiling; reduce heat. Cover and simmer about 10 minutes or until pasta and vegetables are tender. Sprinkle individual servings with cheese.

Nutrition Facts per serving: 290 cal., 14 g total fat (7 g sat. fat), 38 mg chol., 1,302 mg sodium, 26 g carbo., 4 g fiber, 15 g pro.

Make extra batches and freeze in single serving containers for a wholesome meal that's ready in minutes.

MEATBALL STEW

5	cups water
1	14 ½-ounce can diced tomatoes, undrained
2	medium carrots, diced
2	stalks celery, sliced
1	large onion, chopped
⅓	cup quick-cooking barley
3	beef bouillon cubes or 1 tablespoon instant beef bouillon granules
1	teaspoon seasoned salt
1	teaspoon dried basil, crushed
1	bay leaf
36	frozen cooked meatballs (about ½ ounce each)

1 In a large saucepan combine the water, undrained tomatoes, carrots, celery, onion, barley, bouillon, seasoned salt, basil, and bay leaf. Bring to boiling, stirring occasionally.

2 Add frozen meatballs. Cover and simmer for 5 to 10 minutes or until meatballs are heated through, stirring once or twice. Discard bay leaf.

Nutrition Facts per serving: 330 cal., 22 g total fat (9 g sat. fat), 30 mg chol., 1,518 mg sodium, 21 g carbo., 5 g fiber, 13 g pro.

START TO FINISH:
30 minutes
MAKES:
6 to 8 servings

MENU IDEA:
Garlic Dinner Rolls
(see p. 329)

Purchased individual shortcakes served with sliced strawberries and whipped cream

Do you have hungry people at home old enough to work in the kitchen? Keep a stock of frozen meatballs, pasta sauce, and preshredded cheese so that they can whip these up whenever those hunger pangs hit.

SAUCY MEATBALL SANDWICHES

START TO FINISH:

20 minutes

MAKES:

6 servings

18 frozen Italian-style cooked meatballs (about 1 ounce each)

1 26- to 28-ounce jar red pasta sauce

1 medium onion, coarsely chopped

6 hoagie buns, split and toasted

1 cup shredded Italian 4-cheese blend (4 ounces)

1 In a large saucepan combine frozen meatballs, pasta sauce, and onion. Bring to boiling; reduce heat. Cover and simmer about 10 minutes or until meatballs are heated through, stirring occasionally. Spoon hot meatball mixture onto bottom halves of rolls. Spoon any remaining sauce over the meatballs. Sprinkle cheese over the meatballs. Top with bun halves. Let stand for 1 to 2 minutes before serving.

Nutrition Facts per serving: 802 cal., 36 g total fat (14 g sat. fat), 74 mg chol., 2,293 mg sodium, 88 g carbo., 9 g fiber, 32 g pro.

MENU IDEA:

Angel hair pasta, cooked and tossed with olive oil, bottled roasted garlic, and shredded Parmesan cheese

Lemon Meringue Cookie Tarts
(see p. 352)

Serve this sensational salad as a main course for a special luncheon. For an extra special finish to the meal, serve crispy amaretti cookies with ice cream.

ITALIAN WEDDING SALAD

6	ounces dried orzo pasta
32	frozen cooked meatballs (about ½ ounce each), thawed
½	cup bottled Italian salad dressing
1	6-ounce jar marinated artichoke hearts, drained and chopped
1	6-ounce package prewashed baby spinach
¼	cup chopped walnuts, toasted
	Salt
	Black pepper
	Finely shredded Parmesan or Romano cheese (optional)

1 Cook pasta according to package directions; drain well.

2 Meanwhile, in a 4-quart Dutch oven combine meatballs and salad dressing. Cook over medium heat until meatballs are heated through, stirring occasionally. Stir in drained pasta, artichoke hearts, spinach, and walnuts. Heat and stir just until spinach is wilted. Season to taste with salt and pepper. If desired, sprinkle with cheese.

Nutrition Facts per serving: 730 cal., 52 g total fat (15 g sat. fat), 40 mg chol., 1,383 mg sodium, 48 g carbo., 8 g fiber, 23 g pro.

START TO FINISH:
25 minutes
MAKES:
4 servings

MENU IDEA:
Purchased croissants or crescent rolls served with fruit preserves

Vanilla ice cream with Chocolate-Hazelnut Ice Cream Sauce *(see p. 372)*

Vinegar, brown sugar, and spices mix to create a thick and bubbly sauce dotted with fresh berries.

PORK CHOPS WITH RASPBERRIES

START TO FINISH:

25 minutes

MAKES:

4 servings

MENU IDEA:

**Broiled Summer
Squash & Onions**
(see p. 277)

Purchased pecan rolls
served with vanilla
ice cream

¾ cup chicken broth

1 tablespoon packed brown sugar

1 tablespoon white balsamic vinegar

1½ teaspoons cornstarch

 Dash ground allspice

4 pork rib chops, cut ¾ inch thick (about 1½ pounds total)

½ teaspoon salt

¼ teaspoon black pepper

¼ teaspoon dried basil, crushed

1 tablespoon cooking oil

1 cup fresh raspberries

1 In a small bowl stir together broth, brown sugar, balsamic vinegar, cornstarch, and allspice; set aside.

2 Trim fat from chops. Sprinkle both sides of each chop with salt, pepper, and basil. In a 12-inch skillet heat oil over medium heat. Add chops; cook for 8 to 12 minutes or until tender (160°F) and juices run clear, turning once. Transfer chops to a serving platter. Cover and keep warm. Drain fat from skillet.

3 Stir vinegar mixture. Add to skillet. Cook and stir over medium heat until slightly thickened and bubbly. Cook and stir for 2 minutes more. Gently stir in raspberries; heat through. To serve, spoon raspberry mixture over chops.

Nutrition Facts per serving: 206 cal., 9 g total fat (2 g sat. fat), 53 mg chol., 516 mg sodium, 8 g carbo., 2 g fiber, 22 g pro.

Roasted garlic, balsamic salad dressing, honey mustard, and rosemary add a gutsy zing and a little sweetness to these quick-cooking chops.

BALSAMIC & GARLIC PORK

4	boneless pork loin chops, cut ½ inch thick (12 to 16 ounces total)
½	teaspoon dried rosemary, crushed
¼	teaspoon salt
1	tablespoon olive oil
2	teaspoons bottled minced roasted garlic
½	cup bottled balsamic vinaigrette salad dressing
1	tablespoon honey mustard

1 Trim fat from chops. Sprinkle both sides of each chop with rosemary and salt, pressing into surface of meat.

2 In a large nonstick skillet heat oil over medium heat. Add chops; cook for 8 to 12 minutes or until done (160°F) and juices run clear, turning once. Transfer chops to a serving platter. Cover and keep warm.

3 For sauce, in same skillet cook garlic in hot drippings for 30 seconds. Stir in balsamic salad dressing and honey mustard. Bring to boiling. Serve sauce over chops.

Nutrition Facts per serving: 276 cal., 18 g total fat (4 g sat. fat), 54 mg chol., 562 mg sodium, 5 g carbo., 0 g fiber, 22 g pro.

START TO FINISH:
20 minutes
MAKES:
4 servings

MENU IDEA:
Confetti Rice Salad
(see p. 317)

Purchased chocolate pound cake drizzled with caramel or hot fudge sauce

Tempt your family with the mouthwatering aroma of pork chops and vibrantly colored sweet peppers sizzling in a pan.

PORK CHOPS WITH PEPPERS & ONIONS

START TO FINISH:

25 minutes

MAKES:

4 servings

MENU IDEA:

Purchased refrigerated biscuits, baked and served with butter and maple syrup

Amaretto Peaches with Vanilla Yogurt
(see p. 375)

4   pork loin or rib chops, cut $\frac{1}{2}$ to $\frac{3}{4}$ inch thick (about $1\frac{1}{4}$ pounds total)

1   tablespoon olive oil

1   medium red sweet pepper, cut into strips

1   medium green sweet pepper, cut into strips

1   medium yellow sweet pepper, cut into strips

1   large sweet onion, thinly sliced

$\frac{1}{4}$ cup water

$\frac{1}{4}$ cup dry white wine or chicken broth

1   teaspoon snipped fresh rosemary or $\frac{1}{2}$ teaspoon dried rosemary, crushed

$\frac{1}{4}$ teaspoon salt

1 Trim fat from chops. In a large skillet heat oil over medium-high heat. Add chops; cook for 4 to 5 minutes or until brown, turning once. Add sweet peppers and onion to skillet. Add the water, wine, rosemary, and salt. Bring to boiling; reduce heat. Cover and simmer for 4 to 7 minutes or until pork is done (160°F) and juices run clear.

2 Transfer chops to serving plates. Use a slotted spoon to remove pepper mixture from skillet; spoon over chops. If desired, drizzle with some of the skillet juices.

Nutrition Facts per serving: 209 cal., 8 g total fat (2 g sat. fat), 58 mg chol., 205 mg sodium, 10 g carbo., 2 g fiber, 22 g pro.

Just a few ingredients add up to more than a main dish—the less time you spend in the kitchen, the more time you'll have for other things.

CRANBERRY-SAUCED PORK & SWEET POTATOES

4   boneless pork loin chops, cut ¾ inch thick
    (about 1 pound total)

    Salt

    Black pepper

    Nonstick cooking spray

1   17-ounce can vacuum-pack sweet potatoes

1   tablespoon butter or margarine

1   cup orange juice

¼   cup dried cranberries

1 Trim fat from pork. Sprinkle pork lightly with salt and pepper. Lightly coat an unheated large skillet with cooking spray. Preheat skillet over medium-high heat. Add chops; cook for 8 to 12 minutes or until tender (160°F) and juices run clear, turning once.

2 Meanwhile, place sweet potatoes in a medium saucepan. Mash with a potato masher. Stir in butter. Cook and stir over medium heat until potatoes are heated through. If desired, season with additional salt and pepper.

3 Transfer pork to a serving platter; cover to keep warm. Add orange juice and cranberries to skillet. Bring to boiling; reduce heat. Simmer, uncovered, about 7 minutes or until liquid is reduced by half. Spoon sauce over pork. Serve with sweet potatoes.

Nutrition Facts per serving: 352 cal., 9 g total fat (4 g sat. fat), 70 mg chol., 278 mg sodium, 38 g carbo., 3 g fiber, 28 g pro.

START TO FINISH:

20 minutes

MAKES:

4 servings

MENU IDEA:

Parkerhouse
or dinner rolls

Quick Rice Pudding
(see p. 335)

Keep a variety of nuts on hand for adding crunch, taste, and extra nutrients to everyday meals. Nuts can be stored in an airtight container in the refrigerator for up to 4 months or in the freezer up to 6 months.

GALA PORK CHOPS

PREP:
10 minutes

GRILL:
12 minutes

MAKES:
4 servings

MENU IDEA:

Summer Spaghetti
(see p. 280)

Pirouette cookies
served with coffee
ice cream

4	boneless pork loin chops, cut ¾ inch thick (about 1 pound total)
1	teaspoon olive oil
½	teaspoon dried rosemary, crushed
½	teaspoon salt
¼	to ½ teaspoon black pepper
1½	cups sliced, peeled cooking apples
⅓	cup apple juice or apple cider
1	tablespoon lemon juice
1	tablespoon cold water
1½	teaspoons cornstarch
¼	cup crumbled feta cheese (1 ounce)
¼	cup chopped pecans, toasted

1 Trim fat from chops. Rub both sides of each chop lightly with the oil. Sprinkle both sides of each chop with rosemary, salt, and pepper.

2 Place chops on the rack of an uncovered grill directly over medium heat. Grill for 12 to 15 minutes or until tender (160° F) and juices run clear, turning once.

3 Meanwhile, in a medium saucepan stir together apples, apple juice, and lemon juice. Bring to boiling; reduce heat. Cover and simmer for 3 minutes. In a small bowl stir together the cold water and cornstarch. Add to apple mixture. Cook and stir until thickened and bubbly. Cook and stir for 2 minutes more. Serve apple mixture over chops; top with feta and pecans.

BROILER METHOD: Place chops on unheated rack of a broiler pan. Broil 3 to 4 inches from heat for 9 to 11 minutes or until tender (160°F) and juices run clear.

Nutrition Facts per serving: 278 cal., 14 g total fat (4 g sat. fat), 68 mg chol., 421 mg sodium, 11 g carbo., 2 g fiber, 27 g pro.

Tangy, sweet Dijon mustard complements many meats, including pork.

PORK CHOPS DIJON

3   tablespoons Dijon-style mustard

2   tablespoons bottled reduced-calorie Italian salad dressing

¼   teaspoon black pepper

4   pork loin chops, cut ½ inch thick (about 1½ pounds total)
    Nonstick cooking spray

1   medium onion, halved and sliced

1 In a small bowl combine mustard, Italian dressing, and pepper; set aside. Trim fat from the chops. Coat an unheated 10-inch skillet with cooking spray. Preheat the skillet over medium-high heat. Add the chops; cook until brown on both sides, turning once. Remove chops from skillet.

2 Add onion to skillet. Cook and stir over medium heat for 3 minutes. Push onion aside; return chops to skillet. Spread mustard mixture over chops. Cover and cook over medium-low heat about 15 minutes or until done (160°F). Spoon onion over chops.

Nutrition Facts per serving: 163 cal., 5 g total fat (2 g sat. fat), 53 mg chol., 403 mg sodium, 2 g carbo., 0 g fiber, 22 g pro.

START TO FINISH:

30 minutes

MAKES:

4 servings

MENU IDEA:

Steamed asparagus tossed with olive oil and thinly shredded basil

Purchased angel food cake with Golden Citrus Sauce *(see p. 370)*

These deliciously sticky and succulent chops are sure to appeal to even the pickiest eater.

MAPLE-PECAN GLAZED PORK CHOPS

START TO FINISH:

15 minutes

MAKES:

4 servings

4   boneless pork loin chops, cut ¾ inch thick (about 1 pound total)

    Salt

    Black pepper

4   tablespoons butter or margarine, softened

2   tablespoons pure maple syrup or maple-flavored syrup

⅓   cup chopped pecans, toasted

1 Trim fat from chops. Sprinkle chops with salt and pepper. In a 12-inch skillet melt 1 tablespoon of the butter over medium-high heat. Add chops; cook for 8 to 12 minutes or until tender (160°F) and juices run clear, turning once. Transfer chops to a serving platter.

2 Meanwhile, in a small bowl combine the remaining 3 tablespoons butter and the maple syrup. Spread butter mixture evenly over cooked chops. Let stand about 1 minute or until melted. Sprinkle with pecans.

Nutrition Facts per serving: 333 cal., 23 g total fat (10 g sat. fat), 98 mg chol., 310 mg sodium, 8 g carbo., 1 g fiber, 23 g pro.

MENU IDEA:

Baked Pineapple Casserole *(see p. 279)*

Purchased individual cheesecakes topped with warmed cherry preserves

The plums and grapes in this recipe provide color and variety. You can choose a yellow, green, or purple plum to go with the red grapes. Or select seedless green grapes and opt for a red or purple plum.

PORK CHOPS IN PLUM-GRAPE SAUCE

4	boneless pork top loin chops, cut 1 inch thick (about 1¼ pounds total)
¼	teaspoon salt
¼	teaspoon black pepper
2	teaspoons olive oil
⅓	cup water
¼	cup plum jam
1	tablespoon balsamic vinegar
2	teaspoons Dijon-style mustard
½	teaspoon chicken bouillon granules
½	teaspoon bottled minced garlic (1 clove)
1	small plum, seeded and cut into thin wedges
½	cup seedless red grapes, halved

START TO FINISH:
25 minutes
MAKES:
4 servings

❶ Trim fat from chops. Sprinkle chops with salt and pepper. In a large nonstick skillet heat oil over medium heat. Add chops; cook for 8 to 12 minutes or until tender (160°F) and juices run clear, turning once. Transfer chops to a serving platter. Cover and keep warm.

❷ Add the water, jam, balsamic vinegar, mustard, bouillon granules, and garlic to skillet. Whisk over medium heat until bubbly. Remove from heat. Gently stir in plum wedges and grapes. Serve plum-grape mixture over chops.

Nutrition Facts per serving: 305 cal., 10 g total fat (3 g sat. fat), 83 mg chol., 386 mg sodium, 21 g carbo., 1 g fiber, 31 g pro.

MENU IDEA:

Packaged frozen broccoli, cauliflower, and carrots in butter sauce, prepared according to package directions

Dessert Waffles
(see p. 357)

Coating the chops with the corn bread stuffing mix gives them a delightful crispy crust, keeping them juicy and moist inside.

OVEN-FRIED PORK CHOPS

PREP:
10 minutes

BAKE:
20 minutes

MAKES:
4 servings

3   tablespoons butter or margarine

1   egg

2   tablespoons milk

1   cup packaged corn bread stuffing mix

4   pork loin chops, cut ½ inch thick (about 1½ pounds total)

     Applesauce (optional)

1 Place butter in a 13×9×2-inch baking pan; heat in a 425°F oven about 3 minutes or until butter melts.

2 Meanwhile, in a shallow dish beat egg with a fork; stir in milk. Place dry stuffing mix in another shallow dish. Trim fat from chops. Dip pork chops into egg mixture. Coat both sides with stuffing mix. Place chops in the baking pan with the butter.

3 Bake for 20 to 25 minutes or until tender (160°F) and juices run clear, turning once. If desired, serve with applesauce.

Nutrition Facts per serving: 326 cal., 16 g total fat (8 g sat. fat), 131 mg chol., 392 mg sodium, 17 g carbo., 0 g fiber, 26 g pro.

MENU IDEA:

Purchased chunky applesauce sprinkled with cinnamon-sugar

Raspberry & Chocolate Tulips
(see p. 351)

Could there be anything more comforting on a cold evening than succulent smoked pork chops paired with a maple-bourbon sauce? If the bourbon doesn't appeal to you, leave it out. The chops will have enough great flavor left to satisfy eaters of any age.

MAPLE-BOURBON SMOKED CHOPS

2	teaspoons cooking oil
1	medium onion, halved lengthwise and sliced
1/4	cup pure maple syrup or maple-flavored syrup
1	tablespoon bourbon
1	tablespoon Dijon-style mustard
1	teaspoon bottled minced garlic (2 cloves)
1/8	teaspoon crushed red pepper
4	cooked smoked boneless pork chops, cut 3/4 inch thick (about 1 pound total)

START TO FINISH:

30 minutes

MAKES:

4 servings

1 In a large skillet heat oil over medium heat. Add onion; cook for 4 to 5 minutes or until tender, stirring occasionally. Increase heat to medium-high; cook and stir for 3 to 4 minutes more or until onion is golden. Remove onion from skillet with a slotted spoon, reserving drippings. In a medium bowl stir together cooked onion, maple syrup, bourbon, mustard, garlic, and red pepper; set aside.

2 Trim fat from chops. In the same skillet cook chops in reserved drippings over medium heat for 5 minutes. Turn chops over. Return onion mixture to skillet. Cook, uncovered, for 4 to 5 minutes more or until chops are heated through.

3 Serve onion mixture over chops.

Nutrition Facts per serving: 229 cal., 8 g total fat (2 g sat. fat), 60 mg chol., 1,382 mg sodium, 16 g carbo., 0 g fiber, 20 g pro.

MENU IDEA:

Gingery Sugar Snap Peas *(see p. 268)*

Pineapple ice cream served with fresh pineapple wedges and fresh mint leaves

The skillet is one of the most versatile pans you can have in your kitchen—and this recipe makes good use of it. Not only are you cooking meat to golden perfection, you're preparing the veggies at the same time.

SMOKED PORK CHOP SKILLET

START TO FINISH:

25 minutes

MAKES:

4 servings

4 cooked smoked pork chops, cut ¾ inch thick (about 1¾ pounds total)

1 16-ounce package frozen French-style green beans

¼ cup water

1½ teaspoons snipped fresh sage or ½ teaspoon dried leaf sage, crushed

½ cup balsamic vinegar

1 Trim fat from chops. In a large nonstick skillet cook chops over medium heat for 6 to 10 minutes or until lightly browned, turning once. Remove from skillet; keep warm. Add beans, the water, and sage to skillet; return chops to skillet. Cover and cook over medium heat for 5 minutes.

2 Meanwhile, in a small saucepan gently boil balsamic vinegar about 5 minutes or until reduced to ¼ cup. Brush chops with vinegar; drizzle remaining vinegar over the bean mixture.

Nutrition Facts per serving: 257 cal., 14 g total fat (5 g sat. fat), 47 mg chol., 749 mg sodium, 18 g carbo., 3 g fiber, 17 g pro.

MENU IDEA:

Herb-flavored quick-cooking rice mix prepared according to package directions

Baked Fruit Ambrosia
(see p. 336)

The cranberries, pineapple, and mandarin oranges jazz up this dish with vivid color, great taste, and extra nutrients. If you've never tasted basmati rice, now is the time to enjoy this nutty-flavored grain.

SMOKED PORK CHOPS WITH CURRIED FRUIT

4	cooked smoked pork chops, cut ¾ inch thick (about 1¾ pounds total)
1	tablespoon cooking oil
1	8-ounce can pineapple chunks (juice pack)
⅓	cup chopped onion
1	tablespoon butter or margarine
1½	teaspoons curry powder
¾	cup orange juice
1	tablespoon cornstarch
1	cup fresh cranberries
1	11-ounce can mandarin orange sections, drained
	Hot cooked basmati rice or couscous (optional)

START TO FINISH:
20 minutes

MAKES:
4 servings

1 Trim fat from chops. In a 12-inch skillet cook chops in hot oil for 8 to 10 minutes or until heated through, turning once.

2 Meanwhile, for sauce, drain pineapple, reserving juice. In a medium saucepan cook onion in butter until tender. Stir in curry powder. Cook and stir for 1 minute. Stir together reserved pineapple juice, orange juice, and cornstarch. Stir into mixture in saucepan. Add cranberries. Cook and stir over medium heat until thickened and bubbly. Cook and stir for 2 minutes more. Gently stir in pineapple and mandarin oranges; heat through. Serve sauce over pork chops. If desired, serve with rice or couscous.

Nutrition Facts per serving: 422 cal., 20 g total fat (7 g sat. fat), 92 mg chol., 2,162 mg sodium, 28 g carbo., 3 g fiber, 33 g pro.

MENU IDEA:
Fresh baby spinach tossed with toasted nuts, olive oil, and fruit-flavored vinegar

Mocha Mousse Cups
(see p. 363)

This ruby-red chutney is the perfect match for pan-fried pork medallions. If you have any left over, store it in the refrigerator and serve it with other roast meats such as beef or chicken.

PORK MEDALLIONS WITH CRANBERRY & FIG CHUTNEY

START TO FINISH:

20 minutes

MAKES:

2 servings

MENU IDEA:

Quick-cooking long grain and wild rice mix, prepared according to package directions

Chocolate Brownie Pudding *(see p. 339)*

½	cup fresh cranberries or ¼ cup canned whole cranberry sauce
¼	cup apple juice or apple cider
2	tablespoons snipped dried figs
1	tablespoon packed brown sugar or granulated sugar
½	teaspoon snipped fresh rosemary or ¼ teaspoon dried rosemary, crushed
	Salt
	Freshly ground black pepper
6	ounces pork tenderloin
2	teaspoons cooking oil
	Hot cooked rice (optional)

1 For chutney, in a heavy small saucepan stir together cranberries or cranberry sauce, apple juice, figs, sugar, and rosemary. Bring to boiling; reduce heat. Simmer, uncovered, for 5 to 8 minutes or until chutney is of desired consistency, stirring occasionally. Season to taste with salt and pepper. Set aside.

2 Meanwhile, trim fat from meat. Cut meat crosswise into 6 pieces. Press each pork piece with the palm of your hand to make an even thickness. In a large nonstick skillet heat oil over medium-high heat. Add pork pieces; cook for 2 to 3 minutes or until pork is tender and juices run clear, turning once.

3 Serve warm chutney with pork. If desired, serve with hot cooked rice.

Nutrition Facts per serving: 227 cal., 7 g total fat (1 g sat. fat), 55 mg chol., 185 mg sodium, 23 g carbo., 3 g fiber, 18 g pro.

For a special treat, consider corn bread as a charming dinner partner for this Southern-inspired dish. Bake and freeze some corn bread ahead so that it will be ready at a moment's notice.

MOLASSES-GLAZED PORK TENDERLOIN

¼ cup finely chopped prosciutto or 2 slices bacon, coarsely chopped

1 16-ounce package frozen lima beans or two 9-ounce packages frozen Italian green beans

½ cup chopped onion

¾ cup water

1 tablespoon olive oil

12 ounces pork tenderloin, cut into ½-inch slices

½ cup orange juice

3 tablespoons molasses

1 teaspoon cornstarch

½ teaspoon salt

¼ teaspoon black pepper

2 tablespoons snipped fresh parsley

START TO FINISH:

30 minutes

MAKES:

4 servings

MENU IDEA:

Veggie Mash
(see p. 271)

Purchased mixed berry pie served with butter pecan ice cream

1 In a large skillet cook prosciutto or bacon over medium heat until crisp; drain and set aside. In the same skillet cook beans and onion in the water according to lima bean package directions. Drain beans; set aside.

2 Add oil to same skillet; cook pork in hot oil over medium-high heat for 4 to 5 minutes or until tender and juices run clear, turning once.

3 Meanwhile, in a small bowl stir together orange juice, molasses, cornstarch, salt, and pepper. Add to meat in skillet. Cook and stir until thickened and bubbly. Cook and stir about 2 minutes more. Stir bean mixture into skillet mixture; heat through.

4 Serve bean mixture with pork. Top with the prosciutto or bacon; sprinkle with parsley.

Nutrition Facts per serving: 324 cal., 6 g total fat (1 g sat. fat), 52 mg chol., 460 mg sodium, 38 g carbo., 7 g fiber, 29 g pro.

Using frozen sweet potatoes cuts down on time-consuming peeling and chopping.

PORK TENDERLOIN WITH SWEET POTATOES

START TO FINISH:

25 minutes

MAKES:

4 servings

MENU IDEA:

B.L.T. Salad (make half of the recipe) *(see p. 305)*

Purchased cherry or apple coffee cake

12 ounces pork tenderloin, cut into ½-inch slices

1 large onion, cut into wedges

1 tablespoon cooking oil

2 10-ounce or one 16-ounce package(s) frozen candied sweet potatoes, thawed

1 tablespoon snipped fresh thyme or ½ teaspoon dried thyme, crushed

1 In a large skillet cook pork slices and onion wedges in hot oil about 6 minutes or until pork is tender and juices run clear, turning pork once. Remove pork from the skillet; set aside.

2 Stir sweet potatoes with sauce and dried thyme, if using, into onion wedges in skillet. Bring to boiling; reduce heat to medium. Cover and cook about 10 minutes or until potatoes are tender. Return pork to skillet. Heat through. Stir in fresh thyme, if using.

Nutrition Facts per serving: 386 cal., 13 g total·fat (2 g sat. fat), 55 mg chol., 484 mg sodium, 44 g carbo., 4 g fiber, 20 g pro.

Pork and apples are a classic combination—and for good reason! They taste great together, especially in this easy entrée that takes just 15 minutes to bring to the table.

PORK SLICES WITH APPLES

2   tablespoons olive oil or butter

1   teaspoon bottled minced garlic (2 cloves)

1   pound pork tenderloin, cut crosswise into ½-inch slices

1   20-ounce can sliced apples, drained

2   teaspoons snipped fresh thyme or ½ teaspoon dried thyme, crushed

1 In a 12-inch skillet heat oil over medium-high heat. Add garlic; cook for 15 seconds. Carefully place the pork slices into the hot oil. Cook about 4 minutes or until browned and juices run clear, turning once. Add drained apples and thyme. Cover and cook about 1 minute or until apples are heated through.

Nutrition Facts per serving: 292 cal., 11 g total fat (2 g sat. fat), 73 mg chol., 61 mg sodium, 24 g carbo., 2 g fiber, 24 g pro.

START TO FINISH:
15 minutes

MAKES:
4 servings

MENU IDEA:

Frozen sweet peas, cooked and tossed with butter and shredded orange peel

Chocolate-Mint Sandwich Cookies *(see p. 347)*

Pork and pears are delightful in this fresh fall salad. Leaving the pears unpeeled adds color and boosts the fiber content. The nuts add crunch.

SAUTÉED PORK & PEAR SALAD

START TO FINISH:

30 minutes

MAKES:

4 servings

MENU IDEA:

Cracked wheat brown-and-serve rolls, baked

Chocolate ice cream with Mocha Cookies *(see p. 345)*

8   ounces boneless pork top loin roast or pork tenderloin, trimmed and cut into thin bite-size strips

½   teaspoon black pepper

½   teaspoon dried sage, crushed

2   tablespoons olive oil

¼   cup coarsely chopped hazelnuts or almonds, toasted

½   cup unsweetened pineapple juice

1   tablespoon honey

2   teaspoons Dijon-style mustard

1   8-ounce package torn mixed salad greens (about 7 cups)

2   medium pears, cored and sliced

1 Sprinkle pork with pepper and sage. In a large skillet heat 1 tablespoon of the oil over medium-high heat. Add pork. Cook and stir for 2 to 3 minutes or until meat is just slightly pink in the center. Add nuts. Cook and stir for 30 seconds more. Remove pork mixture; cover and keep warm.

2 For dressing, in the same skillet combine the remaining 1 tablespoon oil, the pineapple juice, honey, and mustard. Cook and stir just until bubbly, scraping up any crusty, browned bits from bottom of skillet.

3 Divide salad greens among 4 shallow bowls or dinner plates. Arrange pears on greens. Top with meat mixture and drizzle with dressing.

Nutrition Facts per serving: 282 cal., 15 g total fat (2 g sat. fat), 33 mg chol., 45 mg sodium, 24 g carbo., 4 g fiber, 14 g pro.

These tacos get their pizzazz from chipotle chili powder. If you can't find it at your supermarket, crush a dried chipotle chile pepper. In a real pinch, regular chili powder will do.

SOFT SHELL PORK TACOS

2	teaspoons cooking oil
8	ounces boneless pork loin, trimmed and cut into thin bite-size strips
¼	cup dairy sour cream
¼	teaspoon chipotle chili powder, crushed dried chipotle chile pepper, or chili powder
4	6-inch flour tortillas, warmed*
½	cup shredded lettuce
½	cup diced tomato
½	cup shredded cheddar cheese (2 ounces)
	Bottled salsa

1 In a large skillet heat oil over medium-high heat. Add pork; cook until done. Set aside.

2 In a small bowl combine sour cream and chipotle chili powder, chipotle pepper, or chili powder; set aside.

3 Spoon one-fourth of the pork onto each tortilla just below the center. Top pork with lettuce, tomato, and cheese. Fold top half of each tortilla over filling. Serve with sour cream mixture and salsa.

*NOTE: To warm tortillas, wrap them in white microwave-safe paper towels; microwave on 100% power (high) for 15 to 30 seconds or until tortillas are softened. (Or wrap tortillas in foil. Heat in a 350°F oven for 10 to 15 minutes or until warmed.)

Nutrition Facts per serving: 255 cal., 14 g total fat (6 g sat. fat), 51 mg chol., 243 mg sodium, 13 g carbo., 1 g fiber, 18 g pro.

TEST KITCHEN TIP: For lower-fat tacos, substitute light dairy sour cream and reduced-fat cheddar cheese for the regular sour cream and cheddar cheese.

Nutrition Facts per serving: 240 cal., 11 g total fat (4 g sat. fat), 48 mg chol., 263 mg sodium, 14 g carbo., 1 g fiber, 19 g pro.

START TO FINISH:
25 minutes
MAKES:
4 servings

MENU IDEA:

Fried rice mix prepared according to package directions and sprinkled with shredded cheese

Bananas Suzette over Pound Cake *(see p. 340)*

Look for pork that's been presliced ready for stir-fries. It will save you time and will make this Asian-inspired recipe a snap.

MU SHU-STYLE PORK ROLL-UPS

START TO FINISH:

20 minutes

MAKES:

4 servings

1	teaspoon toasted sesame oil
12	ounces lean boneless pork, trimmed and cut into thin bite-size strips
2	cups loose-pack frozen stir-fry vegetables (any combination)
4	10-inch flour tortillas, warmed*
¼	cup bottled plum or hoisin sauce

1 In a large skillet heat oil over medium-high heat. Add pork; cook and stir for 2 to 3 minutes or just until meat is slightly pink in center. Add the vegetables. Cook and stir for 3 to 4 minutes or until vegetables are crisp-tender.

2 Spread each tortilla with 1 tablespoon of the plum or hoisin sauce. Spoon one-fourth of the meat mixture onto each tortilla just below the center. Fold the bottom edge of each tortilla up and over the filling. Fold in the sides until they meet; roll up over the filling.

MENU IDEA:

Spicy Peanut Noodles
(see p. 282)

Honeydew melon and/or cantaloupe wedges

*NOTE: To warm tortillas, wrap them in white microwave-safe paper towels; microwave on 100% power (high) for 15 to 30 seconds or until tortillas are softened. (Or wrap tortillas in foil. Heat in a 350°F oven for 10 to 15 minutes or until warmed.)

Nutrition Facts per serving: 302 cal., 8 g total fat (2 g sat. fat), 53 mg chol., 311 mg sodium, 34 g carbo., 2 g fiber, 22 g pro.

Make your meal lively by adding some Caribbean heat from Jerk seasoning. It's a heady and fragrant combination of chiles, garlic, onion, and other seasonings, such as thyme, cinnamon, ginger, allspice, and cloves.

JAMAICAN PORK STIR-FRY

2 tablespoons cooking oil

1 16-ounce package loose-pack frozen peas, whole baby carrots, snow peas, and baby corn

12 ounces lean boneless pork, trimmed and cut into thin bite-size strips

2 to 3 teaspoons Jamaican jerk seasoning

¾ cup bottled plum sauce

Hot cooked rice or pasta

Crushed corn chips or chopped peanuts

1 In a wok or large skillet heat oil over medium-high heat. Add frozen vegetables; cook and stir for 5 to 7 minutes or until vegetables are crisp-tender. Remove vegetables from wok.

2 Toss pork strips with Jamaican jerk seasoning; add pork strips to wok. (Add more cooking oil if necessary.) Cook and stir for 2 to 3 minutes or until pork is tender and juices run clear.

3 Add plum sauce to wok. Return vegetables to wok. Stir together to coat all ingredients with sauce. Heat through. Serve over hot cooked rice or pasta. Sprinkle with corn chips or peanuts.

Nutrition Facts per serving: 419 cal., 11 g total fat (2 g sat. fat), 46 mg chol., 269 mg sodium, 51 g carbo., 3 g fiber, 24 g pro.

START TO FINISH:
20 minutes
MAKES:
4 servings

MENU IDEA:

Fresh pineapple wedges served with purchased fruit dip

No-Drip Chocolate Dip *(see p. 369)*

There's no heating up the kitchen with this dinner—not when you cook the ham on the grill and your vegetable of choice in the microwave oven. Presto! You're done!

PEACH-MUSTARD GLAZED HAM

PREP:

10 minutes

GRILL:

6 minutes + 6 minutes

MAKES:

4 servings

2	tablespoons packed brown sugar
2	tablespoons spicy brown mustard
⅓	cup peach nectar or apricot nectar
1	1-pound cooked ham slice, cut ¾ to 1 inch thick
4	medium peaches, peeled and halved lengthwise
2	small green and/or red sweet peppers, each cut crosswise into 4 rings

1 For glaze, in a small bowl combine brown sugar and mustard. Gradually whisk in the nectar until smooth. To prevent ham from curling, make shallow cuts around the edge at 1-inch intervals. Brush 1 side of the ham slice with the glaze.

2 Place ham slice, glazed side down, on the greased rack of an uncovered grill directly over medium-hot heat. Grill for 6 minutes. Turn ham slice. Top with peach halves and pepper rings. Brush ham, peaches, and peppers with glaze. Grill for 6 to 10 minutes more or until heated through, brushing occasionally with glaze.

Nutrition Facts per serving: 284 cal., 7 g total fat (2 g sat. fat), 60 mg chol., 1,468 mg sodium, 31 g carbo., 3 g fiber, 26 g pro.

MENU IDEA:

Peeled baby carrots, cooked and tossed with butter and brown sugar

Cinnamon-Seared Pound Cake
(see p. 341)

Let's face it—plain ham slices can be a little dull. You won't find anything ordinary about this recipe because the ham slice is adorned with an ambrosial sauce of cherries and fresh basil.

HAM SLICE WITH BASIL-CHERRY SAUCE

2   tablespoons butter or margarine

1   1- to 1¼-pound cooked center-cut ham slice, cut ½ inch thick

1   15- to 17-ounce can pitted dark sweet cherries

2   teaspoons cornstarch

2   teaspoons fresh snipped basil or ½ teaspoon dried basil, crushed

1 In a 12-inch skillet melt 1 tablespoon of the butter over medium heat. Add ham; cook for 8 to 10 minutes or until heated through, turning once. Transfer to a serving platter; keep warm.

2 Meanwhile, drain canned cherries, reserving juice; set cherries aside. In a small saucepan stir reserved cherry juice into cornstarch. Cook and stir until thickened and bubbly; cook and stir for 2 minutes more. Add cherries, basil, and remaining 1 tablespoon butter; cook and stir until butter is melted and mixture is heated through. Serve warm over ham.

Nutrition Facts per serving: 338 cal., 18 g total fat (8 g sat. fat), 74 mg chol., 1,285 mg sodium, 20 g carbo., 2 g fiber, 23 g pro.

START TO FINISH:

20 minutes

MAKES:

4 servings

MENU IDEA:

Potatoes & Sugar Snap Peas
(see p. 269)

Purchased bakery or frozen lemon meringue pie

This dish is so good it is reason enough to keep your pantry stocked with beans, olive oil, and garlic. You'll want to make this satisfying supper often.

HAM & BEANS WITH ESCAROLE

START TO FINISH:

20 minutes

MAKES:

4 servings

MENU IDEA:

Purchased refrigerated large southern-style or flaky biscuits, baked and served with honey

Fruit-Filled Nachos *(see p. 358)*

2   15-ounce cans Great Northern beans

1   tablespoon olive oil

1   tablespoon bottled minced garlic (6 cloves)

2   cups cooked smoked ham cut into bite-size strips

3   cups chopped fresh escarole or spinach

1 Drain beans, reserving liquid. In a large nonstick skillet heat oil over medium heat. Add garlic; cook and stir for 1 minute. Add beans and ham to skillet. Cook about 5 minutes or until heated through, stirring occasionally. Stir in escarole or spinach; cover and cook for 2 to 5 minutes more or until greens are wilted. If desired, thin mixture with some of the reserved liquid.

Nutrition Facts per serving: 324 cal., 8 g total fat (2 g sat. fat), 39 mg chol., 1,443 mg sodium, 33 g carbo., 11 g fiber, 29 g pro.

Pasta is the empty canvas of cooking—the possibilities are endless! Here it's topped with a wonderfully rich and cheesy curry-and-ham sauce.

HAM CURRY SAUCE FOR PASTA

12	ounces dried spaghetti
2	tablespoons butter or margarine
3	green onions, sliced
1/2	cup whipping cream
1	3-ounce package cream cheese
1	tablespoon curry powder
1/4	teaspoon salt
1/8	teaspoon black pepper
2	medium tomatoes, diced
3	ounces cooked ham, cut into bite-size pieces
1/4	cup finely shredded Parmesan cheese (1 ounce)

1 Cook spaghetti according to package directions; drain well. Return to pan; cover and keep warm.

2 Meanwhile, for sauce, in a large skillet melt butter over medium heat. Add green onions; cook until tender. Stir in whipping cream, cream cheese, curry powder, salt, and pepper. Cook and stir about 5 minutes or until cream cheese is melted. Stir in tomatoes and ham; cook and gently stir until heated through.

3 Toss sauce with cooked spaghetti. Transfer to a serving bowl; sprinkle with Parmesan cheese.

Nutrition Facts per serving: 592 cal., 30 g total fat (17 g sat. fat), 93 mg chol., 891 mg sodium, 57 g carbo., 3 g fiber, 24 g pro.

START TO FINISH:
30 minutes

MAKES:
5 servings

MENU IDEA:

Quick Focaccia Breadsticks
(see p. 330)

Fresh peach slices topped with vanilla-flavored whipped cream

This creamy, satisfying dish resembles a vegetable-studded fettuccine Alfredo. Instead of the usual heavy cream, this rich-tasting sauce is made with evaporated milk. You save on calories and don't have to give up taste.

PASTA WITH HAM-MUSHROOM SAUCE

START TO FINISH:

30 minutes

MAKES:

4 servings

MENU IDEA:

Baguette-style French bread served with olive oil and cracked black pepper

Coffee & Almond Parfaits *(see p. 342)*

2	cups sliced fresh shiitake or button mushrooms
1	small red or green sweet pepper, cut into thin strips
1	medium onion, chopped
1/2	teaspoon bottled minced garlic (1 clove)
1	tablespoon butter or margarine
1	12-ounce can (1 1/2 cups) evaporated milk
2	tablespoons snipped fresh basil or 1/2 teaspoon dried basil, crushed
4	teaspoons cornstarch
1/4	teaspoon black pepper
4	ounces cooked ham, cut into thin bite-size strips
1	9-ounce package refrigerated fettuccine
	Finely shredded Parmesan cheese (optional)

1 For sauce, in a large skillet cook mushrooms, sweet pepper, onion, and garlic in hot butter until tender. In a medium bowl combine evaporated milk, basil, cornstarch, and black pepper. Stir into vegetable mixture in skillet. Cook and stir over medium heat until bubbly. Cook and stir for 2 minutes more. Stir in ham. Remove from heat.

2 Meanwhile, cook pasta according to package directions. Drain. Serve sauce over pasta. If desired, sprinkle with Parmesan cheese.

Nutrition Facts per serving: 432 cal., 14 g total fat (7 g sat. fat), 116 mg chol., 501 mg sodium, 60 g carbo., 4 g fiber, 20 g pro.

TEST KITCHEN TIP: For a lower-fat sauce, substitute fat-free evaporated milk for the regular evaporated milk.

Nutrition Facts per serving: 385 cal., 10 g total fat (4 g sat. fat), 96 mg chol., 600 mg sodium, 52 g carbo., 3 g fiber, 22 g pro.

Cavatappi is a short, ridged, spiral macaroni. But you can use any tubular pasta that you have on hand.

CAVATAPPI WITH TOMATOES & HAM

1	medium onion, cut into ¼-inch slices
12	red and/or yellow cherry and/or pear tomatoes, halved
8	ounces dried cavatappi or gemelli pasta
¼	teaspoon crushed red pepper (optional)
2	ounces thinly sliced cooked ham, cut into strips
3	tablespoons thinly sliced fresh basil
2	tablespoons garlic-flavor olive oil or olive oil

1 Place onion slices on the foil-lined rack of a broiler pan. Broil onion slices 4 inches from heat for 5 minutes. Add tomato halves to pan; broil about 5 minutes more or until edges are brown.

2 Meanwhile, cook pasta according to package directions, adding crushed red pepper (if desired) to water. Drain well. Return to pan; cover and keep warm.

3 Cut up onion slices. Toss onion pieces and tomato halves with pasta, ham, basil, and oil.

Nutrition Facts per serving: 341 cal., 11 g total fat (2 g sat. fat), 16 mg chol., 381 mg sodium, 47 g carbo., 2 g fiber, 13 g pro.

START TO FINISH:

30 minutes

MAKES:

4 servings

MENU IDEA:

Mozzarella Caprese (make half of the recipe) *(see p. 320)*

Purchased biscotti served with espresso or flavored coffee

Turning whole grain breads, such as rye, into deliciously crunchy croutons is a great way to add fiber to recipes. The rustic and nutty rye stands up well to the zesty honey-mustard salad dressing.

HAM & RYE SALAD

PREP:

10 minutes

BAKE:

10 minutes

MAKES:

4 to 6 servings

MENU IDEA:

Sourdough bread

Caramel Apple Pastry
(see p. 333)

6 slices rye bread

3 tablespoons butter or margarine, melted

1 10-ounce package torn mixed salad greens with carrot

8 ounces cooked ham, cubed

⅔ cup bottled honey-mustard salad dressing

1 Cut rye bread slices into ¾-inch cubes (should have 4 cups); place in a large bowl. Add melted butter and toss to coat. Arrange bread cubes in an even layer in a shallow baking pan. Bake in a 350°F oven for 10 to 15 minutes or until toasted, turning once. Set aside to cool.

2 In a large salad bowl toss together toasted bread cubes, salad greens, and ham. Drizzle with salad dressing. Toss gently to coat.

Nutrition Facts per serving: 503 cal., 36 g total fat (10 g sat. fat), 65 mg chol., 1,602 mg sodium, 29 g carbo., 4 g fiber, 18 g pro.

It's a classic sandwich combination, so why not enjoy it in a soup?

HAM-CHEESE SOUP

1	cup water
1½	cups chopped, peeled potatoes
1	medium carrot, chopped
1	stalk celery, chopped
¼	cup chopped onion
2	tablespoons butter or margarine
2	tablespoons all-purpose flour
1	cup milk
1	cup diced cooked ham (about 5 ounces)
8	ounces process cheese spread, cubed

1 In a large saucepan bring the water to boiling. Add potatoes, carrot, celery, and onion; cover and cook for 12 to 15 minutes or until tender. Do not drain.

2 Meanwhile, in a small saucepan melt butter; stir in flour until smooth. Add milk all at once. Cook and stir over medium heat until mixture is thickened and bubbly. Stir into undrained vegetable mixture; stir in ham and cheese. Stir until cheese melts and mixture is heated through.

Nutrition Facts per serving: 410 cal., 25 g total fat (15 g sat. fat), 88 mg chol., 1,344 mg sodium, 24 g carbo., 2 g fiber, 23 g pro.

START TO FINISH:

30 minutes

MAKES:

4 servings

MENU IDEA:

Sliced fresh red and/ or yellow tomatoes drizzled with olive oil and sprinkled with snipped fresh basil

Triple Dipster Strawberries
(see p. 359)

Add a dash of black pepper, snipped fresh dill, or celery seeds to the filling, if you like.

HAM & POTATO STUFFED PEPPERS

START TO FINISH:

15 minutes

MAKES:

4 servings

2   medium green sweet peppers

1   pint deli potato salad

1   cup diced cooked ham

½   cup loose-pack frozen whole kernel corn, thawed

1   to 2 tablespoons dill pickle relish

1 Cut sweet peppers in half; remove stems, seeds, and membranes. In a large saucepan cook pepper halves in a large amount of boiling water for 3 minutes. Drain. Put pepper halves in bowl of ice water to chill.

2 Meanwhile, stir together potato salad, ham, corn, and pickle relish. Invert pepper halves onto paper towels to drain. Set pepper halves cut sides up. Spoon potato mixture into pepper halves.

Nutrition Facts per serving: 280 cal., 14 g total fat (3 g sat. fat), 106 mg chol., 1,229 mg sodium, 23 g carbo., 3 g fiber, 12 g pro.

MENU IDEA:

Cantaloupe or honeydew melon wedges

Strawberry ice cream with Chocolate-Hazelnut Ice Cream Sauce
(see p. 372)

Have you ever wondered what to do with those convenient-looking tubes of refrigerated polenta you've spotted in the produce section? Here's a delicious answer.

SAUSAGE & POLENTA WITH BALSAMIC VINAIGRETTE

3	uncooked sweet (mild) Italian sausage links, each cut into 4 pieces (about 12 ounces total)
½	of a 16-ounce tube refrigerated polenta (plain or flavored)
1	tablespoon olive oil
6	cups purchased Mediterranean- or Italian-blend torn mixed greens
½	cup apple juice or apple cider
¼	cup balsamic vinegar
2	tablespoons snipped dried tomato (not oil-packed)
¼	cup pine nuts or slivered almonds, toasted (optional)

START TO FINISH:
30 minutes
MAKES:
4 servings

1 In a 10-inch skillet cook sausage over medium heat for 5 minutes, turning to brown evenly. Meanwhile, cut polenta into ¼-inch slices; cut each slice crosswise in half. Brush tops of polenta slices with oil. Arrange in a single layer on a baking sheet. Bake in a 400°F oven for 10 to 12 minutes or until golden brown, turning once.

2 Divide greens among 4 dinner plates; set aside.

3 Remove sausage from skillet; drain off fat and wipe out skillet. Return sausage to skillet; add apple juice, vinegar, and dried tomato. Bring to boiling; reduce heat. Cover and simmer for 8 to 10 minutes or until sausage is cooked through (160°F).*

4 Arrange polenta slices over greens on plates. Add sausage pieces to plates; drizzle with balsamic mixture. If desired, sprinkle with nuts.

*NOTE: The internal color of a sausage piece is not a reliable doneness indicator. A sausage piece cooked to 160°F is safe, regardless of color. To measure the doneness of a sausage piece, insert an instant-read thermometer from an end into the center of the sausage piece.

Nutrition Facts per serving: 380 cal., 22 g total fat (8 g sat. fat), 57 mg chol., 741 mg sodium, 23 g carbo., 4 g fiber, 15 g pro.

MENU IDEA:

Creamy Carrot Soup
(see p. 293)

Purchased pound cake served with canned blueberry pie filling, whipped cream, and shredded orange peel

Seasoned tomatoes and ramen noodles make this dish extra easy while adding lots of snappy flavor.

QUICK SAUSAGE-NOODLE SOUP

START TO FINISH:

20 minutes

MAKES:

4 servings

MENU IDEA:

Honey-Nut Corn Muffins *(see p. 323)*

Purchased individual graham cracker tart shells filled with canned chocolate fudge pudding, topped with whipped cream, and sprinkled with miniature semisweet chocolate pieces

4   cups water

1   14½-ounce can diced tomatoes with green pepper and onion, undrained

8   ounces cooked smoked sausage, halved lengthwise and thinly sliced

1   medium sweet pepper, cut into bite-size strips

2   3-ounce packages chicken-flavored ramen noodles

1 In a large saucepan combine the water, undrained tomatoes, sausage, sweet pepper, and seasoning packets from the noodles. Bring to boiling. Break noodles into quarters; add to saucepan. Return to boiling; cook for 2 to 3 minutes or until noodles are tender.

Nutrition Facts per serving: 462 cal., 27 g total fat (6 g sat. fat), 39 mg chol., 2,001 mg sodium, 36 g carbo., 2 g fiber, 19 g pro.

This is a dish that will have you coming back for more. The smokiness of the sausage is a wonderful counterpart to the tangy, vinegary dressing, and the red cabbage and carrot add intense color and crunch.

GERMAN SWEET & SOUR STIR-FRY

1	pound cooked smoked sausage, cut into 1-inch slices
4	green onions, bias-sliced into 1-inch pieces
2	tablespoons cooking oil
1	tablespoon all-purpose flour
1	tablespoon sugar
½	teaspoon salt
½	teaspoon celery seeds
½	teaspoon dry mustard
¼	teaspoon black pepper
⅔	cup water
¼	cup vinegar
1	10-ounce package shredded red cabbage (5 cups)
2	cups packaged coarsely shredded carrot

1 In a 12-inch skillet cook and stir sliced sausage and green onions in hot oil for 5 minutes; remove from skillet with a slotted spoon.

2 For dressing, stir flour, sugar, salt, celery seeds, dry mustard, and pepper into drippings in skillet. Stir in the water and vinegar. Cook and stir until thickened and bubbly. Stir in the cabbage and carrot. Cover and simmer about 3 minutes or until cabbage is crisp-tender, stirring once. Top with sausage mixture. Cover and cook for 1 to 2 minutes more or until heated through.

Nutrition Facts per serving: 517 cal., 41 g total fat (17 g sat. fat), 50 mg chol., 1,276 mg sodium, 22 g carbo., 4 g fiber, 16 g pro.

TEST KITCHEN TIP: For a lower-fat stir-fry, substitute light smoked sausage for the regular sausage.

Nutrition Facts per serving: 357 cal., 23 g total fat (8 g sat. fat), 70 mg chol., 1,416 mg sodium, 22 g carbo., 4 g fiber, 20 g pro.

START TO FINISH:

20 minutes

MAKES:

4 to 6 servings

MENU IDEA:

Easy Beer Cheese Soup *(see p. 297)*

Purchased German chocolate cake served with vanilla ice cream

After a busy day you want a dinner solution, not a dinner problem. That's where this hearty soup comes in. It's delicious and ready in 20 minutes. Who would have thought chowder could be so easy!

CORN & SAUSAGE CHOWDER

START TO FINISH:

20 minutes

MAKES:

5 servings

1 20-ounce package refrigerated shredded hash brown potatoes
1 14-ounce can reduced-sodium chicken broth
2 cups loose-pack frozen whole kernel corn
2 cups milk
12 ounces cooked smoked sausage, halved lengthwise and sliced
⅓ cup sliced green onions
¼ teaspoon black pepper
   Salt
   Green or red bottled hot pepper sauce

❶ In a 4-quart Dutch oven or saucepan combine potatoes, broth, and corn. Bring just to boiling; reduce heat. Cover and simmer about 10 minutes or just until potatoes are tender, stirring occasionally.

❷ Using a potato masher, slightly mash potatoes. Stir in milk, sausage, green onions, and pepper; heat through. Season to taste with salt and hot pepper sauce.

Nutrition Facts per serving: 444 cal., 23 g total fat (11 g sat. fat), 38 mg chol., 979 mg sodium, 45 g carbo., 3 g fiber, 17 g pro.

TEST KITCHEN TIP: For a lower-fat soup, substitute light smoked sausage for the regular sausage and fat-free milk for the regular milk.

Nutrition Facts per serving: 264 cal., 3 g total fat (0 g sat. fat), 26 mg chol., 1,243 mg sodium, 42 g carbo., 3 g fiber, 19 g pro.

MENU IDEA:

Purchased refrigerated corn bread twists, baked, or purchased corn muffins served with honey

Chocolate-Peanut Butter Fondue
(see p. 368)

Cold weather calls for warming comfort food such as this substantial soup. Even better, it's ready in under a half hour!

KIELBASA SOUP

6¼ cups chicken broth

4 cups water

12 ounces cooked kielbasa or Polish sausage (Polska kielbasa), cut into ¼- to ½-inch slices

2 stalks celery, chopped

2 medium carrots, thinly sliced

2 bay leaves

¼ teaspoon black pepper

4 ounces dried wide noodles (about 2 cups)

1 In a 4-quart Dutch oven combine broth, the water, kielbasa, celery, carrots, bay leaves, and pepper. Bring to boiling. Add noodles. Return to boiling. Cook for 8 to 10 minutes or just until noodles and vegetables are tender. Discard bay leaves.

Nutrition Facts per serving: 347 cal., 22 g total fat (10 g sat. fat), 55 mg chol., 1,819 mg sodium, 23 g carbo., 2 g fiber, 14 g pro.

START TO FINISH:

25 minutes

MAKES:

5 servings

MENU IDEA:

Whole-grain crackers served with assorted cheeses

Hot Taffy Apple Pita Pizza *(see p. 334)*

Maple-flavored sausage and white beans team up in a winning combination that is so simple to prepare. Don't be fooled though—what it lacks in prep time it makes up for in taste.

RANGE-TOP SAUSAGE SOUP

START TO FINISH:

25 minutes

MAKES:

3 or 4 servings

1	7-ounce package (10 links) frozen maple-flavored brown-and-serve sausage links or original brown-and-serve sausage links
1	15-ounce can Great Northern beans, undrained
1	cup sliced cauliflower florets
½	cup water
1	8-ounce can pizza sauce

1 Cut each of the sausage links crosswise into thirds. In a medium saucepan cook the sausage pieces over medium-high heat about 7 minutes or until browned. Stir in the undrained beans, cauliflower, and the water.

2 Bring to boiling; reduce heat. Cover and simmer for 8 to 10 minutes or until cauliflower is tender. Stir in pizza sauce; heat through.

Nutrition Facts per serving: 469 cal., 30 g total fat (10 g sat. fat), 58 mg chol., 1.501 mg sodium, 31 g carbo., 8 g fiber, 21 g pro.

MENU IDEA:

Purchased ready-to-bake garlic bread loaf, baked

Banana Tostadas
(see p. 355)

Green tomatoes give this quick dish a piquant flavor. If you don't have green tomatoes on hand—use red ones. The pasta still will be sensational.

SAUTÉ & SERVE PASTA TOSS

8	ounces dried fusilli or spaghetti
2	tablespoons olive oil or cooking oil
1½	ounces Italian bread, torn into small pieces (1½ cups)
8	ounces bulk Italian sausage or ground beef
2	medium green tomatoes, cut into wedges
1	medium red onion, coarsely chopped
1	medium red, green, or yellow sweet pepper, cut into bite-size pieces
1	26-ounce jar pasta sauce with olives

1 Cook pasta according to package directions; drain well. Return pasta to pan; cover and keep warm.

2 Meanwhile, in a large skillet heat the oil over medium-high heat. Add bread pieces. Cook and stir for 2 to 3 minutes or until bread is toasted. Remove from skillet; set aside.

3 In the same skillet combine sausage or ground beef, green tomatoes, onion, and sweet pepper. Cook and stir over medium heat for 6 to 8 minutes or until vegetables are tender and sausage is brown. Drain off fat. Stir pasta sauce into mixture in skillet. Cook and stir until heated through. Serve sauce over hot cooked pasta; sprinkle with toasted bread pieces.

Nutrition Facts per serving: 595 cal., 23 g total fat (6 g sat. fat), 38 mg chol., 1,023 mg sodium, 71 g carbo., 6 g fiber, 20 g pro.

START TO FINISH:

25 minutes

MAKES:

4 servings

MENU IDEA:

Mixed greens tossed with bottled balsamic vinaigrette salad dressing

Peaches & Cranberries with Sorbet
(make half of the recipe)
(see p. 374)

These brimming-with-flavor wraps spice up pork and succotash with a touch of old Mexico.

PORK WITH BLACK BEANS & SUCCOTASH

START TO FINISH:

30 minutes

MAKES:

4 servings

MENU IDEA:

Mexican Potato Cakes *(see p. 271)*

Assorted sliced fruit, such as papaya, kiwifruit, mango, and/or banana served with strawberry ice cream

8	ounces bulk pork sausage
1	medium onion, chopped
1	small red sweet pepper, chopped
1	10-ounce package frozen succotash or 1 cup loose-pack frozen whole kernel corn plus 1 cup loose-pack frozen lima beans
¼	cup water
1	15-ounce can black beans, rinsed and drained
½	cup bottled salsa
2	tablespoons snipped fresh cilantro
8	6-inch corn tortillas, warmed*
1	small avocado, seeded, peeled, sliced, and halved
	Dairy sour cream (optional)

1 In a large nonstick skillet combine sausage, onion, and sweet pepper; cook about 5 minutes or until meat is brown. Drain off fat. Stir succotash and the water into mixture in skillet.

2 Bring to boiling; reduce heat. Cover and simmer about 15 minutes or until beans in succotash are tender. Stir in black beans and salsa. Heat through. Remove from heat. Stir in cilantro.

3 Serve sausage mixture with tortillas, avocado slices, and, if desired, sour cream.

*NOTE: To warm tortillas, wrap them in white microwave-safe paper towels; microwave on 100% power (high) for 15 to 30 seconds or until tortillas are softened. (Or wrap tortillas in foil. Heat in a 350°F oven for 10 to 15 minutes or until warmed.)

Nutrition Facts per serving: 536 cal., 24 g total fat (7 g sat. fat), 39 mg chol., 774 mg sodium, 68 g carbo., 12 g fiber, 21 g pro.

TEST KITCHEN TIP: For a lower-fat dish, substitute low-fat bulk pork sausage for the regular sausage.

Nutrition Facts per serving: 392 cal., 5 g total fat (1 g sat. fat), 33 mg chol., 717 mg sodium, 66 g carbo., 10 g fiber, 24 g pro.

Perfect for busy nights, this no-fuss skillet meal is sure to appeal to hungry people.

SAUSAGE-CAVATELLI SKILLET

8   ounces dried cavatelli (about 1¾ cups)

1   pound bulk Italian sausage or ground beef

1   medium green sweet pepper, chopped (optional)

1   20-ounce jar spaghetti sauce with mushrooms

1   cup shredded mozzarella cheese (4 ounces)

1 Cook cavatelli according to package directions; drain well.

2 Meanwhile, in a large skillet cook Italian sausage or ground beef and sweet pepper (if desired) until sausage is brown. Drain off fat. Stir spaghetti sauce into sausage in skillet; cook about 2 minutes or until heated through. Stir in drained cavatelli. Sprinkle with cheese. Cover and cook about 2 minutes more or until cheese melts.

Nutrition Facts per serving: 677 cal., 32 g total fat (13 g sat. fat), 93 mg chol., 1,469 mg sodium, 60 g carbo., 4 g fiber, 32 g pro.

START TO FINISH:
20 minutes
MAKES:
4 servings

MENU IDEA:

Torn leaf lettuce, tossed with hard-cooked egg, chopped fresh tomato, seasoned croutons, and bottled salad dressing

Fast & Fruity Banana Split Tarts
(see p. 352)

Chorizo sausage, made with garlic, chili powder, and other spices, is the star here surrounded by the vibrant colors of tomatoes, green chile peppers, corn, and cheddar cheese.

TEX-MEX SKILLET

START TO FINISH:

30 minutes

MAKES:

4 servings

MENU IDEA:

Nacho Corn Soup
(see p. 292)

Mixed fresh berries

8	ounces ground pork
4	ounces uncooked chorizo sausage
1	10-ounce can diced tomatoes and green chile peppers, undrained
1	cup loose-pack frozen whole kernel corn
¾	cup water
1	small red sweet pepper, chopped
1	cup instant rice
½	cup shredded cheddar cheese or Monterey Jack cheese (2 ounces)
	Flour tortillas, warmed* (optional)
	Dairy sour cream (optional)

1 In a large skillet cook pork and sausage until brown. Drain off fat. Stir undrained tomatoes, corn, the water, and sweet pepper into pork mixture in skillet. Bring to boiling.

2 Stir uncooked rice into meat mixture in skillet. Remove from heat. Top with cheese. Cover and let stand about 5 minutes or until rice is tender. If desired, serve in flour tortillas and top with sour cream.

*NOTE: To warm tortillas, wrap them in white microwave-safe paper towels; microwave on 100% power (high) for 15 to 30 seconds or until tortillas are softened. (Or wrap tortillas in foil. Heat in a 350°F oven for 10 to 15 minutes or until warmed.)

Nutrition Facts per serving: 395 cal., 20 g total fat (9 g sat. fat), 66 mg chol., 748 mg sodium, 33 g carbo., 1 g fiber, 21 g pro.

Customize how hot you make this tortellini by choosing sweet or hot Italian sausage and mild, medium, or hot salsa.

HOT & SAUCY TORTELLINI

7   to 8 ounces dried cheese-filled tortellini (about 1¾ cups)

8   ounces bulk Italian sausage

1   16-ounce bottle salsa

1   13- to 14-ounce jar red pasta sauce

2   tablespoons snipped fresh cilantro

1 Cook tortellini according to package directions; drain well. Return tortellini to pan; cover and keep warm.

2 Meanwhile, in a large skillet cook sausage until brown; drain. Stir salsa and pasta sauce into sausage in skillet. Bring to boiling; reduce heat. Cover and simmer for 5 minutes. Stir cooked tortellini and 1 tablespoon of the cilantro into sauce mixture; heat through. Transfer to a serving bowl or platter. Sprinkle with remaining 1 tablespoon cilantro.

Nutrition Facts per serving: 450 cal., 20 g total fat (5 g sat. fat), 38 mg chol., 1,848 mg sodium, 42 g carbo., 3 g fiber, 21 g pro.

START TO FINISH:
25 minutes
MAKES:
4 servings

MENU IDEA:

Cheese-Garlic Crescents *(see p. 328)*

Lemon or mango sorbet served with purchased sugar cookies

Tomatoes are nowhere to be found on this pizza—but it is delicious just the same.

CANADIAN BACON PIZZA

PREP:

15 minutes

BAKE:

15 minutes

MAKES:

4 to 6 servings

MENU IDEA:

Avocado, Grapefruit & Spinach Salad *(see p. 304)*

Sliced fresh peaches, nectarines, and/or apricots topped with vanilla yogurt and sprinkled with brown sugar and ground cinnamon

1   16-ounce package Italian bread shell (Boboli)
1   6-ounce jar marinated artichoke hearts
1   5.2-ounce container semisoft cheese with garlic and herb
1   3.5-ounce package pizza-style Canadian-style bacon (1½-inch-diameter slices)
1   medium sweet pepper, cut into bite-size strips

1 Place the bread shell on a large baking sheet. Drain artichoke hearts, reserving 1 tablespoon of the marinade. Coarsely chop artichokes; set aside. In a small bowl combine cheese and reserved marinade. Spread half of the cheese mixture over bread shell; top with Canadian bacon, sweet pepper, and artichoke hearts. Spoon remaining cheese mixture by teaspoons over toppings. Bake in a 350°F oven about 15 minutes or until heated through.

Nutrition Facts per serving: 529 cal., 24 g total fat (9 g sat. fat), 54 mg chol., 1,136 mg sodium, 58 g carbo., 2 g fiber, 23 g pro.

While the soup simmers, pop some popcorn to garnish the soup.

BEER, CHEESE & BACON SOUP

1	medium onion, finely chopped
½	cup butter or margarine
⅔	cup all-purpose flour
1	teaspoon dry mustard
1	teaspoon paprika
⅛	teaspoon cayenne pepper
4	cups milk
1	12-ounce can beer
1	10½-ounce can condensed chicken broth
3	cups shredded sharp cheddar cheese (12 ounces)
10	slices bacon, crisp-cooked, drained, and crumbled
	Popcorn (optional)

1 In a large saucepan cook onion in hot butter until tender. Stir in flour, dry mustard, paprika, and cayenne pepper. Gradually stir in milk, beer, and broth. Cook, stirring constantly, over medium heat until mixture comes to a boil. Cook and stir for 1 minute more. Reduce heat. Add cheese, stirring until smooth. Stir in bacon. If desired, top individual servings with popcorn.

Nutrition Facts per serving: 463 cal., 34 g total fat (18 g sat. fat), 95 mg chol., 811 mg sodium, 16 g carbo., 1 g fiber, 20 g pro.

START TO FINISH:

15 minutes

MAKES:

8 servings

MENU IDEA:

Purchased refrigerated or frozen biscuits baked and served with a mixture of softened butter, black pepper, and snipped fresh chives

A Billow of Berries 'n' Brownies
(see p. 338)

Keep your pantry stocked with quick flavor boosters, such as canned tomatoes with seasonings, roasted red peppers, and balsamic vinegar. They're ideal for making recipes, such as this one—tender veal loin chops topped with a robust tomato-and-pepper relish.

VEAL CHOPS WITH TOMATO-PEPPER RELISH

START TO FINISH:

20 minutes

MAKES:

4 servings

MENU IDEA:

Purchased frozen potato wedges, baked and tossed with a mixture of grated Parmesan cheese, Italian seasoning, and seasoned salt

Fruited Yogurt Brûlée *(see p. 335)*

1	tablespoon olive oil
1	teaspoon bottled minced garlic (2 cloves)
1	14½-ounce can diced tomatoes with Italian herbs, undrained
1	7-ounce jar roasted red sweet peppers, rinsed, drained, and chopped
¼	teaspoon crushed red pepper
4	veal loin chops, cut 1 inch thick (about 2 pounds total)
	Salt
1	tablespoon balsamic vinegar

1 In a medium saucepan heat oil over medium heat. Add garlic; cook for 1 to 2 minutes or until golden brown. Add undrained tomatoes, roasted red peppers, and crushed red pepper. Bring to boiling; reduce heat. Simmer, uncovered, about 12 minutes or until slightly thickened.

2 Meanwhile, trim fat from chops. Heat a large nonstick skillet over medium-high heat until hot. Reduce heat to medium. Place veal chops in skillet; cook for 12 to 14 minutes or until done (160°F), turning once. Season with salt.

3 Stir balsamic vinegar into tomato mixture; serve with chops.

Nutrition Facts per serving: 236 cal., 8 g total fat (2 g sat. fat), 105 mg chol., 496 mg sodium, 13 g carbo., 2 g fiber, 28 g pro.

Though veal is the traditional meat of choice here, chicken makes an inexpensive substitute.

VEAL MARSALA

4	teaspoons olive oil or cooking oil
3	cups sliced fresh mushrooms
4	veal cutlets (1 pound total)
¼	teaspoon salt
¼	teaspoon black pepper
¾	cup dry Marsala
4	green onions, sliced
1	tablespoon snipped fresh sage or ½ teaspoon dried sage, crushed
1	tablespoon cold water
1	teaspoon cornstarch
⅛	teaspoon salt

1 In a 12-inch skillet heat 2 teaspoons of the oil over medium heat. Add mushrooms; cook and stir for 4 to 5 minutes or until tender. Remove from skillet. Set aside.

2 Sprinkle meat with the ¼ teaspoon salt and the pepper. In the same skillet heat the remaining 2 teaspoons oil over medium-high heat. Add veal, half at a time; cook for 2 to 3 minutes or until done, turning once. Transfer to dinner plates. Keep warm.

3 Add Marsala to drippings in skillet. Bring to boiling. Boil mixture gently for 1 minute, scraping up any browned bits. Return mushrooms to skillet; add green onions and sage. In a small bowl stir together the cold water, cornstarch, and the ⅛ teaspoon salt; add to skillet. Cook and stir until slightly thickened and bubbly; cook and stir for 1 minute more. To serve, spoon the mushroom mixture over meat. Serve immediately.

Nutrition Facts per serving: 219 cal., 8 g total fat (1 g sat. fat), 88 mg chol., 288 mg sodium, 4 g carbo., 1 g fiber, 27 g pro.

START TO FINISH:
30 minutes
MAKES:
4 servings

MENU IDEA:
Glazed Parsnips & Apples *(see p. 267)*

Purchased individual shortcakes topped with sliced bananas, strawberries, and vanilla ice cream, and drizzled with hot fudge sauce

Orange juice, ginger, garlic, and green onions combine to make this intense and tangy citrus sauce. It goes well with pork too.

VEAL WITH ORANGE SAUCE

START TO FINISH:

25 minutes

MAKES:

4 servings

MENU IDEA:

Steamed green beans or sugar snap peas tossed with butter and lemon-pepper

Crunchy Pound Cake Slices *(see p. 343)*

2   medium oranges

12   ounces veal scallopini or boneless veal leg round steak or sirloin steak, cut $1/4$ inch thick

$1/4$ teaspoon salt

$1/4$ teaspoon black pepper

2   teaspoons olive oil

$1/3$ cup sliced green onions

1   teaspoon bottled minced garlic (2 cloves)

1   teaspoon grated fresh ginger

1   cup orange juice

1   tablespoon white wine vinegar

2   teaspoons cornstarch

$1/4$ cup golden raisins

$1/8$ teaspoon salt

     Hot cooked pasta or rice (optional)

1 Finely shred $1/2$ teaspoon peel from 1 of the oranges; set peel aside. Peel and section oranges, discarding seeds. Set orange sections aside.

2 Sprinkle meat with the $1/4$ teaspoon salt and the pepper. In a large nonstick skillet heat oil over medium-high heat. Add veal; cook for 4 to 6 minutes or until brown, turning once. Remove meat from skillet, reserving drippings in skillet. Add green onions, garlic, and ginger to drippings in skillet. Cook and stir over medium heat for 1 minute.

3 In a small bowl stir together orange juice, vinegar, and cornstarch; add to skillet. Cook and stir until slightly thickened and bubbly. Add the orange peel, orange sections, raisins, and the $1/8$ teaspoon salt to skillet. Toss gently to coat. Return meat to skillet; spoon sauce over meat. Heat through. If desired, serve meat over hot cooked pasta or rice.

Nutrition Facts per serving: 196 cal., 4 g total fat (1 g sat. fat), 66 mg chol., 265 mg sodium, 21 g carbo., 2 g fiber, 19 g pro.

Americans always have had a love affair with Italian cooking. The fresh-and-simple appeal of Tuscan cooking and its quick yet stylish dishes, such as this one, fit right into fast-paced lifestyles.

TUSCAN LAMB CHOP SKILLET

8	lamb rib chops, cut 1 inch thick (about 1½ pounds total)
2	teaspoons olive oil
1½	teaspoons bottled minced garlic (3 cloves)
1	19-ounce can cannellini (white kidney) beans, rinsed and drained
1	8-ounce can Italian-style stewed tomatoes, undrained
1	tablespoon balsamic vinegar
2	teaspoons snipped fresh rosemary

1 Trim fat from chops. In a large skillet heat oil over medium heat. Add chops; cook for 9 to 11 minutes or until medium doneness (160°F), turning once. Transfer chops to a plate; keep warm.

2 Stir garlic into drippings in skillet. Cook and stir for 1 minute. Stir in beans, undrained tomatoes, vinegar, and rosemary. Bring to boiling; reduce heat. Simmer, uncovered, for 3 minutes.

3 Divide bean mixture among 4 dinner plates; arrange 2 chops on top of beans on each plate.

Nutrition Facts per serving: 272 cal., 9 g total fat (3 g sat. fat), 67 mg chol., 466 mg sodium, 24 g carbo., 6 g fiber, 30 g pro.

START TO FINISH:

20 minutes

MAKES:

4 servings

MENU IDEA:

Mushroom & Herb Rice *(see p. 288)*

(see p. 288)

Purchased baked mini phyllo tarts filled with canned fruit pie filling and topped with whipped cream

Featuring fresh tarragon and mushrooms, the low-calorie topper makes an ideal accent to the distinctive flavor of the lamb. Try it with other broiled or grilled meats such as pork, chicken, or beef.

LAMB WITH HERBED MUSHROOMS

START TO FINISH:

25 minutes

MAKES:

4 servings

8	lamb loin chops, cut 1 inch thick (about 1½ pounds total)
2	teaspoons olive oil
1	small onion, thinly sliced
2	cups sliced fresh mushrooms
1	tablespoon balsamic vinegar
1	teaspoon bottled minced garlic (2 cloves)
¼	teaspoon salt
¼	teaspoon black pepper
1	teaspoon snipped fresh tarragon or basil or ¼ teaspoon dried tarragon or basil, crushed

1 Trim fat from chops. In a large nonstick skillet heat oil over medium heat. Add chops; cook for 9 to 11 minutes or until medium doneness (160°F), turning once. Transfer chops to a serving platter; keep warm.

2 Stir onion into drippings in skillet. Cook and stir for 2 minutes. Stir in mushrooms, balsamic vinegar, garlic, salt, and pepper. Cook and stir for 3 to 4 minutes or until mushrooms are tender. Stir in tarragon. Spoon mushroom mixture over chops on platter.

Nutrition Facts per serving: 165 cal., 9 g total fat (3 g sat. fat), 48 mg chol., 280 mg sodium, 4 g carbo., 1 g fiber, 16 g pro.

MENU IDEA:

Steamed broccoli tossed with butter and crushed red pepper

Fudge Cookies in Chocolate Cream *(see p. 347)*

The tangy honey-mustard glaze adds just the right amount of sweet and savory flavor to the chops.

HONEY-MUSTARD LAMB CHOPS

8   lamb loin chops, cut 1 inch thick (about 1½ pounds total)

2   medium zucchini and/or yellow summer squash, quartered lengthwise

Salt

Black pepper

2   tablespoons Dijon-style mustard

2   tablespoons honey

1   tablespoon snipped fresh rosemary
    or 1 teaspoon dried rosemary, crushed

1 Trim fat from chops. Season chops and zucchini with salt and pepper. Arrange chops and zucchini, cut sides down, on the unheated rack of a broiler pan. In a small bowl stir together mustard, honey, and rosemary. Brush some of the mustard mixture on top of the chops.

2 Broil chops and zucchini 3 to 4 inches from the heat for 5 minutes. Turn chops and zucchini; brush remaining mustard mixture on the chops and zucchini. Discard any remaining mustard mixture. Broil for 5 to 10 minutes more or until lamb is medium doneness (160°F) and zucchini is tender.

Nutrition Facts per serving: 181 cal., 5 g total fat (2 g sat. fat), 60 mg chol., 302 mg sodium, 12 g carbo., 1 g fiber, 20 g pro.

PREP:

10 minutes

BROIL:

5 minutes + 5 minutes

MAKES:

4 servings

MENU IDEA:

Peas & Carrots with Cumin
(see p. 268)

Purchased apple coffee cake served with caramel-swirl ice cream

Although you can make lamb chops any time of year, the cranberry-orange relish, toasted pecans, and orange juice turn these chops into holiday fare. When you're looking for an alternative to traditional turkey or roast beef, remember this recipe!

LAMB CHOPS WITH CRANBERRY RELISH

PREP:

15 minutes

BROIL:

9 minutes + 1 minute

MAKES:

4 servings

½ cup purchased cranberry-orange relish

¼ cup chopped pecans, toasted

2 tablespoons orange juice

2 teaspoons snipped fresh rosemary or ½ teaspoon dried rosemary, crushed

8 lamb loin chops, cut 1 inch thick (about 1½ pounds total)

   Salt

   Black pepper

1 In a small bowl combine cranberry-orange relish, pecans, orange juice, and rosemary. Set aside.

2 Trim fat from chops. Place chops on the unheated rack of a broiler pan. Season generously with salt and pepper. Broil 3 to 4 inches from the heat for 9 to 11 minutes or until medium doneness (160°F), turning once. Spread pecan mixture over chops. Broil for 1 minute more.

Nutrition Facts per serving: 239 cal., 10 g total fat (2 g sat. fat), 60 mg chol., 137 mg sodium, 18 g carbo., 1 g fiber, 20 g pro.

MENU IDEA:

Purchased refrigerated mashed potatoes, cooked and mixed with dairy sour cream and snipped fresh herbs

Piecrust Cookies
(see p. 344)

Don't worry about precooking the pasta for this simple but satisfying dish. It will cook nicely in the tomato juice and beef broth mixture already in the skillet. How convenient is that?

GREEK-STYLE LAMB SKILLET

12	ounces ground lamb or ground beef
1	14½-ounce can diced tomatoes with onion and garlic, undrained
1	5½-ounce (⅔ cup) can tomato juice
½	cup onion-flavored beef broth
½	teaspoon ground cinnamon
1	cup dried medium shell macaroni or elbow macaroni
1	cup loose-pack frozen cut green beans
½	cup crumbled feta cheese (2 ounces)

START TO FINISH:

30 minutes

MAKES:

4 servings

1 In a large skillet cook ground lamb or beef until brown. Drain off fat. Stir undrained tomatoes, tomato juice, broth, and cinnamon into meat in skillet. Bring to boiling.

2 Stir uncooked macaroni and green beans into meat mixture. Return to boiling; reduce heat. Cover and simmer for 15 to 20 minutes or until macaroni and green beans are tender. Sprinkle with feta cheese.

Nutrition Facts per serving: 411 cal., 21 g total fat (10 g sat. fat), 75 mg chol., 1,013 mg sodium, 32 g carbo., 2 g fiber, 23 g pro.

MENU IDEA:

Sun-dried tomato or garlic-herb focaccia

Miniature Fruit Tarts
(see p. 348)

These burgers are Greek through and through. The feta cheese, tomato slices, and fresh mint are all fabulous and fresh ingredients used often in Greek cooking.

LAMB BURGERS WITH FETA & MINT

PREP:

15 minutes

GRILL:

14 minutes

MAKES:

4 servings

MENU IDEA:

Dutch Treat Coleslaw
(make half of the recipe)
(see p. 309)

Assorted fresh fruits

1½ pounds ground lamb or ground beef

4   lettuce leaves

4   kaiser rolls, split and toasted

½   cup crumbled feta cheese with peppercorns (2 ounces)

4   tomato slices

1   tablespoon snipped fresh mint

1 Shape ground lamb or beef into four ¾-inch-thick patties. Place patties on the greased rack of an uncovered grill directly over medium heat. Grill for 14 to 18 minutes or until done (160°F),* turning once.

2 Place lettuce on roll bottoms. Top with meat patties, feta cheese, tomato slices, mint, and roll tops.

*NOTE: The internal color of a burger is not a reliable doneness indicator. A lamb, beef, veal, or pork patty cooked to 160°F is safe, regardless of color. To measure the doneness of a patty, insert an instant-read thermometer through the side of the patty to a depth of 2 to 3 inches.

BROILER METHOD: Place patties on unheated rack of a broiler pan. Broil 3 to 4 inches from heat for 12 to 14 minutes or until done (160°F)*, turning once.

Nutrition Facts per serving: 554 cal., 30 g total fat (13 g sat. fat), 130 mg chol., 615 mg sodium, 32 g carbo., 1 g fiber, 38 g pro.

POULTRY

2

With its mild flavor, chicken is one of the most versatile meats available. There are so many delicious things you can do with it—pairing it with fruit, for example. This recipe brings together hot, sweet, spicy, and salty ingredients to create a dish that tastes as good as it looks.

SPICY CHICKEN BREASTS WITH FRUIT

START TO FINISH:

30 minutes

MAKES:

4 servings

MENU IDEA:

Sliced carrots, cooked and tossed with brown sugar and butter

Chocolate ice cream with Chocolate-Hazelnut Ice Cream Sauce
(see p. 372)

2   teaspoons Jamaican jerk seasoning

2   fresh serrano chile peppers,* seeded and finely chopped

4   skinless, boneless chicken breast halves (about 1¼ pounds total)

Nonstick cooking spray

½   cup peach nectar

3   green onions, cut into 1-inch pieces

2   cups sliced, peeled peaches

1   cup sliced, pitted plums

1   tablespoon packed brown sugar

⅛   teaspoon salt

½   cup pitted dark sweet cherries

Hot cooked rice (optional)

❶ For rub, in a small bowl combine Jamaican jerk seasoning and half of the serrano peppers. Sprinkle mixture evenly over all sides of chicken breasts; rub in with your fingers. Lightly coat an unheated large skillet with cooking spray. Preheat skillet over medium heat. Add chicken; cook for 8 to 10 minutes or until chicken is tender and no longer pink (170°F), turning once. Transfer to a serving platter; keep warm.

❷ Add 2 tablespoons of the peach nectar and the green onions to skillet. Cook and stir over medium heat for 4 to 5 minutes or just until green onions are tender.

❸ In a medium bowl combine remaining peach nectar, remaining chile pepper, half of the peaches, half of the plums, the brown sugar, and salt. Add to skillet. Cook and stir over medium heat about 2 minutes or until slightly thickened and bubbly. Remove from heat. Stir in cherries and remaining peaches and plums. Spoon over chicken. If desired, serve with hot cooked rice.

*NOTE: Because chile peppers contain volatile oils that can burn your skin and eyes, avoid direct contact with them as much as possible. When working with chile peppers, wear plastic or rubber gloves. If your bare hands do touch the peppers, wash your hands and nails well with soap and warm water.

Nutrition Facts per serving: 264 cal., 2 g total fat (1 g sat. fat), 82 mg chol., 304 mg sodium, 26 g carbo., 3 g fiber, 34 g pro.

Boneless chicken breasts are a boon to busy families because they are quick to cook—and most kids like chicken. A few fresh touches, including a garlic-laced rosemary sauce, take this dish well beyond the ordinary.

ROSEMARY CHICKEN WITH VEGETABLES

4   medium skinless, boneless chicken breast halves (about 1¼ pounds total)

½   teaspoon lemon-pepper seasoning

2   tablespoons olive oil

1   teaspoon bottled minced garlic (2 cloves)

2   medium zucchini and/or yellow summer squash, sliced ¼ inch thick (2½ cups)

½   cup apple juice or apple cider

2   teaspoons snipped fresh rosemary or ½ teaspoon dried rosemary, crushed

1   9-ounce package refrigerated spinach linguine or plain linguine

2   tablespoons dry white wine

2   teaspoons cornstarch

12   cherry tomatoes, halved

START TO FINISH:
30 minutes

MAKES:
4 servings

MENU IDEA:
Purchased refrigerated crescent rolls, baked and served with purchased lemon curd

Cherry Trifles *(see p. 344)*

1 Sprinkle chicken with lemon-pepper seasoning. In a large skillet heat oil over medium heat. Add chicken; cook over medium heat for 8 to 10 minutes or until chicken is tender and no longer pink (170°F), turning once. Transfer chicken to platter; cover and keep warm.

2 Add garlic to skillet; cook for 15 seconds. Add zucchini and/or summer squash, apple juice, and rosemary. Bring to boiling; reduce heat. Cover and simmer for 2 minutes.

3 Meanwhile, cook pasta according to package directions; drain. In a small bowl combine wine and cornstarch; add to zucchini mixture in skillet. Cook and stir until thickened and bubbly; cook for 2 minutes more. Stir in tomatoes. Serve vegetables and pasta with chicken.

Nutrition Facts per serving: 455 cal., 11 g total fat (2 g sat. fat), 132 mg chol., 294 mg sodium, 44 g carbo., 5 g fiber, 43 g pro.

Remember this recipe when asparagus season rolls around. Depending on where you live, the vegetable is usually at its freshest, in-season best from February to June.

LEMON CHICKEN WITH ASPARAGUS

START TO FINISH:

25 minutes

MAKES:

4 servings

MENU IDEA:

Orange Dream Fruit Salad *(see p. 314)*

Vanilla or chocolate ice cream topped with chopped assorted chocolate candy bars

Nonstick cooking spray

4   skinless, boneless chicken breast halves (about 1¼ pounds total)

1   pound fresh asparagus

1   cup water

1   10¾-ounce can condensed cream of chicken or cream of asparagus soup

¾   cup chicken broth

1   tablespoon lemon juice

Hot cooked couscous

1 Lightly coat an unheated large nonstick skillet with cooking spray. Preheat skillet over medium heat. Add chicken; cook in hot skillet for 8 to 10 minutes or until tender and no longer pink (170°F), turning once. Meanwhile, snap off and discard woody bases from asparagus. If desired, scrape off scales.

2 Remove chicken from skillet; cover and keep warm. In the same skillet combine asparagus and the water. Bring to boiling; reduce heat. Cover and simmer for 3 to 5 minutes or until asparagus is crisp-tender. Drain.

3 Meanwhile, in a small saucepan combine cream of chicken or asparagus soup, broth, and lemon juice. Cook and stir until heated through. Serve sauce with chicken, asparagus, and hot cooked couscous.

Nutrition Facts per serving: 354 cal., 8 g total fat (3 g sat. fat), 88 mg chol., 844 mg sodium, 27 g carbo., 3 g fiber, 40 g pro.

Caraway seeds and paprika, traditional Hungarian ingredients, season fast-cooking boneless chicken breasts.

CHICKEN PAPRIKA

¼   cup all-purpose flour

2   to 3 teaspoons paprika

¼   teaspoon salt

4   skinless, boneless chicken breast halves (about 1¼ pounds total)

2   tablespoons butter or margarine

¾   cup whipping cream

½   teaspoon bottled minced garlic (1 clove)

½   teaspoon caraway seeds, crushed

1   tablespoon dry sherry

2   teaspoons lemon juice

    Hot cooked noodles (optional)

START TO FINISH:

25 minutes

MAKES:

4 servings

MENU IDEA:

Steamed or broiled fresh asparagus spears

Raspberry-Cranberry Sauce *(see p. 370)*

1 In a shallow bowl stir together flour, paprika, and salt. Dip chicken in flour mixture to coat.

2 In a large skillet melt butter over medium heat. Add chicken; cook for 8 to 10 minutes or until tender and no longer pink (170°F), turning once. Remove from skillet; cover and keep warm.

3 Stir whipping cream, garlic, and caraway seeds into skillet. Cook and stir until boiling, scraping up browned bits. Cook for 2 to 3 minutes more or until thickened. Stir in sherry and lemon juice. If desired, serve chicken and sauce with noodles.

Nutrition Facts per serving: 409 cal., 25 g total fat (14 g sat. fat), 160 mg chol., 284 mg sodium, 8 g carbo., 1 g fiber, 35 g pro.

A Dijon-style mustard and jalapeño pepper glaze is a tongue-tingling way to dress up succulent chicken breasts. Pounding the breasts to a uniform thickness ensures quick and even cooking. And it is a great stress reliever!

CHICKEN BREASTS WITH JALAPEÑO JELLY

START TO FINISH:

25 minutes

MAKES:

4 servings

MENU IDEA:

Torn romaine lettuce tossed with bottled creamy Caesar salad dressing and seasoned croutons

Butter pecan ice cream with Butter Pecan Sauce *(see p. 371)*

4	skinless, boneless chicken breast halves (about 1¼ pounds total)
	Salt
	Freshly ground black pepper
2	tablespoons butter or margarine
1	tablespoon water
8	stalks celery, bias sliced
¼	cup red jalapeño chile pepper jelly
2	tablespoons lemon juice
1	tablespoon Dijon-style mustard

1 Place each chicken breast half between 2 pieces of plastic wrap. Working from center to edges, pound lightly with the flat side of a meat mallet to about ½-inch thickness. Remove plastic wrap. Sprinkle chicken with salt and pepper.

2 In a 12-inch skillet melt butter over medium-high heat. Add chicken; cook for 8 to 10 minutes or until chicken is tender and no longer pink, turning once. Remove from skillet.

3 For sauce, carefully stir the water into skillet, scraping up browned bits. Add celery; cook and stir for 1 minute. Add jelly, lemon juice, and mustard; cook and stir about 3 minutes more or until slightly thickened. Return chicken to skillet; heat through.

Nutrition Facts per serving: 281 cal., 9 g total fat (4 g sat. fat), 99 mg chol., 236 mg sodium, 16 g carbo., 1 g fiber, 34 g pro.

Don't let the name fool you. Buttermilk is actually quite low in fat and has a subtle tang and creamy texture. It gives body and richness to sauces and gravies without adding extra fat and calories.

CHICKEN WITH BUTTERMILK GRAVY

1/3	cup fine dry seasoned bread crumbs
2	tablespoons grated Parmesan cheese
1/2	teaspoon paprika
6	skinless, boneless chicken breast halves (about 2 pounds total)
3	tablespoons butter or margarine, melted
	Salt (optional)
	Black pepper (optional)
1	1-ounce envelope chicken gravy mix
1	cup buttermilk
1/4	teaspoon dried sage, crushed

1 In a shallow dish combine bread crumbs, Parmesan cheese, and paprika; set aside. Brush chicken with some of the melted butter. If desired, sprinkle with salt and pepper. Dip chicken into crumb mixture, turning to coat evenly.

2 Arrange chicken on the unheated rack of a broiler pan. Drizzle with any remaining melted butter. Broil 4 to 5 inches from the heat for 12 to 15 minutes or until chicken is tender and no longer pink (170°F), turning once.

3 Meanwhile, for gravy, in a small saucepan prepare chicken gravy mix according to package directions, except use the 1 cup buttermilk in place of the water called for in the package directions. Stir sage into gravy. Serve with chicken.

Nutrition Facts per serving: 288 cal., 9 g total fat (5 g sat. fat), 107 mg chol., 644 mg sodium, 10 g carbo., 0 g fiber, 38 g pro.

PREP:
15 minutes

BROIL:
12 minutes

MAKES:
6 servings

MENU IDEA:
Purchased refrigerated large or Southern-style biscuits, baked

Strawberry Shortbread Sandwiches
(see p. 348)

A medley of seasonings—mint, sesame seeds, fennel seeds, and thyme—adds a dynamite flavor to simple chicken breasts.

CHICKEN WITH HERB RUB

START TO FINISH:

25 minutes

MAKES:

4 servings

MENU IDEA:

Creamy Lemon Pasta
(see p. 284)

Iced cinnamon rolls,
warmed and served with
cinnamon or vanilla
ice cream and chopped
toasted pecans

4   skinless, boneless chicken breast halves (about 1¼ pounds)
½   cup snipped fresh mint
2   tablespoons sesame seeds
2   to 4 teaspoons fennel seeds, crushed
2   teaspoons dried thyme, crushed
1   teaspoon salt
¼   teaspoon freshly ground black pepper
1   tablespoon olive oil or cooking oil

1 Place each chicken breast half between 2 pieces of plastic wrap. Working from center to edges, pound lightly with the flat side of a meat mallet to about ½-inch thickness. Remove plastic wrap. For rub, in a small bowl combine mint, sesame seeds, fennel seeds, thyme, salt, and pepper. Sprinkle evenly over chicken; rub in with your fingers.

2 In a very large skillet heat oil over medium heat. Add chicken; cook for 8 to 10 minutes or until tender and no longer pink, turning once.

Nutrition Facts per serving: 228 cal., 8 g total fat (1 g sat. fat), 82 mg chol., 662 mg sodium, 2 g carbo., 1 g fiber, 34 g pro.

Spice up chicken with cayenne pepper, then cool it down with a refreshing yogurt-cucumber sauce. If you're afraid the chicken is too zippy for your palate, start out with half of the cayenne pepper.

CUCUMBER-YOGURT CHICKEN

1	8-ounce carton plain low-fat yogurt
1	cup chopped, peeled seedless cucumber
½	cup finely chopped radishes
2	tablespoons mayonnaise or salad dressing
¼	teaspoon finely shredded lemon peel
1	tablespoon lemon juice
½	teaspoon bottled minced garlic (1 clove)
¼	teaspoon bottled hot pepper sauce
4	skinless, boneless chicken breast halves (about 1¼ pounds total)
¼	teaspoon salt
¼	teaspoon cayenne pepper
2	teaspoons cooking oil

1 For sauce, in a small bowl combine yogurt, cucumber, radishes, mayonnaise, lemon peel, lemon juice, garlic, and hot pepper sauce. Cover and chill until ready to serve.

2 Sprinkle chicken with salt and cayenne pepper. In a large nonstick skillet heat oil over medium-high heat. Add chicken; cook for 8 to 10 minutes or until chicken is tender and no longer pink (170°F), turning once. Serve the chicken with sauce.

Nutrition Facts per serving: 276 cal., 11 g total fat (2 g sat. fat), 91 mg chol., 313 mg sodium, 6 g carbo., 0 g fiber, 36 g pro.

START TO FINISH:

25 minutes

MAKES:

4 servings

MENU IDEA:

Curried Cherry Pilaf *(see p. 285)*

Purchased loaf pound cake iced with canned lemon frosting and garnished with lemon and/or orange wedges

Hear the sizzle of this pan-cooked chicken and know that dinner is just minutes away.

LEMON-BUTTER CHICKEN BREASTS

START TO FINISH:

30 minutes

MAKES:

6 servings

MENU IDEA:

**Steamed Brussels
sprouts or sugar
snap pea pods**
tossed with honey

Caramel Apple Pastry
(see p. 333)

6	medium skinless, boneless chicken breast halves (2 pounds total)
½	cup all-purpose flour
½	teaspoon salt
2	teaspoons lemon-pepper seasoning
⅓	cup butter
2	tablespoons lemon juice
	Hot cooked rice or pilaf (optional)

1 Place each chicken breast half between 2 pieces of plastic wrap. Working from center to edges, pound lightly with the flat side of a meat mallet into a rectangle about ¼ inch thick. Remove plastic wrap. In a shallow bowl combine flour and salt. Coat chicken breasts with flour mixture. Sprinkle chicken breasts with lemon-pepper seasoning.

2 In a 12-inch skillet melt butter over medium-high heat. Add half of the chicken; cook about 6 minutes or until browned and no longer pink, turning once. Remove chicken. Repeat with remaining chicken. Return all of the chicken to the skillet, overlapping chicken breasts slightly. Drizzle lemon juice over the chicken breasts. Cook for 2 to 3 minutes more or until pan juices are slightly reduced. If desired, serve chicken and pan juices over hot cooked rice or pilaf.

Nutrition Facts per serving: 305 cal., 13 g total fat (6 g sat. fat), 116 mg chol., 714 mg sodium, 8 g carbo., 0 g fiber, 36 g pro.

A mixture of orange-tangerine juice concentrate and sesame oil infuses the tender chicken breasts with citrus flavor as they steam.

PULLED CHICKEN-PEANUT SALAD

2	tablespoons frozen orange-tangerine or orange juice concentrate
1	tablespoon water
2	teaspoons toasted sesame oil
¼	teaspoon salt
⅛	teaspoon coarsely ground black pepper
12	ounces skinless, boneless chicken breasts
3	cups watercress sprigs or torn fresh spinach
¼	cup cocktail peanuts

1 In a small bowl combine juice concentrate, the water, sesame oil, salt, and pepper. Reserve 1 tablespoon of the juice concentrate mixture. Cover remaining mixture; set aside.

2 In a large skillet bring ½ inch water to boiling. (Water should come just below the bottom of a steamer basket.) Reduce heat to simmer. Arrange chicken in a single layer in steamer basket. Place basket in skillet. Brush chicken with the reserved 1 tablespoon juice concentrate mixture. Cover. Steam chicken for 10 to 12 minutes or until tender and no longer pink (170°F).

3 Transfer chicken to cutting board. Cool slightly (about 5 minutes). Using a pair of forks, pull chicken into bite-size pieces about 1½ inches long.

4 In a large salad bowl combine chicken, watercress, and peanuts. Stir remaining juice concentrate mixture. Pour over salad and toss to coat.

Nutrition Facts per serving: 186 cal., 8 g total fat (1 g sat. fat), 49 mg chol., 241 mg sodium, 5 g carbo., 1 g fiber, 23 g pro.

START TO FINISH:
25 minutes
MAKES:
4 servings

MENU IDEA:

Sticky Lemon Pinwheels
(see p. 329)

Chocolate frozen yogurt topped with chocolate sprinkles and served with chocolate cream-filled wafer cookies

Peanut butter, coconut milk, and ginger turn everyday chicken into an exotic treat. If you can find it, use light coconut milk. The dish will taste just as nice and you won't miss the extra fat.

QUICK THAI CHICKEN

START TO FINISH:

20 minutes

MAKES:

4 servings

MENU IDEA:

Cooked white rice tossed with a little unsweetened coconut milk, finely chopped green onion, and crushed red pepper

Mocha Cookies *(see p. 345)*

¾   cup purchased unsweetened coconut milk*

¼   cup peanut butter

¼   teaspoon ground ginger

¼   teaspoon black pepper

1   tablespoon cooking oil

4   skinless, boneless chicken breast halves (about 1¼ pounds total)

4   green onions, cut into 1-inch pieces

¼   cup honey-roasted peanuts, coarsely chopped

1 In a small bowl combine coconut milk, peanut butter, ginger, and pepper; set aside.

2 In a large skillet heat oil over medium heat. Add chicken; cook for 8 to 10 minutes or until chicken is tender and no longer pink (170°F), turning once. Remove from skillet; keep warm.

3 For sauce, add green onions to skillet. Cook and stir about 2 minutes or until tender. Stir in peanut butter mixture. Cook and stir until bubbly.

4 To serve, spoon sauce over chicken. Sprinkle with peanuts.

***NOTE:** Look for cans of unsweetened coconut milk in the Asian foods section of your supermarket or at an Asian market.*

Nutrition Facts per serving: 416 cal., 25 g total fat (11 g sat. fat), 82 mg chol., 198 mg sodium, 7 g carbo., 2 g fiber, 39 g pro.

A creamy mushroom sauce, subtly flavored with dry white wine, complements the combination of chicken and artichokes.

CHEESY CHICKEN WITH ARTICHOKES

1	14-ounce can chicken broth
4	skinless, boneless chicken breast halves (about 1¼ pounds total)
1	9-ounce package frozen artichoke hearts
	Nonstick cooking spray
2	cups sliced fresh mushrooms
¼	cup chopped onion
½	teaspoon bottled minced garlic (1 clove)
4	teaspoons cornstarch
¾	cup evaporated milk
⅛	teaspoon salt
⅛	teaspoon ground white pepper
2	tablespoons dry white wine or chicken broth
⅓	cup finely shredded or grated Parmesan cheese

1 Pour the can of broth into a large skillet; bring to boiling. Add chicken. Reduce heat. Cover and cook about 15 minutes or just until chicken is tender and no longer pink. Drain, reserving ¾ cup broth. Cover chicken and keep warm.

2 Meanwhile, cook artichoke hearts according to package directions. Drain and keep warm.

3 For the sauce, wipe out the skillet with a paper towel; lightly coat skillet with cooking spray. Preheat skillet over medium heat. Add mushrooms, onion, and garlic; cook just until onion is tender. Stir in cornstarch. Add reserved broth, evaporated milk, salt, and white pepper; cook and stir until thickened and bubbly. Cook and stir for 2 minutes more. Stir in the 2 tablespoons wine or broth.

4 Place a chicken breast half on each of 4 dinner plates. Arrange artichokes around chicken breasts. Spoon sauce over chicken. Sprinkle with Parmesan cheese.

Nutrition Facts per serving: 477 cal., 19 g total fat (11 g sat. fat), 129 mg chol., 1,395 mg sodium, 17 g carbo., 4 g fiber, 57 g pro.

START TO FINISH:
30 minutes
MAKES:
4 servings

MENU IDEA:
Italian bread, sliced, spread with bottled creamy garlic salad dressing, and toasted

Fruit-Filled Waffle Bowls *(see p. 354)*

A splash of color from the dried fruit and a dash of sweetness from the honey and pumpkin pie spice make this recipe a wonderful choice for a fall supper.

CHICKEN WITH DRIED FRUIT & HONEY

START TO FINISH:

25 minutes

MAKES:

4 servings

8   skinless, boneless chicken thighs (about 1½ pounds total)

½   teaspoon pumpkin pie spice or ¼ teaspoon ground ginger

1   tablespoon butter or margarine

1   cup mixed dried fruit bits

⅓   cup water

¼   cup honey

❶ Sprinkle 1 side of each thigh with pumpkin pie spice or ground ginger. In a 12-inch skillet cook the thighs in hot butter about 4 minutes or until browned, turning once. Stir in dried fruit bits, the water, and honey. Bring to boiling; reduce heat. Cover and simmer for 10 to 15 minutes or until chicken is tender and no longer pink (180°F).

Nutrition Facts per serving: 381 cal., 9 g total fat (4 g sat. fat), 149 mg chol., 171 mg sodium, 41 g carbo., 0 g fiber, 35 g pro.

MENU IDEA:

Steamed broccoli topped with shredded American or cheddar cheese

Double Dippin' Fruit
(see p. 366)

A fruit-based or garlic-seasoned salad dressing works best with the garlic pepper-accented chicken and salad greens.

CHICKEN TOSSED SALAD

4   skinless, boneless chicken breast halves
     (about 1¼ pounds total)

1   tablespoon olive oil

¼   teaspoon garlic-pepper blend

8   cups torn mixed salad greens

1   medium yellow or red sweet pepper, cut into bite-size strips

1   medium tomato, cut into wedges

½   cup bottled salad dressing (such as a berry or roasted garlic vinaigrette or Parmesan-basil Italian)

¼   cup crumbled feta cheese (1 ounce)

¼   cup purchased croutons

1 Brush chicken breasts with oil; sprinkle with garlic-pepper blend. In a medium nonstick skillet cook chicken over medium heat for 8 to 10 minutes or until no longer pink (170°F). Slice the chicken into bite-size strips. Set aside.

2 In a large serving bowl combine greens, sweet pepper, and tomato; add dressing and toss to coat. Top with chicken, feta cheese, and croutons.

Nutrition Facts per serving: 396 cal., 24 g total fat (5 g sat. fat), 88 mg chol., 348 mg sodium, 9 g carbo., 2 g fiber, 36 g pro.

START TO FINISH:
20 minutes
MAKES:
4 servings

MENU IDEA:
Purchased mini muffins, such as lemon-poppy seed, blueberry, and/or banana

Strawberry Dip
(see p. 367)

Cream of chicken soup adds a saucy consistency to this family-friendly dish.

CHICKEN FAJITAS

START TO FINISH:

25 minutes

MAKES:

4 servings

MENU IDEA:

Rice pilaf mix, prepared according to package directions

Tropical Fruit Cups (double the recipe) *(see p. 361)*

2	tablespoons cooking oil
1	medium onion, cut into thin wedges
1	teaspoon bottled minced garlic (2 cloves)
2	medium red and/or green sweet peppers, cut into thin bite-size strips
12	ounces skinless, boneless chicken breasts, cut into bite-size strips
1	10¾-ounce can condensed cream of chicken soup
⅓	cup bottled salsa
8	7- to 8-inch flour tortillas, warmed*
2	cups shredded lettuce
	Dairy sour cream, shredded cheddar cheese, and/or thinly sliced green onion (optional)

1 In a large skillet heat 1 tablespoon of the oil over medium-high heat. Add onion and garlic; cook and stir for 2 minutes. Add sweet peppers; cook and stir for 1 to 2 minutes more or until vegetables are crisp-tender. Remove from skillet.

2 Add remaining 1 tablespoon oil to skillet. Add chicken; cook and stir for 3 to 4 minutes or until chicken is no longer pink. Return vegetables to skillet. Add cream of chicken soup and salsa; cook and stir until heated through.

3 To serve, divide chicken mixture evenly among warmed tortillas. Top with lettuce. If desired, top with sour cream, cheese, and/or green onion. Roll up tortillas.

***NOTE:** To warm tortillas, wrap them in white microwave-safe paper towels; microwave on 100% power (high) for 15 to 30 seconds or until tortillas are softened. (Or wrap tortillas in foil. Heat in a 350°F oven for 10 to 15 minutes or until warmed.)*

Nutrition Facts per serving: 491 cal., 13 g total fat (3 g sat. fat), 56 mg chol., 1,342 mg sodium, 62 g carbo., 5 g fiber, 27 g pro.

Bring out the flavor of the traditional chili seasonings in this hearty soup by serving it with vibrant Tex-Mex toppers, such as coarsely crushed tortilla chips, chopped avocado, diced tomato, shredded Monterey Jack cheese, and snipped fresh cilantro.

CHILI-FLAVORED CHICKEN SOUP

1	15-ounce can whole kernel corn, drained
1	14-ounce can beef broth
1	14-ounce can chicken broth
1	14½-ounce can diced tomatoes, undrained
1	medium onion, chopped
¼	cup chopped green sweet pepper
1	teaspoon chili powder
½	teaspoon ground cumin
¼	teaspoon black pepper
1	pound skinless, boneless chicken breasts, cut into bite-size pieces

1 In a Dutch oven combine corn, beef broth, chicken broth, undrained tomatoes, onion, sweet pepper, chili powder, cumin, and black pepper. Bring to boiling. Stir in chicken pieces. Return to boiling; reduce heat. Cover and simmer for 10 to 12 minutes or until chicken is no longer pink, stirring once or twice.

Nutrition Facts per serving: 173 cal., 2 g total fat (1 g sat. fat), 44 mg chol., 762 mg sodium, 17 g carbo., 2 g fiber, 21 g pro.

PREP:
10 minutes
COOK:
10 minutes
MAKES:
6 servings

MENU IDEA:

Honey-Nut Corn Muffins *(see p. 323)*

Sliced watermelon and/or cantaloupe

Kids will absolutely love these homemade chicken fingers. Ask them to help you dip and coat the strips. It might be a little messy, but it will definitely be more fun!

CRUNCHY RANCH FINGERS

START TO FINISH:

25 minutes

MAKES:

4 servings

MENU IDEA:

Peanut Butter Fruit Salad *(see p. 313)*

Root beer floats— root beer served over scoops of vanilla ice cream and topped with whipped cream

Nonstick cooking spray

1 cup cornflake crumbs

1 tablespoon snipped fresh parsley

¼ teaspoon salt

⅛ teaspoon black pepper

⅓ cup bottled buttermilk ranch salad dressing

1 tablespoon water

12 ounces skinless, boneless chicken breasts, cut into bite-size strips

Bottled buttermilk ranch salad dressing

1 Coat a 15×10×1-inch baking pan with cooking spray; set aside.

2 In a shallow dish combine cornflake crumbs, parsley, salt, and pepper. In another shallow dish stir together the ⅓ cup salad dressing and the water. Dip chicken strips into the dressing mixture, allowing excess to drip off; dip into crumb mixture to coat. Arrange strips in prepared pan. Bake in a 425°F oven for 12 to 15 minutes or until chicken is no longer pink. Serve with additional dressing.

Nutrition Facts per serving: 208 cal., 10 g total fat (2 g sat. fat), 50 mg chol., 444 mg sodium, 11 g carbo., 1 g fiber, 18 g pro.

Pasta and chicken are always good together. Honey and fresh tarragon add a sweet dimension to this lemony chicken dish.

LEMON-TARRAGON CHICKEN TOSS

6	ounces dried fettuccine or linguine
2	cups broccoli or cauliflower florets
½	cup chicken broth
3	tablespoons lemon juice
1	tablespoon honey
2	teaspoons cornstarch
¼	teaspoon ground white pepper
12	ounces skinless, boneless chicken breasts, cut into bite-size strips
2	teaspoons olive oil or cooking oil
1	medium carrot, shredded
1	tablespoon snipped fresh tarragon or ½ teaspoon dried tarragon, crushed

START TO FINISH:

20 minutes

MAKES:

4 servings

1 Cook pasta according to package directions, adding the broccoli or cauliflower for the last 4 minutes of cooking; drain well. Return pasta mixture to pan; cover and keep warm.

2 Meanwhile, in a small bowl combine broth, lemon juice, honey, cornstarch, and white pepper; set aside.

3 In a large nonstick skillet stir-fry chicken in hot oil for 3 to 4 minutes or until no longer pink. Stir cornstarch mixture; add to skillet. Cook and stir until thickened and bubbly. Add carrot and tarragon; cook for 1 minute more.

4 To serve, spoon chicken mixture over pasta mixture.

Nutrition Facts per serving: 322 cal., 5 g total fat (1 g sat. fat), 50 mg chol., 197 mg sodium, 43 g carbo., 3 g fiber, 27 g pro.

MENU IDEA:

Purchased soft breadsticks brushed with melted butter and sprinkled with grated Parmesan cheese

Gooey Brownie Cups *(see p. 339)*

Pesto is a powerful flavor enhancer and it works its magic in this recipe.

PARMESAN-PESTO CHICKEN SOUP

START TO FINISH:

30 minutes

MAKES:

4 servings

2	14-ounce cans chicken broth
1	teaspoon dried Italian seasoning, crushed
1	teaspoon bottled minced garlic (2 cloves)
12	ounces skinless, boneless chicken breasts, cut into bite-size pieces
¾	cup dried small shell macaroni
2	½-inch slices Italian bread, halved crosswise
2	tablespoons purchased basil pesto
¼	cup finely shredded Parmesan cheese (1 ounce)
¾	cup loose-pack frozen shelled peas
2	green onions, thinly sliced

1 In a medium saucepan combine broth, Italian seasoning, and garlic; bring to boiling.

2 Add chicken and macaroni to broth. Return mixture to boiling; reduce heat. Simmer, uncovered, for 8 to 9 minutes or until pasta is tender and chicken is no longer pink, stirring occasionally.

3 Meanwhile, spread 1 side of each halved bread slice with pesto. Sprinkle with cheese. Place on broiler rack. Broil 3 to 4 inches from heat about 2 minutes or just until cheese begins to melt.

4 Stir frozen peas and green onion into broth mixture; cook for 2 minutes more. Ladle into soup bowls. Top each serving with a slice of the cheese-topped bread.

Nutrition Facts per serving: 345 cal., 10 g total fat (2 g sat. fat), 59 mg chol., 1,179 mg sodium, 31 g carbo., 2 g fiber, 31 g pro.

MENU IDEA:

Mixed baby greens tossed with bottled berry vinaigrette salad dressing and toasted nuts

Amaretto Peaches with Vanilla Yogurt *(see p. 375)*

A perennial favorite of all ages, sweet-and-sour chicken can be made quickly—without deep frying!

SWEET & SOUR CHICKEN

1 8-ounce can pineapple chunks (juice pack)

½ cup bottled sweet-and-sour sauce

12 ounces skinless, boneless chicken breasts,
    cut into 1-inch pieces

1 tablespoon soy sauce

4 teaspoons cooking oil

1 medium red sweet pepper, cut into bite-size strips

1 medium carrot, thinly sliced

1 cup fresh pea pods, tips and stems removed

   Hot cooked rice

1 Drain pineapple, reserving 2 tablespoons of the juice; set pineapple chunks aside. In a small bowl stir together reserved pineapple juice and the sweet-and-sour sauce; set aside. In a medium bowl toss chicken with soy sauce; set aside.

2 In a large nonstick skillet heat 3 teaspoons of the oil over medium-high heat. Add sweet pepper and carrot; cook and stir for 3 minutes. Add pea pods. Cook and stir about 1 minute more or until vegetables are crisp-tender. Remove from skillet; set aside.

3 Add remaining 1 teaspoon oil to skillet. Using a slotted spoon, add chicken to skillet. Cook and stir for 3 to 4 minutes or until chicken is no longer pink. Add sweet-and-sour sauce mixture, vegetable mixture, and pineapple chunks; heat through. Serve chicken mixture with hot cooked rice.

Nutrition Facts per serving: 344 cal., 6 g total fat (1 g sat. fat), 49 mg chol., 389 mg sodium, 46 g carbo., 2 g fiber, 24 g pro.

START TO FINISH:

25 minutes

MAKES:

4 or 5 servings

MENU IDEA:

Steamed whole green beans tossed with minced garlic and ground ginger

Lemon Cheesecake Mousse *(see p. 363)*

Chicken may not be the traditional meat choice for chili, but it's a great alternative when you want to try something different. The pre-spiced chili beans with chili gravy make assembling this warming meal the ultimate in convenience.

CHUNKY CHICKEN CHILI

START TO FINISH:

20 minutes

MAKES:

4 servings

	Nonstick cooking spray
12	ounces skinless, boneless chicken thighs, cut into 1-inch pieces
2	15-ounce cans chili beans with spicy chili gravy
1½	cups loose-pack frozen pepper stir-fry vegetables (yellow, green, and red peppers and onion)
¾	cup bottled salsa

1 Coat an unheated large saucepan with cooking spray. Preheat over medium-high heat. Add chicken; cook and stir until browned. Stir in undrained chili beans, frozen vegetables, and salsa.

2 Bring to boiling; reduce heat. Simmer, uncovered, about 7 minutes or until chicken is no longer pink.

Nutrition Facts per serving: 320 cal., 5 g total fat (1 g sat. fat), 70 mg chol., 930 mg sodium, 39 g carbo., 12 g fiber, 29 g pro.

MENU IDEA:

Purchased refrigerated corn bread twists, baked and served with bottled salsa

Banana & Caramel Cream Pies
(see p. 353)

Chicken strips and tofu—cooked in the savory Asian flavors of sesame, oyster sauce, and ginger—turn a simple stir-fry into a satisfying meal.

CHICKEN STIR-FRY WITH SESAME TOFU

1	12- to 16-ounce package firm tub-style tofu (fresh bean curd), drained and cut into ¾-inch cubes
1/3	cup chicken broth
2	tablespoons bottled oyster sauce
2	tablespoons soy sauce
1	teaspoon toasted sesame oil
2	teaspoons cornstarch
2	teaspoons peanut oil
1	tablespoon grated fresh ginger
1	teaspoon bottled minced garlic (2 cloves)
8	ounces skinless, boneless chicken thighs, cut into bite-size strips
2	cups broccoli florets
1	medium red sweet pepper, cut into thin strips
3	green onions, cut into ½-inch pieces
	Hot cooked jasmine rice or regular rice

START TO FINISH:

25 minutes

MAKES:

4 to 6 servings

MENU IDEA:

Fresh pineapple wedges

Snow Angel Cake *(see p. 343)*

1 Place tofu in a medium bowl. In a small bowl stir together broth, oyster sauce, soy sauce, and sesame oil. Drizzle 2 tablespoons of the soy mixture over tofu; toss gently to coat. For sauce, stir cornstarch into the remaining soy mixture. Set aside.

2 Pour peanut oil into a wok or large nonstick skillet. Heat wok or skillet over medium-high heat. Stir-fry ginger and garlic in hot oil for 30 seconds. Add chicken. Stir-fry for 3 to 4 minutes or until chicken is no longer pink. Remove from wok or skillet.

3 Add broccoli, sweet pepper, and green onions to hot wok. Stir-fry about 3 minutes or until vegetables are crisp-tender. Return chicken to wok or skillet. Stir sauce; add to chicken mixture. Cook and stir until thickened and bubbly.

4 Drain tofu; add to chicken mixture. Cook and stir gently about 1 minute or until heated through. Serve over rice.

Nutrition Facts per serving: 340 cal., 10 g total fat (2 g sat. fat), 45 mg chol., 874 mg sodium, 36 g carbo., 3 g fiber, 25 g pro.

It's hard to believe this tasty soup takes only 20 minutes to make.

EASY ORIENTAL CHICKEN SOUP

START TO FINISH:

20 minutes

MAKES:

3 servings

MENU IDEA:

Mixed Greens Salad with Ginger Vinaigrette
(see p. 305)

Assorted fresh berries topped with whipped cream and crushed shortbread cookies

1   tablespoon cooking oil

8   ounces skinless, boneless chicken thighs or breasts, cut into thin bite-size strips

3   cups water

½   of a 16-ounce package (2 cups) loose-pack frozen broccoli, carrots, and water chestnuts

1   3-ounce package chicken-flavor ramen noodles

2   tablespoons reduced-sodium or regular soy sauce

1 In a large saucepan heat oil over medium-high heat. Add chicken; cook and stir for 2 to 3 minutes or until no longer pink. Remove from heat. Drain off fat.

2 Carefully add the water, vegetables, and seasoning packet from ramen noodles to chicken in saucepan. Bring to boiling. Break up noodles; add to soup. Reduce heat. Cover and simmer for 3 minutes. Stir in soy sauce.

Nutrition Facts per serving: 254 cal., 8 g total fat (1 g sat. fat), 63 mg chol., 829 mg sodium, 22 g carbo., 5 g fiber, 22 g pro.

Chicken breast strips double-dipped in a lemon-and-herb flour, then flash-fried in a skillet have all the crunch of traditional fried chicken. This salad is especially delicious in the summer when strawberries are at their sweet and juicy peak.

CHICKEN SALAD WITH STRAWBERRIES

¾   cup all-purpose flour

4   tablespoons snipped fresh purple or green basil

1   tablespoon finely shredded lemon peel

2   eggs, beaten

1   pound skinless, boneless chicken breasts, cut into thin bite-size strips

2   tablespoons cooking oil

4   cups torn mixed spring salad greens

1   head radicchio, torn into bite-size pieces

2   cups sliced fresh strawberries

½   cup bottled balsamic vinaigrette salad dressing

6   butterhead (Bibb or Boston) lettuce leaves

1 In a shallow dish combine flour, 2 tablespoons of the basil, and the lemon peel. Place eggs in another shallow dish. Dip chicken into flour mixture, then into eggs, and then again into flour mixture to coat.

2 In a heavy 12-inch skillet heat cooking oil over medium-high heat. Add chicken; cook and stir for 6 to 8 minutes or until chicken is no longer pink. (If necessary, reduce heat to medium to prevent overbrowning and add more oil as needed during cooking.) Cool slightly.

3 Meanwhile, in a large bowl toss together greens, radicchio, strawberries, and remaining 2 tablespoons basil. Drizzle vinaigrette over greens mixture; toss gently to coat. To serve, line salad bowls with lettuce leaves. Add greens mixture. Top with chicken.

Nutrition Facts per serving: 261 cal., 13 g total fat (2 g sat. fat), 79 mg chol., 295 mg sodium, 16 g carbo., 2 g fiber, 21 g pro.

START TO FINISH:

30 minutes

MAKES:

6 servings

MENU IDEA:

Sourdough rolls
served with flavored cream cheese

Cookies & Cream
(see p. 350)

Premade pizza shells are indispensable for the busy home cook—especially if you have hungry kids to feed. The topping possibilities are endless! This recipe features a fresh combination of pesto, a blend of cheeses, mushrooms, and chicken strips.

MUSHROOM-TOMATO PESTO PIZZA

PREP:

15 minutes

BAKE:

10 minutes

MAKES:

4 servings

1	12-inch Italian bread shell (Boboli)
½	cup purchased dried tomato pesto
1	cup shredded four-cheese pizza blend (4 ounces)
1	6-ounce package refrigerated Italian-seasoned cooked chicken breast strips
1½	cups sliced fresh shiitake, crimini, and/or button mushrooms

1 Place the bread shell on a 12-inch pizza pan. Spread pesto over bread shell. Sprinkle with half of the cheese. Top with the chicken strips and mushrooms. Sprinkle with remaining cheese. Bake in a 400°F oven for 10 to 15 minutes or until pizza is heated through and cheese is melted.

Nutrition Facts per serving: 585 cal., 24 g total fat (8 g sat. fat), 55 mg chol., 1,382 mg sodium, 64 g carbo., 4 g fiber, 33 g pro.

MENU IDEA:

Mixed greens tossed with bottled balsamic vinaigrette, chopped fresh tomatoes, and bottled sliced pepperoncini

Cherry-Bananas Foster *(see p. 360)*

Daikon is a large Asian radish with a pleasant, sweet, and zesty flavor and a mild bite. It is available year-round in many supermarkets and in Asian specialty stores.

ASIAN CHICKEN SANDWICH

1	2- to 2¼-pound deli-roasted chicken
8	8- to 10-inch flour tortillas
½	cup bottled hoisin sauce
¼	cup finely chopped peanuts
¼	cup finely chopped green onions
½	cup shredded daikon, well drained
3	tablespoons soy sauce
3	tablespoons Chinese black vinegar or rice vinegar
1	tablespoon water
1	teaspoon chili oil or toasted sesame oil

START TO FINISH:
30 minutes
MAKES:
8 servings

1 Remove skin from chicken and discard. Remove chicken from bones and shred chicken (you should have about 4 cups); set aside.

2 Spread one side of each tortilla with some of the hoisin sauce; sprinkle with peanuts and green onions. Top with shredded chicken and shredded daikon. Roll up; halve crosswise.

3 In a small bowl combine soy sauce, vinegar, the water, and chili oil or sesame oil. Serve as a dipping sauce with chicken roll-ups.

Nutrition Facts per serving: 283 cal., 9 g total fat (2 g sat. fat), 50 mg chol., 869 mg sodium, 26 g carbo., 1 g fiber, 20 g pro.

MENU IDEA:
Asian Pea Pod Salad (double the recipe) *(see p. 304)*

Vanilla ice cream, sliced strawberries, and a dash of cinnamon placed in a blender container and blended until nearly smooth

Fruit salsa makes a nice change from the regular tomato version. It complements the chicken and gives these tostadas a tangy touch.

SWEET CHICKEN TOSTADAS

START TO FINISH:

20 minutes

MAKES:

4 servings

8	tostada shells
½	cup dairy sour cream
1	cup bottled fruit salsa
1½	cups finely chopped, cooked chicken (about 8 ounces)
1	cup shredded Monterey Jack cheese with jalapeño chile peppers (4 ounces)

1 Spread one side of each tostada shell with 1 tablespoon of the sour cream, spreading to edges. Spread 2 tablespoons of the salsa evenly on top of sour cream on each tostada. Top each with 3 tablespoons of the chopped chicken and 2 tablespoons of the shredded cheese.

2 Place 4 of the tostadas on a large cookie sheet. Place on an unheated broiler rack. Broil 4 to 5 inches from the heat for 1 to 1½ minutes or until cheese is melted. Repeat with remaining tostadas. Serve warm.

Nutrition Facts per serving: 511 cal., 26 g total fat (12 g sat. fat), 89 mg chol., 488 mg sodium, 42 g carbo., 4 g fiber, 27 g pro.

MENU IDEA:

Mexican Vegetable Soup *(see p. 302)*

Purchased mango or lemon sorbet

Make dinner fun with different colored tortillas. The kids will love filling up their red, green, or white shells with the tomatoes, chicken, cheese, nuts, and basil leaves.

DRIED TOMATO & BASIL CHICKEN WRAPS

½ of a 3-ounce package (about ¾ cup) dried tomatoes (not oil-packed)

3 cups shredded roasted or grilled chicken (about 1 pound)

1 cup shredded mozzarella or Monterey Jack cheese (4 ounces)

½ cup chopped pecans, toasted

⅓ cup bottled creamy Italian or ranch salad dressing

6 10-inch dried tomato, spinach, and/or plain flour tortillas, warmed*

1 cup large fresh basil leaves

START TO FINISH:

20 minutes

MAKES:

6 servings

1 Soak dried tomatoes in enough hot water to cover for 10 minutes. Drain and chop tomatoes.

2 In a large bowl combine chopped dried tomatoes, chicken, cheese, pecans, and salad dressing.

3 Line each tortilla with some of the basil leaves. Divide chicken mixture among the tortillas. Fold in sides and roll up; cut each diagonally in half to serve.

*NOTE: To warm tortillas, wrap them in white microwave-safe paper towels; microwave on 100% power (high) for 15 to 30 seconds or until tortillas are softened. (Or wrap tortillas in foil. Heat in a 350°F oven for 10 to 15 minutes or until warmed.)

Nutrition Facts per serving: 449 cal., 24 g total fat (6 g sat. fat), 73 mg chol., 701 mg sodium, 29 g carbo., 3 g fiber, 30 g pro.

MENU IDEA:

Salt-and-vinegar potato chips or kettle-cooked potato chips

Fast & Fruity Banana Split Tarts *(see p. 352)*

Lime juice, fresh ginger, and pumpkin seeds update chicken salad with a breezy tropical flavor. To keep your kitchen cool and save time, pick up a ready-to-eat roasted chicken from your local supermarket on your way home from work or from picking up the kids.

GINGER-LIME CHICKEN SALAD

START TO FINISH:

25 minutes

MAKES:

2 servings

MENU IDEA:

Croissants served
with jam or preserves

Mango Parfait
(see p. 365)

¼   cup light mayonnaise dressing or salad dressing

1   tablespoon chopped red onion

1   tablespoon lime juice

1   teaspoon grated fresh ginger

1   small clove garlic, quartered

1½   cups roasted chicken breast cut into bite-size strips

1   stalk celery, cut lengthwise into thin ribbons

1   tablespoon salted pumpkin seeds or chopped peanuts

1 For dressing, in a blender combine mayonnaise dressing, red onion, lime juice, ginger, and garlic. Cover and blend until onion is finely chopped and mixture is combined.

2 Place chicken in a medium bowl. Pour dressing over chicken; toss to coat.

3 Divide celery between 2 dinner plates. Top with the chicken mixture; sprinkle with pumpkin seeds.

Nutrition Facts per serving: 306 cal., 16 g total fat (3 g sat. fat), 99 mg chol., 276 mg sodium, 7 g carbo., 1 g fiber, 34 g pro.

This soup is a quick-to-fix solution for leftover cooked chicken or turkey. A small amount of wine deepens the flavor of this popular classic. Substitute chicken broth for the wine, if desired.

CHICKEN-VEGETABLE SOUP

1	stalk celery, chopped
1	medium carrot, thinly sliced
½	cup sliced leek or chopped onion
1	tablespoon butter or margarine
1	14-ounce can chicken broth
¼	cup all-purpose flour
2	cups milk
1	tablespoon snipped fresh thyme or basil or 1 teaspoon dried thyme or basil, crushed
¼	teaspoon salt
1½	cups chopped cooked chicken or turkey (about 8 ounces)
¼	cup dry white wine or chicken broth
	Cracked black pepper

1 In a large saucepan cook celery, carrot, and leek or onion in hot butter until tender. In a medium bowl gradually stir the 14-ounce can of chicken broth into the flour; stir into vegetables in saucepan. Add milk, dried herb (if using), and salt. Cook and stir until slightly thickened and bubbly; cook and stir for 1 minute more.

2 Stir in chicken, wine or the ¼ cup chicken broth, and fresh herb (if using). Cook about 2 minutes more or until heated through. Sprinkle individual servings with pepper.

Nutrition Facts per serving: 246 cal., 10 g total fat (4 g sat. fat), 66 mg chol., 700 mg sodium, 15 g carbo., 1 g fiber, 21 g pro.

START TO FINISH:

30 minutes

MAKES:

4 servings

MENU IDEA:

Bacon & Chive Biscuits *(see p. 326)*

Vanilla frozen yogurt served in waffle cone bowls and sprinkled with crushed peanut brittle

Creamy Brie and tender chicken are combined with crunchy toasted pecans and juicy ripe pears, then topped with a sweet and tangy raspberry vinaigrette in this elegant, yet easy-to-make salad.

FRUITED CHICKEN & BRIE SALAD

START TO FINISH:

30 minutes

MAKES:

4 servings

3	tablespoons sugar
½	cup pecan or walnut halves
6	cups torn butterhead (Bibb or Boston) lettuce
2	cups cooked chicken cut into strips
1	4½-ounce round Brie, chilled and cut in small cubes
2	ripe pears, cut into thin wedges
½	cup bottled raspberry vinaigrette or other vinaigrette

1 Place sugar in a heavy medium skillet. Cook, without stirring, over medium-high heat until sugar begins to melt, shaking skillet occasionally. Reduce heat to low. Stir with a wooden spoon until sugar is golden brown and completely melted. Add nuts, stirring to coat. Spoon onto buttered foil to cool; break nuts apart.

2 Divide lettuce evenly among 4 dinner plates. Arrange chicken, Brie, and pears on lettuce. Drizzle with vinaigrette; sprinkle with nuts.

Nutrition Facts per serving: 496 cal., 27 g total fat (8 g sat. fat), 94 mg chol., 293 mg sodium, 37 g carbo., 4 g fiber, 29 g pro.

MENU IDEA:

Sticky Lemon Pinwheels
(see p. 329)

Purchased New York-style cheesecake

Buttery, flaky croissants enfold the moist, warm honey-and-chicken filling, making a wonderful main dish for a special luncheon or for when you want to treat your family.

HONEY CHICKEN SANDWICHES

3 tablespoons honey

2 teaspoons snipped fresh thyme
   or ½ teaspoon dried thyme, crushed

1 small red onion, halved and thinly sliced

12 ounces thinly sliced cooked chicken, halved crosswise

4 purchased croissants, halved horizontally and toasted

1 In a medium skillet combine honey and thyme; stir in red onion. Cook and stir over medium-low heat just until hot (do not boil). Stir in chicken; heat through. Arrange chicken mixture in halved croissants.

Nutrition Facts per serving: 445 cal., 18 g total fat (8 g sat. fat), 118 mg chol., 498 mg sodium, 40 g carbo., 2 g fiber, 29 g pro.

START TO FINISH:
20 minutes
MAKES:
4 servings

MENU IDEA:
Apple & Sweet Pepper Slaw
(see p. 308)

Bottled iced coffee drink, blended with ice and topped with whipped cream

This scrumptious fruit-and-chicken salad makes a guaranteed-to-be-gone addition to any buffet table.

PRIZEWINNING SUNDAY SALAD

START TO FINISH:

20 minutes

MAKES:

6 to 8 servings

1	20-ounce can pineapple chunks, drained
2	cups cubed cooked chicken breast (about 10 ounces)
2	cups cubed cooked ham (about 10 ounces)
4	stalks celery, diced
1	medium green sweet pepper, chopped
¾	cup slivered almonds
½	cup mayonnaise or salad dressing
2	to 3 tablespoons lemon juice
½	teaspoon ground ginger
½	teaspoon ground nutmeg
	Dash salt
	Lettuce leaves

MENU IDEA:

Sliced fresh watermelon and honeydew melon

Ultimate Chocolate Sundaes *(see p. 376)*

1 In a large bowl combine pineapple chunks, chicken, ham, celery, sweet pepper, and almonds.

2 For dressing, in a small bowl combine mayonnaise, lemon juice, ginger, nutmeg, and salt. Pour dressing over salad; toss lightly to coat. Serve on lettuce-lined plates.

Nutrition Facts per serving: 461 cal., 29 g total fat (5 g sat. fat), 78 mg chol., 901 mg sodium, 22 g carbo., 4 g fiber, 30 g pro.

Try this Tex-Mex-style combination for a quick supper after the kids' ball practice or music lessons.

SIMPLE SALSA SKILLET

1	green sweet pepper, cut into bite-size strips
1	red sweet pepper, cut into bite-size strips
1	tablespoon cooking oil
2	cups cubed cooked potatoes
1	16-ounce jar salsa
1	15½-ounce can whole kernel corn, drained
1	15- or 16-ounce can black beans, rinsed and drained
1½	cups cubed cooked chicken (about 8 ounces)
	Dairy sour cream (optional)

1 In a large skillet cook sweet pepper strips in hot oil for 2 minutes. Add potatoes, salsa, corn, black beans, and chicken. Stir gently.

2 Cover and cook over medium-low heat about 10 minutes or until heated through, stirring occasionally. If desired, serve with sour cream.

Nutrition Facts per serving: 365 cal., 9 g total fat (2 g sat. fat), 47 mg chol., 959 mg sodium, 53 g carbo., 10 g fiber, 27 g pro.

START TO FINISH:
25 minutes
MAKES:
4 to 6 servings

MENU IDEA:
Purchased corn bread or corn muffins

Piecrust Cookies
(see p. 344)

Simple definitely describes this soup. In just 15 minutes you can have hot and nourishing soup on the table. It doesn't get much simpler, or satisfying, than this!

SIMPLY RAMEN CHICKEN SOUP

START TO FINISH:

15 minutes

MAKES:

4 servings

2	14-ounce cans reduced-sodium chicken broth
2	3-ounce packages chicken-flavor ramen noodles
½	teaspoon dried oregano or basil, crushed
1	10-ounce package frozen cut broccoli
2	cups shredded cooked chicken or turkey (about 10 ounces)
¼	cup sliced almonds, toasted

① In a large saucepan combine broth, seasoning packets from ramen noodles, and oregano. Bring to boiling. Break up noodles. Add noodles and broccoli to mixture in saucepan. Return to boiling; reduce heat. Simmer, uncovered, for 3 minutes. Stir in chicken; heat through. Sprinkle individual servings with almonds.

Nutrition Facts per serving: 416 cal., 18 g total fat (2 g sat. fat), 62 mg chol., 1,300 mg sodium, 32 g carbo., 3 g fiber, 30 g pro.

MENU IDEA:

Crackers served with purchased semisoft cheese with herbs

Quick Strawberry Shortcakes
(see p. 337)

Thanks to bottled stir-fry sauce, this is a quick meal you can whip up during the busy workweek. If you like, substitute regular button mushrooms for shiitakes. Many supermarkets sell mushrooms and vegetables, such as red peppers and pea pods, already washed and ready for stir-frying.

GINGER NOODLE BOWL

2	cups dried Chinese egg noodles or fine egg noodles (4 ounces)
⅓	cup bottled stir-fry sauce
¼	teaspoon ground ginger
2	teaspoons peanut oil or cooking oil
1	cup fresh sugar snap peas or pea pods, tips and stems removed and cut up
1	cup sliced fresh shiitake mushrooms
1	small red sweet pepper, cut into bite-size strips
1	cup cooked chicken breast cut into strips (about 5 ounces)
2	tablespoons broken cashews

1 Cook noodles according to package directions. Drain; set aside. In a small bowl stir together stir-fry sauce and ginger; set aside.

2 In a large skillet heat oil over medium-high heat. Add sugar snap peas, mushrooms, and sweet pepper; cook and stir for 3 to 5 minutes or until crisp-tender. Add cooked noodles, stir-fry sauce mixture, chicken, and cashews; heat through.

Nutrition Facts per serving: 362 cal., 10 g total fat (2 g sat. fat), 77 mg chol., 734 mg sodium, 42 g carbo., 4 g fiber, 25 g pro.

START TO FINISH:

25 minutes

MAKES:

3 servings

MENU IDEA:

Summer Fruit with Sesame Dressing
(see p. 314)

Purchased brownies, crumbled and layered with whipped cream, canned chocolate pudding, and toasted chopped nuts

Nothing goes better with hot summer days than a cool pasta salad chockful of colorful vegetables and other wonderful ingredients. Simply double the recipe if you have a crowd to feed.

CHICKEN & PASTA SALAD WITH TOMATOES

PREP:
15 minutes

CHILL:
10 minutes

MAKES:
4 servings

MENU IDEA:

Sun-dried tomato or cheese focaccia

Blueberry-Lemon Tarts *(see p. 353)*

1   16-ounce package frozen pasta and vegetables in a seasoned sauce (such as pasta, broccoli, peas, and carrots in onion and herb seasoned sauce)

1   cup chopped cooked chicken or turkey (about 5 ounces)

½   cup dairy sour cream dip with chives

2   medium tomatoes, coarsely chopped

½   cup shredded cheddar cheese (2 ounces)

1 In a 2-quart saucepan cook frozen pasta and vegetables according to package directions.

2 Meanwhile, in a large bowl stir together chicken and sour cream dip with chives. Gently fold the undrained cooked pasta mixture and the tomatoes into the chicken mixture. Cover and chill in freezer for 10 minutes.

3 To serve, sprinkle with cheddar cheese.

Nutrition Facts per serving: 335 cal., 17 g total fat (10 g sat. fat), 67 mg chol., 785 mg sodium, 24 g carbo., 5 g fiber, 21 g pro.

This bow tie-and-chicken salad can be served either hot or chilled.

CILANTRO CHICKEN PASTA WITH TOMATOES

8	ounces dried bow tie or penne pasta
1	9-ounce package frozen chopped, cooked chicken breast, thawed
2	medium tomatoes, chopped
2	green onions, sliced
⅓	cup snipped fresh cilantro
¾	cup bottled French salad dressing
1	tablespoon balsamic vinegar
2	slices packaged ready-to-serve cooked bacon, crumbled
¼	teaspoon salt
¼	teaspoon cracked black pepper

START TO FINISH:
20 minutes
MAKES:
4 servings

1 Cook pasta according to package directions. Drain. In a large bowl combine drained pasta, cooked chicken, tomatoes, green onions, and cilantro.

2 In a small bowl stir together French dressing, balsamic vinegar, crumbled bacon, salt, and pepper. Pour over pasta mixture; toss to coat. Return to pan and heat through. Serve immediately.

MAKE·AHEAD DIRECTIONS: Prepare as directed. Cover and chill for up to 24 hours.

Nutrition Facts per serving: 558 cal., 24 g total fat (6 g sat. fat), 57 mg chol., 894 mg sodium, 56 g carbo., 3 g fiber, 29 g pro.

MENU IDEA:
Sautéed sugar snap peas and mushrooms tossed with butter and lemon-pepper seasoning

Bananas Suzette over Pound Cake
(see p. 340)

With just five ingredients and 10 minutes of preparation time, you can't beat this soup for a hurry-up meal.

MINESTRONE IN MINUTES

START TO FINISH:

10 minutes

MAKES:

2 servings

1   18- to 19-ounce can ready-to-serve minestrone soup

1   cup chopped cooked chicken breast (5 ounces)

½   teaspoon bottled roasted minced garlic

1   cup fresh baby spinach leaves

2   tablespoons shredded Parmesan cheese

1 In a large saucepan combine minestrone soup, cooked chicken, and roasted minced garlic. Cook over medium heat until heated through.

2 Add spinach leaves; stir just until wilted. Heat through. Sprinkle Parmesan cheese on individual servings.

Nutrition Facts per serving: 357 cal., 13 g total fat (7 g sat. fat), 82 mg chol., 1,623 mg sodium, 23 g carbo., 5 g fiber, 37 g pro.

MENU IDEA:

Assorted purchased melba toast, bagel chips, and/or crackers

Fun-Day Sundae Parfait *(see p. 377)*

Cream of chicken soup is wonderfully creamy and chicken-y, and blends well with so many flavors. Here it takes on an especially intriguing flair, thanks to a touch of curry powder.

CURRIED CHICKEN & CORN CHOWDER

1	17-ounce can cream-style corn
2	cups milk
1	10¾-ounce can condensed cream of chicken soup
¾	cup chopped green or red sweet pepper
1	tablespoon dried minced onion
2	to 3 teaspoons curry powder
1	9¾- or 10-ounce can chunk-style chicken or 1½ cups frozen diced cooked chicken
	Coarsely chopped peanuts (optional)

1 In a large saucepan stir together undrained corn, milk, cream of chicken soup, sweet pepper, dried minced onion, and curry powder. Bring to boiling, stirring frequently.

2 Stir in undrained canned chicken or frozen chicken; cook about 2 minutes or until heated through. If desired, sprinkle with peanuts.

Nutrition Facts per serving: 324 cal., 11 g total fat (4 g sat. fat), 49 mg chol., 1,201 mg sodium, 39 g carbo., 3 g fiber, 24 g pro.

START TO FINISH:
15 minutes

MAKES:
4 servings

MENU IDEA:
Parmesan Corn Bread Swirls *(see p. 328)*

Fresh strawberries served with purchased fruit dip

Fast and festive, here is a versatile alternative to cooking a whole turkey—either for the holidays or for everyday eating.

TURKEY STEAKS WITH CRANBERRY-ORANGE SAUCE

START TO FINISH:

25 minutes

MAKES:

4 servings

MENU IDEA:

Honey-Glazed Carrots
(see p. 262)

Purchased pumpkin bars or pumpkin pie

2   turkey breast tenderloins, halved horizontally (about 1 pound total)

Salt

Black pepper

2   tablespoons butter or margarine

1   6-ounce package quick-cooking long grain and wild rice mix

1   10-ounce package frozen cranberry-orange relish, thawed

2   tablespoons orange liqueur or orange juice

1 Sprinkle turkey with salt and pepper. In a large skillet melt butter over medium heat. Add turkey; cook for 10 to 12 minutes or until no longer pink (170°F), turning once.

2 Meanwhile, cook rice mix according to package directions.

3 Transfer turkey to a serving platter. Keep warm. Remove skillet from heat; let cool for 2 minutes. Carefully add cranberry-orange relish to drippings in skillet; add liqueur or orange juice. Return to heat; cook and stir over low heat until heated through. Spoon sauce over turkey. Serve with rice.

Nutrition Facts per serving: 481 cal., 8 g total fat (4 g sat. fat), 84 mg chol., 941 mg sodium, 68 g carbo., 0 g fiber, 31 g pro.

Turkey breast tenderloins are a great-tasting change from chicken or beef—and they are low in fat.

TURKEY TENDERLOIN WITH BEAN & CORN SALSA

2	turkey breast tenderloins, halved horizontally (about 1 pound total)
	Salt
	Black pepper
¼	cup red jalapeño chile pepper jelly
1¼	cups purchased black bean and corn salsa
2	tablespoons snipped fresh cilantro

1 Place turkey on the unheated rack of a broiler pan. Sprinkle with salt and pepper. Broil 4 to 5 inches from heat for 5 minutes.

2 Meanwhile, in a small saucepan melt jelly. Remove 2 tablespoons of the jelly. Turn turkey and brush with the 2 tablespoons jelly. Discard remainder of jelly used as brush-on. Broil 4 to 6 minutes more or until no longer pink (170°F).

3 Transfer turkey to a serving plate. Spoon jelly remaining in saucepan over turkey; cover and keep warm. In a small saucepan heat salsa. Spoon salsa over the turkey. Sprinkle with cilantro.

Nutrition Facts per serving: 196 cal., 2 g total fat (1 g sat. fat), 66 mg chol., 377 mg sodium, 16 g carbo., 1 g fiber, 27 g pro.

START TO FINISH:
25 minutes

MAKES:
4 servings

MENU IDEA:
Holy Guacamole Soup
(see p. 299)

Purchased angel food cake, sliced and spread with purchased lemon curd, served with whipped cream and finely crushed lemon drop candies

An aromatic basil-flavored spread takes these sandwiches out of an ordinary realm and puts them into an extraordinary one. Fresh basil is the key here; dried simply doesn't work.

ITALIAN TURKEY SANDWICHES

START TO FINISH:

20 minutes

MAKES:

4 sandwiches

MENU IDEA:

Purchased frozen seasoned potato wedges, cooked according to package directions and served with warm spaghetti or pizza sauce

Mocha Cookies
(see p. 345)

1/3   cup fine dry bread crumbs

2   teaspoons dried Italian seasoning, crushed

2   turkey breast tenderloins, halved horizontally (about 1 pound total)

2   teaspoons olive oil

2   tablespoons snipped fresh basil

1/4   cup mayonnaise or salad dressing

8   1/2-inch slices Italian bread, toasted

1   cup bottled roasted red and/or yellow sweet peppers, cut into thin strips

1 In a large resealable plastic bag combine bread crumbs and Italian seasoning. Place a turkey tenderloin piece in the bag; seal and shake to coat. Repeat with remaining turkey tenderloin pieces.

2 In a 12-inch nonstick skillet heat oil over medium heat. Add turkey; cook about 10 minutes or until tender and no longer pink (170°F), turning once.

3 In a small bowl stir 1 tablespoon of the basil into mayonnaise. Spread mayonnaise mixture on one side of each of 4 of the bread slices; top with turkey pieces, sweet pepper strips, and the remaining 1 tablespoon basil. Top with remaining bread slices.

Nutrition Facts per sandwich: 457 cal., 18 g total fat (3 g sat. fat), 78 mg chol., 728 mg sodium, 39 g carbo., 3 g fiber, 33 g pro.

TEST KITCHEN TIP: For a lower-fat sandwich, substitute light mayonnaise dressing for the mayonnaise.

Nutrition Facts per sandwich: 399 cal., 11 g total fat (2 g sat. fat), 73 mg chol., 671 mg sodium, 40 g carbo., 3 g fiber, 33 g pro.

Balsamic vinegar, aged several years before it gets to store shelves, possesses an earthy sweetness. For this recipe, a small amount of honey and crushed red pepper combine with the vinegar, giving the turkey an intense spicy-sweet flavor.

BALSAMIC TURKEY WITH ZUCCHINI

2   tablespoons balsamic vinegar

2   tablespoons cooking oil

1   tablespoon honey

⅛   to ¼ teaspoon crushed red pepper

2   turkey breast tenderloins, halved horizontally
     (about 1 pound total)

     Salt

     Black pepper

2   medium zucchini, halved lengthwise and
     cut into ¼-inch slices

     Hot cooked pasta or rice

½   cup chopped tomato

     Shredded fresh basil

START TO FINISH:

25 minutes

MAKES:

4 servings

MENU IDEA:

Packaged corn bread mix combined with a little snipped fresh basil before baking

Amaretto Peaches with Vanilla Yogurt
(see p. 375)

1 For dressing, in a small bowl stir together balsamic vinegar, 1 tablespoon of the oil, the honey, and crushed red pepper; set aside. Lightly sprinkle turkey with salt and pepper.

2 In a large nonstick skillet heat remaining 1 tablespoon oil over medium-high heat. Add turkey; cook for 8 to 10 minutes or until tender and no longer pink (170°F), turning once. Remove from skillet; cover and keep warm.

3 Add zucchini to skillet; cook and stir about 3 minutes or until crisp-tender. Cut turkey into bite-size pieces. In a large bowl combine turkey, zucchini, and dressing. Spoon over hot cooked pasta or rice. Sprinkle with tomato and basil.

Nutrition Facts per serving: 328 cal., 9 g total fat (2 g sat. fat), 68 mg chol., 96 mg sodium, 30 g carbo., 2 g fiber, 31 g pro.

For an attractive and mouthwatering presentation, be sure to use different colored sweet peppers including red, green, and yellow.

TURKEY & PEPPERS

START TO FINISH:

25 minutes

MAKES:

4 servings

MENU IDEA:

Sliced fresh pineapple and kiwifruit

Fudge Cookies in Chocolate Cream
(see p. 347)

4 ¼- to ⅜-inch-thick turkey breast slices (cutlets) (about 12 ounces total)

   Salt

   Black pepper

1 tablespoon olive oil

2 medium red, green, and/or yellow sweet peppers, cut into thin strips

1 medium onion, halved lengthwise and sliced

1 fresh jalapeño chile pepper, seeded and thinly sliced*

¾ cup chicken broth

1 tablespoon all-purpose flour

1 teaspoon paprika

   Hot cooked brown rice (optional)

1 Sprinkle turkey lightly with salt and black pepper. In a large nonstick skillet heat oil over medium-high heat. Add turkey; cook for 4 to 5 minutes or until turkey is tender and no longer pink, turning once. (If necessary, reduce heat to medium to prevent overbrowning.) Transfer turkey to a serving platter; cover and keep warm.

2 Add sweet peppers, onion, and chile pepper to skillet. Cover and cook for 4 to 5 minutes or until vegetables are crisp-tender, stirring occasionally.

3 In a screw-top jar combine broth, flour, and paprika; shake well. Add to chile pepper mixture. Cook and stir over medium heat until thickened and bubbly. Cook and stir for 1 minute more. Spoon the chile pepper mixture over turkey. If desired, serve with hot cooked brown rice.

*NOTE: Because chile peppers contain volatile oils that can burn your skin and eyes, avoid direct contact with them as much as possible. When working with chile peppers, wear plastic or rubber gloves. If your bare hands do touch the peppers, wash your hands and nails well with soap and warm water.

Nutrition Facts per serving: 164 cal., 4 g total fat (1 g sat. fat), 53 mg chol., 324 mg sodium, 8 g carbo., 2 g fiber, 23 g pro.

Five-spice powder lends a wonderfully exotic and aromatic element to this stir-fry. Used extensively in Chinese cooking, the powder is a pungent mixture of five ground spices—cinnamon, cloves, fennel seeds, star anise, and Szechwan peppercorns. You can find it in Asian markets and most supermarkets.

FIVE-SPICE TURKEY STIR-FRY

1	4.4-ounce package beef lo-mein noodle mix
12	ounces turkey breast tenderloin, cut into thin bite-size strips
¼	teaspoon five-spice powder
¼	teaspoon salt
¼	teaspoon black pepper
2	tablespoons cooking oil
½	of a 16-ounce package frozen pepper stir-fry vegetables (yellow, green, and red peppers and onion)
2	tablespoons chopped honey-roasted peanuts or plain peanuts

1 Prepare noodle mix according to package directions. Set aside. In a small bowl toss together turkey strips, five-spice powder, salt, and pepper; set aside.

2 Pour 1 tablespoon of the oil into a wok or large skillet. Heat over medium-high heat. Carefully add frozen vegetables to wok; cook and stir for 3 minutes. Remove vegetables from wok. Add remaining 1 tablespoon oil to hot wok. Add turkey mixture to wok or skillet; cook and stir for 2 to 3 minutes or until turkey is done. Return cooked vegetables to wok or skillet. Cook and stir about 1 minute more or until heated through.

3 To serve, divide noodle mixture among 4 dinner plates. Top with turkey mixture; sprinkle with peanuts.

Nutrition Facts per serving: 314 cal., 11 g total fat (2 g sat. fat), 76 mg chol., 670 mg sodium, 26 g carbo., 3 g fiber, 27 g pro.

START TO FINISH:
25 minutes

MAKES:
4 servings

MENU IDEA:
Mixed Greens Salad with Ginger Vinaigrette
(see p. 305)

Strawberry frozen yogurt topped with sliced strawberries

When you think tacos, you may automatically think of beef. Here turkey replaces beef with results that are just as tasty. The recipe doubles easily for feeding the family.

TURKEY TACO SALAD

START TO FINISH:

30 minutes

MAKES:

2 servings

MENU IDEA:

Sliced roma tomatoes drizzled with olive oil and sprinkled with snipped fresh cilantro

Dessert Waffles
(see p. 357)

6	ounces uncooked ground turkey or lean ground beef or pork
½	teaspoon bottled minced garlic (1 clove)
½	cup bottled salsa or taco sauce
½	cup canned red kidney beans, rinsed and drained
2	tablespoons water
1	teaspoon chili powder
	Dash ground cumin
2	8-inch flour tortillas
1	tablespoon butter or margarine, melted
2	cups torn lettuce
1	medium tomato, chopped
½	of a small avocado, seeded, peeled, and chopped
¼	cup sliced pitted ripe olives
¼	cup shredded cheddar cheese (1 ounce)
	Dairy sour cream (optional)
	Bottled salsa or taco sauce (optional)

1 In a medium skillet cook ground turkey and garlic over medium heat about 5 minutes or until turkey is no longer pink. Drain off fat. Stir in the ½ cup salsa or taco sauce, kidney beans, the water, chili powder, and cumin. Bring to boiling; reduce heat. Cover and simmer for 10 minutes.

2 Meanwhile, lightly brush both sides of the tortillas with melted butter. Place tortillas in a single layer on an ungreased baking sheet. Bake in a 400°F oven for 7 to 10 minutes or until tortillas are lightly browned.

3 In a medium bowl combine lettuce, tomato, avocado, and olives. Add the hot meat mixture; toss gently to combine.

4 To serve, transfer the tortillas to 2 dinner plates. Spoon lettuce mixture on top of tortillas. Sprinkle with cheese. If desired, serve with sour cream and additional salsa or taco sauce.

Nutrition Facts per serving: 482 cal., 27 g total fat (10 g sat. fat), 97 mg chol., 866 mg sodium, 35 g carbo., 9 g fiber, 26 g pro.

Golden hominy gives this chili a twist. It provides lots of corn flavor and a splash of yellow color.

TURKEY CHILI WITH A TWIST

12   ounces uncooked turkey Italian sausage
     (remove casings, if present) or uncooked ground turkey

 2   15-ounce cans chili beans with chili gravy

 1   15-ounce can golden hominy, drained

 1   cup bottled salsa with lime

⅔   cup water

⅓   cup sliced green onions

1 In a large saucepan cook the turkey sausage until brown. Stir in undrained chili beans, hominy, salsa, and the water. Heat through. Sprinkle with sliced green onions.

Nutrition Facts per serving: 470 cal., 11 g total fat (3 g sat. fat), 45 mg chol., 1,897 mg sodium, 64 g carbo., 16 g fiber, 28 g pro.

START TO FINISH:

20 minutes

MAKES:

4 or 5 servings

MENU IDEA:

Assorted vegetable dippers or crackers served with purchased vegetable dip

Apricot-Peach Cobbler *(see p. 332)*

The seasonings in this zesty turkey sausage-and-squash medley work with just about any flavor of red pasta sauce. Use whichever is your favorite.

SPICY TURKEY PASTA SAUCE

START TO FINISH:

25 minutes

MAKES:

4 servings

8   ounces uncooked turkey Italian sausage (remove casings, if present)

1   cup cut-up pattypan squash or yellow summer squash

1   small red sweet pepper, cut into thin strips

¼   cup chopped red onion

1   14-ounce jar red pasta sauce (any flavor)

1   9-ounce package refrigerated fettuccine or linguine

2   tablespoons shredded Parmesan cheese (optional)

1 In a large skillet cook sausage, squash, sweet pepper, and onion over medium heat until sausage is brown. Drain off fat. Stir in pasta sauce; heat through.

2 Meanwhile, cook pasta according to package directions; drain.

3 Serve sausage mixture over pasta. If desired, sprinkle with Parmesan cheese.

Nutrition Facts per serving: 350 cal., 10 g total fat (3 g sat. fat), 115 mg chol., 866 mg sodium, 49 g carbo., 5 g fiber, 20 g pro.

MENU IDEA:

Mixed greens tossed with bottled Italian salad dressing

Cannoli *(see p. 356)*

Busy week ahead? Time to raid your pantry! Chances are you already have some of these ingredients in your refrigerator and cupboards. If not, be sure to stock up so you're ready to whip up this incredibly satisfying supper in no time flat.

TURKEY-BISCUIT PIE

1	10¾-ounce can condensed cream of chicken soup
½	cup milk
¼	cup dairy sour cream
6	ounces cooked turkey breast, cubed
1½	cups loose-pack frozen mixed vegetables
½	teaspoon dried basil, crushed
⅛	teaspoon black pepper
1	package (5 or 6) refrigerated biscuits, quartered

1 In a medium saucepan stir together cream of chicken soup, milk, and sour cream. Stir in turkey, mixed vegetables, basil, and pepper. Cook and stir over medium heat until boiling.

2 Spoon turkey mixture into a lightly greased 1½-quart casserole. Top with quartered biscuits.

3 Bake in a 450°F oven, uncovered, for 12 to 15 minutes or until biscuits are browned.

Nutrition Facts per serving: 335 cal., 14 g total fat (5 g sat. fat), 49 mg chol., 1,049 mg sodium, 33 g carbo., 3 g fiber, 20 g pro.

PREP:
15 minutes

BAKE:
12 minutes

MAKES:
4 servings

MENU IDEA:

Chunky applesauce sprinkled with ground cinnamon

Strawberry Shortbread Sandwiches
(see p. 348)

Need a quick meal? This soup is a creative way to use leftover turkey. The ravioli adds some fun and will satisfy kids of all ages.

TURKEY RAVIOLI SOUP

START TO FINISH:

25 minutes

MAKES:

6 servings

MENU IDEA:

Sourdough rolls
served with a mixture of softened butter and purchased basil pesto

Double Dippin' Fruit
(see p. 366)

6	cups chicken broth
1	medium red sweet pepper, chopped
1	medium onion, chopped
1½	teaspoons dried Italian seasoning, crushed
1	9-ounce package refrigerated cheese ravioli
1½	cups cooked turkey cut into bite-size pieces (about 8 ounces)
2	cups shredded fresh spinach
	Finely shredded Parmesan cheese (optional)

1 In a Dutch oven combine broth, sweet pepper, onion, and Italian seasoning. Bring to boiling; reduce heat. Cover and simmer for 5 minutes.

2 Add ravioli and turkey. Return to boiling; reduce heat. Simmer, uncovered, about 6 minutes or just until ravioli is tender. Stir in spinach. If desired, sprinkle with Parmesan cheese.

Nutrition Facts per serving: 204 cal., 4 g total fat (2 g sat. fat), 48 mg chol., 1,204 mg sodium, 22 g carbo., 2 g fiber, 20 g pro.

How do you turn baby spinach into a meal? Add cubed turkey, grapefruit and orange sections, and sliced almonds. Toss them all together with a homemade poppy seed dressing and enjoy.

TURKEY & SPINACH SALAD

8	cups fresh baby spinach or torn fresh spinach
8	ounces cooked turkey, cubed
2	grapefruit, peeled and sectioned
2	oranges, peeled and sectioned
¼	cup orange juice
2	tablespoons olive oil
1	teaspoon honey
½	teaspoon poppy seeds
¼	teaspoon salt
¼	teaspoon dry mustard
2	tablespoons sliced almonds, toasted (optional)

1 Place spinach in a large bowl. Add turkey, grapefruit sections, and orange sections.

2 For dressing, in a screw-top jar combine orange juice, oil, honey, poppy seeds, salt, and dry mustard. Cover and shake well. Pour the dressing over salad; toss gently. If desired, sprinkle with almonds.

Nutrition Facts per serving: 228 cal., 10 g total fat (2 g sat. fat), 43 mg chol., 261 mg sodium, 16 g carbo., 8 g fiber, 20 g pro.

START TO FINISH:
25 minutes
MAKES:
4 servings

MENU IDEA:
Blueberry Gems
(see p. 323)

Purchased apple crisp
served with caramel
ice cream

If your family loves chili, this quick-fixing saucy mixture served over corn muffins will appeal to everyone.

SPICY TURKEY & BEANS

START TO FINISH:

30 minutes

MAKES:

6 servings

1	7- to 8½-ounce package corn muffin mix
1	to 2 teaspoons chili powder
2	15½-ounce cans pinto and/or small red beans, rinsed and drained
1	15-ounce can tomato sauce
1	10-ounce can chopped tomatoes and green chile peppers, undrained
1	cup chopped cooked turkey (about 5 ounces)
½	cup shredded cheddar or Monterey Jack cheese (2 ounces)

1 In a medium bowl combine corn muffin mix and ½ teaspoon of the chili powder. Prepare and bake muffins according to package directions, making 6 muffins.

2 Meanwhile, in a medium saucepan combine remaining ½ to 1½ teaspoons chili powder, beans, tomato sauce, undrained tomatoes and green chile peppers, and turkey. Cook and stir for 8 to 10 minutes or until heated through. Split corn muffins; spoon bean mixture over muffins. Sprinkle with cheese.

Nutrition Facts per serving: 385 cal., 9 g total fat (2 g sat. fat), 28 mg chol., 1,328 mg sodium, 57 g carbo., 8 g fiber, 22 g pro.

MENU IDEA:

Peanut Butter Fruit Salad *(see p. 313)*

Purchased pound cake topped with vanilla frozen yogurt and strawberry ice cream topping

What will you enjoy more—how easy this soup is to assemble or its smoky, Southwestern flavor?

SMOKED TURKEY CHUCKWAGON SOUP

2   14-ounce cans reduced-sodium chicken broth

1   15-ounce can white hominy, drained

1   11-ounce can condensed tomato rice soup

2   cups chopped smoked turkey (about 10 ounces)

½   cup chopped yellow sweet pepper

⅓   cup bottled salsa

1   teaspoon ground cumin

1½   cups crushed tortilla chips (about 2½ ounces)

Dairy sour cream (optional)

1 In a large saucepan combine broth, hominy, tomato rice soup, smoked turkey, sweet pepper, salsa, and cumin. Bring to boiling; reduce heat. Simmer, uncovered, about 5 minutes or until sweet pepper is tender. Top individual servings with tortilla chips and, if desired, sour cream.

Nutrition Facts per serving: 318 cal., 10 g total fat (2 g sat. fat), 38 mg chol., 2,013 mg sodium, 39 g carbo., 5 g fiber, 20 g pro.

START TO FINISH:

20 minutes

MAKES:

4 servings

MENU IDEA:

Assorted sliced fresh melon

Gooey Brownie Cups
(see p. 339)

Sharp blue cheese and sweet mandarin orange sections give this pasta salad some punch.

SMOKED TURKEY & BLUE CHEESE PASTA SALAD

START TO FINISH:

25 minutes

MAKES:

4 servings

1   cup medium dried bow ties or medium shell macaroni (about 2½ ounces)

½   cup crumbled blue cheese (2 ounces)

⅓   cup bottled balsamic vinaigrette or oil and vinegar salad dressing

6   ounces smoked turkey, cut into bite-size pieces

3   cups torn mixed salad greens

¼   cup walnut or pecan pieces

1   11-ounce can mandarin orange sections, drained

1 Cook pasta in lightly salted water according to package directions. Drain in colander. Rinse with cold water; drain again.

2 Meanwhile, in a large bowl combine blue cheese and vinaigrette. Add smoked turkey, salad greens, and nuts. Add pasta; toss gently to coat. Top individual servings with mandarin orange sections.

Nutrition Facts per serving: 284 cal., 16 g total fat (4 g sat. fat), 29 mg chol., 887 mg sodium, 25 g carbo., 2 g fiber, 14 g pro.

MENU IDEA:

Purchased refrigerated soft breadsticks, baked

Purchased pound cake with Apricot-Orange Sauce
(see p. 372)

Looking for something to serve after the game or for Sunday football in front of the television? This turkey chili soup will have your sports fans coming back for seconds.

BEER-CHILI BEAN SOUP

1	15-ounce can hot-style chili beans with chili gravy
1	12-ounce can (1½ cups) beer
1	11¼-ounce can condensed chili beef soup
1½	cups chopped cooked turkey (about 8 ounces)
1	cup hot water
1	teaspoon dried minced onion
1	teaspoon Worcestershire sauce
½	teaspoon garlic powder
	Shredded cheddar cheese
	Dairy sour cream (optional)

START TO FINISH:
20 minutes
MAKES:
4 servings

1 In a large saucepan combine undrained chili beans, beer, chili beef soup, turkey, the hot water, dried minced onion, Worcestershire sauce, and garlic powder.

2 Bring to boiling; reduce heat. Simmer, uncovered, for 5 minutes. Serve with cheese and, if desired, sour cream.

Nutrition Facts per serving: 353 cal., 10 g total fat (5 g sat. fat), 57 mg chol., 1,154 mg sodium, 35 g carbo., 12 g fiber, 27 g pro.

MENU IDEA:
Packaged corn muffin mix, baked and served with honey
Cherry Trifles
(see p. 344)

There are extra vegetables and some fragrant snipped fresh rosemary in this comforting classic.

TURKEY & RICE SOUP

START TO FINISH:

30 minutes

MAKES:

6 servings

2   14-ounce cans chicken broth

1½   cups water

1   teaspoon snipped fresh rosemary
     or ¼ teaspoon dried rosemary, crushed

¼   teaspoon black pepper

1   medium carrot, thinly sliced

1   stalk celery, thinly sliced

1   small onion, chopped

1   cup instant rice

½   cup loose-pack frozen cut green beans

2   cups chopped cooked turkey or chicken (about 10 ounces)

1   14½-ounce can diced tomatoes, undrained

MENU IDEA:

Cracked wheat or rye crackers

Strawberry Dip
(see p. 367)

1 In a large saucepan or Dutch oven combine broth, the water, rosemary, and pepper. Add carrot, celery, and onion. Bring to boiling.

2 Stir in uncooked rice and green beans. Return to boiling; reduce heat. Cover and simmer for 10 to 12 minutes or until vegetables are tender. Stir in turkey or chicken and undrained tomatoes; heat through.

Nutrition Facts per serving: 232 cal., 3 g total fat (1 g sat. fat), 37 mg chol., 705 mg sodium, 32 g carbo., 2 g fiber, 18 g pro.

Cooked smoked turkey sausage has a long shelf life when stored in the refrigerator. Keep some on hand for cool days that call for this creamy and delicious soup.

TURKEY-BEAN SOUP

START TO FINISH:

30 minutes

MAKES:

4 servings

2	15-ounce cans Great Northern or white kidney (cannellini) beans, rinsed and drained
1	10¾-ounce can condensed cream of celery soup
8	ounces cooked smoked turkey sausage, halved lengthwise and sliced
1½	cups milk
1	teaspoon dried minced onion
1	teaspoon bottled minced garlic (2 cloves) or ¼ teaspoon garlic powder
½	teaspoon dried thyme, crushed
⅛	to ¼ teaspoon black pepper

❶ In a large saucepan combine beans, cream of celery soup, and turkey sausage; stir in milk, dried minced onion, garlic or garlic powder, thyme, and pepper.

❷ Bring to boiling over medium-high heat, stirring occasionally; reduce heat. Cover and simmer for 10 minutes, stirring occasionally.

Nutrition Facts per serving: 434 cal., 11 g total fat (3 g sat. fat), 54 mg chol., 1,129 mg sodium, 57 g carbo., 11 g fiber, 29 g pro.

MENU IDEA:

Quick Focaccia Breadsticks
(see p. 330)

Sliced green and/or red apples served with purchased caramel dip

This pasta dish salutes Tuscany, a region in Italy known for its fabulous combinations that make the most of delicious cannellini, or white kidney, beans. To help busy cooks, this recipe calls for convenient canned beans instead of dried beans which require a long soaking time.

WHITE BEAN & SAUSAGE RIGATONI

START TO FINISH:

20 minutes

MAKES:

4 servings

8	ounces dried rigatoni
1	15-ounce can white kidney (cannellini), Great Northern, or navy beans, rinsed and drained
1	14½-ounce can Italian-style stewed tomatoes, undrained
6	ounces cooked smoked turkey sausage, cut into ½-inch slices
⅓	cup snipped fresh basil
¼	cup shaved or finely shredded Asiago cheese (1 ounce)

① Cook pasta according to package directions, except do not add salt to the cooking water; drain well. Return pasta to saucepan.

② Meanwhile, in a large saucepan combine beans, undrained tomatoes, and sausage; heat through. Add bean mixture and basil to pasta; toss gently to combine. Sprinkle individual servings with cheese.

Nutrition Facts per serving: 401 cal., 6 g total fat (1 g sat. fat), 32 mg chol., 964 mg sodium, 67 g carbo., 5 g fiber, 25 g pro.

MENU IDEA:

Steamed asparagus with Blue Cheese Sauce for Vegetables *(see p. 279)*

Purchased pound cake drizzled with orange liqueur or orange juice concentrate and served with whipped cream

This has to be the fastest salad you'll ever prepare! Toss fresh crunchy cabbage slaw, tender cooked turkey, sweet mandarin oranges, and crispy ramen noodles with a vibrant orange vinaigrette dressing and you're ready to eat.

QUICK & CRUNCHY TURKEY SALAD

1	16-ounce package shredded cabbage with carrot (coleslaw mix)
6	ounces sliced cooked turkey breast, cubed
1	3-ounce package ramen noodles (any flavor)
⅔	cup bottled orange vinaigrette salad dressing
1	11-ounce can mandarin orange sections, drained

1 In a large salad bowl combine cabbage mixture and turkey. Remove seasoning packet from noodles; reserve for another use. Crumble noodles and add to cabbage mixture. Pour the dressing over the salad; toss to coat. Gently fold in orange sections.

Nutrition Facts per serving: 527 cal., 23 g total fat (1 g sat. fat), 15 mg chol., 1,552 mg sodium, 67 g carbo., 3 g fiber, 17 g pro.

START TO FINISH:
10 minutes

MAKES:
4 servings

MENU IDEA:

Broccoli-Cheddar Salad *(see p. 320)*

Purchased pecan or sticky rolls, warmed and served with cinnamon ice cream

There is nothing like the savory flavors of turkey, ham, Swiss cheese, and sweet-tangy honey mustard nestled between French toast slices.

MOCK MONTE CRISTO SANDWICHES

PREP:

10 minutes

BAKE:

15 minutes

MAKES:

6 half sandwiches

MENU IDEA:

Mashed Potato Soup (double the recipe) *(see p. 301)*

Purchased angel food cake served with assorted mixed berries

6   slices frozen French toast

2   tablespoons honey mustard

3   ounces sliced cooked turkey breast

3   ounces sliced cooked ham

3   ounces thinly sliced Swiss cheese

1 Lightly grease a baking sheet; set aside. To assemble sandwiches, spread 1 side of each of the frozen French toast slices with honey mustard. Layer 3 of the toast slices, mustard sides up, with the turkey, ham, and cheese. Cover with remaining toast slices, mustard sides down.

2 Place sandwiches on prepared baking sheet. Bake in a 400°F oven for 15 to 20 minutes or until sandwiches are heated through, turning sandwiches once. Cut each sandwich in half diagonally.

Nutrition Facts per half sandwich: 221 cal., 9 g total fat (4 g sat. fat), 75 mg chol., 704 mg sodium, 21 g carbo., 1 g fiber, 14 g pro.

Take advantage of the latest convenience products to cut the prep time for this colorful and flavor-packed sandwich. Buy presliced mushrooms, prewashed spinach leaves, and precooked bacon, if they are available.

CALIFORNIA CLUB SANDWICH

1	8-ounce tub cream cheese
2	tablespoons honey mustard
1	6½-ounce jar marinated artichoke hearts, drained and chopped
¼	cup chopped pitted ripe olives, pitted green olives, or Greek black olives
1	16-ounce loaf crusty French bread
2	cups loosely packed fresh spinach leaves, stems removed
2	cups sliced fresh mushrooms
1	small red onion, thinly sliced
8	ounces thinly sliced cooked turkey breast
4	slices bacon, crisp-cooked, drained, and crumbled
¼	cup roasted and salted sunflower seeds

1 In a small bowl stir together cream cheese and honey mustard. Gently stir in artichokes and olives; set aside.

2 Cut bread loaf in half lengthwise. Hollow out bottom half of bread loaf, leaving a ½-inch-thick shell (reserve bread crumbs for another use). Spread bread shell with ⅔ cup of the cream cheese mixture. Layer spinach leaves, sliced mushrooms, red onion, and turkey into bottom half of loaf. Sprinkle with bacon and sunflower seeds.

3 Spread another ⅔ cup cream cheese mixture onto cut side of top half of bread loaf. Reserve any remaining cream cheese mixture for another use. Place top half of bread, cream cheese mixture side down, on top of sandwich. Cut into 4 serving-portions.

Nutrition Facts per serving: 665 cal., 34 g total fat (16 g sat. fat), 85 mg chol., 1,941 mg sodium, 62 g carbo., 5 g fiber, 31 g pro.

START TO FINISH:

25 minutes

MAKES:

4 servings

MENU IDEA:

Purchased pasta salad

Citrus Freeze
(see p. 381)

A creamy cheese and honey mustard spread serves as an irresistible base for sliced ham, turkey, and cheese. Team this hearty and healthful sandwich with a favorite soup for a super-satisfying lunch or supper.

DELI SANDWICH STACKS

START TO FINISH:

20 minutes

MAKES:

4 half sandwiches

MENU IDEA:

Tomato-Barley Soup with Garden Vegetables
(see p. 294)

Purchased brownies topped with whipped cream and maraschino cherries

½ of a 4-ounce container semisoft cheese with garlic and herb

2 tablespoons honey mustard

¼ teaspoon lemon-pepper seasoning

6 slices marble rye, cracked wheat, or seven-grain bread

2 small plum tomatoes, thinly sliced

⅓ cup sliced canned banana chile peppers, well drained

1 cup loosely packed fresh spinach leaves or 4 lettuce leaves

4 thin slices Colby or Monterey Jack cheese

4 ounces thinly sliced cooked turkey breast

4 ounces thinly sliced cooked ham

1 In a small bowl combine semisoft cheese, honey mustard, and lemon-pepper seasoning. Spread the cheese mixture evenly onto 1 side of each of 4 of the bread slices.

2 To assemble sandwiches, divide tomatoes, sliced banana peppers, spinach or lettuce, and Colby cheese among the 4 bread slices, spread sides up. Top 2 stacks with turkey and 2 stacks with ham. Arrange the stacks with ham on top of the stacks with turkey. Top with remaining 2 bread slices. Cut stacks diagonally in half. If desired, secure each half with a wooden pick.

Nutrition Facts per half sandwich: 378 cal., 17 g total fat (9 g sat. fat), 69 mg chol., 916 mg sodium, 31 g carbo., 4 g fiber, 24 g pro.

Chutney adds a subtle heat to the dressing for these turkey-and-Gouda cheese sandwiches.

TURKEY & CHUTNEY SANDWICHES

¼   cup bottled chutney

3   tablespoons mayonnaise or salad dressing

2   pita bread rounds, halved crosswise

4   small romaine leaves

4   ounces thinly sliced cooked turkey

3   ounces very thinly sliced smoked Gouda cheese

1   medium carrot, coarsely shredded

¼   cup shredded fresh basil leaves

1 Cut up any large pieces of chutney. In a small bowl stir together the chutney and mayonnaise.

2 Line the pita halves with romaine leaves. Fill with turkey, Gouda cheese, carrot, and basil. Top with mayonnaise mixture.

Nutrition Facts per serving: 303 cal., 15 g total fat (5 g sat. fat), 46 mg chol., 627 mg sodium, 26 g carbo., 2 g fiber, 15 g pro.

START TO FINISH:

20 minutes

MAKES:

4 servings

MENU IDEA:

Kettle-cooked potato chips

Triple Dipster Strawberries
(see p. 359)

Citrus mayonnaise is an unusual but refreshing choice that really perks up the relatively mild taste of turkey and Swiss cheese.

TURKEY SUB WITH CITRUS MAYONNAISE

START TO FINISH:

15 minutes

MAKES:

4 servings

1	orange
½	cup mayonnaise or salad dressing
4	sourdough rolls, split
8	to 12 ounces thinly sliced cooked peppered turkey or cooked smoked turkey
4	slices Swiss or provolone cheese (3 to 4 ounces total)

1 Finely shred 1 teaspoon peel from the orange. Cut the orange in half; squeeze 2 tablespoons juice from orange halves. Discard seeds and any remaining orange. For citrus mayonnaise, in a small bowl combine mayonnaise, orange juice, and orange peel.

2 If desired, toast rolls. Spread citrus mayonnaise on the cut sides of each roll. Place bottom halves of rolls on a serving platter, mayonnaise sides up. Layer turkey and cheese on rolls. Top with remaining halves of rolls, mayonnaise sides down.

Nutrition Facts per serving: 436 cal., 30 g total fat (7 g sat. fat), 61 mg chol., 1,123 mg sodium, 21 g carbo., 1 g fiber, 21 g pro.

MENU IDEA:

Purchased vinaigrette coleslaw

Tropical Fruit Shortcakes
(see p. 337)

FISH & SEAFOOD

3

Mild tasting with a firm texture, halibut is an excellent choice for the zesty mustard sauce.

BROILED HALIBUT WITH DIJON CREAM

PREP:

10 minutes

BROIL:

8 minutes

MAKES:

4 servings

4	fresh or frozen halibut steaks, cut 1 inch thick (1 to 1½ pounds)
1	teaspoon Greek-style or Mediterranean seasoning blend
¼	teaspoon coarsely ground black pepper
¼	cup dairy sour cream
¼	cup creamy Dijon-style mustard blend
1	tablespoon milk
½	teaspoon dried oregano, crushed

1 Thaw fish, if frozen. Rinse fish; pat dry with paper towels. Grease the rack of an unheated broiler pan; place fish on rack. Sprinkle fish with Greek-style seasoning blend and pepper.

2 Broil 4 inches from the heat for 8 to 12 minutes or until fish flakes easily when tested with a fork, turning once. Invert fish onto serving platter.

3 Meanwhile, for sauce, in a small bowl stir together sour cream, mustard blend, milk, and oregano. Serve sauce over fish.

Nutrition Facts per serving: 168 cal., 5 g total fat (2 g sat. fat), 42 mg chol., 300 mg sodium, 4 g carbo., 0 g fiber, 24 g pro.

MENU IDEA:

Mushroom & Herb Rice *(see p. 288)*

Vanilla ice cream drizzled with pourable cherry all-fruit topping and sprinkled with dried cherries or cranberries

Cooking the couscous in a mixture of chicken broth and orange juice gives it a boost of color and extra flavor.

SPICY FISH KABOBS WITH COUSCOUS

1½	pounds fresh or frozen halibut or sea bass steaks
1	teaspoon ground cumin
1	teaspoon ground coriander
¾	teaspoon salt
½	teaspoon black pepper
⅛	teaspoon cayenne pepper
3	tablespoons butter or margarine
¼	cup orange juice
1	10-ounce package (1½ cups) quick-cooking couscous
1	14-ounce can chicken broth or vegetable broth
½	cup orange juice
2	medium zucchini, cut into ½-inch slices
1	medium yellow summer squash, cut into ½-inch slices

1 Thaw fish, if frozen. Rinse fish; pat dry with paper towels. Cut fish into 1-inch cubes. Set aside.

2 In a small bowl combine cumin, coriander, salt, black pepper, and cayenne pepper. In a medium saucepan melt butter over medium heat; add spice mixture and cook for 1 minute. Transfer 2 tablespoons of the mixture to a small bowl. Stir the ¼ cup orange juice into mixture in bowl. Stir couscous into remaining mixture in saucepan. Cook for 1 minute more. Stir broth and the ½ cup orange juice into saucepan. Bring to boiling. Cover and remove from heat. Set aside.

3 Grease the rack of an unheated broiler pan; set aside. On six long skewers, alternately thread fish cubes, zucchini slices, and yellow summer squash slices. Brush with the reserved butter and spice mixture.

4 Place kabobs on the prepared rack of broiler pan. Broil 3 to 4 inches from heat for 6 to 10 minutes or until fish flakes easily when tested with a fork, turning once. Serve with couscous.

Nutrition Facts per serving: 391 cal., 9 g total fat (4 g sat. fat), 53 mg chol., 678 mg sodium, 43 g carbo., 4 g fiber, 32 g pro.

PREP:
20 minutes
BROIL:
6 minutes
MAKES:
6 servings

MENU IDEA:
Speedy Southwestern-Style Tomato Soup
(see p. 293)
Fresh pineapple wedges

Versatile catfish can be fried, poached, steamed, baked, or grilled. Here it's cut into sticks, coated with crushed cornflakes, and oven-baked—perfect for dipping in the ranch sauce.

CRUNCHY CATFISH & ZUCCHINI STICKS

PREP:

15 minutes

BAKE:

12 minutes

MAKES:

4 servings

MENU IDEA:

Tricolor rotini pasta, cooked and tossed with butter, Parmesan cheese, and snipped fresh basil

Strawberry-Mango Milk Shake (double the recipe) *(see p. 381)*

1   pound fresh or frozen catfish fillets

1   medium zucchini or yellow summer squash

4   cups cornflakes

1   cup bottled ranch salad dressing

2   teaspoons bottled hot pepper sauce

❶ Thaw fish, if frozen. Rinse fish; pat dry with paper towels. Bias-cut fish into 1-inch-thick strips. Cut zucchini in half crosswise. Cut each half lengthwise into six wedges.

❷ Grease a 15×10×1-inch baking pan; set aside. Place the cornflakes in a large resealable plastic bag. Seal and crush slightly; set aside. In a large bowl combine ranch dressing and hot pepper sauce. Set aside half of the dressing mixture for dipping sauce. Add catfish and zucchini strips to remaining dressing in bowl; stir gently to coat.

❸ Add one-third of the zucchini strips to the bag with the crushed cornflakes. Seal; shake to coat. Remove zucchini and place in a single layer in prepared baking pan. Repeat to coat remaining zucchini and the fish.

❹ Bake in a 425°F oven for 12 to 15 minutes or until fish flakes easily when tested with a fork and crumbs are golden brown. Serve with reserved dipping sauce.

Nutrition Facts per serving: 545 cal., 40 g total fat (7 g sat. fat), 58 mg chol., 779 mg sodium, 24 g carbo., 0 g fiber, 20 g pro.

Simply prepared with fruity olive oil and tangy margarita mix concentrate, this dish can be on the table in 20 minutes.

LIME-POACHED MAHI MAHI

4   6-ounce fresh or frozen mahi mahi or catfish fillets, ½ to ¾ inch thick

2   teaspoons seasoned pepper

1   tablespoon olive oil

⅓   cup frozen margarita mix concentrate, thawed

    Hot cooked rice

1 Thaw fish, if frozen. Skin fish, if necessary. Rinse fish; pat dry with paper towels.

2 Rub both sides of each fish fillet with seasoned pepper. In a large nonstick skillet heat oil over medium-high heat. Add fish; cook for 2 to 4 minutes or until lightly browned on both sides, turning once. Reduce heat to medium-low. Carefully add margarita mix concentrate to skillet.

3 Cover and cook for 6 to 8 minutes or until fish flakes easily when tested with a fork. Serve with rice.

Nutrition Facts per serving: 336 cal., 5 g total fat (1 g sat. fat), 124 mg chol., 150 mg sodium, 41 g carbo., 0 g fiber, 34 g pro.

START TO FINISH:
20 minutes
MAKES:
4 servings

MENU IDEA:

Steamed sugar snap peas tossed with butter and shredded orange peel

Tropical Fruit Shortcakes
(see p. 337)

Bottled teriyaki and hoisin sauces give this Asian-inspired dish outstanding flavor.

FISH WITH BLACK BEAN SAUCE

START TO FINISH:

30 minutes

MAKES:

6 servings

MENU IDEA:

Cooked sliced carrots tossed with snipped fresh chives

Purchased pound cake with Golden Citrus Sauce
(see p. 370)

1½   pounds fresh or frozen skinless sea bass
      or orange roughy fillets

1   15-ounce can black beans, rinsed and drained

3   tablespoons bottled teriyaki sauce

2   tablespoons bottled hoisin sauce

     Nonstick cooking spray

     Hot cooked rice

1 Thaw fish, if frozen. Rinse fish; pat dry with paper towels. Cut into 6 serving-size pieces; set aside. In a blender or food processor combine drained beans, teriyaki sauce, and hoisin sauce. Cover and blend or process until nearly smooth.

2 Lightly coat an unheated 12-inch skillet with cooking spray. Preheat skillet over medium-high heat. Carefully place fish portions in skillet and cook about 4 minutes or until browned on both sides, turning once. Add bean mixture to fish. Bring to boiling; reduce heat to medium. Cover and simmer about 8 minutes or until fish flakes easily when tested with a fork. Serve with rice.

Nutrition Facts per serving: 276 cal., 3 g total fat (1 g sat. fat), 46 mg chol., 617 mg sodium, 35 g carbo., 4 g fiber, 28 g pro.

If sea bass isn't available, substitute any mild, fairly lean white-fleshed fish, such as mahi mahi or sole.

SEA BASS WITH CHILI OIL

1¼	pounds fresh or frozen sea bass fillets
2	medium carrots
5	cups chopped cabbage (about 1½ pounds)
2	tablespoons water
1	tablespoon lemon juice
½	teaspoon salt
¼	teaspoon black pepper
2	to 3 teaspoons bottled chili oil
2	teaspoons grated fresh ginger
1	teaspoon bottled minced garlic (2 cloves)
	Bottled chili oil (optional)
	Lemon wedges (optional)

START TO FINISH:
30 minutes
MAKES:
4 servings

MENU IDEA:
Spicy Peanut Noodles
(see p. 282)
Mango sorbet

1 Thaw fish, if frozen. Rinse fish; pat dry with paper towels. Cut fish into 4 serving-size pieces; set aside. Using a vegetable peeler, cut the carrots into long thin ribbons (about 1 cup). In a 12-inch skillet combine carrot ribbons, cabbage, the water, lemon juice, ¼ teaspoon of the salt, and the pepper.

2 Sprinkle fish pieces with the remaining ¼ teaspoon salt. In a small bowl stir together the 2 to 3 teaspoons chili oil, the ginger, and garlic; spread over fish pieces. Place fish pieces on top of vegetable mixture in skillet.

3 Bring skillet mixture just to boiling; reduce heat. Cover and simmer for 9 to 12 minutes or until fish flakes easily when tested with a fork. To serve, transfer fish and vegetable mixture to 4 serving plates. If desired, drizzle with additional chili oil and serve with lemon wedges.

Nutrition Facts per serving: 196 cal., 5 g total fat (1 g sat. fat), 58 mg chol., 415 mg sodium, 9 g carbo., 3 g fiber, 28 g pro.

Fish in a salad? Why not! Coating the tilapia with sesame seeds before cooking makes it look attractive and gives it an agreeable crunch.

SESAME-COATED TILAPIA SALAD

START TO FINISH:

20 minutes

MAKES:

4 servings

1	pound fresh or frozen tilapia fillets
¼	cup all-purpose flour
¼	cup sesame seeds
½	teaspoon black pepper
⅔	cup bottled honey-Dijon salad dressing
2	tablespoons cooking oil
1	5-ounce package fresh baby spinach and red leaf lettuce or baby spinach with radicchio

1 Thaw fish, if frozen. Rinse fish; pat dry with paper towels. Cut fish into 4 serving-size pieces.

2 In a shallow bowl combine flour, sesame seeds, and pepper. Transfer 2 tablespoons of the salad dressing to a small bowl. Brush all sides of the fish pieces with the 2 tablespoons salad dressing. Firmly press both sides of each fish piece into sesame seed mixture.

3 In a 12-inch skillet heat oil over medium heat. Add coated fish; cook about 6 minutes or until fish flakes easily when tested with a fork, turning once.

4 Divide spinach mixture among 4 dinner plates; top each with a fish piece. Drizzle with the remaining salad dressing.

Nutrition Facts per serving: 418 cal., 30 g total fat (3 g sat. fat), 0 mg chol., 247 mg sodium, 16 g carbo., 4 g fiber, 22 g pro.

MENU IDEA:

Honeydew melon and/or cantaloupe wedges

Quick Rice Pudding
(see p. 335)

Originally from the waters surrounding Africa, tilapia is raised commercially everywhere from North America to Asia. In this recipe, the sweet, mild fish—sometimes called Hawaiian sun fish—fries up crisp and tender, and soaks up all the glorious flavor of the sassy sauce.

TILAPIA WITH CHILI CREAM SAUCE

1	pound fresh or frozen tilapia or other firm-flesh fish fillets, ½ to 1 inch thick
2	tablespoons cornmeal
2	tablespoons all-purpose flour
	Nonstick cooking spray
1	teaspoon cooking oil
2	teaspoons butter or margarine
2	teaspoons all-purpose flour
1	teaspoon chili powder
¼	teaspoon salt
¼	teaspoon ground cumin
¾	cup half-and-half or light cream
2	tablespoons snipped fresh parsley or cilantro (optional)

START TO FINISH:

25 minutes

MAKES:

4 servings

1 Thaw fish, if frozen. Rinse fish; pat dry with paper towels. Cut into 4 serving-size pieces. In a small bowl stir together cornmeal and the 2 tablespoons flour. Sprinkle over both sides of each fish piece. Lightly coat an unheated 12-inch nonstick skillet with cooking spray. Add the oil to skillet. Preheat over medium-high heat. Add fish pieces. Cook over medium to medium-high heat for 4 to 6 minutes or until fish flakes easily when tested with a fork, turning once. Remove fish from skillet. Cover and keep warm.

2 For sauce, melt butter in the same skillet. Stir in the 2 teaspoons flour, the chili powder, salt, and cumin. Stir in half-and-half. Cook and stir until thickened and bubbly. Cook and stir for 1 minute more. To serve, spoon sauce over fish. If desired, sprinkle with parsley.

Nutrition Facts per serving: 229 cal., 11 g total fat (4 g sat. fat), 22 mg chol., 240 mg sodium, 11 g carbo., 1 g fiber, 21 g pro.

TEST KITCHEN TIP: For a lower-fat dish, substitute fat-free half-and-half for the regular half-and-half.

Nutrition Facts per serving: 187 cal., 4 g total fat (2 g sat. fat), 60 mg chol., 258 mg sodium, 12 g carbo., 1 g fiber, 23 g pro.

MENU IDEA:

Frozen or canned Spanish-style rice, prepared according to package or can directions

Tropical Fruit Cups (double the recipe) *(see p. 361)*

This snappy salsa-flavored sauce brings out the best in delicate orange roughy or red snapper. You can also use sea bass, sole, or whitefish. For a tasty change of pace, try this with a fruit salsa.

SIMPLE SALSA FISH

PREP:

15 minutes

BROIL:

4 to 6 minutes per ¹/₂-inch thickness + 1 minute

MAKES:

4 servings

MENU IDEA:

Summer Squash with Peppers *(see p. 276)*

Chocolate or vanilla ice cream topped with sliced bananas and flaked coconut

1	pound fresh or frozen skinless orange roughy or red snapper fillets, ¹/₂ to 1 inch thick
¹/₃	cup bottled salsa
¹/₂	teaspoon bottled minced garlic (1 clove)
1	14-ounce can vegetable broth
1	cup quick-cooking couscous
¹/₄	cup thinly sliced green onions or coarsely snipped fresh cilantro
	Lime or lemon wedges

1 Thaw fish, if frozen. Rinse fish; pat dry with paper towels. Measure thickness of fish. Set aside. In a small bowl combine salsa and garlic; set aside.

2 In a small saucepan bring broth to boiling. Stir in couscous; cover and remove from heat. Let stand about 5 minutes or until liquid is absorbed. Stir in green onions or cilantro.

3 Grease rack of an unheated broiler pan; place fish on rack. Broil about 4 inches from the heat until fish flakes easily when tested with a fork (allow 4 to 6 minutes per ¹/₂-inch thickness of fish). Turn 1-inch-thick fillets over halfway through broiling. Spoon salsa mixture over fish; broil about 1 minute more or until salsa is heated through.

4 Arrange fish on couscous mixture. Serve with lime wedges.

Nutrition Facts per serving: 295 cal., 3 g total fat (0 g sat. fat), 42 mg chol., 549 mg sodium, 39 g carbo., 7 g fiber, 30 g pro.

The ultimate in cold weather comfort food, this chowder will warm your family in a flash. By using some ready-made ingredients, such as cream of shrimp soup and frozen hash brown potatoes, you can have steaming bowls of soup on the table in less than 30 minutes.

SEAFOOD CHOWDER

12	ounces fresh or frozen fish fillets (such as salmon, orange roughy, or cod)
3	cups loose-pack frozen diced hash brown potatoes with onions and peppers
1	cup water
1	12-ounce can evaporated milk
1	10¾-ounce can condensed cream of shrimp or cream of potato soup
⅓	of a 3-ounce can (⅓ cup) cooked bacon pieces
2	teaspoons snipped fresh dillweed or ¾ teaspoon dried dillweed
¼	teaspoon black pepper
1	2-ounce jar diced pimiento, drained

1 Thaw fish, if frozen. Rinse fish; pat dry with paper towels. Cut fish into 1-inch pieces. Set aside.

2 Meanwhile, in a large saucepan combine hash brown potatoes and the water. Bring to boiling; reduce heat. Cover and simmer about 5 minutes or until tender.

3 Stir in evaporated milk, cream of shrimp or cream of potato soup, bacon, dillweed, and pepper. Return to boiling. Add fish and pimiento; reduce heat. Cover and simmer for 3 to 5 minutes or until fish flakes easily when tested with a fork.

Nutrition Facts per serving: 366 cal., 15 g total fat (7 g sat. fat), 86 mg chol., 1,045 mg sodium, 27 g carbo., 2 g fiber, 30 g pro.

START TO FINISH:

25 minutes

MAKES:

4 servings

MENU IDEA:

Whole-grain dinner rolls, brushed with butter and toasted

Quick Apple Crisp
(see p. 332)

Feta, the world's favorite Greek cheese, lends its tangy flavor to sweet salmon and tender pasta. Add to the Greek flair by using kalamata olives, which have a wonderfully pungent, salty flavor.

SALMON WITH FETA & PASTA

START TO FINISH:

25 minutes

MAKES:

5 servings

MENU IDEA:

Baguette-style French bread, sliced, brushed with olive oil and cracked black pepper, and toasted

Blueberry-Lemon Tarts (see p. 353)

12	ounces fresh or frozen skinless salmon fillet
8	ounces dried rotini pasta
	Nonstick cooking spray
1	teaspoon bottled minced garlic (2 cloves)
	Salt
4	large plum tomatoes, chopped (2 cups)
1	cup sliced green onions
⅓	cup sliced pitted ripe olives
3	tablespoons snipped fresh basil
½	teaspoon coarsely ground black pepper
2	teaspoons olive oil
1	4-ounce package crumbled feta cheese

1 Thaw fish, if frozen. Rinse fish; pat dry with paper towels. Cut into 1-inch pieces. Cook rotini according to package directions. Drain well. Return to pan. Cover and keep warm.

2 Meanwhile, lightly coat an unheated large nonstick skillet with cooking spray. Preheat skillet over medium-high heat. Add garlic. Cook and stir for 15 seconds. Lightly sprinkle fish pieces with salt. Add fish to skillet. Cook fish for 4 to 6 minutes or until fish flakes easily when tested with a fork, turning occasionally. Stir in tomatoes, green onions, olives, basil, and pepper. Heat through.

3 In a large bowl toss together hot pasta and oil. Add salmon mixture and feta cheese; gently toss to combine.

Nutrition Facts per serving: 373 cal., 13 g total fat (5 g sat. fat), 56 mg chol., 443 mg sodium, 41 g carbo., 3 g fiber, 24 g pro.

Browning the butter lends a subtle nutty flavor that complements the maple syrup and orange peel, giving the salmon a sweet richness.

BROWNED BUTTER SALMON

4   fresh or frozen salmon or halibut steaks, cut 1 inch thick (about 1½ pounds total)

Salt

Black pepper

2   tablespoons butter or margarine

2   tablespoons pure maple syrup

1   teaspoon finely shredded orange peel

1 Thaw fish, if frozen. Rinse fish and pat dry with paper towels. Sprinkle both sides of each fish steak with salt and pepper; set aside. In a small saucepan cook the butter over medium heat about 3 minutes or until golden brown, stirring occasionally. Remove from heat. Cool for 10 minutes. Stir in maple syrup and orange peel (mixture may thicken).

2 Meanwhile, line unheated broiler pan with foil; grease rack. Place fish on prepared rack of broiler pan. Spread both sides of each fish steak with the browned butter mixture. Broil 4 inches from the heat for 5 minutes. Using a wide spatula, carefully turn fish over. Broil for 3 to 7 minutes more or until fish flakes easily when tested with a fork.

Nutrition Facts per serving: 277 cal., 12 g total fat (5 g sat. fat), 105 mg chol., 322 mg sodium, 7 g carbo., 0 g fiber, 34 g pro.

PREP:
20 minutes

BROIL:
5 minutes + 3 minutes

MAKES:
4 servings

MENU IDEA:

Candied Sweet Potatoes *(see p. 273)*

New York-style cheesecake served with mixed fresh berries

Fresh dill, smoked salmon, and pasta make a delightful combination in this main dish salad.

SMOKED SALMON & PASTA

START TO FINISH:

25 minutes

MAKES:

4 servings

- - - - - - - - - - - - - - - -

MENU IDEA:

Cheese-Garlic Crescents *(see p. 328)*

Iced cappuccino
topped with
whipped cream and
chocolate shavings

- - - - - - - - - - - - - - - -

8   ounces dried pasta (such as rotini, cut ziti, mostaccioli, penne, or medium shell pasta)

1   cup cherry tomatoes, halved

¼   cup snipped fresh chives

⅓   cup olive oil

2   tablespoons lemon juice

4   teaspoons finely chopped shallot

⅓   cup snipped fresh dill

⅛   teaspoon salt

     Dash freshly ground black pepper

4   ounces smoked salmon, flaked, and skin and bones removed

1   small red onion, thinly sliced and separated into rings

½   cup dairy sour cream

1 Cook pasta according to package directions. Drain well. Rinse with cold water; drain again. In a large bowl combine pasta, cherry tomatoes, and chives.

2 For dressing, in a small bowl stir together oil, lemon juice, shallot, dill, salt, and pepper. Pour dressing over pasta mixture. Toss lightly to coat. Spoon into a serving dish. Top with salmon, red onion, and sour cream.

Nutrition Facts per serving: 474 cal., 25 g total fat (6 g sat. fat), 17 mg chol., 316 mg sodium, 48 g carbo., 2 g fiber, 14 g pro.

Salmon and broccoli make a great pair because they taste wonderful together and are chockful of nutrients.

SALMON-BROCCOLI CHOWDER

2½	cups milk
1	10¾-ounce can condensed broccoli-cheese soup or cream of chicken soup
¾	cup shredded sharp cheddar cheese or process American cheese (3 ounces)
1	cup loose-pack frozen cut broccoli
½	cup loose-pack frozen whole kernel corn
1	15-ounce can salmon, drained, flaked, and skin and bones removed

1 In a medium saucepan stir together milk and broccoli-cheese or cream of chicken soup. Stir in cheese. Stir in broccoli and corn. Cook and stir just until mixture boils. Stir in salmon. Heat through.

Nutrition Facts per serving: 401 cal., 22 g total fat (10 g sat. fat), 65 mg chol., 1,257 mg sodium, 19 g carbo., 2 g fiber, 31 g pro.

START TO FINISH:

20 minutes

MAKES:

4 servings

MENU IDEA:

Citrus Salad with Glazed Pecans
(see p. 311)

Purchased shortbread or butter cookies

Easy-to-prepare and enjoy, these savory biscuits will be a dish your family will ask for often. If you prefer, you can omit the sherry.

SALMON-SAUCED BISCUITS

START TO FINISH:

30 minutes

MAKES:

4 servings

MENU IDEA:

Mixed fresh fruit salad

Chocolate-Mint Sandwich Cookies
(see p. 347)

4   frozen individual ready-to-bake biscuits
    or 4 English muffins, split

1   10-ounce container refrigerated Alfredo pasta sauce

1   9- to 10-ounce package frozen cut asparagus, thawed

1   4-ounce can (drained weight) mushroom stems
    and pieces, drained

1   teaspoon lemon juice

¼   teaspoon dried dillweed

1   6-ounce can skinless, boneless salmon, drained and flaked

1   tablespoon dry sherry

1 Bake biscuits according to package directions or toast English muffins. Cool biscuits slightly; split biscuits.

2 Meanwhile, in a medium saucepan combine Alfredo pasta sauce, thawed asparagus, mushrooms, lemon juice, and dillweed. Cook and stir over medium heat until bubbly and heated through. Remove from heat; stir in salmon and sherry.

3 Spoon salmon mixture over biscuit or English muffin halves.

Nutrition Facts per serving: 498 cal., 33 g total fat (3 g sat. fat), 59 mg chol., 1,158 mg sodium, 31 g carbo., 3 g fiber, 18 g pro.

To toast the sesame seeds, place them in a single layer in a glass pie plate or on a cookie sheet. Cook them in a 350°F oven for 2 to 4 minutes or until seeds are a golden color and smell toasted. Keep a close watch, though, as they burn easily.

SESAME SEARED TUNA

4	6-ounce fresh or frozen tuna fillets, about ¾ inch thick
1	tablespoon olive oil
⅓	cup bottled hoisin sauce
3	tablespoons orange juice
1	tablespoon sesame seeds, toasted

START TO FINISH:

20 minutes

MAKES:

4 servings

1 Thaw fish, if frozen. Rinse fish; pat dry with paper towels. In a large skillet heat oil over medium-high heat. Add fish; cook about 8 minutes or until tuna flakes easily when tested with a fork (tuna can be slightly pink in the center), turning once.

2 Meanwhile, in a small saucepan stir together hoisin sauce and orange juice; heat through. Remove fish to serving plates; drizzle with sauce and sprinkle with sesame seeds.

Nutrition Facts per serving: 271 cal., 7 g total fat (1 g sat. fat), 76 mg chol., 297 mg sodium, 9 g carbo., 0 g fiber, 41 g pro.

MENU IDEA:

Sautéed green beans tossed with minced garlic and black pepper

Bananas Suzette over Pound Cake *(see p. 340)*

This easy tuna recipe gives you maximum flavor with minimum cleanup.

TUNA & PASTA ALFREDO

START TO FINISH:

25 minutes

MAKES:

6 servings

3	cups dried mini lasagna, broken mafalda, or medium noodles
1	tablespoon butter or margarine
2	cups chopped broccoli rabe or broccoli
1	medium red sweet pepper, chopped
1	10-ounce container refrigerated Alfredo pasta sauce
2	teaspoons snipped fresh dillweed
1	to 2 tablespoons milk (optional)
1	9½-ounce can tuna (water-pack), drained and broken into chunks
½	cup sliced almonds, toasted (optional)

MENU IDEA:

Frozen or refrigerated large biscuits, prepared according to package directions and sprinkled with shredded Asiago or Parmesan cheese

Lemon Meringue Cookie Tarts
(see p. 352)

1 Cook pasta according to package directions; drain well. Return pasta to hot pan. Cover and keep warm.

2 Meanwhile, in a large saucepan melt butter over medium heat. Add broccoli rabe or broccoli and sweet pepper; cook until tender. Stir in Alfredo sauce and dillweed. If necessary, stir in enough of the milk to make sauce of desired consistency. Gently stir cooked pasta and tuna into broccoli rabe mixture. Heat through.

3 To serve, if desired, sprinkle with almonds.

Nutrition Facts per serving: 387 cal., 12 g total fat (5 g sat. fat), 63 mg chol., 568 mg sodium, 48 g carbo., 3 g fiber, 20 g pro.

Everyone loves a good mac and cheese! In this version canned tuna is added to a quick mac and cheese dinner mix. It's so easy to prepare and so satisfying.

CREAMY TUNA MAC

1	7¼-ounce package macaroni and cheese dinner mix
1	cup loose-pack frozen peas
½	cup ranch-, onion-, or chive-flavor sour cream dip
1	6-ounce can solid white tuna, drained and broken into chunks
	Crushed potato chips (optional)

1 Cook macaroni from dinner mix according to package directions, except add peas for the last 2 minutes of cooking. Drain. Continue according to dinner mix package directions.

2 Stir dip into macaroni mixture; stir tuna into mixture. Heat through. If desired, sprinkle with crushed potato chips.

Nutrition Facts per serving: 368 cal., 9 g total fat (4 g sat. fat), 47 mg chol., 888 mg sodium, 50 g carbo., 2 g fiber, 23 g pro.

START TO FINISH:
25 minutes
MAKES:
4 to 6 servings

MENU IDEA:
Curried Carrots
(see p. 261)

Ice cream served in sugar ice cream cones and sprinkled with chopped nuts, miniature chocolate pieces, or colored sprinkles

Tuna, tomato, and curry powder give store-bought coleslaw a special touch.

CURRIED TUNA CUPS

START TO FINISH:

15 minutes

MAKES:

4 servings

1½ cups purchased creamy coleslaw

1 small tomato, seeded and chopped

1 teaspoon curry powder

1 6-ounce can tuna, drained and flaked

4 large butterhead (Bibb or Boston) lettuce leaves

¼ cup chopped peanuts

Dairy sour cream dip with chives (optional)

1 In a small bowl stir together coleslaw, tomato, and curry powder. Gently fold in tuna.

2 To serve, spoon the tuna mixture onto lettuce leaves. Sprinkle with peanuts. If desired, top with dip.

Nutrition Facts per serving: 148 cal., 7 g total fat (1 g sat. fat), 21 mg chol., 213 mg sodium, 9 g carbo., 2 g fiber, 14 g pro.

MENU IDEA:

Assorted sliced fresh vegetables served with purchased sour cream dip

Fresh Strawberry Fool *(see p. 364)*

Refrigerated or frozen tortellini ranks with canned soup as a great convenience product.

TUNA TORTELLINI SOUP

3   cups milk

2   10¾-ounce cans condensed cream of potato soup

1   cup loose-pack frozen peas

1   teaspoon dried basil, crushed

1   9-ounce package refrigerated cheese tortellini

1   12-ounce can tuna (water pack), drained and flaked

⅓   cup dry white wine

1 In a large saucepan combine milk, cream of potato soup, peas, and basil; bring just to boiling. Add tortellini. Simmer, uncovered, for 6 to 8 minutes or until tortellini is tender, stirring frequently to prevent sticking. Stir in tuna and wine; heat through.

Nutrition Facts per serving: 351 cal., 9 g total fat (4 g sat. fat), 59 mg chol., 1,267 mg sodium, 38 g carbo., 2 g fiber, 27 g pro.

START TO FINISH:

20 minutes

MAKES:

6 servings

MENU IDEA:

B.L.T. Salad
(see p. 305)

Purchased individual graham cracker tart crusts filled with canned lemon pie filling and topped with vanilla yogurt or whipped cream

A sprinkling of crushed red pepper will give this orange-flavored shrimp stir-fry extra kick.

STIR-FRY HOISIN & CITRUS SHRIMP

START TO FINISH:

25 minutes

MAKES:

4 servings

MENU IDEA:

Gingery Sugar Snap Peas *(see p. 268)*

Lemon or orange sorbet

---

12   ounces fresh or frozen large shrimp, peeled and deveined

2   tablespoons cooking oil

1   teaspoon bottled minced garlic (2 cloves)

1   medium red sweet pepper, cut into thin bite-size strips

⅓   cup orange juice

3   tablespoons bottled hoisin sauce

1½   cups shredded fresh spinach

    Hot cooked rice

    Crushed red pepper (optional)

1 Thaw shrimp, if frozen. Rinse shrimp; pat dry with paper towels. Set aside.

2 In a large skillet heat 1 tablespoon of the oil over medium-high heat. Add garlic; cook and stir for 15 seconds. Add sweet pepper; cook and stir about 3 minutes or until sweet pepper is crisp-tender. Remove sweet pepper with a slotted spoon.

3 Add remaining 1 tablespoon oil to skillet. Add shrimp; stir-fry about 3 minutes or until shrimp are opaque. Remove shrimp with a slotted spoon. Add orange juice and hoisin sauce to the skillet. Bring to boiling. Simmer, uncovered, about 1 minute or until slightly thickened. Return shrimp and sweet pepper to skillet along with spinach; toss just until combined.

4 Serve shrimp mixture over hot cooked rice. If desired, sprinkle with crushed red pepper.

Nutrition Facts per serving: 306 cal., 9 g total fat (1 g sat. fat), 129 mg chol., 372 mg sodium, 34 g carbo., 1 g fiber, 20 g pro.

The fresh flavors of cilantro and lime juice add a touch of lightness to this spectacular slaw. It's refreshing to serve in the winter when your family's spirits and taste buds need a lift.

ISLAND-STYLE SEAFOOD SLAW

1	12-ounce package frozen peeled, cooked shrimp, thawed
6	cups packaged shredded cabbage with carrot (coleslaw mix)
2	medium red and/or yellow sweet peppers, cut into thin bite-size strips
⅓	cup thinly sliced green onions
¼	cup snipped fresh cilantro
¾	cup mayonnaise or salad dressing
1	teaspoon finely shredded lime peel
3	tablespoons lime juice
¼	teaspoon salt
⅛	teaspoon cayenne pepper
¼	cup honey-roasted peanuts (optional)

START TO FINISH:

20 minutes

MAKES:

4 servings

MENU IDEA:

Sliced mango, papaya, pineapple and/or kiwifruit

Mocha Mousse Cups
(see p. 363)

1 Rinse shrimp; pat dry with paper towels. In a very large bowl toss together shrimp, coleslaw mix, sweet peppers, green onions, and cilantro.

2 For dressing, in a small bowl stir together mayonnaise, lime peel, lime juice, salt, and cayenne pepper. Pour dressing over salad; toss to coat. Serve immediately. If desired, sprinkle with peanuts.

Nutrition Facts per serving: 432 cal., 34 g total fat (5 g sat. fat), 196 mg chol., 622 mg sodium, 11 g carbo., 4 g fiber, 20 g pro.

TEST KITCHEN TIP: For a lower-fat slaw, substitute light mayonnaise dressing for the mayonnaise or salad dressing.

Nutrition Facts per serving: 327 cal., 17 g total fat (3 g sat. fat), 185 mg chol., 613 mg sodium, 21 g carbo., 5 g fiber, 25 g pro.

Shrimp and grits are a Southern classic—and with good reason. This combination is delectable as part of a hearty breakfast or brunch or for an intriguing, mouthwatering dinner.

SHRIMP GRAVY

START TO FINISH:

30 minutes

MAKES:

4 to 6 servings

1½ pounds fresh or frozen medium shrimp

5 slices bacon

1 cup thinly sliced green onions

1 medium green sweet pepper, chopped

2 teaspoons bottled minced garlic (4 cloves)

1 tablespoon all-purpose flour

¼ teaspoon garlic salt

¼ teaspoon black pepper

12 ounces fresh mushrooms, sliced (4½ cups)

Hot cooked grits

MENU IDEA:

Purchased corn bread or corn muffin mix, prepared according to package directions

Purchased brownies with Raspberry-Cranberry Sauce *(see p. 370)*

❶ Thaw shrimp, if frozen. Peel and devein shrimp. Rinse shrimp; pat dry with paper towels. Set aside.

❷ In a large skillet cook bacon until crisp. Remove bacon from skillet; drain on paper towels. Reserve 2 tablespoons of the drippings in the skillet. Crumble bacon; set aside.

❸ Heat reserved bacon drippings over medium heat. Add green onions, sweet pepper, and garlic; cook until tender. Stir in flour, garlic salt, and black pepper. Stir in sliced mushrooms and shrimp. Cover and cook about 5 minutes or until shrimp are opaque and mushrooms are tender, stirring occasionally.

❹ Serve immediately with hot cooked grits. Top each serving with crumbled bacon.

Nutrition Facts per serving: 353 cal., 12 g total fat (4 g sat. fat), 209 mg chol., 887 mg sodium, 32 g carbo., 2 g fiber, 29 g pro.

A simplified version of paella, a Spanish classic, this meal-in-minutes shrimp medley requires only one pan.

SPANISH-STYLE RICE WITH SEAFOOD

1	5.6- to 6.2-ounce package Spanish-style rice mix
1¾	cups water
1	tablespoon butter or margarine
	Several dashes bottled hot pepper sauce
1	12-ounce package frozen peeled, deveined shrimp
1	cup loose-pack frozen peas
1	medium tomato, chopped

1 In a large skillet stir together rice mix, the water, butter, and hot pepper sauce. Bring to boiling; reduce heat. Cover and simmer for 5 minutes.

2 Stir shrimp into rice mixture. Return to boiling; reduce heat. Cover and simmer for 2 to 3 minutes more or until shrimp are opaque. Remove from heat. Stir in peas. Cover and let stand for 10 minutes. Sprinkle with tomato.

Nutrition Facts per serving: 282 cal., 5 g total fat (2 g sat. fat), 137 mg chol., 897 mg sodium, 36 g carbo., 3 g fiber, 23 g pro.

START TO FINISH:
25 minutes

MAKES:
4 servings

MENU IDEA:

Flour tortillas, sprinkled with shredded Mexican blend cheese, toasted, and cut into wedges

Double Dippin' Fruit *(see p. 366)*

Fresh jalapeño peppers spice up this dish that pairs plump, juicy shrimp, garlic, and tomatoes, all tossed with perfectly cooked linguine. Tailor the amount of jalapeño to suit your family's taste.

SPICY JALAPEÑO-SHRIMP PASTA

START TO FINISH:

30 minutes

MAKES:

4 servings

....

MENU IDEA:

Broiled Summer Squash & Onions *(see p. 277)*

Canned apple pie filling, warmed, sprinkled with granola, and topped with butter pecan ice cream

....

12	ounces fresh or frozen large shrimp in shells
8	ounces dried linguine
2	tablespoons olive oil
1	or 2 fresh jalapeño chile peppers, finely chopped*
1	teaspoon bottled minced garlic (2 cloves)
½	teaspoon salt
⅛	teaspoon black pepper
2	cups chopped tomatoes and/or cherry tomatoes, halved or quartered
	Finely shredded Parmesan cheese (optional)

1 Thaw shrimp, if frozen. Peel and devein shrimp. Rinse shrimp; pat dry with paper towels. Cook linguine according to package directions; drain well. Return to pan. Cover and keep warm.

2 In a large skillet heat oil over medium-high heat. Add chile peppers, garlic, salt, and black pepper; cook and stir for 1 minute. Add shrimp; cook about 3 minutes more or until shrimp are opaque. Stir in tomatoes; heat through.

3 Toss cooked linguine with shrimp mixture. If desired, sprinkle with Parmesan cheese.

*NOTE: Because chile peppers contain volatile oils that can burn your skin and eyes, avoid direct contact with them as much as possible. When working with chile peppers, wear plastic or rubber gloves. If your bare hands do touch the peppers, wash your hands and nails well with soap and warm water.

Nutrition Facts per serving: 363 cal., 9 g total fat (1 g sat. fat), 97 mg chol., 396 mg sodium, 48 g carbo., 3 g fiber, 21 g pro.

Prepared polenta is the base for this delicious main dish. It's so full of flavor you can feel good about serving it to family or friends.

SAUCY SHRIMP OVER POLENTA

START TO FINISH:

25 minutes

MAKES:

6 servings

18	fresh or frozen peeled and deveined, cooked shrimp, tails removed (about 8 ounces)
1	16-ounce tube refrigerated cooked polenta, cut crosswise into 12 slices
1	tablespoon cooking oil
2	cups loose-pack frozen whole kernel corn
4	medium plum tomatoes, chopped (about 1½ cups)
3	tablespoons balsamic vinegar
1	teaspoon dried thyme, crushed
½	teaspoon ground cumin
¼	teaspoon salt

1 Thaw shrimp, if frozen. Rinse shrimp; pat dry with paper towels. Set aside. In a large skillet cook polenta slices in hot oil for 5 to 8 minutes or until golden brown, turning once. Transfer to a serving platter; keep warm.

2 In the same large skillet combine corn, tomatoes, balsamic vinegar, thyme, cumin, and salt. Cook and stir about 5 minutes or until heated through. Stir in shrimp. Cook and stir until heated through.

3 Using a slotted spoon, spoon shrimp mixture over polenta slices.

Nutrition Facts per serving: 196 cal., 3 g total fat (1 g sat. fat), 74 mg chol., 483 mg sodium, 30 g carbo., 4 g fiber, 12 g pro.

MENU IDEA:

Steamed buttered sugar snap pea or snow pea pods

No-Drip Chocolate Dip *(see p. 369)*

Couscous mix and canned seasoned tomatoes make this shrimp dish as easy as it is delicious.

MEDITERRANEAN SHRIMP & COUSCOUS

START TO FINISH:

25 minutes

MAKES:

4 servings

1	pound fresh or frozen medium shrimp
1	14½-ounce can diced tomatoes with garlic and onion, undrained
¾	cup water
1	5.6-ounce package toasted pine nut couscous mix
½	cup golden raisins

1 Thaw shrimp, if frozen. Peel and devein shrimp. Rinse shrimp; pat dry with paper towels. Set aside.

2 In a large skillet combine undrained tomatoes, the water, and the seasoning packet from the couscous mix; bring to boiling. Stir in shrimp; cook over high heat for 2 to 3 minutes or until shrimp are opaque. Stir in couscous and raisins. Remove from heat. Cover and let stand about 5 minutes or until liquid is absorbed.

Nutrition Facts per serving: 338 cal., 4 g total fat (1 g sat. fat), 129 mg chol., 967 mg sodium, 53 g carbo., 6 g fiber, 25 g pro.

MENU IDEA:

Baguette-style French bread, sliced and toasted

Miniature Fruit Tarts *(see p. 348)*

This sweet, succulent crabmeat mixed with lemon and dill will please young and old alike.

LEMONY CRAB BOW TIE PASTA SALAD

3	cups dried bow tie pasta
½	cup dairy sour cream
¼	cup mayonnaise or salad dressing
2	tablespoons lemon juice
½	teaspoon sugar
½	teaspoon black pepper
½	teaspoon dried dillweed
¼	teaspoon salt
½	of a medium cucumber, seeded and finely chopped (about ¾ cup)
1	stalk celery, finely chopped
1	small carrot, shredded
2	green onions, sliced
1	pound cooked crabmeat, cut into bite-size pieces, or two 6- or 8-ounce packages flake- or chunk-style imitation crabmeat

1 Cook pasta according to package directions. Drain; rinse with cold water. Drain again; set aside.

2 Meanwhile, in a large bowl stir together sour cream, mayonnaise, lemon juice, sugar, pepper, dillweed, and salt. Add cooked pasta, cucumber, celery, carrot, and green onions; toss to coat. Add crabmeat; toss gently to combine.

Nutrition Facts per serving: 263 cal., 13 g total fat (3 g sat. fat), 107 mg chol., 391 mg sodium, 17 g carbo., 1 g fiber, 19 g pro.

TEST KITCHEN TIP: For a lower-fat salad, substitute light mayonnaise dressing for the mayonnaise or salad dressing and light dairy sour cream for the regular sour cream.

Nutrition Facts per serving: 218 cal., 7 g total fat (2 g sat. fat), 86 mg chol., 385 mg sodium, 20 g carbo., 1 g fiber, 19 g pro.

START TO FINISH:
25 minutes
MAKES:
6 servings

MENU IDEA:
Parmesan Corn Bread Swirls
(see p. 328)

Fresh strawberries topped with whipped cream and shredded orange peel

The distinctive smoky flavor of the chipotle chile pepper gives the sauce for these subtly seasoned crab cakes zing. If you haven't used chipotle peppers in adobo sauce before, start with half of a pepper, taste, and then add the other half if you wish.

CHIPOTLE-TOPPED CRAB CAKES

START TO FINISH:

30 minutes

MAKES:

4 servings

1	egg, slightly beaten
¾	cup soft bread crumbs (1 slice)
1	green onion, sliced
2	tablespoons mayonnaise or salad dressing
1	tablespoon milk
½	teaspoon lemon-pepper seasoning
2	6- to 7-ounce cans crabmeat, drained, flaked, and cartilage removed
	Nonstick cooking spray
4	cups torn mixed salad greens
1	recipe Chipotle Sauce
	Lime wedges

❶ In a large bowl stir together egg, bread crumbs, green onion, mayonnaise, milk, and lemon-pepper seasoning. Add crabmeat; mix well. Shape into 8 patties.

❷ Lightly coat an unheated large nonstick skillet with cooking spray. Preheat over medium heat. Add patties. Cook for 6 to 8 minutes or until browned on both sides, turning once. Serve over greens with Chipotle Sauce. Pass lime wedges.

CHIPOTLE SAUCE: In a small bowl stir together ⅓ cup mayonnaise or salad dressing; ¼ cup dairy sour cream; 2 tablespoons milk; 2 teaspoons snipped fresh cilantro; 1 canned chipotle chile pepper in adobo sauce, drained and finely chopped;* and dash salt.

*NOTE: Because chile peppers contain volatile oils that can burn your skin and eyes, avoid direct contact with them as much as possible. When working with chile peppers, wear plastic or rubber gloves. If your bare hands do touch the peppers, wash your hands and nails well with soap and warm water.

Nutrition Facts per serving: 348 cal., 25 g total fat (5 g sat. fat), 153 mg chol., 719 mg sodium, 7 g carbo., 1 g fiber, 21 g pro.

TEST KITCHEN TIP: For lower-fat crab cakes and sauce, substitute light mayonnaise dressing for the mayonnaise or salad dressing and light dairy sour cream for the regular sour cream.

Nutrition Facts per serving: 255 cal., 13 g total fat (3 g sat. fat), 144 mg chol., 739 mg sodium, 12 g carbo., 1 g fiber, 22 g pro.

MENU IDEA:

Skewered bite-size pieces of fresh fruit, such as pineapple, grapes, strawberries, banana, melon, and/or kiwifruit

Triple Dipster Strawberries
(see p. 359)

Canned soups make this crab bisque extra fast and easy, but just as rich as made-from-scratch versions.

CRAB BISQUE

1 10¾-ounce can condensed cream of asparagus soup
1 10¾-ounce can condensed cream of mushroom soup
2¾ cups milk
1 cup half-and-half or light cream
1 6- to 7-ounce can crabmeat, drained, flaked, and cartilage removed
3 tablespoons dry sherry or milk

1 In a large saucepan combine cream of asparagus soup, cream of mushroom soup, milk, and half-and-half. Cook over medium heat just until boiling, stirring frequently. Stir in crabmeat and dry sherry; heat through.

Nutrition Facts per serving: 227 cal., 12 g total fat (6 g sat. fat), 63 mg chol., 921 mg sodium, 16 g carbo., 1 g fiber, 12 g pro.

START TO FINISH:
20 minutes
MAKES:
6 servings

MENU IDEA:
Purchased sourdough rolls

A Billow of Berries 'n' Brownies
(see p. 338)

This citrus-flavored dish is an enticing and refreshing way to serve scallops or delicate fish.

LIME-SAUCED SEAFOOD

START TO FINISH:

30 minutes

MAKES:

4 servings

MENU IDEA:

Quick-cooking couscous mix with herbs, prepared according to package directions

Banana & Caramel Cream Pies *(see p. 353)*

1	pound fresh or frozen sea scallops, skinless salmon fillet, whitefish fillet, or mahi mahi fillet
2	tablespoons all-purpose flour
$\frac{1}{2}$	teaspoon freshly ground black pepper
2	tablespoons butter or margarine
$\frac{1}{4}$	cup orange marmalade
2	tablespoons lime juice
1	tablespoon soy sauce
$\frac{1}{2}$	teaspoon grated fresh ginger
$\frac{1}{4}$	teaspoon cayenne pepper
4	cups sliced bok choy or Chinese cabbage
$\frac{1}{2}$	cup coarsely shredded carrot
1	lime, cut into wedges

1 Thaw scallops or fish, if frozen. Rinse scallops or fish; pat dry with paper towels. If using scallops, in a resealable plastic bag combine flour and pepper. Add scallops; toss to coat. If using fish, cut into 4 serving-size pieces; sprinkle with pepper (omit flour).

2 In a large skillet melt butter over medium heat. Add scallops or fish pieces. Cook scallops about 4 minutes or until golden brown, turning once. (Cook fish pieces for 8 to 12 minutes or until fish flakes easily when tested with a fork, turning once.) Use a slotted spoon to remove scallops or fish from skillet, reserving drippings in skillet.

3 Add orange marmalade, lime juice, soy sauce, ginger, and cayenne pepper to skillet; heat through. Remove from heat. Add bok choy and carrot to skillet. Toss to coat. Serve with scallops or fish and lime wedges.

Nutrition Facts per serving: 250 cal., 7 g total fat (4 g sat. fat), 54 mg chol., 864 mg sodium, 25 g carbo., 3 g fiber, 23 g pro.

The sweetness of the papaya complements the delicate flavor of the scallops, and the freshly made salsa makes them extra colorful.

SEARED SCALLOPS WITH TROPICAL SALSA

12	ounces fresh or frozen scallops
1	cup finely chopped strawberry papaya or papaya
½	cup seeded and finely chopped cucumber
1	small tomato, seeded and chopped
2	tablespoons snipped fresh cilantro
1	fresh jalapeño chile pepper, seeded and finely chopped*
4	teaspoons lime juice
1	teaspoon olive oil
	Salt
	Black pepper
1	teaspoon butter or margarine
½	teaspoon bottled minced garlic (1 clove)

START TO FINISH:
25 minutes

MAKES:
4 servings

MENU IDEA:

Cooked linguine or fettuccine tossed with olive oil, lime juice, and minced garlic

Fast & Fruity Banana Split Tarts
(see p. 352)

1 Thaw scallops, if frozen. Rinse scallops; pat dry with paper towels. Set aside. For salsa, in a small bowl stir together papaya, cucumber, tomato, cilantro, chile pepper, lime juice, and oil. Let stand at room temperature for at least 15 minutes to allow flavors to blend.

2 Meanwhile, halve any large scallops. Lightly sprinkle with salt and black pepper.

3 In a large nonstick skillet melt butter over medium heat. Add garlic; cook for 30 seconds. Add scallops. Cook and stir for 2 to 3 minutes or until scallops are opaque. Use a slotted spoon to remove scallops; drain on paper towels. Serve scallops with the salsa.

*NOTE: Because chile peppers contain volatile oils that can burn your skin and eyes, avoid direct contact with them as much as possible. When working with chile peppers, wear plastic or rubber gloves. If your bare hands do touch the peppers, wash your hands and nails well with soap and warm water.

Nutrition Facts per serving: 116 cal., 3 g total fat (0 g sat. fat), 31 mg chol., 151 mg sodium, 8 g carbo., 1 g fiber, 15 g pro.

A tantalizing combination of olive, orange, and licorice flavors makes these scallops a captivating headliner for a party menu.

SCALLOPS WITH ANISE-ORANGE TAPENADE

START TO FINISH:

20 minutes

MAKES:

4 servings

12	fresh or frozen sea scallops (about 1¼ pounds)
⅓	cup pitted kalamata olives, coarsely chopped
1	green onion, sliced
½	teaspoon finely shredded orange peel
2	teaspoons orange juice
¼	teaspoon anise seeds, crushed
⅛	teaspoon cayenne pepper
	Nonstick cooking spray

1 Thaw scallops, if frozen. Rinse scallops; pat dry with paper towels. Set aside.

2 For tapenade, in a small bowl combine olives, green onion, orange peel, orange juice, anise seeds, and cayenne pepper.

3 Coat an unheated large nonstick skillet with cooking spray. Preheat over medium-high heat. Add scallops to skillet; cook for 3 to 6 minutes or until scallops are opaque, turning once.

4 Serve cooked scallops with tapenade.

Nutrition Facts per serving: 145 cal., 3 g total fat (0 g sat. fat), 47 mg chol., 353 mg sodium, 5 g carbo., 1 g fiber, 24 g pro.

MENU IDEA:

Asparagus Salad with Tarragon Vinaigrette *(see p. 303)*

Purchased unfrosted sugar cookies frosted with canned cream cheese frosting and sprinkled with colored coarse sugar and snipped dried cranberries

Tossing in chunks of fresh sweet lobster is a decadent and delicious way to dress up pasta and beans. For convenience, see if your supermarket will cook the lobster for you. Or in a pinch, substitute frozen cooked lobster.

WHITE BEANS & PASTA WITH LOBSTER

8	ounces dried cavatappi, fusilli, or rotini
1	15- to 19-ounce can white kidney (cannellini) beans, rinsed and drained
½	cup chicken broth
1	tablespoon olive oil
3	cloves garlic, thinly sliced
6	medium plum tomatoes, coarsely chopped (about 2 cups)
12	ounces cooked lobster, cut into 1-inch pieces, or 12 ounces fresh or frozen cod fillets, cooked and cut into 1-inch pieces
½	cup snipped fresh flat-leaf parsley
½	to 1 teaspoon cracked black pepper
½	teaspoon salt

1 Cook pasta according to package directions; drain well.

2 In a blender or food processor combine ¾ cup of the drained beans and the broth; cover and blend or process until smooth. Add to the pan used for cooking the pasta; bring to boiling. Return pasta to pan.

3 Meanwhile, in a large skillet heat oil over medium heat. Add garlic; cook for 1 minute. Add tomatoes; cook for 1 minute more. Add remaining beans, the lobster, parsley, pepper, and salt. Heat through.

4 Add tomato mixture to hot pasta; toss to coat.

Nutrition Facts per serving: 602 cal., 9 g total fat (1 g sat. fat), 102 mg chol., 1,051 mg sodium, 87 g carbo., 10 g fiber, 49 g pro.

START TO FINISH:

30 minutes

MAKES:

3 or 4 servings

MENU IDEA:

Steamed broccoli rabe or broccoli tossed with butter and shredded Asiago cheese

Cherry-Bananas Foster *(see p. 360)*

Herbs, especially the basil, dillweed, and thyme trio, make this salad a standout. Feel free to try your favorites. Serve the salad with garlic bread or crusty sourdough rolls and glasses of iced tea.

PEACHY LOBSTER PASTA SALAD

START TO FINISH:

30 minutes

MAKES:

4 to 6 servings

MENU IDEA:

Garlic bread loaf, toasted

Cannoli *(see p. 356)*

6	ounces dried medium shell macaroni
½	cup snipped mixed fresh herbs (such as basil, dillweed, and thyme)
¼	cup olive oil
1	teaspoon finely shredded lime peel
3	tablespoons lime juice
3	tablespoons orange juice
1	tablespoon honey
1	teaspoon bottled minced garlic (2 cloves)
¼	teaspoon salt
¼	teaspoon black pepper
3	medium peaches, peeled and sliced
2	cups cut-up, cooked lobster or crabmeat (cartilage removed) or flake-style imitation lobster (about 12 ounces)
1	cup watercress
	Salt
	Black pepper

1 Cook pasta according to package directions; drain well. Rinse with cold water; drain again.

2 Meanwhile, in a large salad bowl combine herbs, oil, lime peel, lime juice, orange juice, honey, garlic, the ¼ teaspoon salt, and the ¼ teaspoon pepper. Add peach slices. Toss gently to combine. Add cooked pasta, lobster, and watercress. Toss gently to combine. Season with additional salt and pepper.

Nutrition Facts per serving: 422 cal., 15 g total fat (2 g sat. fat), 61 mg chol., 509 mg sodium, 49 g carbo., 3 g fiber, 24 g pro.

Canned clams are something every busy cook should keep in the pantry—especially if your family loves good chowder, like this one.

CLAM CHOWDER

2   10¾-ounce cans condensed cream of celery soup

2   cups loose-pack frozen diced hash brown potatoes with onion and peppers

1   8-ounce bottle clam juice

1   6½-ounce can minced or chopped clams, undrained

2   teaspoons Worcestershire sauce

1   teaspoon dried thyme, crushed

1   cup half-and-half or light cream

3   slices packaged ready-to-serve cooked bacon, chopped

Black pepper (optional)

1 In a large saucepan combine cream of celery soup, hash browns, clam juice, undrained clams, Worcestershire sauce, and thyme. Bring to boiling; reduce heat. Cover and simmer about 15 minutes or until potatoes are tender, stirring frequently.

2 Stir in half-and-half; heat through. Sprinkle individual servings with bacon. If desired, season to taste with pepper.

Nutrition Facts per serving: 383 cal., 20 g total fat (9 g sat. fat), 62 mg chol., 1,410 mg sodium, 29 g carbo., 3 g fiber, 19 g pro.

PREP:
15 minutes
COOK:
15 minutes
MAKES:
4 to 6 servings

MENU IDEA:

Rye or pumpernickel bread, spread with herb butter and toasted

Caramel Apple Pastry *(see p. 333)*

This recipe gives clams an Asian flair by teaming them with sweet peppers, fresh ginger, garlic, red pepper flakes, and soy sauce.

ASIAN-STYLE NOODLES WITH CLAMS

START TO FINISH:

30 minutes

MAKES:

4 servings

8	ounces dried linguine
½	cup shredded fresh spinach
1	teaspoon toasted sesame oil
2	6½-ounce cans chopped or minced clams
2	teaspoons cornstarch
1	tablespoon olive oil
2	cups thin short strips red and/or yellow sweet peppers
1	tablespoon grated fresh ginger
½	teaspoon bottled minced garlic (1 clove)
¼	teaspoon crushed red pepper
1	tablespoon soy sauce

1 Cook linguine according to package directions; drain well. Return to hot pan. Stir in spinach and sesame oil. Cover and keep warm.

2 Meanwhile, drain clams, reserving liquid. Measure ¾ cup of the clam liquid (if necessary, add enough water to clam liquid to equal ¾ cup). Stir liquid into cornstarch; set aside. In a large skillet heat olive oil over medium-high heat. Add sweet pepper, ginger, garlic, and crushed red pepper; cook for 3 minutes. Stir in clam liquid mixture and soy sauce. Cook and stir over medium heat until bubbly; cook and stir for 1 minute more. Stir in clams. Cook and stir about 1 minute more or until clams are heated through.

3 Serve clam mixture over linguine mixture.

Nutrition Facts per serving: 414 cal., 7 g total fat (1 g sat. fat), 62 mg chol., 340 mg sodium, 53 g carbo., 3 g fiber, 32 g pro.

MENU IDEA:

Mixed Greens Salad with Ginger Vinaigrette *(see p. 305)*

Purchased frozen individual cheesecakes drizzled with warmed fruit preserves and topped with fresh sliced fruit

MEATLESS

Mustard greens, tomato, and fontina cheese make this simple omelet a masterpiece. Remember it when you have leftover brown rice.

TOMATO-BROWN RICE FRITTATA

START TO FINISH:

30 minutes

MAKES:

4 servings

MENU IDEA:

Purchased muffins
served with maple
butter or jam

Baked Fruit Ambrosia
(see p. 336)

6	egg whites
3	eggs
¼	teaspoon salt
⅛	teaspoon black pepper
½	cup cooked brown rice
¼	cup chopped onion
½	teaspoon bottled minced garlic (1 clove)
1	tablespoon olive oil
2	cups packed fresh mustard greens, stems trimmed and torn into 1-inch pieces
1	medium tomato, seeded and chopped
⅓	cup shredded fontina, provolone, or Gruyère cheese

1 In a medium bowl beat together egg whites, eggs, salt, and pepper. Stir in brown rice; set aside. In a large broilerproof skillet cook onion and garlic in oil until tender. Stir in mustard greens; cook and stir about 2 minutes or until wilted. Stir in tomato; cook for 1 minute more.

2 Pour egg mixture into skillet over vegetables. Cook over medium-low heat. As mixture sets, run a spatula around edge of skillet, lifting egg mixture so uncooked portion flows underneath. Continue cooking and lifting edge until egg mixture is almost set (surface will be moist). Sprinkle with cheese. Place the skillet under broiler 4 to 5 inches from heat. Broil for 1 to 2 minutes or just until top is set and cheese is melted.

Nutrition Facts per serving: 197 cal., 11 g total fat (4 g sat. fat), 172 mg chol., 370 mg sodium, 11 g carbo., 2 g fiber, 14 g pro.

Don't worry if you are short on mushrooms or pea pods—simply open the refrigerator and make use of whatever vegetables you do have.

THYME-MUSHROOM OMELETS

¼ cup butter

1 cup sliced fresh mushrooms

½ cup sliced fresh or thawed frozen pea pods

2 green onions, sliced

1½ teaspoons snipped fresh thyme
or ¼ teaspoon dried thyme, crushed

4 eggs

¼ cup water

¼ teaspoon salt

⅛ teaspoon black pepper

½ cup shredded Gruyère or Swiss cheese (2 ounces)

1 For mushroom filling, in a small skillet melt 2 tablespoons of the butter over medium heat; add mushrooms, pea pods, green onions, and thyme. Cook until mushrooms and pea pods are tender, stirring occasionally.

2 Meanwhile, for omelets, in a small bowl combine eggs, the water, salt, and pepper. Using a fork, beat until combined but not frothy. Heat an 8-inch nonstick skillet with flared sides over medium-high heat until skillet is hot.

3 Add 1 tablespoon of the remaining butter to skillet. When butter has melted, add half of the egg mixture to skillet; lower heat to medium. Immediately begin stirring the eggs gently but continuously with a wooden or plastic spatula until mixture resembles small pieces of cooked egg surrounded by liquid egg. Stop stirring. Cook for 30 to 60 seconds more or until egg mixture is set but still shiny.

4 Spoon half of the mushroom filling across the center of the omelet. Sprinkle with half of the cheese. Using a spatula, lift and fold unfilled half of omelet over filling. Remove from the heat. Transfer to a warm plate. Keep warm while making another omelet with remaining eggs, butter, mushroom filling, and cheese.

Nutrition Facts per omelet: 509 cal., 44 g total fat (21 g sat. fat), 518 mg chol., 705 mg sodium, 5 g carbo., 1 g fiber, 24 g pro.

START TO FINISH:

25 minutes

MAKES:

2 omelets

MENU IDEA:

Orange-pineapple juice over crushed ice served with orange wedges

Dessert Waffles (make a half recipe) *(see p. 357)*

This open-face omelet calls on many easy-to-use ingredients—feta cheese that's already crumbled, pitted and sliced olives, bottled minced garlic, and roasted red sweet peppers from a jar—to make a colorful, simple dish that's perfect for brunch, lunch, or a light supper.

MEDITERRANEAN FRITTATA

START TO FINISH:

30 minutes

MAKES:

6 servings

MENU IDEA:

Refrigerated or frozen diced hash browns, prepared according to package directions and tossed with snipped fresh chives and cracked black pepper

Vanilla ice cream with Apricot-Orange Sauce *(see p. 372)*

3	tablespoons olive oil
1	large onion, chopped
1	teaspoon bottled minced garlic (2 cloves)
8	eggs
¼	cup half-and-half, light cream, or milk
½	cup crumbled feta cheese (2 ounces)
½	of a 7-ounce jar (½ cup) roasted red sweet peppers, drained and chopped
½	cup sliced kalamata or pitted ripe olives
¼	cup slivered fresh basil
⅛	teaspoon black pepper
½	cup purchased onion-and-garlic croutons, coarsely crushed
2	tablespoons finely shredded Parmesan cheese

1 In a 10-inch broilerproof skillet heat 2 tablespoons of the oil over medium heat. Add onion and garlic; cook just until onion is tender.

2 Meanwhile, in a large bowl beat together eggs and half-and-half. Stir in feta cheese, roasted sweet peppers, olives, basil, and black pepper. Pour over onion mixture in skillet. Cook over medium heat. As mixture sets, run a spatula around the edge of the skillet, lifting egg mixture so the uncooked portion flows underneath. Continue cooking and lifting edge until egg mixture is almost set (surface will be moist). Reduce heat as necessary to prevent overcooking.

3 In a small bowl combine crushed croutons, Parmesan cheese, and the remaining 1 tablespoon oil; sprinkle mixture over frittata.

4 Place skillet under broiler. Broil 4 to 5 inches from heat for 1 to 2 minutes or just until top is set. Cut frittata in wedges to serve.

Nutrition Facts per serving: 242 cal., 19 g total fat (6 g sat. fat), 297 mg chol., 339 mg sodium, 7 g carbo., 1 g fiber, 12 g pro.

Although this great-tasting omelet makes a terrific brunch dish, you also can team it with a light mixed green salad for a delicious dinner.

SPECIAL OCCASION OMELET

Bacon drippings or olive oil

⅓ cup chopped green sweet pepper

⅓ cup chopped red sweet pepper

1 fresh jalapeño chile pepper, seeded and finely chopped*

1 medium tomato, seeded and chopped

6 eggs

¼ cup whipping cream

¼ cup shredded cheddar cheese (1 ounce)

¼ cup shredded Swiss cheese (1 ounce)

START TO FINISH:

30 minutes

MAKES:

4 servings

1 For filling, in 10-inch nonstick skillet with flared sides heat 1 tablespoon bacon drippings or oil over medium heat. Add sweet peppers and chile pepper; cook for 2 to 3 minutes or until tender. Stir in tomato. Remove filling from skillet; set aside.

2 In a medium bowl combine the eggs and whipping cream; beat with a whisk or rotary beater. In same skillet heat 1 teaspoon bacon drippings or oil over medium heat. Add half of the egg mixture. Immediately begin stirring egg mixture gently but continuously with a wooden or plastic spatula until mixture resembles small pieces of cooked egg surrounded by liquid egg. Stop stirring. Cook for 30 to 60 seconds more or until egg mixture is set but still shiny.

3 Spoon half of the vegetable mixture across the center of the omelet. Sprinkle with half of the cheddar cheese and half of the Swiss cheese. Fold sides over. Heat for 1 to 2 minutes more to melt the cheese. Transfer omelet to a serving plate; keep warm.

4 Repeat with another 1 teaspoon bacon drippings or oil and remaining egg mixture, filling, and cheeses.

*NOTE: Because chile peppers contain volatile oils that can burn your skin and eyes, avoid direct contact with them as much as possible. When working with chile peppers, wear plastic or rubber gloves. If your bare hands do touch the peppers, wash your hands and nails well with soap and warm water.

Nutrition Facts per serving: 280 cal., 23 g total fat (11 g sat. fat), 359 mg chol., 166 mg sodium, 5 g carbo., 0 g fiber, 14 g pro.

MENU IDEA:

Purchased frozen pancakes, prepared according to package directions and served with maple or fruit syrup and toasted chopped pecans

Fresh Strawberry Fool *(see p. 364)*

Large supermarkets stock a variety of flavored tortillas. Use whichever flavor catches your fancy.

EGG & VEGETABLE SALAD WRAPS

START TO FINISH:

30 minutes

MAKES:

6 wraps

MENU IDEA:

Sliced honeydew melon and/or cantaloupe

Raspberry Cheesecake Shake
(see p. 382)

4   hard-cooked eggs, chopped
1   cup chopped cucumber
1   cup chopped zucchini or yellow summer squash
½   cup chopped red onion
½   cup shredded carrot
¼   cup mayonnaise or salad dressing
2   tablespoons Dijon-style mustard
1   tablespoon milk
1   teaspoon snipped fresh tarragon or basil
⅛   teaspoon paprika
6   leaf lettuce leaves
6   10-inch spinach, vegetable, or plain flour tortillas
2   plum tomatoes, thinly sliced

1 In a large bowl combine eggs, cucumber, zucchini or yellow summer squash, red onion, and carrot. For dressing, in a small bowl stir together mayonnaise, mustard, milk, tarragon, and paprika. Pour the dressing over egg mixture; toss gently to coat.

2 For each wrap, place a lettuce leaf on a tortilla. Place 3 or 4 tomato slices on top of lettuce on each tortilla, slightly off center. Spoon about ⅔ cup of the egg mixture on top of the tomato slices. Fold in 2 opposite sides of the tortilla; roll up from the bottom. To serve, cut each tortilla roll in half diagonally.

Nutrition Facts per wrap: 355 cal., 15 g total fat (3 g sat. fat), 148 mg chol., 613 mg sodium, 41 g carbo., 5 g fiber, 12 g pro.

TEST KITCHEN TIP: For a lower-fat wrap, substitute fat-free mayonnaise dressing or salad dressing for the mayonnaise or salad dressing and fat-free milk for the milk.

Nutrition Facts per wrap: 307 cal., 8 g total fat (1 g sat. fat), 143 mg chol., 769 mg sodium, 46 g carbo., 2 g fiber, 13 g pro.

If you think one egg salad sandwich is like another, you'll be surprised and delighted when you taste this one. It is dressed up with Colby Jack cheese and sweet red pepper.

EGG SALAD SANDWICHES

4	hard-cooked eggs, chopped
¼	cup shredded Colby Jack cheese (1 ounce)
2	tablespoons sweet or dill pickle relish
2	tablespoons finely chopped red sweet pepper
¼	cup mayonnaise or salad dressing
1	tablespoon prepared mustard
10	slices whole wheat and/or white bread
5	small romaine leaves
	Halved cherry tomatoes and/or thin bite-size carrot strips (optional)

1 In a medium bowl stir together eggs, cheese, relish, and sweet pepper. Stir in mayonnaise and mustard.

2 If desired, use large cookie cutters to cut bread slices into shapes. Top 5 slices of the bread with lettuce leaves. Spread on egg mixture. Top with remaining bread slices. If desired, garnish sandwiches with cherry tomatoes and/or carrots, using wooden toothpicks to secure.

Nutrition Facts per sandwich: 431 cal., 20 g total fat (4 g sat. fat), 183 mg chol., 551 mg sodium, 50 g carbo., 6 g fiber, 14 g pro.

TEST KITCHEN TIP: For a lower-fat sandwich, substitute reduced-fat Colby Jack cheese for the Colby Jack cheese and light mayonnaise dressing or salad dressing for the mayonnaise or salad dressing.

Nutrition Facts per sandwich: 365 cal., 11 g total fat (3 g sat. fat), 176 mg chol., 599 mg sodium, 54 g carbo., 6 g fiber, 15 g pro.

START TO FINISH:
20 minutes

MAKES:
5 sandwiches

MENU IDEA:
Tortilla or corn chips
Chewy Granola Bars
(see p. 345)

Roasted sweet peppers and cheese with jalapeños kick up the flavor of a hollandaise sauce mix. Sprinkle the finished dish with grated Parmesan cheese if you like.

PASTA WITH PEPPER-CHEESE SAUCE

START TO FINISH:

25 minutes

MAKES:

4 to 6 servings

8   ounces dried medium shell, mostaccioli, or cut ziti pasta

1   0.9- to 1.25-ounce package hollandaise sauce mix

1   7-ounce jar roasted red sweet peppers, drained and chopped

½   cup shredded Monterey Jack cheese with jalapeño chile peppers (2 ounces)

1 Cook pasta according to package directions; drain well. Return pasta to pan. Cover and keep warm.

2 Meanwhile, prepare hollandaise sauce according to package directions, except use only 2 tablespoons butter or margarine. Stir in roasted sweet peppers. Remove pan from heat. Add cheese to sauce, stirring until cheese melts. Add sauce to pasta in pan; toss to coat.

Nutrition Facts per serving: 384 cal., 13 g total fat (8 g sat. fat), 36 mg chol., 407 mg sodium, 53 g carbo., 2 g fiber, 13 g pro.

MENU IDEA:

Quick Focaccia Breadsticks
(see p. 330)

Raspberry sherbet
sprinkled with fresh raspberries and served with purchased cream-filled vanilla wafers

Creamy garlicky Alfredo sauce instead of pizza sauce is a great change of pace for pizza.
Buy two or three Italian bread shells and freeze them for quick-to-fix, satisfying pizzas.

ALFREDO & SWEET PEPPER PIZZA

1	16-ounce Italian bread shell (Boboli)
½	of a 10-ounce container (about ⅔ cup) refrigerated Alfredo pasta sauce
½	teaspoon dried Italian seasoning, crushed
1	8-ounce package shredded 4-cheese pizza cheese (2 cups)
1	16-ounce package frozen pepper stir-fry vegetables (yellow, green, and red peppers and onion), thawed and well drained

1 Place bread shell on an ungreased baking sheet. In a small bowl stir together Alfredo sauce and Italian seasoning. Spread Alfredo sauce mixture over bread shell.

2 Sprinkle bread shell with 1 cup of the cheese. Top with stir-fry vegetables. Sprinkle with remaining 1 cup cheese. Bake in a 425°F oven about 10 minutes or until heated through.

Nutrition Facts per serving: 626 cal., 30 g total fat (8 g sat. fat), 63 mg chol., 1,136 mg sodium, 60 g carbo., 3 g fiber, 30 g pro.

PREP:
15 minutes

BAKE:
10 minutes

MAKES:
4 servings

MENU IDEA:

Mixed greens tossed with seasoned croutons, tomato wedges, and bottled Italian salad dressing

Quick Strawberry Shortcakes
(see p. 337)

This comfort food classic is made even better with the addition of mushrooms and caramelized onions. Sourdough bread complements the bold flavors of the berry-balsamic vinegar and the onions.

GRILLED CHEESE WITH CARAMELIZED ONIONS

START TO FINISH:

30 minutes

MAKES:

4 sandwiches

MENU IDEA:

Fruited Wild Rice & Spinach Salad
(see p. 319)

Chocolate fudge ice cream sprinkled with toasted sliced almonds

6	tablespoons butter or margarine, softened
1	large onion, sliced
1	cup sliced fresh mushrooms
1	teaspoon berry-balsamic vinegar
⅛	teaspoon salt
8	slices sourdough bread
8	slices cheddar cheese, Swiss cheese, Monterey Jack cheese, and/or other desired cheese

1 In a large skillet melt 2 tablespoons of the butter over medium heat. Add onion slices; cook about 10 minutes or until onion is soft and golden brown, stirring occasionally. Stir in mushrooms. Cook and stir for 2 minutes more. Remove from heat. Sprinkle onions and mushrooms with balsamic vinegar and salt.

2 Butter 1 side of each slice of the bread with 1 tablespoon of the remaining butter. Place 2 slices of the desired cheese on the unbuttered side of each of 4 slices of the sourdough bread. Top each with some of the onion-mushroom mixture and another slice of sourdough bread, buttered side up. In a large skillet cook sandwiches over medium heat for 4 to 6 minutes or until cheese is melted, turning once.

Nutrition Facts per sandwich: 552 cal., 39 g total fat (22 g sat. fat), 108 mg chol., 861 mg sodium, 32 g carbo., 2 g fiber, 20 g pro.

This rich and creamy sauce clings nicely to the linguine noodles while the asparagus adds color and the walnuts add delightful crunch.

LINGUINE WITH GORGONZOLA SAUCE

1   9-ounce package refrigerated linguine

1   pound fresh asparagus, trimmed and cut into 1-inch pieces, or one 10-ounce package frozen cut asparagus

1   cup half-and-half or light cream

1   cup crumbled Gorgonzola or other blue cheese (4 ounces)

¼   teaspoon salt

2   tablespoons chopped walnuts, toasted

1 Cook pasta and asparagus according to package directions for the pasta; drain well. Return pasta and asparagus to pan. Cover and keep warm.

2 Meanwhile, for sauce, in a medium saucepan combine half-and-half, ¾ cup of the Gorgonzola cheese, and the salt. Bring to boiling over medium heat; reduce heat. Simmer, uncovered, for 3 minutes, stirring frequently.

3 Pour sauce over pasta mixture; toss gently to coat. Transfer to a warm serving dish. Sprinkle with remaining ¼ cup Gorgonzola cheese and the walnuts.

Nutrition Facts per serving: 399 cal., 20 g total fat (11 g sat. fat), 111 mg chol., 590 mg sodium, 39 g carbo., 3 g fiber, 18 g pro.

START TO FINISH:

20 minutes

MAKES:

4 servings

MENU IDEA:

Cooked peeled baby carrots tossed with butter and brown sugar

Crunchy Pound Cake Slices *(see p. 343)*

Topping bowls of this chowder with cheesy slices of toasted rye bread is a simple way to add eye appeal that invites hungry eaters to dig in.

POTATO-CAULIFLOWER CHOWDER

START TO FINISH:
30 minutes

MAKES:
6 servings

MENU IDEA:

Peanut Butter Fruit Salad *(see p. 313)*

Purchased unfrosted brownies spread with canned chocolate frosting and sprinkled with mini marshmallows and chopped nuts

1	large onion, chopped
2	tablespoons butter or margarine
4	cups chicken or vegetable broth
2	cups diced, peeled Yukon gold or white potatoes
2½	cups cauliflower florets
1	cup half-and-half, light cream, or milk
2	tablespoons all-purpose flour
2½	cups shredded Jarlsberg cheese or Swiss cheese (10 ounces)
	Salt
	Black pepper
3	slices dark rye or pumpernickel bread, halved crosswise (optional)
½	cup shredded Jarlsberg cheese or Swiss cheese (2 ounces) (optional)
2	tablespoons snipped fresh flat-leaf parsley (optional)

1 In a large saucepan or Dutch oven cook onion in hot butter until tender. Carefully add broth and potatoes. Bring to boiling; reduce heat. Cover and simmer for 6 minutes. Add cauliflower. Return to boiling; reduce heat. Cover and simmer for 4 to 6 minutes or until vegetables are tender.

2 In a small bowl whisk half-and-half into flour until smooth; add to soup mixture. Cook and stir until mixture is thickened and bubbly. Reduce heat to low. Add the 2½ cups cheese, stirring until melted. Do not allow mixture to boil. Season to taste with salt and pepper.

3 Meanwhile, if using bread, if desired, trim crusts from bread. Place the halved bread slices on a baking sheet. Bake in a 350°F oven about 3 minutes or until crisp on top. Turn slices over. If desired, sprinkle with the ½ cup cheese and the parsley. Bake about 5 minutes more or until cheese melts.

4 Float cheese-topped bread slices on individual servings.

Nutrition Facts per serving: 267 cal., 17 g total fat (12 g sat. fat), 58 mg chol., 533 mg sodium, 14 g carbo., 2 g fiber, 15 g pro.

*These packed-full-of-veggies quesadillas are quick, colorful, and irresistible.
The diced peaches add a hint of sweetness.*

BEAN & CHEESE QUESADILLAS

½   of a 16-ounce can refried beans (¾ cup)

1   8-ounce can whole kernel corn, drained

¼   cup bottled salsa

1   canned chipotle chile pepper in adobo sauce,
    drained and chopped* (optional)

8   8-inch flour tortillas

2   tablespoons cooking oil

1   cup packaged shredded broccoli (broccoli slaw mix)

1   4- to 4¼-ounce can or container diced peaches, drained

1   cup finely shredded Mexican cheese blend (4 ounces)
    Purchased guacamole dip, dairy sour cream,
    and/or bottled salsa

1 In a small bowl combine refried beans, corn, the ¼ cup salsa, and, if
desired, chipotle chile pepper. Brush 1 side of each tortilla with some of the
oil. Spread bean mixture over the unoiled side of 4 of the tortillas; set aside.

2 In another bowl combine broccoli slaw and peaches. Top bean mixture
on tortillas with broccoli mixture. Top with cheese. Top with remaining
tortillas, oiled sides up; press down lightly. Place on a large baking sheet.

3 Bake in a 400°F oven for 12 to 15 minutes or until golden brown and
cheese is melted. Cut into quarters to serve. Serve with guacamole dip,
sour cream, and/or additional salsa.

*NOTE: Because chile peppers contain volatile oils that can burn your skin
and eyes, avoid direct contact with them as much as possible. When working
with chile peppers, wear plastic or rubber gloves. If your bare hands do touch
the peppers, wash your hands and nails well with soap and warm water.

Nutrition Facts per serving: 444 cal., 21 g total fat (7 g sat. fat), 25 mg chol., 825 mg sodium,
50 g carbo., 5 g fiber, 14 g pro.

PREP:
15 minutes

BAKE:
12 minutes

MAKES:
4 servings

MENU IDEA:
**Tomato-Barley Soup
with Garden
Vegetables**
(see p. 294)

Vanilla frozen yogurt
served with sliced
fresh mango

The name says it all—this Alfredo-sauced macaroni laced with toasted nuts is easy and cheesy!

EASY CHEESY MACARONI

START TO FINISH:

20 minutes

MAKES:

4 servings

8   ounces dried penne, rotini, or gemelli pasta

2   cups loose-pack frozen cauliflower, broccoli, and carrots

1   10-ounce container refrigerated light Alfredo pasta sauce

¼   cup milk

1   cup shredded cheddar cheese (4 ounces)

½   cup finely shredded Parmesan cheese (2 ounces)

¼   cup chopped walnuts, toasted

1 In a 4-quart Dutch oven cook pasta according to package directions, adding frozen vegetables for the last 4 minutes of cooking; drain well. Return to Dutch oven; cover and keep warm.

2 Meanwhile, in a medium saucepan combine Alfredo sauce and milk; heat and stir just until bubbly. Gradually add cheddar and Parmesan cheeses, stirring until melted. Add cheese mixture to pasta mixture in Dutch oven; stir to coat. Heat through. Top with toasted walnuts.

Nutrition Facts per serving: 586 cal., 28 g total fat (15 g sat. fat), 70 mg chol., 1,054 mg sodium, 57 g carbo., 3 g fiber, 26 g pro.

MENU IDEA:

Rosy Tangerine-Scented Cabbage *(see p. 260)*

Sliced green and/or red apples served with caramel dip and sprinkled with granola

Brimming with zesty pickled vegetables and herbed cheese, this stuffed focaccia makes an instant meal. Save time by buying prewashed spinach from the produce department and getting the cheese at the deli counter so you can have it very thinly sliced or shaved.

CHEESE & VEGETABLE-FILLED FOCACCIA

1/3	cup mayonnaise or salad dressing
2	tablespoons honey mustard
1	8- to 10-inch tomato or onion focaccia bread, halved horizontally
1	cup lightly packed fresh spinach leaves
6	ounces dilled Havarti cheese, very thinly sliced
1	16-ounce jar pickled mixed vegetables, drained and chopped

1 In a small bowl stir together mayonnaise and honey mustard. Spread mayonnaise mixture over bottom half of focaccia. Top with spinach leaves and half of the cheese. Spoon vegetables over; top with remaining cheese. Replace bread top. Cut into quarters.

Nutrition Facts per serving: 364 cal., 32 g total fat (2 g sat. fat), 67 mg chol., 1,251 mg sodium, 10 g carbo., 0 g fiber, 10 g pro.

START TO FINISH:

20 minutes

MAKES:

4 servings

MENU IDEA:

Creamy Carrot Soup
(see p. 293)

Fresh strawberries
topped with vanilla or strawberry frozen yogurt and served with purchased sugar cookies

This inventive way to serve ravioli is sure to please all of the pasta lovers in your family.

RAVIOLI SKILLET LASAGNA

START TO FINISH:

25 minutes

MAKES:

4 servings

2	cups bottled light chunky-style spaghetti sauce
⅓	cup water
1	9-ounce package refrigerated or frozen cheese or meat-filled ravioli
1	egg
1	15-ounce carton ricotta cheese
¼	cup grated Romano or Parmesan cheese (1 ounce)
1	10-ounce package frozen chopped spinach, thawed and well drained
	Grated Romano or Parmesan cheese

1 In a 10-inch skillet combine spaghetti sauce and the water. Bring to boiling. Stir in the ravioli. Cover and cook over medium heat about 5 minutes or until ravioli are nearly tender, stirring once to prevent sticking.

2 Meanwhile, in a medium bowl beat egg with a fork. Stir in ricotta cheese and the ¼ cup Romano cheese. Dot ravioli with spinach. Spoon ricotta mixture on top of spinach. Cover and cook over low heat about 10 minutes or until ricotta layer is set and pasta is just tender. Sprinkle individual servings with additional Romano cheese.

Nutrition Facts per serving: 433 cal., 14 g total fat (3 g sat. fat), 131 mg chol., 501 mg sodium, 49 g carbo., 3 g fiber, 36 g pro.

MENU IDEA:

Garlic bread loaf, sprinkled with grated Romano or Parmesan cheese and toasted

Caramel Apple Sundaes *(see p. 378)*

Ground meat with garlic, tomatoes, and vegetables make up a traditional Bolognese sauce. In this vegetarian version, fiber-rich cereal creates a texture in the sauce that is remarkably similar to ground meat. The cereal softens as the sauce stands, so for a chewier texture, serve immediately.

SPAGHETTI WITH VEGETARIAN SAUCE "BOLOGNESE"

6	ounces dried spaghetti
1	tablespoon olive oil
1	medium carrot, finely chopped
1	stalk celery, thinly sliced
1	medium onion, finely chopped
1½	teaspoons bottled minced garlic (3 cloves)
½	teaspoon dried oregano, crushed
¼	teaspoon salt
¼	teaspoon black pepper
1	14½-ounce can stewed tomatoes, undrained and cut up
1	8-ounce can tomato sauce
¼	cup water
¾	cup Grape Nuts® cereal
	Grated Parmesan or Romano cheese (optional)

1 Cook spaghetti according to package directions; drain well. Return to hot pan; cover and keep warm.

2 Meanwhile, in a medium saucepan heat oil over medium-high heat. Add carrot, celery, onion, garlic, oregano, salt, and pepper; cook about 5 minutes or until onion is tender. Add undrained tomatoes, tomato sauce, and the water. Bring to boiling; reduce heat. Cover and simmer for 5 minutes. Stir in cereal; return to boiling. Remove from heat.

3 Divide the hot pasta among 4 dinner plates. Spoon sauce over. If desired, sprinkle with Parmesan cheese.

Nutrition Facts per serving: 340 cal., 5 g total fat (1 g sat. fat), 0 mg chol., 733 mg sodium, 65 g carbo., 6 g fiber, 10 g pro.

START TO FINISH:
30 minutes
MAKES:
4 servings

MENU IDEA:
Refrigerated soft breadsticks, brushed with olive oil, sprinkled with dried Italian seasoning, and prepared according to package directions

Blueberries & Orange Cream
(see p. 365)

Turn the heat to low or take the skillet off of the burner before adding the sour cream to the sauce. The sour cream will curdle if it gets too hot.

CREAMY PENNE & MUSHROOMS

START TO FINISH:

25 minutes

MAKES:

4 servings

8	ounces dried penne pasta
3	cups sliced fresh button mushrooms (8 ounces)
1½	cups sliced fresh shiitake mushrooms (4 ounces)
2	teaspoons bottled minced garlic (4 cloves)
1	tablespoon butter or margarine
½	cup dry white wine
1	teaspoon instant chicken bouillon granules
¼	teaspoon coarsely ground black pepper
½	cup light dairy sour cream
¼	cup finely shredded Parmesan cheese (1 ounce)

MENU IDEA:

Lemon-Almond Broccoli *(see p. 257)*

Purchased individual shortcakes topped with canned apple pie filling and drizzled with purchased caramel sauce

1 Cook pasta according to package directions; drain. Return to hot pan; cover and keep warm.

2 In a large skillet cook and stir mushrooms and garlic in hot butter for 3 minutes. Stir in white wine, bouillon granules, and pepper. Bring to boiling; reduce heat. Simmer, uncovered, for 5 minutes. Reduce heat to low. Stir in sour cream; add hot cooked pasta. Cook and stir until heated through (do not boil).

3 To serve, transfer pasta to shallow pasta bowls or dinner plates. Sprinkle individual servings with Parmesan cheese.

Nutrition Facts per serving: 360 cal., 9 g total fat (5 g sat. fat), 24 mg chol., 408 mg sodium, 51 g carbo., 2 g fiber, 14 g pro.

Plain feta cheese packs plenty of tanginess on its own, but the versions made with herbs or peppercorns intensify the taste of this colorful fettuccine one-dish meal.

FETTUCCINE-VEGETABLE TOSS

1	9-ounce package refrigerated spinach fettuccine
1	tablespoon olive oil
1	green onion, chopped
4	small red and/or yellow tomatoes, chopped (2 cups)
1	medium carrot, finely chopped
¼	cup oil-packed dried tomatoes, drained and snipped
½	cup crumbled garlic-and-herb feta cheese, peppercorn feta cheese, or plain feta cheese (2 ounces)

1 Cook pasta according to package directions; drain well. Return to hot pan; cover and keep warm.

2 Meanwhile, in a large skillet heat oil over medium heat. Add green onion; cook for 30 seconds. Stir in fresh tomatoes, carrot, and dried tomatoes. Cover and cook for 5 minutes, stirring once. Spoon tomato mixture over cooked pasta. Sprinkle with feta cheese; toss gently.

Nutrition Facts per serving: 311 cal., 11 g total fat (4 g sat. fat), 73 mg chol., 250 mg sodium, 44 g carbo., 2 g fiber, 13 g pro.

START TO FINISH:
20 minutes
MAKES:
4 servings

MENU IDEA:
Seeded Dinner Rolls
(see p. 330)

Purchased lemon cake served with whipped cream and fresh blueberries

Zippy dried tomatoes, sweet fresh basil, and creamy goat cheese make a terrific pasta main dish. It's hard to believe you can have a meal this amazing on the table in just 25 minutes!

LINGUINE TOSS

START TO FINISH:

25 minutes

MAKES:

3 servings

MENU IDEA:

Garlic and tomato focaccia

Chocolate Brownie Pudding *(see p. 339)*

1   tablespoon olive oil

2   cups thinly sliced onions

1   teaspoon bottled minced garlic (2 cloves)

½   cup chicken broth or vegetable broth

¼   cup dry white wine

¼   teaspoon salt

⅛   teaspoon black pepper

1   9-ounce package refrigerated spinach linguine or plain linguine

1   cup broccoli florets

⅓   cup thin bite-size strips dried tomatoes (not oil-packed)

⅓   cup snipped fresh basil

3   tablespoons pine nuts, toasted

2   ounces mild goat cheese, crumbled

1 In a large skillet heat oil over medium-low heat. Add onions and garlic. Cover and cook for 10 to 15 minutes or until onions begin to brown, stirring frequently.

2 Remove cover; cook for 2 minutes more. Add broth, wine, salt, and pepper. Cook, uncovered, for 2 minutes.

3 Meanwhile, cook linguine, broccoli, and dried tomatoes in boiling water according to package directions for linguine; drain.

4 In a large bowl combine hot linguine mixture, hot onion mixture, basil, pine nuts, and cheese; toss gently.

Nutrition Facts per serving: 493 cal., 18 g total fat (6 g sat. fat), 77 mg chol., 619 mg sodium, 65 g carbo., 6 g fiber, 20 g pro.

Pasta is so incredibly versatile because it goes well with just about any other ingredient. Here curly rotini, asparagus, red peppers, pattypan squash, and thyme are a winning combination.

ROTINI & SWEET PEPPER PRIMAVERA

1	pound fresh asparagus
8	ounces dried rotini or gemelli pasta
2	small red and/or yellow sweet peppers, cut into 1-inch pieces
1	cup halved baby pattypan squash or sliced yellow summer squash
1	10-ounce container refrigerated light Alfredo pasta sauce
2	teaspoons snipped fresh thyme or ¾ teaspoon dried thyme, crushed
⅛	to ¼ teaspoon crushed red pepper
	Coarsely cracked black pepper (optional)

START TO FINISH:
25 minutes

MAKES:
4 servings

1 Snap off and discard woody bases from asparagus. If desired, scrape off scales. Bias-slice asparagus into 1-inch pieces. (You should have about 2 cups.)

2 Cook pasta according to package directions, adding asparagus, sweet peppers, and squash to the pasta for the last 3 minutes of cooking. Drain well. Return the pasta and vegetables to hot pan; cover and keep warm.

3 Meanwhile, in a small saucepan stir together Alfredo sauce, thyme, and crushed red pepper. Cook and stir over medium heat about 5 minutes or until mixture is heated through. Pour over pasta and vegetables; toss gently to coat. If desired, sprinkle with black pepper.

Nutrition Facts per serving: 421 cal., 12 g total fat (6 g sat. fat), 31 mg chol., 622 mg sodium, 66 g carbo., 2 g fiber, 15 g pro.

MENU IDEA:

Mixed baby greens tossed with bottled berry vinaigrette salad dressing, fresh berries, and chopped nuts

Chocolate-Mint Sandwich Cookies *(see p. 347)*

This easy entrée has all the wonderful tomato, mint, and lemon flavors of the traditional Middle Eastern favorite, tabbouleh.

TABBOULEH-STYLE COUSCOUS WITH TOFU

START TO FINISH:

25 minutes

MAKES:

6 servings

MENU IDEA:

Mixed fresh fruit tossed with a little lemonade and snipped fresh mint

Chocolate-Coconut Cheesecake
(see p. 356)

1⅓	cups chicken broth or vegetable broth
1	cup quick-cooking couscous
2	tablespoons olive oil
1	16-ounce package extra-firm tofu (fresh bean curd), drained and cut into ½-inch cubes
⅔	cup sliced green onions
1	teaspoon bottled minced garlic (2 cloves)
1½	cups chopped tomatoes
¼	cup snipped fresh basil
¼	cup lemon juice
1	tablespoon snipped fresh mint
¼	teaspoon black pepper
½	cup crumbled feta cheese (2 ounces)

1 In a medium saucepan bring broth to boiling. Stir in couscous. Remove saucepan from heat. Cover and let stand about 5 minutes or until liquid is absorbed.

2 Meanwhile, in a large nonstick skillet heat 1 tablespoon of the oil over medium-high heat. Add tofu, green onions, and garlic. Cook for 8 to 10 minutes or until tofu is light brown, turning carefully. (If necessary, reduce heat to medium to prevent overbrowning.)

3 In a large bowl combine couscous, tofu mixture, the remaining 1 tablespoon oil, the tomatoes, basil, lemon juice, mint, and black pepper; toss gently to coat. Sprinkle individual servings with feta cheese.

Nutrition Facts per serving: 276 cal., 11 g total fat (3 g sat. fat), 9 mg chol., 329 mg sodium, 30 g carbo., 3 g fiber, 14 g pro.

With this no-hassle recipe, you can enjoy a Chinese classic at home in just minutes.

VEGETABLE FRIED RICE

1	teaspoon toasted sesame oil or cooking oil
2	eggs, slightly beaten
1/3	cup rice vinegar
1/4	cup soy sauce
1/8	teaspoon ground ginger
1/8	teaspoon crushed red pepper
1	tablespoon cooking oil
1	cup sliced fresh mushrooms
1	teaspoon bottled minced garlic (2 cloves)
2	8.8-ounce pouches cooked long grain rice
1/2	cup loose-pack frozen peas
1	2-ounce jar diced pimientos, drained
1/4	cup chopped peanuts (optional)

1 In a large skillet heat sesame oil over medium heat. Add half of the egg, lifting and tilting the skillet to form a thin layer (egg may not completely cover the bottom of the skillet). Cook about 1 minute or until set. Invert skillet over a baking sheet to remove cooked egg; cut into strips and set aside. Repeat with remaining egg. In a small bowl stir together vinegar, soy sauce, ginger, and crushed red pepper; set aside.

2 In the same skillet heat cooking oil over medium-high heat. Add mushrooms and garlic; cook about 3 minutes or until mushrooms are tender. Stir in vinegar mixture. Stir in rice, frozen peas, and pimientos. Cook and stir about 2 minutes or until heated through and liquid is nearly evaporated. Stir in egg strips. If desired, sprinkle individual servings with chopped peanuts.

Nutrition Facts per serving: 314 cal., 10 g total fat (1 g sat. fat), 106 mg chol., 999 mg sodium, 45 g carbo., 3 g fiber, 10 g pro.

START TO FINISH:
20 minutes
MAKES:
4 servings

MENU IDEA:
Asian Pea Pod Salad
(see p. 304)

Instant pistachio pudding mix, prepared according to package directions and topped with flaked coconut

A little like a creamy risotto, this dish gets its wonderful richness from sweet and nutty Gruyère cheese and pungent and slightly sweet, pink peppercorns.

CREAMY BARLEY & BROCCOLI

START TO FINISH:

25 minutes

MAKES:

4 servings

MENU IDEA:

Sweet Saucy Carrots & Pecans *(see p. 261)*

Purchased angel food cake topped with whipped cream and fresh raspberries and/or sliced peaches

1	14-ounce can vegetable broth
1	cup quick-cooking barley
2	cups broccoli florets
2	tablespoons butter or margarine
2	tablespoons all-purpose flour
¼	teaspoon salt
	Dash ground allspice
1½	cups milk
¾	cup shredded Gruyère cheese (3 ounces)
	Cracked pink peppercorns

1 In a medium saucepan bring broth to boiling. Stir in barley. Return to boiling; reduce heat. Cover and simmer for 10 to 12 minutes or until barley is tender and most of the liquid is absorbed, adding broccoli for the last 5 minutes of cooking.

2 Meanwhile, for sauce, in a small saucepan melt butter over medium heat. Stir in flour, salt, and allspice. Add milk all at once. Cook and stir over medium heat until thickened and bubbly. Cook and stir for 1 minute more. Add ½ cup of the cheese, stirring until melted.

3 Gently stir the sauce into barley mixture. Divide the barley mixture among 4 shallow bowls. Sprinkle with the remaining ¼ cup cheese; sprinkle with cracked pink peppercorns.

Nutrition Facts per serving: 352 cal., 15 g total fat (8 g sat. fat), 47 mg chol., 718 mg sodium, 39 g carbo., 5 g fiber, 15 g pro.

A fresh combination of Great Northern beans, sweet juicy red tomatoes, and fragrant basil makes a quick-and-easy meatless main dish. The bow tie pasta adds an element of fun.

WHITE BEANS WITH TOMATO, BASIL & PARMESAN

8	ounces dried bow tie pasta
1	tablespoon olive oil
1½	teaspoons bottled minced garlic (3 cloves)
2	15-ounce cans Great Northern or white kidney (cannellini) beans, rinsed and drained
2	large tomatoes, chopped (about 3 cups)
¼	cup snipped fresh basil or 2 teaspoons dried basil, crushed
1	tablespoon lemon juice
¼	teaspoon salt (optional)
½	cup grated Parmesan cheese (2 ounces)
	Freshly ground black pepper

1 Cook pasta according to package directions; drain well. Return to hot pan; cover and keep warm.

2 Meanwhile, in a large nonstick skillet heat oil over medium-low heat. Add garlic; cook, stirring occasionally, for 1 to 2 minutes or until golden brown. Stir in beans, tomatoes, and basil. Cook, uncovered, for 5 minutes. Stir in lemon juice and, if desired, salt.

3 Serve bean mixture over hot cooked pasta. Sprinkle individual servings with Parmesan cheese and freshly ground pepper.

Nutrition Facts per serving: 480 cal., 9 g total fat (3 g sat. fat), 10 mg chol., 247 mg sodium, 77 g carbo., 12 g fiber, 25 g pro.

START TO FINISH:

30 minutes

MAKES:

4 servings

MENU IDEA:

Honey & Poppy Seed Biscuits *(see p. 326)*

Coffee or mocha ice cream served with purchased fudge stick cookies

The great taste of summer garden vegetables simmers in this stew. It combines eggplant, green beans, tomatoes, onion, and sweet pepper, all cooked with basil in fruity olive oil. For a fun presentation, serve the colorful stew in hollowed eggplant halves.

CHUNKY RATATOUILLE STEW

START TO FINISH:

25 minutes

MAKES:

4 servings

1	tablespoon olive oil
1	large onion, chopped
½	cup chopped green sweet pepper
½	of a small eggplant, peeled and chopped (2 cups)
1	cup loose-pack frozen cut green beans
1	14-ounce can beef broth or vegetable broth
½	cup water
2	tablespoons dry red wine
1	14½-ounce can diced tomatoes with roasted garlic, undrained
1	4½-ounce jar (drained weight) whole mushrooms, drained
1	tablespoon snipped fresh basil or ½ teaspoon dried basil, crushed
¾	cup shredded provolone cheese (3 ounces)

MENU IDEA:

Cooked angel hair pasta tossed with olive oil, snipped fresh chives, and snipped sun-dried tomatoes

Blueberry-Lemon Tarts *(see p. 353)*

1 In a Dutch oven heat oil over medium heat. Add onion and sweet pepper. Cook and stir until tender. Stir in eggplant, green beans, broth, the water, and wine. Bring to boiling; reduce heat. Cover and simmer for 8 to 10 minutes or until vegetables are tender.

2 Stir in undrained tomatoes, mushrooms, and basil; heat through. Sprinkle individual servings with provolone cheese.

Nutrition Facts per serving: 199 cal., 9 g total fat (4 g sat. fat), 16 mg chol., 1,107 mg sodium, 19 g carbo., 4 g fiber, 9 g pro.

Thai basil is a tropical version of sweet basil that's used in Thai and other Asian cooking. Its flavor boasts a hint of licorice. Look for it in Asian specialty markets.

STIR-FRIED VEGETABLES IN THAI PEANUT SAUCE

½	cup chicken broth or vegetable broth
1	fresh jalapeño chile pepper, seeded and finely chopped*
½	teaspoon bottled minced garlic (1 clove)
¼	cup peanut butter
2	tablespoons rice vinegar
2	tablespoons reduced-sodium soy sauce
1	teaspoon toasted sesame oil
1	tablespoon cooking oil
2	medium carrots, cut into thin bite-size strips
1	small onion, cut into thin wedges
2	cups shredded napa cabbage
1	small cucumber, seeded and cut into thin bite-size strips
1	tablespoon snipped fresh Thai basil or fresh mint
	Hot cooked rice
¼	cup coarsely chopped unsalted dry roasted peanuts

START TO FINISH:
30 minutes
MAKES:
4 servings

MENU IDEA:
Steamed snow pea pods tossed with a dash of toasted sesame oil

Fruited Yogurt Brûlée *(see p. 335)*

1 For sauce, in a small saucepan stir together broth, jalapeño pepper, and garlic. Bring to boiling; reduce heat. Cover and simmer about 2 minutes or until jalapeño pepper is tender. Add peanut butter; stir until combined. Remove from heat. Stir in rice vinegar, soy sauce, and sesame oil; set aside.

2 Pour cooking oil into a wok or large skillet. Heat wok over medium-high heat. Stir-fry carrots and onion in hot oil about 4 minutes or until vegetables are crisp-tender.

3 Add the sauce, napa cabbage, cucumber, and basil. Reduce heat to medium-low. Cook and stir for 1 to 2 minutes or until heated through. Serve immediately over hot cooked rice. Sprinkle individual servings with peanuts.

*NOTE: Because chile peppers contain volatile oils that can burn your skin and eyes, avoid direct contact with them as much as possible. When working with chile peppers, wear plastic or rubber gloves. If your bare hands do touch the peppers, wash your hands and nails well with soap and warm water.

Nutrition Facts per serving: 338 cal., 18 g total fat (3 g sat. fat), 0 mg chol., 592 mg sodium, 36 g carbo., 3 g fiber, 10 g pro.

The addition of shredded Havarti cheese keeps the polenta creamy, providing a luxurious base for the chunky mushroom and tomato sauce.

POLENTA WITH PORTOBELLO MUSHROOM SAUCE

START TO FINISH:

25 minutes

MAKES:

2 servings

MENU IDEA:

Crusty Italian bread, sliced, spread with butter and bottled roasted garlic, and toasted

Mango Parfait *(see p. 365)*

1	tablespoon olive oil
1	8-ounce fresh portobello mushroom, stem removed, quartered, and sliced (2½ cups)
1	medium onion, finely chopped
1½	teaspoons bottled minced garlic (3 cloves)
2	tablespoons dry red wine
2	teaspoons snipped fresh oregano or ½ teaspoon dried oregano, crushed
3	plum tomatoes, chopped
1	cup water
⅓	cup cornmeal
1	tablespoon butter or margarine
⅛	teaspoon salt
⅓	cup shredded Havarti or brick cheese

1 In a large skillet heat oil over medium-high heat. Add mushroom, onion, and garlic. Cook and stir for 4 to 5 minutes or until mushroom is tender. Add wine and, if using, dried oregano. Bring to boiling; reduce heat. Cover and simmer for 5 minutes to blend flavors. Stir in tomatoes and, if using, fresh oregano; heat through. Remove from heat; cover and keep warm.

2 Meanwhile, for polenta, in a small bowl stir together ½ cup of the water and the cornmeal; set aside. In a small saucepan combine the remaining ½ cup water, the butter, and salt; bring just to boiling. Slowly add the cornmeal mixture, stirring constantly. Reduce heat to low. Cook and stir about 10 minutes or until polenta is thick. Stir in cheese.

3 To serve, divide the polenta between 2 shallow bowls. Top with the mushroom mixture.

Nutrition Facts per serving: 377 cal., 21 g total fat (4 g sat. fat), 31 mg chol., 345 mg sodium, 33 g carbo., 8 g fiber, 12 g pro.

This zesty bowl-of-red is a blend of both Tex-Mex and Italian flavors.

SPICY VEGETARIAN CHILI & POLENTA

1	medium onion, chopped
1	tablespoon olive oil
1	cup loose-pack frozen hash brown potatoes
1	cup chopped zucchini
1	10-ounce can diced tomatoes and green chile peppers, undrained
1	8-ounce can tomato sauce
2	teaspoons chili powder
1	teaspoon bottled minced garlic (2 cloves)
1	15-ounce can kidney beans, rinsed and drained
1	16-ounce tube refrigerated cooked polenta, cut into 8 slices
½	cup shredded Monterey Jack cheese (2 ounces)
	Dairy sour cream (optional)

1 For chili, in a large skillet cook onion in hot oil until tender, stirring often. Stir in potatoes, zucchini, undrained tomatoes and chile peppers, tomato sauce, chili powder, and garlic. Bring to boiling; reduce heat. Cover and simmer for 15 minutes. Stir in beans. Simmer, uncovered, about 5 minutes more or until desired consistency.

2 Meanwhile, heat polenta according to package directions. Serve with chili. Sprinkle individual servings with Monterey Jack cheese. If desired, pass sour cream.

Nutrition Facts per serving: 350 cal., 9 g total fat (3 g sat. fat), 15 mg chol., 1,251 mg sodium, 58 g carbo., 12 g fiber, 17 g pro.

PREP:
10 minutes
COOK:
15 minutes + 5 minutes
MAKES:
4 servings

MENU IDEA:

Pineapple, honeydew melon, and/or cantaloupe wedges

Purchased apple pie with Butter Pecan Sauce *(see p. 371)*

There is nothing more energizing than a hot steaming bowl of hearty soup on a cold day.

MINESTRONE

START TO FINISH:

25 minutes

MAKES:

8 servings

MENU IDEA:

Sourdough rolls

A Billow of
Berries 'n' Brownies
(see p. 338)

3 14-ounce cans chicken broth or vegetable broth

2 14½-ounce cans stewed tomatoes, undrained

1 15-ounce can white kidney (cannellini) beans,
rinsed and drained

1 15-ounce can garbanzo beans (chickpeas), rinsed and drained

1 6-ounce can tomato paste

2 teaspoons dried Italian seasoning, crushed

2 cups loose-pack frozen mixed vegetables
(such as Italian blend)

2 cups fresh spinach leaves, cut into strips

2 cups cooked medium pasta (such as medium shell macaroni
or mostaccioli)

Finely shredded Parmesan cheese (optional)

1 In a 4-quart Dutch oven combine broth, undrained tomatoes, white kidney beans, garbanzo beans, tomato paste, and Italian seasoning. Bring to boiling; add mixed vegetables. Reduce heat. Cover and simmer about 10 minutes or until vegetables are tender.

2 Stir in spinach and cooked pasta; heat through. If desired, sprinkle with Parmesan cheese.

MAKE-AHEAD DIRECTIONS: Prepare Minestrone as directed through step 1. Cover and chill for up to 24 hours. To serve, reheat soup over medium heat. Stir in spinach and cooked pasta; heat through.

Nutrition Facts per serving: 219 cal., 2 g total fat (0 g sat. fat), 2 mg chol., 1,081 mg sodium, 41 g carbo., 8 g fiber, 12 g pro.

These vibrant and fun tostados can do double duty—as a main dish or as an appetizer for a Mexican-inspired meal.

STACKED VEGGIE TOSTADOS

1	medium zucchini, thinly sliced
1	medium onion, thinly sliced
1	4-ounce can (drained weight) sliced mushrooms, undrained
¼	cup thinly sliced celery
4	6- or 7-inch corn tortillas or whole wheat flour tortillas
2	tablespoons cooking oil
1	cup shredded cheddar cheese (4 ounces)
½	cup dairy sour cream
1	medium tomato, chopped
1	avocado, seeded, peeled, and chopped (optional)
	Bottled taco sauce, hot pepper sauce, and/or salsa (optional)

1 In a medium saucepan combine zucchini, onion, undrained mushrooms, and celery. Bring to boiling; reduce heat. Cover and simmer for 4 to 5 minutes or until crisp-tender, stirring gently once. Drain well.

2 In a skillet cook the tortillas in hot oil about 1 minute or until crisp, turning once. Drain tortillas on paper towels.

3 Arrange tortillas on a heavy baking sheet. Divide vegetable mixture among tortillas. Sprinkle with cheese.

4 Broil 4 to 5 inches from heat for 1½ to 2 minutes or until cheese melts. Serve with sour cream, tomato, and, if desired, avocado. If desired, pass taco sauce, hot sauce, and/or salsa.

Nutrition Facts per serving: 311 cal., 22 g total fat (10 g sat. fat), 40 mg chol., 363 mg sodium, 20 g carbo., 3 g fiber, 11 g pro.

START TO FINISH:
30 minutes
MAKES:
4 servings

MENU IDEA:
Mexican Vegetable Soup *(see p. 302)*

Lemon and/or orange sherbet topped with crushed purchased shortbread cookies

This range-top version of Parmigiana satisfies diners as much as the classic long-baking casserole. A bonus topping of heady basil and crunchy walnuts gives the dish extra appeal.

SKILLET EGGPLANT PARMIGIANA

START TO FINISH:

30 minutes

MAKES:

4 servings

1	medium eggplant (1 pound)
1/4	cup seasoned fine dry bread crumbs
1/2	cup grated Parmesan cheese (2 ounces)
1	egg
1	tablespoon water
2	tablespoons olive oil or cooking oil
1 1/4	cups bottled meatless spaghetti sauce
1	cup shredded mozzarella cheese (4 ounces)
1/4	cup snipped fresh basil
2	tablespoons finely chopped walnuts

MENU IDEA:

Spinach, Red Onion & Cherry Tomato Salad *(see p. 307)*

Purchased carrot cake

1 If desired, peel eggplant. Cut eggplant into 3/4-inch slices. In a shallow dish combine bread crumbs and 1/4 cup of the Parmesan cheese. In another shallow dish whisk together egg and the water. Dip eggplant slices into the egg mixture and then into the crumb mixture to coat.

2 In a 12-inch skillet heat oil over medium heat. Add eggplant slices; cook for 6 to 8 minutes or until golden brown, turning once. Add spaghetti sauce; sprinkle with mozzarella cheese and remaining 1/4 cup Parmesan cheese. Reduce heat to medium-low. Cover and cook for 5 minutes.

3 Sprinkle basil and walnuts over eggplant just before serving.

Nutrition Facts per serving: 295 cal., 20 g total fat (7 g sat. fat), 48 mg chol., 850 mg sodium, 18 g carbo., 5 g fiber, 15 g pro.

You'll love this delectable breakfast or brunch dish. Let the kids help dip and coat the fruit-and-cheese-stuffed toasts.

STUFFED FRENCH TOAST

½   cup cream cheese (about 5 ounces)

2   tablespoons strawberry or apricot spreadable fruit

8   1-inch slices French bread

2   egg whites

1   egg

¾   cup milk

½   teaspoon vanilla

⅛   teaspoon apple pie spice

    Nonstick cooking spray

½   cup strawberry or apricot spreadable fruit

1 In a small bowl combine cream cheese and the 2 tablespoons spreadable fruit. Using a serrated knife, form a pocket in each bread slice by making a horizontal cut halfway between the top and bottom of the crust edge, slicing not quite all the way through. Fill each pocket with about 1 tablespoon of the cream cheese mixture.

2 In a small bowl beat together egg whites, egg, milk, vanilla, and apple pie spice. Lightly coat an unheated nonstick griddle with cooking spray. Heat griddle over medium heat.

3 Dip stuffed bread slices into egg mixture, turning to coat both sides. Place bread slices on hot griddle. Cook about 3 minutes or until golden brown on both sides, turning once.

4 Meanwhile, in a small saucepan heat the ½ cup spreadable fruit until melted, stirring frequently. Serve over French toast.

MAKE-AHEAD DIRECTIONS: Prepare as directed through step 1. Place in an airtight storage container. Cover; refrigerate overnight. In the morning, continue as directed in steps 2 through 4.

Nutrition Facts per slice: 266 cal., 8 g total fat (4 g sat. fat), 44 mg chol., 381 mg sodium, 43 g carbo., 2 g fiber, 8 g pro.

TEST KITCHEN TIP: For a lower-fat French toast, substitute fat-free cream cheese for the cream cheese and fat-free milk for the milk.

Nutrition Facts per slice: 150 cal., 1 g total fat (0 g sat. fat), 30 mg chol., 163 mg sodium, 29 g carbo., 0 g fiber, 7 g pro.

START TO FINISH:

25 minutes

MAKES:

8 slices

MENU IDEA:

Scrambled eggs with mushrooms and shredded cheese

Tropical Fruit Cups (double the recipe) *(see p. 361)*

For a special touch, top these easy-to-make, moist pancakes with fresh fruit and then pass maple or fruit-flavored syrup.

CRUMB GRIDDLE CAKES

PREP:

15 minutes

COOK:

2 minutes per batch

MAKES:

10 standard-size or 20 small pancakes

MENU IDEA:

Assorted fresh fruit

Caramel Hot Chocolate
(see p. 401)

$^{1}/_{2}$ cup all-purpose flour

1 tablespoon baking powder

1 tablespoon sugar (optional)

$^{1}/_{2}$ teaspoon salt

$1^{1}/_{2}$ cups milk

2 eggs

1 tablespoon butter, melted

7 slices white bread, torn into pieces

Maple syrup (optional)

1 In a small bowl stir together flour, baking powder, sugar (if desired), and salt; set aside.

2 In a blender combine milk, eggs, and butter. Cover and blend until combined. Gradually add bread, blending until smooth. Add flour mixture; blend until combined.

3 For each standard-size pancake, pour about $^{1}/_{4}$ cup of the batter onto a hot, lightly greased griddle or heavy skillet. (For small pancakes, use 2 tablespoons batter per pancake.) Cook over medium heat for 2 to 3 minutes or until pancakes are golden brown, turning to second sides when pancakes have bubbly surfaces and edges are slightly dry. Serve warm. If desired, pass syrup.

Nutrition Facts per 1 standard-size pancake: 112 cal., 4 g total fat (2 g sat. fat), 49 mg chol., 374 mg sodium, 15 g carbo., 1 g fiber, 5 g pro.

These burritos are similar to thin French pancakes called crêpes, except that there is no flour in the egg mixture. Slightly mashing the beans helps them absorb the flavors of the other savory ingredients.

KNIFE & FORK BREAKFAST BURRITO

1	cup canned black beans, rinsed and drained
1/3	cup bottled chunky salsa
4	eggs
2	tablespoons milk
1/4	teaspoon black pepper
1/8	teaspoon salt
	Nonstick cooking spray or cooking oil
1	medium tomato, thinly sliced
1/2	cup crumbled queso fresco (Mexican-style) cheese or shredded Monterey Jack cheese (2 ounces)
1/4	cup dairy sour cream
4	teaspoons snipped fresh mint
	Bottled chunky salsa (optional)

START TO FINISH:
25 minutes
MAKES:
4 servings

1 In a small saucepan mash the beans slightly. Stir in the 1/3 cup salsa. Heat through over low heat. Cover and keep warm while making egg "tortillas."

2 In a medium bowl whisk together eggs, milk, pepper, and salt. Coat an unheated 10-inch nonstick omelet pan (or skillet with flared sides) with cooking spray, or brush lightly with a little cooking oil. Preheat pan over medium heat until a drop of water sizzles.

3 For each of the egg "tortillas" pour about 1/4 cup of the egg mixture into the pan. Lift and tilt pan to spread egg mixture over bottom. Return to heat. Cook for 1 1/2 to 2 minutes or until lightly browned on bottom (do not turn).

4 Loosen edges of the egg "tortilla" with spatula; carefully slide out onto a serving plate, browned side down. On one half of the "tortilla," spread one-fourth of the bean-salsa mixture. Top with one-fourth of the tomato and some of the cheese. Fold in half and then into quarters to form the burrito. Keep warm while preparing remaining "tortillas" and assembling remaining burritos. Top with sour cream and the remaining cheese; sprinkle with mint. If desired, serve with additional salsa.

Nutrition Facts per serving: 179 cal., 9 g total fat (4 g sat. fat), 223 mg chol., 389 mg sodium, 14 g carbo., 4 g fiber, 14 g pro.

MENU IDEA:

Frozen crisp potato rounds or potato wedges, prepared according to package directions

Strawberry Dip
(see p. 367)

This meatless version of eggs Benedict features French bread instead of the traditional English muffin. A no-cook mustard and sour cream sauce is a quick alternative to Hollandaise.

FRENCH BREAD EGG BREAKFAST

START TO FINISH:

20 minutes

MAKES:

4 servings

MENU IDEA:

Baked Fruit Ambrosia
(see p. 336)

Espresso or
flavored coffee

¼   cup dairy sour cream or crème fraîche

1   teaspoon lemon juice

¾   to 1 teaspoon dry mustard

3   to 4 teaspoons milk

4   eggs

4   ½-inch slices artisinal French bread, lightly toasted

4   ounces thinly sliced smoked salmon (optional)
    Salt
    Black pepper

1 In a small bowl combine sour cream or crème fraîche, lemon juice, and dry mustard. Add enough milk to make desired consistency. Set aside.

2 Lightly grease 4 cups of an egg poaching pan. Place poacher cups over the pan of boiling water (water should not touch bottoms of cups); reduce heat to simmering. Break an egg into a measuring cup. Carefully slide egg into a poacher cup. Repeat with remaining eggs. Cover and cook for 6 to 8 minutes or until the whites are completely set and yolks begin to thicken but are not hard. Run a knife around edges to loosen eggs. Invert poacher cups to remove eggs.

3 If desired, top each bread slice with smoked salmon. Top with poached egg. Top with sour cream mixture. Season with salt and pepper.

SAUCEPAN METHOD: Lightly grease a 2-quart saucepan with cooking oil or shortening. Half fill the pan with water. Bring the water to boiling; reduce heat to simmering (bubbles should begin to break surface). Break an egg into a measuring cup. Carefully slide egg into simmering water, holding the lip of the cup as close to the water as possible. Repeat with remaining eggs, allowing each egg an equal amount of space. Simmer eggs, uncovered, for 3 to 5 minutes or until whites are completely set and yolks begin to thicken but are not hard. Remove eggs with a slotted spoon.

Nutrition Facts per serving: 172 cal., 8 g total fat (3 g sat. fat), 217 mg chol., 303 mg sodium, 14 g carbo., 1 g fiber, 9 g pro.

The fantastic cloudlike texture of these pancakes makes them worth the extra effort of pulling out the mixer to whip the egg whites.

LEMON SOUFFLÉ PANCAKES

1	cup all-purpose flour
2	teaspoons baking powder
2	teaspoons finely shredded lemon peel
¼	teaspoon salt
1	egg yolk
¾	cup milk
¼	cup butter, melted
3	egg whites
	Maple syrup
	Butter (optional)

1 In a medium bowl stir together flour, baking powder, lemon peel, and salt. Make a well in the center of flour mixture; set aside. In a small bowl use a fork to beat egg yolk slightly. Stir in milk and melted butter. Add egg yolk mixture all at once to the flour mixture. Stir just until moistened (batter should be lumpy).

2 In a medium bowl beat egg whites with an electric mixer on medium speed until stiff peaks form (tips stand straight). Gently fold egg whites into flour mixture, leaving a few fluffs of egg white. Do not overmix.

3 For each 4-inch pancake, pour ¼ cup of the batter onto a hot, lightly greased griddle or heavy skillet. (Or for each dollar-size [2-inch] pancake, pour about 1 tablespoon of the batter onto a hot, lightly greased griddle or heavy skillet.) Cook over medium heat about 4 minutes or until pancakes are golden brown, turning to second side when pancakes have bubbly surfaces and edges are slightly dry. Serve warm with maple syrup. If desired, serve with butter.

Nutrition Facts per 4-inch pancake: 131 cal., 7 g total fat (4 g sat. fat), 44 mg chol., 209 mg sodium, 12 g carbo., 0 g fiber, 4 g pro.

PREP:

20 minutes

COOK:

4 minutes per batch

MAKES:

eight 4-inch pancakes or twenty 2-inch pancakes

MENU IDEA:

Soft-cooked or scrambled eggs

Amaretto Peaches with Vanilla Yogurt
(see p. 375)

Canned pumpkin is the magic ingredient that makes these pancakes moist and hard to resist.

PUMPKIN PANCAKES WITH ORANGE SYRUP

START TO FINISH:

30 minutes

MAKES:

8 pancakes

MENU IDEA:

Refrigerated or frozen diced potatoes with onions and peppers, prepared according to package directions

Hot Gingered Cider *(see p. 401)*

2   cups all-purpose flour
2   tablespoons packed brown sugar
1   tablespoon baking powder
½   teaspoon salt
½   teaspoon pumpkin pie spice
1½ cups milk
1   cup canned pumpkin
2   eggs, beaten
2   tablespoons cooking oil
    Nonstick cooking spray
1   recipe Orange Syrup
1   orange, peeled and sectioned (optional)

1 In a medium bowl stir together flour, brown sugar, baking powder, salt, and pumpkin pie spice. Make a well in the center of flour mixture.

2 In another medium bowl combine milk, pumpkin, eggs, and oil. Add the milk mixture all at once to flour mixture. Stir just until moistened (batter should be lumpy).

3 Lightly coat an unheated nonstick griddle or heavy skillet with cooking spray. Preheat over medium heat. For each pancake, pour about ¼ cup of the batter onto the hot griddle or skillet. Cook over medium heat about 4 minutes or until pancakes are golden brown, turning to second sides when pancakes have bubbly surfaces and edges are slightly dry. Serve warm with Orange Syrup and, if desired, orange sections.

ORANGE SYRUP: In a small saucepan stir together 1 cup orange juice, 2 tablespoons honey, 2½ teaspoons cornstarch, and ¼ teaspoon ground cinnamon. Cook and stir until thickened and bubbly. Cook and stir for 2 minutes more. Serve warm.

Nutrition Facts per pancake: 233 cal., 6 g total fat (1 g sat. fat), 57 mg chol., 278 mg sodium, 38 g carbo., 2 g fiber, 7 g pro.

SIDE DISHES

Lemon peel and ginger are delicious accents to the fresh taste of the asparagus in this luscious serve-along.

GINGER-CREAM ASPARAGUS

START TO FINISH:

15 minutes

MAKES:

4 servings

12	ounces fresh asparagus
½	cup half-and-half or light cream
1	teaspoon cornstarch
¼	teaspoon ground ginger
¼	teaspoon finely shredded lemon peel
	Salt
	Black pepper

1 Snap off and discard woody bases from asparagus. If desired, scrape off scales. In a large skillet cook asparagus, uncovered, in boiling salted water for 3 to 5 minutes or until crisp-tender. Drain.

2 Meanwhile, for sauce, in a small saucepan combine half-and-half, cornstarch, ginger, and lemon peel. Cook and stir over medium heat until thickened and bubbly. Cook and stir for 2 minutes more. Season to taste with salt and pepper. Serve sauce over asparagus.

Nutrition Facts per serving: 51 cal., 4 g total fat (2 g sat. fat), 11 mg chol., 86 mg sodium, 4 g carbo., 1 g fiber, 2 g pro.

Parmesan cheese is something no busy cook should be without. Nicely pungent and salty, it adds a quick flavor boost to crisp-tender asparagus.

ROASTED ASPARAGUS PARMESAN

PREP:

10 minutes

BAKE:

15 minutes

MAKES:

6 servings

2	pounds fresh asparagus
2	tablespoons olive oil
	Salt
	Black pepper
½	cup finely grated Parmesan cheese (2 ounces)

1 Snap off and discard woody bases from asparagus spears. If desired, scrape off scales. Place asparagus in a 15×10×1-inch baking pan. Drizzle with oil, tossing gently to coat. Spread out into a single layer. Sprinkle with salt and pepper.

2 Bake in a 400°F oven about 15 minutes or until asparagus is crisp-tender. Transfer to a serving platter; sprinkle with Parmesan cheese.

Nutrition Facts per serving: 95 cal., 7 g total fat (2 g sat. fat), 8 mg chol., 102 mg sodium, 4 g carbo., 2 g fiber, 5 g pro.

Smoky ham provides a sweet contrast to the pleasantly zingy red wine vinegar dressing.
Use a combination of green and yellow wax beans for extra color.

BEANS & HOT HAM DRESSING

1   pound whole fresh green and/or yellow wax beans,
    ends trimmed

2   tablespoons olive oil

½   cup diced cooked smoked ham or Canadian-style bacon

1   cup cooked or canned garbanzo beans (chickpeas),
    rinsed and drained

2   tablespoons finely chopped shallot

3   tablespoons red wine vinegar

START TO FINISH:

25 minutes

MAKES:

6 to 8 servings

1 In a covered large saucepan cook green and/or yellow beans in a small amount of boiling salted water about 3 minutes or until crisp-tender. Drain well. Transfer to a serving bowl; keep warm.

2 Meanwhile, in a medium skillet heat 1 tablespoon of the oil over medium heat. Add ham or Canadian-style bacon; cook for 3 minutes, stirring occasionally. Add garbanzo beans and shallot. Cook and stir for 2 to 3 minutes more or until pieces of ham are crisp and golden brown. Reduce heat to medium-low. Push mixture to one side of skillet.

3 Carefully add vinegar to skillet. Heat just until bubbly, scraping up browned bits from bottom of skillet. Stir in the remaining 1 tablespoon oil. Stir together garbanzo bean mixture and vinegar mixture. Pour over green and/or yellow beans; toss gently to coat.

Nutrition Facts per serving: 120 cal., 6 g total fat (1 g sat. fat), 7 mg chol., 303 mg sodium, 11 g carbo., 4 g fiber, 7 g pro.

Toasty sesame seeds and savory teriyaki sauce top two favorite vegetables—green beans and carrots. Serve it for dinner tonight alongside chicken or fish.

TERIYAKI GREEN BEANS WITH CARROTS

START TO FINISH:

30 minutes

MAKES:

6 to 8 servings

1	pound fresh green beans, cut into 1-inch pieces (4 cups)
3	medium carrots, cut into bite-size strips (2 cups)
1	tablespoon butter or margarine
1	teaspoon cornstarch
3	tablespoons bottled teriyaki sauce
1	tablespoon water
1	teaspoon sesame seeds, toasted (optional)

1 In a covered medium saucepan cook green beans in a small amount of boiling salted water about 10 minutes or until crisp-tender, adding carrots for the last 5 minutes of cooking. Drain; set vegetables aside.

2 In the same saucepan melt butter; stir in cornstarch. Add teriyaki sauce and the water. Cook and stir until thickened and bubbly. Return vegetables to saucepan; toss gently to coat. Heat through. If desired, sprinkle each serving with sesame seeds.

Nutrition Facts per serving: 62 cal., 2 g total fat (1 g sat. fat), 5 mg chol., 550 mg sodium, 9 g carbo., 3 g fiber, 2 g pro.

Baked beans are without a doubt the ultimate comfort food of the vegetable world. Instead of cooking them from scratch, this recipe starts with a can of pork and beans and adds more beans, bacon, maple syrup, and dry mustard.

SAUCEPAN BAKED BEANS

PREP:

10 minutes

COOK:

10 minutes

MAKES:

6 servings

1	16-ounce can pork and beans in tomato sauce
1	15-ounce can navy or Great Northern beans, rinsed and drained
¼	cup ketchup
2	tablespoons maple syrup or packed brown sugar
2	teaspoons dry mustard
¼	cup purchased cooked bacon pieces

1 In a medium saucepan combine pork and beans, navy beans, ketchup, maple syrup or brown sugar, and dry mustard. Bring mixture to boiling; reduce heat. Simmer, uncovered, about 10 minutes or until desired consistency, stirring frequently. Stir in bacon.

Nutrition Facts per serving: 211 cal., 3 g total fat (1 g sat. fat), 5 mg chol., 870 mg sodium, 39 g carbo., 8 g fiber, 11 g pro.

Baby bok choy—a mild vegetable with pale-green stalks and leaves—is becoming as popular as it is adorable. It's also simple to cook as this quick and easy recipe demonstrates. Look for baby bok choy in Asian specialty markets or large supermarkets throughout the spring and summer.

PAN-FRIED BABY BOK CHOY

12   ounces baby bok choy (4 to 8 pieces) or 1 small bunch regular bok choy, quartered lengthwise

2   tablespoons peanut oil or cooking oil

½   cup coarse soft sourdough bread crumbs

½   teaspoon bottled minced garlic (1 clove)

1   tablespoon soy sauce

2   teaspoons sesame seeds, toasted

START TO FINISH:
15 minutes
MAKES:
4 servings

1 Cut any large pieces of baby bok choy in half lengthwise. Rinse bok choy in cold running water. Shake gently to remove water. Drain well. Set aside.

2 In a large skillet heat oil over medium heat. Add bread crumbs; cook about 1 minute or just until beginning to brown. Add garlic. Cook and stir about 1 minute more or until crumbs are golden brown. Using a slotted spoon, remove crumb mixture from skillet. Set aside. Add bok choy to hot skillet. Cook, uncovered, for 3 to 5 minutes or until stalks are just heated through and leaves are wilted, turning often. Transfer to a serving dish. Toss with crumbs; drizzle with soy sauce. Sprinkle with sesame seeds.

Nutrition Facts per serving: 96 cal., 8 g total fat (1 g sat. fat), 0 mg chol., 314 mg sodium, 4 g carbo., 1 g fiber, 3 g pro.

Fast and fresh, this crunchy, walnut-topped stir-fry is a great Asian-style complement to grilled chicken and cooked rice.

BROCCOLI & PEPPERS WITH WALNUTS

START TO FINISH:

25 minutes

MAKES:

6 servings

¼   cup chicken broth

2   tablespoons bottled oyster sauce

1   teaspoon finely shredded lemon peel

⅛   teaspoon cayenne pepper

4   teaspoons cooking oil

½   cup coarsely chopped walnuts

½   teaspoon bottled minced garlic (1 clove)

1   pound broccoli, cut into 1-inch pieces

1   medium red sweet pepper, cut into bite-size strips

1 In a small bowl combine broth, oyster sauce, lemon peel, and cayenne pepper; set aside.

2 In a large nonstick skillet heat 2 teaspoons of the oil; add walnuts and garlic. Cook and stir for 2 to 3 minutes or until nuts are lightly toasted; transfer to a bowl. Set aside.

3 Heat remaining 2 teaspoons oil in same skillet over medium-high heat; add broccoli and sweet pepper. Stir-fry for 2 to 3 minutes or until crisp-tender.

4 Stir broth mixture; add to skillet. Cook and stir for 1 minute more. Transfer to serving bowl. Sprinkle with walnut mixture.

Nutrition Facts per serving: 124 cal., 10 g total fat (1 g sat. fat), 0 mg chol., 199 mg sodium, 7 g carbo., 3 g fiber, 4 g pro.

Beautiful preserved lemons, with their silken texture and distinctive flavor, give baby broccoli the regal treatment in this dish. Baby broccoli, also called Broccolini, is a cross between broccoli and Chinese kale. Because of its tender stem, it needs little preparation and can be cooked quickly.

LEMON-BRAISED BABY BROCCOLI

1	cup chicken broth
1	tablespoon snipped fresh dill
2	slices preserved lemon*
$1/8$	teaspoon crushed red pepper
$1/8$	teaspoon black pepper
2	tablespoons butter or margarine
1	pound baby broccoli or broccoli rabe

START TO FINISH:

30 minutes

MAKES:

8 servings

1 In a large skillet combine broth, dill, preserved lemon, crushed red pepper, and black pepper. Bring to boiling; reduce heat. Cover and simmer for 15 minutes. Add butter to skillet; add baby broccoli. Cover and cook over medium heat for 6 to 8 minutes or until the baby broccoli is tender. Drain, if desired; transfer to a serving bowl.

***TEST KITCHEN TIP:** If desired, substitute 2 teaspoons finely shredded lemon peel, 1 teaspoon olive oil, and $1/2$ teaspoon kosher salt for the preserved lemon.

Nutrition Facts per serving: 44 cal., 3 g total fat (2 g sat. fat), 8 mg chol., 885 mg sodium, 4 g carbo., 1 g fiber, 2 g pro.

Toasted nuts and broccoli are an appealing combination that is quick and easy to put together. Here a dash of lemon peel makes the broccoli even better while the nuts add some satisfying crunch.

LEMON-ALMOND BROCCOLI

8	ounces broccoli, cut into $3/4$-inch pieces, or 2 cups loose-pack frozen cut broccoli
1	tablespoon butter or margarine
$3/4$	cup sliced fresh mushrooms
1	green onion, thinly sliced
2	tablespoons slivered almonds or chopped pecans, toasted
$1/2$	teaspoon finely shredded lemon peel

START TO FINISH:

20 minutes

MAKES:

4 servings

1 If using fresh broccoli, in a covered medium saucepan cook broccoli in a small amount of boiling lightly salted water about 8 minutes or until crisp-tender. If using frozen broccoli, cook according to package directions. Drain. Meanwhile, for sauce, in a small saucepan melt butter over medium heat. Add mushrooms and green onion; cook until tender, stirring occasionally. Remove from heat. Stir in nuts and lemon peel. Toss with broccoli.

Nutrition Facts per serving: 69 cal., 6 g total fat (2 g sat. fat), 8 mg chol., 34 mg sodium, 4 g carbo., 2 g fiber, 3 g pro.

Glazing vegetables is a fast and simple way to perk them up. Here the spicy-sweet chutney gives Brussels sprouts added appeal.

GLAZED BRUSSELS SPROUTS

START TO FINISH:

15 minutes

MAKES:

3 servings

1 10-ounce package frozen Brussels sprouts

2 tablespoons mango chutney

1 tablespoon butter or margarine

1 Cook Brussels sprouts according to package directions; drain well. In the same saucepan combine chutney and butter; cook and stir over medium-low heat until melted. Return Brussels sprouts to chutney mixture in the saucepan. Stir to coat. Season to taste with *salt* and *pepper.*

Nutrition Facts per serving: 110 cal., 4 g total fat (3 g sat. fat), 11 mg chol., 159 mg sodium, 17 g carbo., 4 g fiber, 4 g pro.

Zesty lemon brightens up the flavor of fresh cooked Brussels sprouts.

BRUSSELS SPROUTS WITH LEMON SAUCE

START TO FINISH:

25 minutes

MAKES:

6 servings

3 cups fresh Brussels sprouts (12 ounces)

¾ cup chicken broth

1 teaspoon butter or margarine

½ teaspoon bottled minced garlic (1 clove)

2 tablespoons chicken broth

1½ teaspoons cornstarch

½ teaspoon finely shredded lemon peel

1 tablespoon lemon juice

⅛ teaspoon black pepper

2 teaspoons snipped fresh dill

1 Trim stems and remove any wilted outer leaves from Brussels sprouts; wash. Cut any large sprouts in half lengthwise.

2 In a medium saucepan combine Brussels sprouts, the ¾ cup broth, the butter, and garlic. Bring to boiling; reduce heat. Cover and simmer for 7 to 10 minutes or until Brussels sprouts are crisp-tender. Using a slotted spoon, transfer sprouts to a serving bowl. Keep warm.

3 Meanwhile, for sauce, in a small bowl combine the 2 tablespoons broth, the cornstarch, lemon peel, lemon juice, and pepper. Gradually add lemon mixture to hot broth mixture in saucepan. Cook and stir over medium heat until mixture is thickened and bubbly. Cook and stir for 2 minutes more. Stir in dill. Pour sauce over Brussels sprouts.

Nutrition Facts per serving: 31 cal., 1 g total fat (0 g sat. fat), 2 mg chol., 158 mg sodium, 5 g carbo., 2 g fiber, 2 g pro.

Add zing to cabbage with butter, balsamic vinegar, and orange marmalade.

ORANGE-BALSAMIC CABBAGE

½   cup orange marmalade

3   tablespoons balsamic vinegar

3   tablespoons butter or margarine, melted

1   2- to 2½-pound cabbage, cored and cut into coarse chunks

1   large onion, coarsely chopped

2   tablespoons water

1 For sauce, in a small bowl stir together orange marmalade, balsamic vinegar, and melted butter; set aside.

2 In a 3-quart microwave-safe casserole with microwave-safe cover combine cabbage and onion. Sprinkle with the water. Place cover on casserole.

3 Microwave on 100% power (high) for 10 to 12 minutes or until cabbage is crisp-tender, stirring once halfway through cooking.

4 Lift cabbage and onion to serving platter with a slotted spoon. Drizzle with some of the sauce. Pass the remaining sauce.

Nutrition Facts per serving: 85 cal., 3 g total fat (2 g sat. fat), 8 mg chol., 53 mg sodium, 14 g carbo., 3 g fiber, 1 g pro.

PREP:

15 minutes

MICROWAVE:

10 minutes

MAKES:

12 servings

Red cabbage adds the wonderful deep pinky-purple color that makes this dish appealing!

ROSY TANGERINE-SCENTED CABBAGE

START TO FINISH:

20 minutes

MAKES:

4 servings

2   tangerines

1   tablespoon lemon juice

1   teaspoon olive oil

4   cups shredded red cabbage

1   large red onion, cut into thin slivers

1   tablespoon sugar

¼   teaspoon coarsely ground peppercorn blend

1   tablespoon finely snipped fresh cilantro

1 Finely shred ½ teaspoon peel from one of the tangerines; set peel aside. Peel, seed, and section tangerines over a bowl to catch the juice.

2 In a large nonstick skillet combine 1 tablespoon of the tangerine juice, the lemon juice, and oil. Bring to boiling. Add red cabbage and onion. Reduce heat to medium. Cover and cook for 3 to 5 minutes or until cabbage is slightly wilted but still crisp, stirring occasionally. Remove from heat. Stir in sugar, coarsely ground peppercorn blend, and ½ teaspoon *salt*. Gently stir in tangerine peel and sections and the cilantro.

Nutrition Facts per serving: 72 cal., 1 g total fat (0 g sat. fat), 0 mg chol., 300 mg sodium, 15 g carbo., 3 g fiber, 2 g pro.

Cauliflower gets the spice treatment with fragrant coriander, cumin, and crushed red pepper.

SPICED CAULIFLOWER WITH TOMATOES

START TO FINISH:

20 minutes

MAKES:

6 servings

5   cups cauliflower florets

1   tablespoon butter or margarine

1   teaspoon ground coriander

½   teaspoon ground cumin

¼   teaspoon salt

⅛   teaspoon crushed red pepper

2   plum tomatoes, chopped

1 In a covered medium saucepan cook cauliflower in a small amount of boiling salted water for 8 to 10 minutes or until crisp-tender. Drain; set aside. In the same saucepan melt butter over medium heat. Stir in coriander, cumin, salt, and crushed red pepper. Cook and stir for 1 minute more. Remove from heat. Stir in tomatoes and cauliflower.

Nutrition Facts per serving: 46 cal., 2 g total fat (1 g sat. fat), 5 mg chol., 138 mg sodium, 6 g carbo., 3 g fiber, 2 g pro.

Keep a supply of frozen vegetables on hand for days when you need speedy side dishes such as these can't miss carrots.

CURRIED CARROTS

1	16-ounce package frozen crinkle-cut carrots
¼	cup chopped onion
2	tablespoons butter or margarine
1	teaspoon sugar
1	teaspoon curry powder
½	teaspoon salt
⅛	teaspoon cayenne pepper
	Dash ground allspice or nutmeg

START TO FINISH:
15 minutes
MAKES:
6 servings

1 In a covered medium saucepan cook carrots and onion in a small amount of boiling salted water for 5 to 7 minutes or until crisp-tender. Drain; set aside.

2 In the same saucepan melt butter over medium heat. Stir in sugar, curry powder, salt, cayenne pepper, and allspice. Stir in carrot mixture; heat through.

Nutrition Facts per serving: 73 cal., 4 g total fat (2 g sat. fat), 11 mg chol., 275 mg sodium, 9 g carbo., 2 g fiber, 1 g pro.

Here is a spectacular way to serve convenient baby carrots.

SWEET SAUCY CARROTS & PECANS

1	16-ounce package peeled baby carrots
2	tablespoons orange marmalade
1	tablespoon butter or margarine
½	teaspoon salt
2	tablespoons pecan pieces, toasted

START TO FINISH:
20 minutes
MAKES:
4 servings

1 In a covered large saucepan cook the carrots in a small amount of boiling water for 8 to 10 minutes or until crisp-tender. Drain. Return carrots to pan. Add orange marmalade, butter, and salt. Stir until carrots are coated. Top with the pecans.

Nutrition Facts per serving: 124 cal., 6 g total fat (2 g sat. fat), 8 mg chol., 365 mg sodium, 19 g carbo., 4 g fiber, 2 g pro.

Honey and a hint of ginger perk up these microwaved carrots.

HONEY-GLAZED CARROTS

START TO FINISH:

15 minutes

MAKES:

4 servings

1   16-ounce package peeled baby carrots

2   tablespoons water

2   tablespoons honey

1   tablespoon butter or margarine

⅛   teaspoon ground ginger

1 In a microwave-safe baking dish or casserole combine carrots and the water. Microwave, covered, on 100% power (high) for 7 to 9 minutes or until crisp-tender, stirring once after 4 minutes. Drain off water.

2 Add honey, butter, and ginger to the carrots in baking dish or casserole. Microwave, covered, on 100% power (high) for 1 to 2 minutes more or until butter is melted. Stir until combined.

Nutrition Facts per serving: 102 cal., 3 g total fat (2 g sat. fat), 8 mg chol., 65 mg sodium, 19 g carbo., 3 g fiber, 1 g pro.

If you think preparing scalloped corn takes too much time for weeknight dinners, try this skillet version. Thick and cheesy, it's ready to serve in just 10 minutes.

SKILLET SCALLOPED CORN

START TO FINISH:

10 minutes

MAKES:

3 servings

2   teaspoons butter or margarine

⅓   cup crushed wheat or rye crackers

1   11-ounce can whole kernel corn with sweet peppers, drained

2   1-ounce slices process Swiss cheese, torn

¼   cup milk

⅛   teaspoon onion powder

    Dash black pepper

1 For crumb topping, in a large skillet melt butter over medium heat. Add 1 tablespoon of the crushed crackers to the skillet. Cook and stir until lightly browned; remove and set aside.

2 In the same skillet combine remaining crushed crackers, corn, cheese, milk, onion powder, and pepper. Cook, stirring frequently, until cheese melts. Transfer to a serving dish; sprinkle with crumb topping.

Nutrition Facts per serving: 199 cal., 9 g total fat (5 g sat. fat), 25 mg chol., 697 mg sodium, 24 g carbo., 3 g fiber, 8 g pro.

It's hard to believe that fresh corn on the cob can be improved—but it can! Sprinkled with one of three spectacular spice blends, corn takes on an extraordinary flavor that will have everyone coming back for more.

CORN SMORGASBORD

12   fresh ears of corn
 1   recipe Mexicali Spice Blend, Italian Spice Blend,
       and/or Herb Spice Blend
¾   cup butter, melted

START TO FINISH:

30 minutes

MAKES:

12 servings

1 Remove husks from corn. Remove silks; rinse corn. In a covered large Dutch oven cook corn in enough boiling lightly salted water to cover for 5 to 7 minutes or until tender. Drain.

2 Meanwhile, prepare desired spice blend(s). Place spice blend(s) in shaker container(s) or small bowl(s).

3 To serve, brush corn with some of the butter. Sprinkle with desired spice blend. Drizzle with remaining butter. (Store any remaining spice blend(s) in airtight containers in the refrigerator for up to 1 month.)

MEXICALI SPICE BLEND: In a small bowl stir together 3 tablespoons chili powder; 3 tablespoons grated Parmesan cheese; 1 tablespoon garlic powder; 1 tablespoon ground cumin; 1 tablespoon dried oregano, crushed; and ½ teaspoon salt. Makes about 9 tablespoons.

Nutrition Facts per serving (with 1 teaspoon Mexicali Spice Blend): 194 cal., 14 g total fat (6 g sat. fat), 33 mg chol., 169 mg sodium, 18 g carbo., 3 g fiber, 3 g pro.

ITALIAN SPICE BLEND: In a small bowl stir together 2 tablespoons grated Parmesan cheese; 1 tablespoon black pepper; 1 tablespoon fennel seeds, ground; 1 tablespoon dried oregano, crushed; 1 teaspoon garlic powder; and ¼ teaspoon salt. If desired, grind the mixture in a coffee grinder to make a powder. Makes about 6 tablespoons.

Nutrition Facts per serving (with 1 teaspoon Italian Spice Blend): 191 cal., 13 g total fat (6 g sat. fat), 33 mg chol., 142 mg sodium, 18 g carbo., 3 g fiber, 3 g pro.

HERB SPICE BLEND: In a small bowl stir together 3 tablespoons grated Romano or Parmesan cheese; 2 tablespoons dried basil, crushed; 2 teaspoons dried tarragon, crushed; 1 tablespoon garlic powder; and ¼ teaspoon salt. If desired, grind the mixture in a coffee grinder to make a powder. Makes about 6 tablespoons.

Nutrition Facts per serving (with 1 teaspoon Herb Spice Blend): 190 cal., 13 g total fat (6 g sat. fat), 33 mg chol., 143 mg sodium, 17 g carbo., 3 g fiber, 3 g pro.

A fusion of hoisin sauce with vegetables gives this side its Asian kick.

EAST-WEST VEGGIES

START TO FINISH:

20 minutes

MAKES:

6 servings

1 tablespoon butter or margarine

1 tablespoon olive oil

1 medium onion, cut into thin wedges

6 green onions, cut into 1-inch pieces

3 tablespoons bottled hoisin sauce

1 teaspoon paprika

1 15¼-ounce can whole kernel corn, drained

1 15-ounce can black beans, rinsed and drained

¾ cup chopped celery

½ cup finely chopped red sweet pepper

1 In a large skillet heat butter and oil over medium heat. Add onion wedges; cook about 4 minutes or until tender. Stir in green onions, hoisin sauce, and paprika. Cook and stir for 1 minute more.

2 Add corn, beans, celery, and red sweet pepper. Cook and stir until heated through.

Nutrition Facts per serving: 166 cal., 5 g total fat (2 g sat. fat), 5 mg chol., 574 mg sodium, 28 g carbo., 5 g fiber, 6 g pro.

Garlic, white wine, and herbs give the mild-tasting mushrooms lots of intense flavor.

SKILLET MUSHROOMS

1	tablespoon butter or margarine
1	tablespoon olive oil
1	teaspoon bottled minced garlic (2 cloves)
2	8-ounce packages fresh mushrooms, quartered
¼	cup dry white wine or chicken broth
½	teaspoon dried oregano or marjoram, crushed

START TO FINISH:
15 minutes
MAKES:
6 servings

1 In a large skillet heat butter and oil over medium heat. Add garlic; cook and stir for 1 minute. Increase heat to medium-high. Add mushrooms to skillet. Cook for 6 to 8 minutes or until almost tender, stirring occasionally.

2 Carefully add wine or broth and oregano to skillet. Cook for 2 minutes more or until mushrooms are tender and the liquid has evaporated. Stir in ¼ teaspoon *salt* and ⅛ teaspoon *pepper.*

Nutrition Facts per serving: 67 cal., 6 g total fat (2 g sat. fat), 5 mg chol., 115 mg sodium, 3 g carbo., 1 g fiber, 2 g pro.

Granny Smith apples add a delightfully tart, fresh taste to these mushrooms.

SAUTÉED APPLES & MUSHROOMS

2	tablespoons butter
2	medium Granny Smith apples and/or Rome Beauty apples, cored and cut into ½-inch wedges (about 2½ cups)
3	shallots, sliced (about ⅓ cup)
1	teaspoon dried thyme, crushed
8	ounces small fresh mushrooms
1	tablespoon lemon juice
¼	teaspoon salt
⅛	teaspoon freshly ground black pepper

START TO FINISH:
20 minutes
MAKES:
4 or 5 servings

1 In a large skillet melt 1 tablespoon of the butter over medium heat. Add apples, shallots, and thyme. Cover and cook about 5 minutes or just until apples are tender, stirring occasionally. Transfer to a large bowl. In the same skillet cook and stir mushrooms in the remaining 1 tablespoon hot butter about 5 minutes or until mushrooms are tender. If necessary, simmer, uncovered, until liquid has evaporated. Stir in apple mixture, lemon juice, salt, and pepper. Cook and stir until heated through.

Nutrition Facts per serving: 120 cal., 7 g total fat (3 g sat. fat), 16 mg chol., 193 mg sodium, 14 g carbo., 2 g fiber, 2 g pro.

Green onions, coleslaw mix, sweet pepper, pea pods, and enoki mushrooms make an appetizing filling for napa cabbage or flour tortillas.

ENOKI MUSHROOM & VEGETABLE CUPS

START TO FINISH:

25 minutes

MAKES:

4 servings

2 teaspoons olive oil

1 teaspoon toasted sesame oil

1 cup fresh pea pods, trimmed and halved crosswise

1 medium red sweet pepper, cut into thin strips

6 green onions, cut into 1-inch pieces

2 3.2-ounce packages fresh enoki mushrooms

3 cups packaged shredded cabbage with carrot (coleslaw mix)

¼ cup bottled hoisin sauce

4 napa cabbage cups or 8-inch flour tortillas, warmed

1 In a large skillet combine olive oil and sesame oil; heat over medium heat. Add pea pods, sweet pepper, and green onions; cook and stir for 2 to 3 minutes or until vegetables are crisp-tender. Stir in enoki mushrooms, coleslaw mix, and hoisin sauce. Heat through.

2 Divide mushroom mixture among cabbage cups or tortillas. Insert wooden skewers through cabbage cups to hold their shape, or roll up tortillas. Serve immediately.

Nutrition Facts per serving: 240 cal., 4 g total fat (1 g sat. fat), 0 mg chol., 677 mg sodium, 45 g carbo., 6 g fiber, 5 g pro.

Parsnips are a versatile root vegetable that can be prepared by almost any cooking method, including baking, boiling, frying, and steaming. Pairing them with apples and brown sugar is a winning combination guaranteed to have you enjoying them more often.

GLAZED PARSNIPS & APPLES

¾ cup apple cider or apple juice

1 pound small parsnips, peeled and cut into ¼-inch slices

2 tablespoons butter or margarine

2 tablespoons packed brown sugar

2 medium cooking apples, cored and thinly sliced

1 In a large skillet bring apple cider just to boiling. Add parsnips; reduce heat. Cover and simmer for 7 to 8 minutes or until crisp-tender. Remove parsnips and any liquid from skillet.

2 In the same skillet combine butter and brown sugar. Cook, uncovered, over medium-high heat about 1 minute or until mixture begins to thicken. Add apples and undrained parsnips; cook, uncovered, about 2 minutes or until glazed, stirring frequently.

Nutrition Facts per serving: 206 cal., 7 g total fat (4 g sat. fat), 16 mg chol., 74 mg sodium, 38 g carbo., 7 g fiber, 1 g pro.

START TO FINISH:

20 minutes

MAKES:

4 or 5 servings

This side dish is so simple—just assemble, sauté, simmer, and serve!

PEAS & ONIONS

1 tablespoon olive oil

1 medium onion, coarsely chopped

1 teaspoon bottled minced garlic (2 cloves)

1 16-ounce package frozen tiny peas

½ cup chicken broth

½ teaspoon fennel seeds or dried basil, crushed

¼ teaspoon salt

⅛ teaspoon black pepper

1 In a large skillet heat oil over medium heat. Add onion and garlic; cook for 3 minutes, stirring occasionally. Add peas, broth, fennel seeds or basil, salt, and pepper.

2 Bring to boiling; reduce heat. Simmer, uncovered, about 5 minutes or until peas are tender and most of the liquid has evaporated.

Nutrition Facts per serving: 87 cal., 3 g total fat (0 g sat. fat), 0 mg chol., 264 mg sodium, 12 g carbo., 3 g fiber, 4 g pro.

START TO FINISH:

15 minutes

MAKES:

6 servings

A light coating of sweet peach preserves, soy sauce, and ginger will tempt even the most finicky eater to enjoy the pleasures of crisp-tender sugar snap peas.

GINGERY SUGAR SNAP PEAS

START TO FINISH:

15 minutes

MAKES:

6 servings

3 cups fresh sugar snap peas or loose-pack frozen sugar snap peas

1 tablespoon butter or margarine

1 tablespoon peach preserves

1 teaspoon soy sauce

Dash ground ginger

Dash black pepper

1 Remove strings and tips from fresh sugar snap peas. In a covered medium saucepan cook fresh peas in a small amount of boiling salted water for 2 to 4 minutes or until crisp-tender. (Or cook frozen sugar snap peas according to package directions.) Drain well; set aside.

2 In the same saucepan melt butter over low heat; stir in preserves, soy sauce, ginger, and pepper. Return sugar snap peas to saucepan, stirring to coat.

Nutrition Facts per serving: 78 cal., 2 g total fat (1 g sat. fat), 5 mg chol., 85 mg sodium, 11 g carbo., 3 g fiber, 3 g pro.

Good friends and good food go together like peas and carrots. Invite a few friends over to take part in an Indian-style feast that includes this colorful dish. Or if it's just the family around the table, serve this deliciously seasoned side with roasted or grilled meats.

PEAS & CARROTS WITH CUMIN

START TO FINISH:

20 minutes

MAKES:

4 servings

2 tablespoons cooking oil

1 teaspoon cumin seeds, crushed

1 medium onion, chopped

$1/2$ teaspoon bottled minced garlic (1 clove)

$1/4$ teaspoon ground coriander

$1/8$ to $1/4$ teaspoon crushed red pepper

$11/2$ cups loose-pack frozen peas

3 medium carrots, cut into thin bite-size strips

1 In a large nonstick skillet heat oil over medium heat. Add cumin seeds; cook for 10 seconds. Add onion, garlic, coriander, and crushed red pepper. Cook and stir for 4 to 5 minutes or until onion is tender. Add peas and carrots. Cook and stir for 4 to 6 minutes or until carrots are tender. Stir in $1/2$ teaspoon *salt*.

Nutrition Facts per serving: 131 cal., 7 g total fat (1 g sat. fat), 0 mg chol., 368 mg sodium, 13 g carbo., 4 g fiber, 3 g pro.

Cream cheese flavored with chives and onion makes instant potatoes incredibly satisfying. The microwave oven makes them even more "instant."

CREAMY MASHED POTATOES

2	cups water
¾	to 1 cup milk
2	tablespoons butter or margarine
¼	teaspoon salt
2	cups instant mashed potato flakes
½	of an 8-ounce tub cream cheese with chives and onion
	Butter or margarine (optional)
	Snipped fresh chives (optional)

1 In a 1½-quart microwave-safe casserole combine the water, ¾ cup of the milk, the 2 tablespoons butter, and the salt. Stir in potato flakes. Microwave, covered, on 100% power (high) for 4 to 5 minutes or until liquid is absorbed.

2 Stir to rehydrate potatoes. Stir in cream cheese. If necessary, stir in enough of the remaining ¼ cup milk to make desired consistency. Microwave, covered, on 100% power (high) about 1 minute or until heated through. If desired, top with additional butter and chives.

Nutrition Facts per serving: 171 cal., 11 g total fat (7 g sat. fat), 31 mg chol., 240 mg sodium, 15 g carbo., 0 g fiber, 3 g pro.

PREP:
10 minutes
MICROWAVE:
4 minutes + 1 minute
MAKES:
6 servings

Thin and crisp fresh pea pods are an excellent substitute when sugar snap peas aren't in season. Just add the pea pods for the last minute of cooking time. They are so tender they don't need much time in the pot.

POTATOES & SUGAR SNAP PEAS

8	small red potatoes (1½ pounds total), quartered
12	ounces fresh sugar snap peas
1	tablespoon olive oil
½	teaspoon dried thyme, crushed, or dried dillweed
¼	teaspoon salt

1 In a covered medium saucepan cook potatoes in a small amount of boiling lightly salted water for 12 minutes. Add sugar snap peas. Cook, covered, about 3 minutes more or until sugar snap peas are crisp-tender and potatoes are tender; drain. Add oil, thyme, and salt. Toss to coat.

Nutrition Facts per serving: 128 cal., 3 g total fat (0 g sat. fat), 0 mg chol., 102 mg sodium, 22 g carbo., 4 g fiber, 4 g pro.

PREP:
10 minutes
COOK:
12 minutes + 3 minutes
MAKES:
6 servings

Kids will eat up the unusual and fun hue of these mashed potatoes. If you can't find purple potatoes in your supermarket, substitute Yukon gold potatoes for a golden dish.

ROYAL PURPLE MASHED POTATOES

START TO FINISH:

20 minutes

MAKES:

4 to 6 servings

1 ½	pounds purple potatoes
¼	teaspoon dried thyme, crushed
¼	teaspoon salt
⅛	teaspoon freshly ground black pepper
3	tablespoons milk

1 Peel potatoes, if desired; quarter potatoes. In a covered medium saucepan cook potatoes in a small amount of boiling water about 15 minutes or until tender; drain.

2 Mash potatoes with a potato masher or fork. Add thyme, salt, and pepper. Gradually beat in milk to make potatoes light and fluffy, adding an extra tablespoon or two of milk if necessary.

Nutrition Facts per serving: 113 cal., 0 g total fat (0 g sat. fat), 0 mg chol., 101 mg sodium, 25 g carbo., 1 g fiber, 3 g pro.

Shape these into mini-sized cakes for the little ones at your table. To tone down the heat, use less of the green chile peppers.

MEXICAN POTATO CAKES

1	egg
1	20-ounce package refrigerated shredded hash brown potatoes
1	4-ounce can diced green chile peppers, drained
1	cup finely shredded cheddar cheese (4 ounces)
¼	teaspoon salt
⅛	teaspoon black pepper
3	tablespoons cooking oil
	Bottled salsa (optional)
	Dairy sour cream (optional)

START TO FINISH:

25 minutes

MAKES:

6 servings

1 In a large bowl beat egg with a whisk; stir in potatoes, chile peppers, ½ cup of the cheese, the salt, and black pepper. Form potato mixture into six patties (each 4 inches in diameter).

2 In a 12-inch skillet heat oil over medium to medium-high heat. (Add additional oil during cooking, if necessary.) Cook potato patties in hot oil for 8 to 10 minutes or until browned and crisp, turning once. Sprinkle cakes with remaining ½ cup cheese. Cook about 1 minute more or until cheese melts. If desired, serve with salsa and sour cream.

Nutrition Facts per serving: 237 cal., 14 g total fat (5 g sat. fat), 55 mg chol., 339 mg sodium, 20 g carbo., 1 g fiber, 9 g pro.

Do you have kids who won't eat their vegetables? Here is a brilliant solution—disguise them! Whipped up with rich and creamy onion dip, this mash is so good they'll be asking for seconds.

VEGGIE MASH

6	medium carrots, sliced
4	medium red potatoes (1¼ pounds total), cut into cubes
1	cup coarsely chopped broccoli
½	of an 8-ounce container onion-flavor dairy sour cream dip
½	teaspoon seasoned pepper

PREP:

15 minutes

COOK:

15 minutes

MAKES:

6 servings

1 In a covered Dutch oven or large saucepan cook carrots and potatoes in enough boiling salted water to cover about 15 minutes or until tender, adding broccoli for the last 3 minutes of cooking. Drain vegetables; return to pan. Mash with a potato masher or beat with an electric mixer on low speed. Add dip and seasoned pepper. Beat until fluffy.

Nutrition Facts per serving: 146 cal., 3 g total fat (2 g sat. fat), 0 mg chol., 173 mg sodium, 27 g carbo., 5 g fiber, 4 g pro.

Fruity mango chutney and creamy yogurt are the perfect toppers for these jalapeño-laced sweet potato and corn patties.

INDIAN-STYLE SWEET POTATO PATTIES

START TO FINISH:

30 minutes

MAKES:

4 servings

1	egg
1	fresh jalapeño chile pepper, seeded and finely chopped*
1	teaspoon bottled minced garlic (2 cloves)
1	teaspoon ground cumin
½	teaspoon ground ginger
¼	teaspoon salt
1	large sweet potato, peeled and coarsely shredded
1	cup loose-pack frozen whole kernel corn, thawed
½	cup fine dry bread crumbs or cornflake crumbs
½	cup firmly packed fresh spinach leaves, finely chopped
⅓	cup sliced green onions
¼	cup snipped fresh cilantro
2	teaspoons olive oil
½	cup mango chutney
½	cup plain low-fat yogurt

1 In a large bowl beat egg with a whisk; stir in jalapeño pepper, garlic, cumin, ginger, and salt.

2 Place shredded sweet potato on several layers of clean, white paper towels; firmly press to remove excess moisture. Add sweet potato, corn, bread crumbs or cornflake crumbs, spinach, green onions, and cilantro to egg mixture; mix well. Shape potato mixture into 8 patties (each 3 inches in diameter).

3 In a large nonstick skillet heat oil over medium heat. Cook patties, half at a time, in hot oil about 8 minutes or until golden brown, turning once. Serve sweet potato patties with chutney and yogurt.

*NOTE: Because chile peppers contain volatile oils that can burn your skin and eyes, avoid direct contact with them as much as possible. When working with chile peppers, wear plastic or rubber gloves. If your bare hands do touch the peppers, wash your hands and nails well with soap and warm water.

Nutrition Facts per serving: 293 cal., 5 g total fat (1 g sat. fat), 54 mg chol., 503 mg sodium, 59 g carbo., 4 g fiber, 7 g pro.

A Southern classic, these potatoes will please everyone in the family.

CANDIED SWEET POTATOES

1	17- or 18-ounce can sweet potatoes, drained
2	tablespoons packed brown sugar
¼	teaspoon ground allspice
1	tablespoon butter or margarine, cut up
2	tablespoons chopped nuts

PREP:
10 minutes
BAKE:
20 minutes
MAKES:
4 servings

1 Cut up sweet potatoes; divide among four 6-ounce custard cups. Sprinkle with brown sugar and allspice. Dot with butter. Sprinkle with nuts.

2 Bake, uncovered, in a 375°F oven about 20 minutes or until potatoes are heated through.

Nutrition Facts per serving: 187 cal., 6 g total fat (2 g sat. fat), 8 mg chol., 88 mg sodium, 33 g carbo., 2 g fiber, 3 g pro.

You can never go wrong with tomatoes. Baking them with flavorful ingredients such as Romano cheese and marjoram turns them into a warm, juicy, and family-pleasing side dish.

HERBED-YOGURT BAKED TOMATOES

2	large tomatoes
½	cup plain low-fat yogurt
2	teaspoons all-purpose flour
½	teaspoon dried marjoram, crushed
3	tablespoons grated Romano or Parmesan cheese

PREP:
10 minutes
BAKE:
20 minutes
MAKES:
4 servings

1 Remove cores from tomatoes; halve tomatoes crosswise. Place tomato halves, cut sides up, in an ungreased 2-quart square baking dish.

2 In a small bowl combine yogurt, flour, and marjoram. Spoon about 2 tablespoons of the yogurt mixture onto each tomato half. Sprinkle cheese over the yogurt mixture. Bake in a 350°F oven for 20 to 25 minutes or until tomatoes are heated through.

Nutrition Facts per serving: 55 cal., 2 g total fat (1 g sat. fat), 6 mg chol., 71 mg sodium, 7 g carbo., 1 g fiber, 4 g pro.

Use fresh rather than frozen okra for this colorful dish because it has a better texture and flavor.

SKILLET TOMATOES & OKRA

START TO FINISH:

30 minutes

MAKES:

4 servings

2	slices bacon
1	tablespoon butter or margarine
1	small onion, cut into thin wedges
1	teaspoon bottled minced garlic (2 cloves)
8	ounces fresh whole okra, cut into $\frac{1}{2}$-inch pieces (about 2 cups)
$\frac{1}{2}$	teaspoon salt
$\frac{1}{4}$	teaspoon freshly ground black pepper
4	small tomatoes, cut into thin wedges
2	teaspoons lime juice
2	tablespoons snipped fresh basil

1 In a large skillet cook bacon until crisp. Remove bacon to paper towels, reserving 1 tablespoon of the drippings in the skillet. Crumble bacon; set aside.

2 Add butter to drippings in skillet. Add onion and garlic; cook over medium heat until onion is tender.

3 Stir in okra, salt, and pepper. Cover and cook over low heat about 15 minutes or until okra is almost tender. Add tomatoes to skillet. Cook and stir about 3 minutes or until heated through. Drizzle with lime juice and sprinkle with crumbled bacon and basil.

Nutrition Facts per serving: 126 cal., 8 g total fat (3 g sat. fat), 14 mg chol., 400 mg sodium, 11 g carbo., 3 g fiber, 3 g pro.

Deep purplish-black kalamata olives add a tangy rich note to this Greek-style side dish. Look for them in the pickle section of the supermarket or at the deli counter.

WILTED SPINACH WITH OLIVES

Nonstick cooking spray

3   tablespoons pitted kalamata olives (about 12)

8   cups lightly packed fresh spinach and/or mustard greens, stems removed

1   ounce feta cheese, cut into small wedges or crumbled

1 Coat an unheated large nonstick skillet with cooking spray. Preheat over medium heat. Add olives. Cook for 3 minutes, stirring occasionally. Remove olives from skillet; set aside. Increase heat to medium-high.

2 Add spinach and/or mustard greens to skillet, adding gradually if necessary. Cook for 1 to 2 minutes or just until wilted, tossing occasionally with tongs or 2 wooden spoons. Transfer to a serving platter. Top with olives and feta cheese.

Nutrition Facts per serving: 83 cal., 5 g total fat (2 g sat. fat), 12 mg chol., 392 mg sodium, 6 g carbo., 4 g fiber, 5 g pro.

20 minutes

MAKES:

2 servings

Take advantage of summer's abundant crop of mild and sweet squash. With their thin, edible skins and tender flesh, they barely take any time to cook.

SUMMER SQUASH WITH PEPPERS

PREP:
15 minutes

ROAST:
15 minutes

MAKES:
6 servings

2   pounds zucchini and/or yellow summer squash, cut into bite-size chunks

1   green sweet pepper, cut into strips

2   tablespoons olive oil

1½ teaspoons Greek-style or Mediterranean-style seasoning blend

¼   teaspoon black pepper

1 In a large shallow roasting pan combine squash pieces and sweet pepper strips. Drizzle with oil and sprinkle with seasoning blend and pepper; toss to coat. Roast, uncovered, in a 425°F oven about 15 minutes or just until tender, stirring once.

Nutrition Facts per serving: 66 cal., 5 g total fat (1 g sat. fat), 0 mg chol., 25 mg sodium, 6 g carbo., 2 g fiber, 2 g pro.

These sesame seed and soy-accented zucchini strips are particularly tasty in summer when your garden is overflowing with the popular green squash.

SESAME ZUCCHINI

START TO FINISH:
15 minutes

MAKES:
4 servings

1   tablespoon cooking oil

2   shallots, halved lengthwise and thinly sliced

1   teaspoon bottled minced garlic (2 cloves)

2   medium zucchini, cut into bite-size strips

1   tablespoon sesame seeds, toasted

1   tablespoon soy sauce

1   teaspoon toasted sesame oil (optional)

⅛   teaspoon crushed red pepper

1 In a large skillet heat cooking oil over medium heat. Add shallots and garlic; cook and stir for 30 seconds. Add zucchini; cook for 5 to 7 minutes more or just until vegetables are tender, stirring occasionally.

2 Add sesame seeds, soy sauce, sesame oil (if using), and crushed red pepper. Cook and stir for 1 minute more.

Nutrition Facts per serving: 70 cal., 5 g total fat (1 g sat. fat), 0 mg chol., 239 mg sodium, 6 g carbo., 1 g fiber, 2 g pro.

Bottled vinaigrettes and other salad dressings are really convenient as fast and flavorful marinades for vegetables. You get great taste without having to fuss over the food.

BROILED SUMMER SQUASH & ONIONS

¼ cup bottled olive oil vinaigrette or balsamic vinaigrette salad dressing

½ teaspoon dried basil or oregano, crushed

⅛ teaspoon black pepper

2 medium yellow summer squash or zucchini, quartered lengthwise

1 small onion, cut into thin wedges

1 In a small bowl whisk together salad dressing, basil, and pepper. Brush summer squash and onion with some of the salad dressing mixture.

2 Place summer squash and onion on unheated rack of a broiler pan. Broil about 4 inches from the heat for 8 to 10 minutes or until crisp-tender, turning and brushing occasionally with salad dressing mixture.

3 Cut broiled vegetables into bite-size pieces; transfer to a serving bowl. Toss with any remaining salad dressing mixture.

Nutrition Facts per serving: 91 cal., 8 g total fat (1 g sat. fat), 0 mg chol., 77 mg sodium, 4 g carbo., 1 g fiber, 1 g pro.

PREP:
10 minutes
BROIL:
8 minutes
MAKES:
4 servings

For a silky, smooth texture, take your time and make sure each piece of butter is completely melted before adding the next.

CREAMY WINE SAUCE FOR VEGETABLES

START TO FINISH:

30 minutes

MAKES:

about 1³/₄ cups

½ cup dry white wine

⅓ cup finely chopped shallots

2 tablespoons white wine vinegar

3 tablespoons whipping cream

1½ cups (3 sticks) cold unsalted butter, cut into 2-tablespoon pieces

Salt

White pepper

Desired cooked vegetables

1 In a medium saucepan* combine wine, shallots, and vinegar. Bring to boiling; reduce heat to medium. Boil gently, uncovered, for 7 to 9 minutes or until mixture is reduced to ¼ cup.

2 Using a wire whisk, stir in whipping cream, then the butter, one piece at a time, allowing each piece to melt before adding the next. Allow about 10 minutes for adding butter. If desired, strain sauce. Season to taste with salt and white pepper. Serve immediately over desired cooked vegetables.

***NOTE:** Because the vinegar may react with aluminum and cause curdling, be sure to use a stainless-steel saucepan and wire whisk.*

Nutrition Facts per 3 tablespoons unstrained sauce: 318 cal., 34 g total fat (22 g sat. fat), 93 mg chol., 40 mg sodium, 1 g carbo., 0 g fiber, 1 g pro.

LEMONY WINE SAUCE: Prepare as directed, except substitute lemon juice for the vinegar. If desired, garnish with finely shredded lemon peel.

Nutrition Facts per 3 tablespoons unstrained sauce: 318 cal., 34 g total fat (22 g sat. fat), 93 mg chol., 40 mg sodium, 2 g carbo., 0 g fiber, 1 g pro.

CREAMY MUSTARD SAUCE: Prepare as directed, except whisk in 2 teaspoons Dijon-style mustard before serving.

Nutrition Facts per 3 tablespoons unstrained sauce: 320 cal., 34 g total fat (22 g sat. fat), 93 mg chol., 67 mg sodium, 2 g carbo., 0 g fiber, 1 g pro.

Add pizzazz to plain cooked vegetables with this intensely flavored blue cheese sauce.

BLUE CHEESE SAUCE FOR VEGETABLES

1   3-ounce package cream cheese, cut up
½   cup milk
⅛   teaspoon white pepper or black pepper
⅓   cup crumbled blue cheese
2   teaspoons snipped fresh chives
    Desired cooked vegetables

1 In a small saucepan combine cream cheese, milk, and pepper; heat over medium-low heat until cream cheese is melted, whisking to make smooth. Stir in blue cheese and chives. Heat through. Serve over desired cooked vegetables.

Nutrition Facts per 2 tablespoons sauce: 65 cal., 6 g total fat (4 g sat. fat), 17 mg chol., 116 mg sodium, 1 g carbo., 0 g fiber, 3 g pro.

START TO FINISH:
10 minutes
MAKES:
about 1 cup sauce

This easy fruit-and-cheese side dish brings out the best in pork, poultry, or fish.

BAKED PINEAPPLE CASSEROLE

1   15¼-ounce can pineapple chunks (juice pack)
½   cup sugar
3   tablespoons all-purpose flour
1   cup shredded cheddar cheese (4 ounces)
½   cup crushed rich round crackers (about 12 crackers)
3   tablespoons butter or margarine, melted

1 Grease 1-quart au gratin dish or casserole; set aside. Drain pineapple, reserving juice (you should have about ⅔ cup juice). In a medium bowl stir together sugar and flour. Stir in reserved juice until smooth. Stir in pineapple and cheese. Pour into prepared dish.

2 In a small bowl stir together crackers and melted butter; sprinkle over pineapple mixture. Bake in a 325°F oven for 20 to 25 minutes or until top is golden brown.

Nutrition Facts per serving: 426 cal., 21 g total fat (10 g sat. fat), 45 mg chol., 375 mg sodium, 53 g carbo., 1 g fiber, 9 g pro.

PREP:
10 minutes
BAKE:
20 minutes
MAKES:
4 to 6 servings

Orecchiette is Italian for "little ears" and refers to the disk shape of the pasta. Your family is sure to enjoy it as it is a nice change from spaghetti and other more common pasta shapes.

SPICY PASTA & BROCCOLI

START TO FINISH:

25 minutes

MAKES:

4 servings

12 ounces dried orecchiette pasta or medium shell pasta (about 4 cups)

2 tablespoons olive oil

3 cups chopped broccoli florets

1 cup chicken with Italian herbs broth

¼ to ½ teaspoon crushed red pepper

1 Cook the pasta according to package directions; drain well. Return pasta to pan. Drizzle 1 tablespoon of the olive oil over pasta; toss to coat. Cover and keep warm.

2 Meanwhile, in a large skillet heat the remaining 1 tablespoon oil over medium-high heat. Add broccoli; cook and stir for 3 minutes. Add broth and crushed red pepper. Bring to boiling; reduce heat. Cover and simmer for 2 to 3 minutes more or until broccoli is crisp-tender. Combine pasta and broccoli mixture; toss to mix.

Nutrition Facts per serving: 404 cal., 9 g total fat (1 g sat. fat), 0 mg chol., 214 mg sodium, 67 g carbo., 4 g fiber, 14 g pro.

Even though it has a pared-down ingredient list and a speedy preparation time, this recipe rewards you with magnificent flavors. Serve it with roasted meats or fish.

SUMMER SPAGHETTI

START TO FINISH:

20 minutes

MAKES:

4 servings

8 ounces dried spaghetti

2 cups cut-up fresh vegetables (such as sliced yellow summer squash, halved baby sunburst squash, chopped carrots, and sliced green onions)

2 tablespoons butter, melted, or olive oil

¼ cup finely shredded Asiago or Parmesan cheese (1 ounce)

⅛ teaspoon freshly ground black pepper

1 Cook pasta according to package directions. Meanwhile, place the vegetables in a colander. Pour pasta mixture over vegetables in colander; drain.

2 Transfer pasta and vegetable mixture to a serving bowl. Drizzle with butter or olive oil; toss to coat. Sprinkle with cheese and pepper.

Nutrition Facts per serving: 320 cal., 10 g total fat (6 g sat. fat), 24 mg chol., 152 mg sodium, 48 g carbo., 3 g fiber, 10 g pro.

Simple pasta dishes, such as this one tossed with tiny super-sweet tomatoes, are popular in Italy. If small tomatoes aren't available, use fresh ripe plum or Roma tomatoes, cut into wedges.

BROKEN PASTA WITH ITALIAN PARSLEY

6	ounces dried lasagna noodles (about 7 noodles)
2	tablespoons olive oil*
½	teaspoon snipped fresh rosemary*
⅔	cup red and/or gold grape tomatoes, teardrop tomatoes, or cherry tomatoes, halved lengthwise
¼	cup snipped fresh flat-leaf parsley
	Salt
	Coarsely ground black pepper
	Parmesan or other hard cheese, crumbled

START TO FINISH:
20 minutes
MAKES:
4 servings

1 Break lasagna noodles into irregular pieces (2 to 3 inches long). In a Dutch oven or large saucepan bring 3 quarts (12 cups) salted water to boiling. Add broken lasagna noodles. Cook, uncovered, for 8 to 10 minutes or until tender but still firm (al dente). Drain and rinse pasta.

2 Meanwhile, in a small bowl stir together oil and snipped rosemary.

3 Toss the cooked pasta with oil-rosemary mixture, tomatoes, and parsley. Season to taste with salt and pepper. Top with crumbled cheese.

*NOTE: If desired, substitute 2 tablespoons purchased rosemary-flavor oil for the oil and rosemary mixture.

Nutrition Facts per serving: 251 cal., 10 g total fat (2 g sat. fat), 6 mg chol., 77 mg sodium, 33 g carbo., 1 g fiber, 7 g pro.

To streamline preparation, buy freshly grated Parmesan cheese. If you like, use light ricotta cheese to save on a few fat calories.

RICOTTA & ROASTED RED PEPPER PASTA

START TO FINISH:

25 minutes

MAKES:

8 servings

12	ounces dried bow tie pasta
¼	cup butter or margarine
½	cup ricotta cheese
¼	cup freshly grated Parmesan cheese (1 ounce)
1	teaspoon bottled minced garlic (2 cloves)
¼	teaspoon crushed red pepper
¼	teaspoon salt
¾	cup coarsely chopped fresh basil
1	7-ounce jar roasted red sweet peppers, drained and chopped (⅔ cup)

1 Cook pasta according to package directions; drain well. Return pasta to hot pan; cover and keep warm.

2 Meanwhile, for sauce, in a small saucepan melt butter over medium-low heat. Add ricotta cheese, Parmesan cheese, garlic, crushed red pepper, and salt. Cook and stir just until heated through. Stir in basil and roasted peppers. Add sauce to warm pasta; toss until coated. Serve immediately.

Nutrition Facts per serving: 256 cal., 10 g total fat (6 g sat. fat), 26 mg chol., 198 mg sodium, 34 g carbo., 2 g fiber, 9 g pro.

What could be more fun than curly ramen noodles teamed with bright vegetables and crunchy peanuts? Ready in just 15 minutes, this recipe has it all.

SPICY PEANUT NOODLES

START TO FINISH:

15 minutes

MAKES:

4 servings

1	9-ounce package frozen cut green beans
2	3-ounce packages Oriental-flavor ramen noodles
1	medium red or yellow sweet pepper, cut into bite-size strips
½	cup bottled peanut sauce or stir-fry sauce
¼	cup chopped peanuts

1 In a large saucepan bring 5 cups *water* to boiling. Add green beans; cook, uncovered, for 3 minutes. Add ramen noodles with seasoning from packets and sweet pepper strips. Cook, uncovered, about 3 minutes more or until noodles and vegetables are tender. Drain. Return noodle mixture to saucepan. Stir in peanut sauce. Heat through. Sprinkle with peanuts.

Nutrition Facts per serving: 372 cal., 19 g total fat (2 g sat. fat), 0 mg chol., 1,269 mg sodium, 40 g carbo., 3 g fiber, 11 g pro.

If your kids are old enough, have them chop and slice the vegetables as you boil the pasta and cook the garlic and onion. No kids around? Buy pre-chopped and sliced veggies at the supermarket.

SUMMER SQUASH PRIMAVERA

12	ounces dried linguine, spiral macaroni, cut ziti, or penne pasta
2½	teaspoons bottled minced garlic (5 cloves)
2	green onions, sliced
2	tablespoons olive oil
2	to 3 medium carrots, sliced
1	medium red sweet pepper, sliced
1	medium yellow sweet pepper, sliced
1	small zucchini, chopped
¼	teaspoon salt
¼	teaspoon black pepper
1	cup chicken broth
1	cup snipped fresh basil
½	cup finely shredded Parmesan cheese (2 ounces)
2	tablespoons pine nuts, toasted

START TO FINISH:

25 minutes

MAKES:

8 to 10 servings

1 Cook pasta according to package directions; drain well. Return to pan; cover and keep warm.

2 Meanwhile, in a large skillet cook garlic and onion in hot oil for 30 seconds. Stir in carrots and sweet peppers. Cook and stir for 3 minutes more.

3 Stir in zucchini, salt, and black pepper. Cook and stir for 3 minutes more. Stir in broth. Bring to boiling; reduce heat. Cover and simmer about 1 minute or just until vegetables are tender.

4 Stir vegetable mixture and basil into pasta; toss gently. Transfer to serving dish. Sprinkle with cheese and pine nuts.

Nutrition Facts per serving: 365 cal., 15 g total fat (7 g sat. fat), 24 mg chol., 776 mg sodium, 39 g carbo., 3 g fiber, 20 g pro.

Luscious whipping cream and a hint of citrus give this pasta dish a touch of elegance.

CREAMY LEMON PASTA

START TO FINISH:

15 minutes

MAKES:

6 servings

9   ounces refrigerated fettuccine or 6 ounces dried fettuccine

¾   cup freshly grated Parmesan cheese (3 ounces)

½   cup whipping cream

1   teaspoon finely shredded lemon peel

    Salt

    Black pepper

1 Cook pasta according to package directions. Drain well. Add half of the cheese, the whipping cream, and lemon peel. Toss gently to coat.

2 Transfer to a serving dish. Top with remaining cheese. Season to taste with salt and pepper.

Nutrition Facts per serving: 245 cal., 12 g total fat (8 g sat. fat), 85 mg chol., 265 mg sodium, 24 g carbo., 1 g fiber, 10 g pro.

Cooked rice is like a blank canvas just waiting for color and flavor to jazz it up. This recipe pairs it with vibrant stir-fry vegetables and roasted cashews. In a pinch, roasted peanuts also will work.

CASHEW VEGETABLE STIR-FRY

START TO FINISH:

15 minutes

MAKES:

4 servings

1   16-ounce package frozen stir-fry vegetables

1   tablespoon cooking oil

⅓   cup bottled stir-fry sauce

    Hot cooked rice

¾   cup dry roasted cashews

1 In a large skillet stir-fry the vegetables in hot oil about 5 minutes or until crisp-tender. Add stir-fry sauce; stir-fry for 1 to 2 minutes more or until heated through. Serve over rice. Top with cashews.

Nutrition Facts per serving: 393 cal., 16 g total fat (3 g sat. fat), 0 mg chol., 720 mg sodium, 54 g carbo., 4 g fiber, 9 g pro.

Fennel with its fresh and delicate hint of licorice becomes even sweeter when cooked with curry powder and tart red cherries in this festive dish.

CURRIED CHERRY PILAF

1	8-ounce fennel bulb with top leaves
1	medium onion, chopped
1	tablespoon butter or margarine
1	14-ounce can chicken broth
1	cup long grain rice
½	cup water
½	teaspoon curry powder
½	cup dried tart red cherries, halved

1 Cut off upper stalks of fennel, reserving the top feathery leaves. Remove wilted outer layer of stalks; cut off a thin layer from base. Wash fennel bulb and chop (you should have about 1 cup).

2 In a medium saucepan cook chopped fennel and onion in hot butter about 3 minutes or until crisp-tender. Carefully stir in broth, uncooked rice, the water, and curry powder. Bring to boiling; reduce heat. Cover and simmer about 15 minutes or until rice is tender.

3 Snip 1 tablespoon of the reserved fennel leaves. Stir dried cherries and snipped fennel leaves into rice mixture. Remove from heat. Cover and let stand for 5 minutes.

Nutrition Facts per serving: 179 cal., 2 g total fat (1 g sat. fat), 6 mg chol., 294 mg sodium, 35 g carbo., 2 g fiber, 3 g pro.

START TO FINISH:

30 minutes

MAKES:

6 to 8 servings

Do you have a pot and 15 minutes to spare? If so, you can whip up this side dish that goes well with grilled or roasted meats. It also can be used as a filling for tortillas.

CHILI RICE

PREP:

10 minutes

STAND:

5 minutes

MAKES:

6 servings

1   14½-ounce can diced tomatoes with onion and garlic, undrained

1   cup water

1   4-ounce can diced green chile peppers, undrained

1   teaspoon chili powder

¼   teaspoon salt

2   cups instant white rice

1 In a medium saucepan combine undrained tomatoes, the water, undrained chile peppers, chili powder, and salt. Bring to boiling; stir in uncooked rice.

2 Remove from heat; cover and let rice mixture stand for 5 minutes. Stir before serving.

Nutrition Facts per serving: 147 cal., 1 g total fat (0 g sat. fat), 0 mg chol., 488 mg sodium, 32 g carbo., 0 g fiber, 4 g pro.

The aromatic spice combination of cardamom, cinnamon, and cloves gives ordinary green peas and white rice a sweet touch reminiscent of the flavors found in Indian cooking.

GREEN PEA & RICE AMANDINE

START TO FINISH:

30 minutes

MAKES:

8 servings

1   tablespoon butter or margarine

¼   teaspoon ground cardamom

¼   teaspoon ground cinnamon

¼   teaspoon salt

    Dash ground cloves

    Dash white pepper

⅔   cup long grain rice

2   cups loose-pack frozen peas

2   tablespoons slivered almonds, toasted

1 In a medium saucepan combine 1⅓ cups *water*, butter, cardamom, cinnamon, salt, cloves, and white pepper. Bring to boiling. Add the uncooked rice; return to boiling. Cover and simmer about 15 minutes or until most of the liquid is absorbed. Stir in the peas. Cover and let stand for 5 minutes. Transfer to a serving dish; sprinkle with almonds.

Nutrition Facts per serving: 108 cal., 3 g total fat (1 g sat. fat), 4 mg chol., 131 mg sodium, 17 g carbo., 2 g fiber, 3 g pro.

Rice has never had it so good—or so tasty! Fragrant garlicky pesto, fresh lemon, and sweet, crisp, plump sugar snap peas give rice the ultimate spring treatment.

LEMON PESTO RICE WITH SUGAR SNAP PEAS

¼ cup dry sherry

3 tablespoons purchased basil pesto

1 teaspoon finely shredded lemon peel

1 tablespoon lemon juice

1 tablespoon olive oil

2 stalks celery, sliced

¾ cup coarsely chopped walnuts

1½ teaspoons bottled minced garlic (3 cloves)

½ teaspoon salt

8 ounces fresh sugar snap peas, halved crosswise if desired

3 cups hot cooked rice

Freshly ground black pepper

Finely shredded Parmesan cheese

START TO FINISH:

25 minutes

MAKES:

8 servings

1 In a small bowl stir together sherry, basil pesto, lemon peel, and lemon juice; set aside.

2 In a large skillet heat oil over medium-high heat. Add celery; cook and stir for 3 to 4 minutes or until tender. Stir in walnuts, garlic, and salt; cook and stir for 30 seconds. Add sugar snap peas; cook and stir about 2 minutes more or until peas are crisp-tender.

3 Stir cooked rice into vegetable mixture. Add pesto mixture. Stir to coat well. Heat through. Sprinkle with pepper and Parmesan cheese.

Nutrition Facts per serving: 234 cal., 13 g total fat (3 g sat. fat), 4 mg chol., 242 mg sodium, 23 g carbo., 2 g fiber, 6 g pro.

The pairing of mushrooms with rice and Italian seasoning makes a savory side dish that takes almost no time at all to go from skillet to plate.

MUSHROOM & HERB RICE

START TO FINISH:

20 minutes

MAKES:

4 servings

1 tablespoon olive oil or butter

8 ounces fresh mushrooms, sliced

1 8.8-ounce pouch cooked whole grain brown rice or long grain rice

1/3 cup shredded carrot

2 green onions, chopped

2 tablespoons water

1 teaspoon dried Italian seasoning or thyme, crushed

1/4 teaspoon salt

1/4 cup finely shredded Parmesan cheese (1 ounce)

1 In a large skillet heat oil or butter over medium heat. Add mushrooms; cook until almost tender. Add rice, carrot, green onions, the water, Italian seasoning, and salt. Cook until heated through and vegetables are tender, stirring occasionally. Top individual servings with Parmesan cheese.

Nutrition Facts per serving: 299 cal., 8 g total fat (3 g sat. fat), 4 mg chol., 241 mg sodium, 50 g carbo., 3 g fiber, 11 g pro.

Give plain couscous some punch with fresh vegetables and an herb. It's perfect for everyday eating or as a company-special side dish.

SAVORY COUSCOUS

START TO FINISH:

20 minutes

MAKES:

8 servings

1 1/2 cups sliced fresh mushrooms

1/2 cup shredded carrot

1/3 cup thinly sliced green onions

1 tablespoon butter or margarine

2 teaspoons instant chicken bouillon granules

2 teaspoons snipped fresh basil or thyme or 1/2 teaspoon dried basil or thyme, crushed

1 10-ounce package quick-cooking couscous

1 In a medium saucepan combine 2 cups *water*, mushrooms, carrot, green onions, butter, bouillon granules, and dried herb (if using). Bring to boiling. Stir in couscous and fresh herb (if using). Remove from heat. Cover; let stand about 5 minutes or until liquid is absorbed. Fluff with fork before serving.

Nutrition Facts per serving: 158 cal., 2 g total fat (1 g sat. fat), 4 mg chol., 241 mg sodium, 29 g carbo., 2 g fiber, 5 g pro.

Take your choice of green or ripe olives for this Mediterranean-style substitute for potatoes.

ZUCCHINI-OLIVE COUSCOUS

1	teaspoon bottled minced garlic (2 cloves)
1	tablespoon olive oil
3	cups chicken broth
1	cup pimiento-stuffed green olives, pitted green olives, and/or pitted ripe olives, cut up
1	10-ounce package quick-cooking couscous
3	medium zucchini, halved lengthwise and thinly sliced (about 3¾ cups)
2	teaspoons finely shredded lemon peel
¼	teaspoon freshly ground black pepper
4	green onions, sliced
2	tablespoons snipped fresh parsley
	Lemon wedges (optional)

START TO FINISH:

25 minutes

MAKES:

8 servings

1 In a large saucepan cook garlic in hot oil for 1 minute, stirring frequently. Add broth and olives; bring to boiling. Stir in couscous, zucchini, lemon peel, and pepper. Cover; remove from heat. Let stand for 5 minutes.

2 To serve, gently stir in green onions and parsley. If desired, serve with lemon wedges.

Nutrition Facts per serving: 190 cal., 5 g total fat (1 g sat. fat), 0 mg chol., 762 mg sodium, 31 g carbo., 3 g fiber, 6 g pro.

The term couscous refers to both the grainlike pieces—similar to tiny pasta—and to the finished dish. Serve this medley as an accompaniment to stew or with broiled or grilled chicken or pork.

FRUIT & NUT COUSCOUS

START TO FINISH:

15 minutes

MAKES:

4 servings

1	cup quick-cooking couscous
¼	teaspoon salt
1	cup boiling water
1	teaspoon butter or margarine
¼	cup slivered almonds
¼	cup snipped dried apricots
½	teaspoon finely shredded orange peel

1 In a medium bowl combine couscous and salt. Gradually add boiling water. Let stand about 5 minutes or until liquid is absorbed.

2 Meanwhile, in a small skillet melt butter over medium heat. Add almonds; stir until almonds are light golden brown. Remove almonds from skillet to cool. Fluff couscous with a fork; add apricots, orange peel, and toasted almonds. Fluff again. Serve immediately.

Nutrition Facts per serving: 250 cal., 5 g total fat (1 g sat. fat), 2 mg chol., 163 mg sodium, 42 g carbo., 4 g fiber, 8 g pro.

Dress up onion soup mix with fresh mushrooms and thinly sliced onion for a soup that tastes like it came from the kitchen of a French bistro.

PRONTO BEEFY MUSHROOM SOUP

1	small red or yellow onion, thinly sliced
1	8-ounce package sliced fresh mushrooms
2	tablespoons butter or margarine
1	14-ounce can beef broth
1½	cups water
1	envelope (½ of a 1.8- to 2.2-ounce package) onion-mushroom soup mix or beefy onion soup mix
1	to 2 tablespoons dry sherry (optional)

1 In a 2-quart saucepan cook onion and mushrooms in hot butter for 5 minutes. Stir in broth, the water, and dry soup mix. Cook and stir over medium-high heat until bubbly. Reduce heat. Simmer, uncovered, for 5 minutes. If desired, stir in sherry.

Nutrition Facts per serving: 104 cal., 8 g total fat (4 g sat. fat), 16 mg chol., 861 mg sodium, 7 g carbo., 1 g fiber, 3 g pro.

START TO FINISH:
20 minutes
MAKES:
4 servings

If your kids love nachos, they will adore this quick-to-fix and spicy soup.

NACHO CORN SOUP

START TO FINISH:

15 minutes

MAKES:

4 servings

2	cups milk
1	11-ounce can whole kernel corn with sweet peppers, drained
1	11-ounce can condensed nacho cheese soup
½	of a 4-ounce can (2 tablespoons) diced green chile peppers, undrained
1	tablespoon dried minced onion
¼	teaspoon ground cumin
¼	teaspoon dried oregano, crushed
	Tortilla chips, broken (optional)

1 In a large saucepan stir together milk, corn, nacho cheese soup, chile peppers, dried minced onion, cumin, and oregano. Cook over medium heat until heated through, stirring frequently.

2 If desired, top individual servings with tortilla chips.

Nutrition Facts per serving: 219 cal., 8 g total fat (4 g sat. fat), 20 mg chol., 898 mg sodium, 29 g carbo., 4 g fiber, 10 g pro.

For a touch of elegance, swirl sour cream or yogurt onto this rich, delicate-flavored soup.
Put the sour cream or yogurt into a plastic squeeze bottle to make the swirling easy.

CREAMY CARROT SOUP

2	cups half-and-half, light cream, or milk
4	teaspoons all-purpose flour
2	6-ounce jars junior carrot baby food
1½	teaspoons instant chicken bouillon granules
½	teaspoon curry powder or ¼ teaspoon dried dillweed
⅛	teaspoon onion salt
⅛	teaspoon black pepper

START TO FINISH:
15 minutes
MAKES:
4 servings

1 In a medium saucepan stir together half-and-half and flour. Stir in carrot baby food, chicken bouillon granules, curry powder or dillweed, onion salt, and pepper. Cook and stir over medium-high heat until thickened and bubbly. Cook and stir for 1 minute more.

Nutrition Facts per serving: 195 cal., 14 g total fat (9 g sat. fat), 44 mg chol., 471 mg sodium, 14 g carbo., 2 g fiber, 5 g pro.

Purchased tomato soup will never be the same! Southwestern-style seasonings give it extra character and punch. For even more flavor, pass additional snipped cilantro to sprinkle on top.

SPEEDY SOUTHWESTERN-STYLE TOMATO SOUP

1	32-ounce jar ready-to-serve tomato soup
1	14½-ounce can Mexican-style stewed tomatoes, undrained
⅛	teaspoon ground cumin
	Dash cayenne pepper or several dashes bottled hot pepper sauce
2	tablespoons snipped fresh cilantro
¼	cup dairy sour cream

START TO FINISH:
10 minutes
MAKES:
5 or 6 servings

1 In a large saucepan combine tomato soup, undrained tomatoes, cumin, and cayenne pepper or hot pepper sauce. Cover and cook over medium heat until heated through, stirring occasionally. Stir in cilantro. Top individual servings with sour cream.

Nutrition Facts per serving: 125 cal., 2 g total fat (1 g sat. fat), 7 mg chol., 788 mg sodium, 23 g carbo., 2 g fiber, 3 g pro.

Start with a can of soup; add zucchini, carrot, and green beans for freshness and color and barley for extra flavor. Serve the combo with crusty rolls and a cheese-and-meat tray, and Sunday night's supper is on the table!

TOMATO-BARLEY SOUP WITH GARDEN VEGETABLES

START TO FINISH:

30 minutes

MAKES:

4 servings

2	14-ounce cans vegetable broth
¾	cup quick-cooking barley
¾	cup thinly sliced carrot
1	teaspoon dried thyme, crushed
⅛	teaspoon black pepper
1	19-ounce can ready-to-serve tomato basil soup
2	cups coarsely chopped zucchini and/or yellow summer squash
1	cup loose-pack frozen cut green beans

1 In a large saucepan combine broth, barley, carrot, thyme, and pepper. Bring to boiling; reduce heat. Cover and simmer for 10 minutes.

2 Stir in tomato basil soup, zucchini, and green beans. Return to boiling; reduce heat. Cover and simmer for 8 to 10 minutes more or until vegetables and barley are tender.

Nutrition Facts per serving: 197 cal., 3 g total fat (0 g sat. fat), 0 mg chol., 1,265 mg sodium, 40 g carbo., 6 g fiber, 7 g pro.

Bacon lends a hint of smokiness to this elegant ginger-accented soup.

PUMPKIN SOUP

3   slices bacon, chopped

1   large onion, chopped

1   29-ounce can pumpkin

2   14-ounce cans chicken broth

1   cup applesauce

2   teaspoons grated fresh ginger

½   teaspoon salt

½   teaspoon black pepper

½   cup dairy sour cream

1 In a 4-quart Dutch oven cook bacon until crisp. Using a slotted spoon, remove bacon, reserving 1 tablespoon of the drippings in skillet. Drain bacon well on paper towels. Set aside.

2 In the same Dutch oven cook onion in the reserved drippings about 5 minutes or until tender. Stir in pumpkin, broth, applesauce, ginger, salt, and pepper. Cook and stir until heated through. Stir in sour cream; heat through. Sprinkle individual servings with cooked bacon.

Nutrition Facts per serving: 132 cal., 6 g total fat (3 g sat. fat), 10 mg chol., 612 mg sodium, 18 g carbo., 4 g fiber, 4 g pro.

START TO FINISH:
25 minutes
MAKES:
8 servings

Blue cheese adds a superb pungency to this creamy soup.

CRÈME OF BLUE CHEESE SOUP

¼	cup butter or margarine
1	medium onion, chopped
⅓	cup chopped celery
⅓	cup dry sherry or dry white wine
¼	cup all-purpose flour
1¾	cups chicken broth or reduced-sodium chicken broth
1	cup whipping cream
1½	cups shredded mozzarella cheese (6 ounces)
½	cup finely shredded Parmesan cheese (2 ounces)
1½	cups crumbled blue cheese (6 ounces)

1 In a large saucepan melt butter over medium heat. Add onion and celery; cook for 3 to 5 minutes or just until tender. Add sherry. Bring to simmering; simmer, uncovered, about 4 minutes or until sherry has evaporated.

2 Sprinkle flour over butter mixture; cook and stir until well mixed. Add broth all at once. Cook and stir until thickened and bubbly. Add whipping cream. Bring to simmering; reduce heat. Simmer, uncovered, for 5 minutes, stirring often. Turn heat to low.

3 Add mozzarella cheese, stirring until melted. Add Parmesan cheese, stirring until melted. Remove from heat. Add blue cheese, stirring until melted. Serve immediately.

Nutrition Facts per serving: 478 cal., 39 g total fat (25 g sat. fat), 124 mg chol., 1,011 mg sodium, 10 g carbo., 0 g fiber, 19 g pro.

Beer adds extra depth of flavor to food. Here it highlights the tangy cheddar cheese.

EASY BEER CHEESE SOUP

2	cups loose-pack frozen cauliflower, broccoli, and carrots
1/2	cup beer
1	tablespoon dried minced onion
1	10¾-ounce can condensed cream of celery soup
1	cup milk
1½	cups shredded cheddar cheese (6 ounces)
	Purchased croutons (optional)

START TO FINISH:
20 minutes
MAKES:
4 servings

1 In a medium saucepan combine vegetables, beer, and minced onion. Bring to boiling; reduce heat. Cover and simmer for 5 to 7 minutes or just until vegetables are tender. Stir in cream of celery soup and milk. Heat through. Add cheese, stirring until melted. If desired, top individual servings with croutons.

Nutrition Facts per serving: 292 cal., 20 g total fat (11 g sat. fat), 51 mg chol., 910 mg sodium, 13 g carbo., 2 g fiber, 15 g pro.

This fresh variation on egg drop soup makes a lovely starter to a multicourse feast, or it can be a light lunch when teamed with a salad or sandwich.

LEMON, EGG & PARMESAN SOUP

8	cups chicken broth
2	tablespoons finely shredded lemon peel (set aside)
2	tablespoons lemon juice
1/3	cup grated Parmesan cheese
	Salt
	White pepper
3	eggs, beaten
2	tablespoons snipped fresh marjoram or oregano

START TO FINISH:
15 minutes
MAKES:
8 servings

1 In a Dutch oven or large saucepan combine broth and lemon juice. Bring to simmering. Stir in lemon peel and Parmesan cheese. Season to taste with salt and white pepper.

2 Pour the beaten eggs into the soup in a steady steam while stirring 2 or 3 times to create shreds. Stir in marjoram.

Nutrition Facts per serving: 84 cal., 4 g total fat (1 g sat. fat), 82 mg chol., 861 mg sodium, 2 g carbo., 0 g fiber, 8 g pro.

Spinach, potato, and curry powder make this sour cream medley irresistible.

CURRIED SPINACH SOUP

START TO FINISH:

30 minutes

MAKES:

8 servings

6   tablespoons butter or margarine
1   large potato, peeled and chopped
4   green onions, sliced
1   pound fresh spinach, washed and stems trimmed (12 cups)
1/3 cup all-purpose flour
2   teaspoons curry powder
4   cups chicken broth
1   tablespoon lemon juice
1   8-ounce carton dairy sour cream
    Purchased croutons (optional)

1 In a large saucepan melt 2 tablespoons of the butter over medium heat. Add potato and green onions; cook about 10 minutes or until potatoes are tender. Slowly add the spinach, one-fifth at a time, stirring just until spinach is limp and dark green after each addition. In a food processor or blender process or blend the spinach mixture, half at a time, until smooth.

2 In the same saucepan melt remaining 4 tablespoons butter over medium heat. Stir in flour and curry powder; cook and stir for 2 minutes. Slowly add broth, whisking until combined. Stir in spinach mixture and lemon juice. Cook and stir over medium heat until slightly thickened and bubbly; cook and stir for 1 minute more. In a medium bowl stir about 1 cup of the hot mixture into sour cream. Return mixture to saucepan. Heat through but do not boil. If desired, top individual servings with croutons.

Nutrition Facts per serving: 192 cal., 15 g total fat (9 g sat. fat), 37 mg chol., 488 mg sodium, 10 g carbo., 6 g fiber, 5 g pro.

Ripe, creamy avocados, zesty lime juice, tomato salsa, and aromatic cumin give this soup a definite Southwestern appeal.

HOLY GUACAMOLE SOUP

1	tablespoon cooking oil
1	tablespoon butter or margarine
1	medium red onion, chopped
1	medium yellow onion, chopped
2	tablespoons bottled minced garlic (12 cloves)
3	medium avocados, pitted, peeled, and mashed (about 1¾ cups)
1	14-ounce can chicken broth or vegetable broth
1½	cups whipping cream
1	cup bottled salsa
2	tablespoons lime juice
2	tablespoons lemon juice
1	tablespoon ground cumin
	Assorted toppers (such as avocado slices, chopped tomato, tortilla chips, dairy sour cream, and/or cooked, peeled, and deveined shrimp) (optional)

1 In a large saucepan heat oil and butter over medium heat. Add red onion, yellow onion, and garlic; cook about 5 minutes or until tender, stirring frequently. Stir in mashed avocados, broth, whipping cream, salsa, lime juice, lemon juice, and cumin. Heat through. If desired, serve with assorted toppers.

Nutrition Facts per serving: 353 cal., 34 g total fat (17 g sat. fat), 88 mg chol., 420 mg sodium, 12 g carbo., 3 g fiber, 4 g pro.

START TO FINISH:

25 minutes

MAKES:

6 to 8 servings

This hearty potato-and-leek soup is equally delicious hot or chilled.

POTATO SOUP WITH CHIVES & GARLIC OLIVE OIL

START TO FINISH:

20 minutes

MAKES:

6 servings

1½	cups refrigerated diced red skinned potatoes or new potatoes, peeled and quartered
½	cup chopped leek*
½	teaspoon bottled minced garlic (1 clove)
2	14-ounce cans chicken broth
6	fresh chives, cut into 1-inch pieces
⅛	teaspoon white pepper
1	cup half-and-half, light cream, or milk
	Snipped fresh chives
1	recipe Garlic Olive Oil

1 In a large saucepan combine potatoes, leek, and garlic. Stir in 1 cup of the broth. Bring to boiling; reduce heat. Cover and simmer about 5 minutes (about 10 minutes if using new potatoes) or until potatoes are tender.

2 Using a handheld mixer, puree undrained potato mixture. (Or add potato mixture to a blender. Cover; blend on low speed until nearly smooth, adding additional broth if necessary. Return mixture to saucepan.) Add chive pieces and white pepper. Whisk in remaining broth and the half-and-half. Heat through.

3 Top individual servings with snipped chives and some of the Garlic Olive Oil.

GARLIC OLIVE OIL: In a small skillet heat ½ teaspoon bottled minced garlic (1 clove) in 2 tablespoons olive oil until garlic begins to brown. Strain to remove garlic. Discard any unused oil (do not store).

*NOTE: Use the white part of the leek plus just a little of the green top to give the soup a pleasant hint of color. To clean the leeks, remove any outer leaves that have wilted and slice the leek lengthwise in half. Holding the leek under a faucet with the root end up, rinse the leek under cold running water, lifting and separating the leaves with your fingers to allow the grit to flow down through the top of the leek. Continue rinsing until all the grit is removed.

Nutrition Facts per serving: 137 cal., 9 g total fat (3 g sat. fat), 16 mg chol., 622 mg sodium, 10 g carbo., 1 g fiber, 3 g pro.

Thick, creamy, and topped with a dollop of sour cream, this creative soup is like having a well-dressed mashed potato in a bowl!

MASHED POTATO SOUP

1 20-ounce package refrigerated mashed potatoes

1 14-ounce can chicken broth

2 green onions, sliced

2 ounces Swiss, cheddar, or smoked Gouda cheese, shredded (½ cup)

Dairy sour cream (optional)

1 In a medium saucepan combine mashed potatoes, broth, and green onions. Cook over medium-high heat just until mixture reaches boiling, whisking to make nearly smooth. Add cheese; whisk until cheese is melted. If desired, serve with sour cream.

Nutrition Facts per serving: 239 cal., 9 g total fat (4 g sat. fat), 17 mg chol., 917 mg sodium, 27 g carbo., 2 g fiber, 11 g pro.

START TO FINISH:

15 minutes

MAKES:

3 servings

Torn spinach gives this meatless, cumin-accented soup a welcome freshness. Fiber-rich chickpeas and sweet nutty jicama—that stays crunchy when it's cooked—offer an unexpected flavor twist.

MEXICAN VEGETABLE SOUP

START TO FINISH:

25 minutes

MAKES:

4 servings

1	teaspoon cumin seeds
¼	teaspoon chili powder
2	14-ounce cans vegetable broth or chicken broth
1	15-ounce can garbanzo beans (chickpeas), rinsed and drained
1	cup peeled jicama cut into bite-size pieces
⅓	cup sliced green onions
3	cups torn fresh spinach
¼	cup crushed baked tortilla chips

1 In a 2-quart saucepan combine cumin seeds and chili powder. Heat and stir over medium heat for 1 to 2 minutes or until slightly fragrant. Remove from heat; carefully add broth and garbanzo beans.

2 Bring to boiling; stir in jicama and green onions. Return to boiling. Stir in spinach. Sprinkle individual servings with crushed tortilla chips.

Nutrition Facts per serving: 201 cal., 3 g total fat (0 g sat. fat), 0 mg chol., 1,599 mg sodium, 33 g carbo., 9 g fiber, 11 g pro.

Coconut milk is the magic ingredient that sets this soup apart from the ordinary. It makes a perfect starter for a Caribbean-inspired barbecue or buffet. Or simply enjoy this soup any time you want a taste of the islands.

SHRIMP & COCONUT SOUP

START TO FINISH:

15 minutes

MAKES:

5 servings

6	ounces fresh or frozen peeled, deveined small shrimp
2	14-ounce cans chicken broth
4	ounces dried angel-hair pasta or vermicelli, broken into 2-inch pieces
1	tablespoon curry powder
1	cup purchased coconut milk
	Sliced green onion or snipped fresh chives

1 Thaw shrimp, if frozen. Rinse shrimp; pat dry with paper towels. In a large saucepan bring broth to boiling. Add uncooked pasta and curry powder; return to boiling. Boil gently for 3 minutes. Add shrimp; cook for 2 to 3 minutes or until shrimp are opaque and pasta is tender. Stir in coconut milk; heat through. Sprinkle with green onion or chives.

Nutrition Facts per serving: 222 cal., 10 g total fat (8 g sat. fat), 53 mg chol., 704 mg sodium, 20 g carbo., 1 g fiber, 12 g pro.

A salad can't shine without a great dressing. Adorn the greens with this wonderfully piquant vinaigrette that features the bold flavors of rice vinegar, Dijon mustard, and tarragon.

ASPARAGUS SALAD WITH TARRAGON VINAIGRETTE

1	pound fresh asparagus
2	tablespoons rice vinegar
2	tablespoons dry sherry or orange juice
1	teaspoon sugar
1	teaspoon snipped fresh tarragon or ¼ teaspoon dried tarragon, crushed
½	teaspoon Dijon-style mustard
⅛	teaspoon salt
⅛	teaspoon freshly ground black pepper
2	tablespoons olive oil
6	cups torn mixed salad greens
1	tablespoon sesame seeds, toasted

START TO FINISH:

25 minutes

MAKES:

4 servings

1 Snap off and discard woody bases from asparagus. If desired, scrape off scales. In a covered medium saucepan cook asparagus in a small amount of boiling water for 2 to 4 minutes or until crisp-tender. Transfer asparagus spears to a bowl filled with ice water; set aside.

2 For dressing, in a food processor or blender combine rice vinegar, dry sherry or orange juice, sugar, tarragon, mustard, salt, and pepper. With processor or blender running, slowly add oil in a thin, steady stream. (This should take about 1 minute.) Continue processing or blending until well mixed.

3 To serve, drizzle about half of the dressing over the greens; toss to coat. Divide greens among 4 salad plates. Pat asparagus dry with paper towels; arrange on top of greens. Drizzle asparagus with remaining dressing. Sprinkle with sesame seeds.

Nutrition Facts per serving: 127 cal., 9 g total fat (1 g sat. fat), 0 mg chol., 103 mg sodium, 7 g carbo., 3 g fiber, 4 g pro.

The buttery avocados, crisp spinach, juicy raspberries, and subtly sweet-tart grapefruits make this salad hard to resist. Use pink or red grapefruits for a sweeter salad and lovely visual appeal.

AVOCADO, GRAPEFRUIT & SPINACH SALAD

START TO FINISH:

20 minutes

MAKES:

6 servings

1   6-ounce package fresh baby spinach or 8 cups fresh baby spinach and/or assorted torn greens

1   cup fresh raspberries

2   grapefruits, peeled and sectioned

2   avocados, pitted, peeled, and sliced
    Several dashes chili powder

¼   cup raspberry vinegar

¼   cup avocado oil or olive oil

2   teaspoons sugar (optional)

1 On a large serving platter or individual salad plates, arrange spinach or mixed greens, raspberries, grapefruit sections, and avocado slices. Sprinkle with chili powder.

2 In a small bowl whisk together raspberry vinegar, oil, and, if desired, sugar. Drizzle over the spinach mixture.

Nutrition Facts per serving: 220 cal., 19 g total fat (3 g sat. fat), 0 mg chol., 58 mg sodium, 13 g carbo., 9 g fiber, 3 g pro.

Fresh pea pods make this salad a real treat. Look for plump, crisp pods with a bright green color.

ASIAN PEA POD SALAD

START TO FINISH:

20 minutes

MAKES:

6 servings

6   cups torn romaine

2   cups fresh pea pods, trimmed and halved crosswise

⅓   cup bottled Italian salad dressing

1   tablespoon bottled hoisin sauce

1   tablespoon sesame seeds, toasted

1 In a large salad bowl toss together romaine and pea pods. In a small bowl stir together salad dressing and hoisin sauce. Pour salad dressing mixture over romaine mixture; toss to coat. Sprinkle with sesame seeds.

Nutrition Facts per serving: 98 cal., 7 g total fat (1 g sat. fat), 0 mg chol., 153 mg sodium, 6 g carbo., 2 g fiber, 2 g pro.

If you think you'll miss the bread, top the salad with baked whole wheat croutons or serve with fresh crusty rolls.

B.L.T. SALAD

START TO FINISH:
20 minutes
MAKES:
8 servings

5	cups torn mixed salad greens or fresh spinach
2	cups grape or cherry tomatoes, halved
8	ounces bacon (about 10 slices), crisp-cooked, drained, and crumbled
2	hard-cooked eggs, peeled and chopped
1/3	cup bottled poppy seed salad dressing

1 In a large bowl top greens with tomatoes, bacon, and chopped eggs. Drizzle with dressing. Toss well.

Nutrition Facts per serving: 126 cal., 10 g total fat (3 g sat. fat), 62 mg chol., 231 mg sodium, 4 g carbo., 1 g fiber, 5 g pro.

To make squash ribbons, draw a vegetable peeler down the length of the squash, cutting it into thin bands.

MIXED GREENS SALAD WITH GINGER VINAIGRETTE

START TO FINISH:
20 minutes
MAKES:
4 servings

1/4	cup salad oil
1/4	cup rice vinegar
2	teaspoons honey
1	teaspoon soy sauce
1	teaspoon grated fresh ginger
4	cups mixed baby salad greens
4	ounces fresh enoki mushrooms
1	small yellow summer squash or zucchini, cut into thin ribbons
1	small tomato, chopped

1 For vinaigrette, in a screw-top jar combine oil, rice vinegar, honey, soy sauce, and ginger. Cover and shake well.

2 On 4 salad plates, arrange greens, mushrooms, squash, and tomato. Drizzle with vinaigrette.

MAKE·AHEAD TIP: Prepare vinaigrette up to 1 week ahead. Cover and store in the refrigerator. Shake well before using.

Nutrition Facts per serving: 98 cal., 7 g total fat (1 g sat. fat), 0 mg chol., 51 mg sodium, 8 g carbo., 2 g fiber, 2 g pro.

Peppery watercress and arugula are given the tropical touch with the addition of juicy, sweet-tart mango both on the plate and in the dressing. When buying mangoes, choose ripe fruit that has a yellow skin blushed with red patches.

SALAD WITH MANGO DRESSING

30 minutes

MAKES:

8 to 10 servings

1	head red or green leaf lettuce, torn into bite-size pieces (about 10 cups)
3	ounces arugula, trimmed and torn into bite-size pieces (about 2½ cups)
½	cup watercress leaves
3	tablespoons snipped fresh basil
3	mangoes
¼	cup rice vinegar
3	tablespoons salad oil
2	tablespoons honey
1	teaspoon snipped fresh mint
1	teaspoon snipped fresh chives
	Salt
	Black pepper

1 In a large salad bowl toss together lettuce, arugula, watercress, and basil; set aside. Pit, peel, and slice mangoes. Chop enough of the sliced mangoes to make ½ cup; set remaining sliced mangoes aside.

2 For dressing, in a blender or food processor combine the ½ cup chopped mango, the rice vinegar, oil, honey, mint, and chives. Cover and blend or process until smooth. Season to taste with salt and pepper.

3 Drizzle about half of the dressing over lettuce mixture; toss gently to coat. Arrange salad on salad plates. Top with mango slices and drizzle with remaining dressing. Sprinkle with additional pepper.

Nutrition Facts per serving: 130 cal., 6 g total fat (0 g sat. fat), 0 mg chol., 29 mg sodium, 21 g carbo., 3 g fiber, 2 g pro.

Baby spinach dressed up with a fresh tarragon vinaigrette and a sprinkling of blue cheese is the perfect serve-along for chicken or pork.

SPINACH, RED ONION & CHERRY TOMATO SALAD

⅓	cup olive oil
3	tablespoons rice vinegar
2	tablespoons snipped fresh tarragon
1	tablespoon finely chopped shallot
¼	teaspoon salt
	Dash black pepper
8	cups fresh baby spinach
1	cup cherry tomatoes and/or yellow pear-shape cherry tomatoes, halved or quartered
¼	cup thinly sliced red onion
2	ounces blue cheese, crumbled

1 For dressing, in a screw-top jar combine oil, rice vinegar, tarragon, shallot, salt, and pepper. Cover and shake well.

2 Arrange the spinach and tomatoes on a platter. Top with red onion and blue cheese. Drizzle with dressing.

Nutrition Facts per serving: 236 cal., 22 g total fat (5 g sat. fat), 13 mg chol., 449 mg sodium, 5 g carbo., 2 g fiber, 5 g pro.

START TO FINISH:

20 minutes

MAKES:

4 servings

With the lively colors, appealing crunchiness, and creamy sweet dressing in this recipe, you won't want to make plain coleslaw again!

APPLE & SWEET PEPPER SLAW

START TO FINISH:

20 minutes

MAKES:

3 or 4 servings

1/3   cup plain fat-free yogurt or fat-free mayonnaise dressing or salad dressing

1/4   of a 0.4-ounce package buttermilk ranch salad dressing mix (about 1 teaspoon)

1   teaspoon honey

2   cups shredded red and/or green cabbage

1   small red or green sweet pepper, cut into thin strips (about 1/2 cup)

1   small apple, chopped

1   carrot, shredded

1/4   cup thinly sliced celery

1 For dressing, in a small bowl stir together yogurt, dry dressing mix, and honey. If desired, thin with a little water.

2 In a large bowl combine cabbage, sweet pepper, apple, carrot, and celery. Pour dressing over cabbage mixture. Toss to coat. Serve immediately.

Nutrition Facts per serving: 70 cal., 0 g total fat (0 g sat. fat), 1 mg chol., 109 mg sodium, 16 g carbo., 3 g fiber, 2 g pro.

Crisp packaged coleslaw mix, juicy canned pineapple bits, and bottled mayonnaise dressing make this as fast to make as it is good. Don't plan to have leftovers!

PINEAPPLE COLESLAW

START TO FINISH:

10 minutes

MAKES:

4 servings

1 1/2   cups packaged shredded cabbage with carrot (coleslaw mix)

1/4   cup well-drained canned pineapple tidbits (juice pack)

2   tablespoons vanilla low-fat yogurt

2   tablespoons light mayonnaise dressing or salad dressing

1/4   cup honey-roasted peanuts, chopped

1 In a small bowl combine coleslaw mix, pineapple, yogurt, and mayonnaise dressing; toss to mix. Sprinkle with peanuts.

Nutrition Facts per serving: 75 cal., 4 g total fat (1 g sat. fat), 2 mg chol., 109 mg sodium, 9 g carbo., 1 g fiber, 2 g pro.

This quick-to-prepare slaw is a perfect addition to summer picnics or backyard barbecues.

DUTCH TREAT COLESLAW

¼	to ⅓ cup sugar
¼	cup vinegar
2	tablespoons water
¼	cup salad oil
1	teaspoon celery seeds
⅛	teaspoon salt
⅛	teaspoon black pepper
¼	cup dairy sour cream
8	cups shredded cabbage with carrot (coleslaw mix)
1	small green sweet pepper, chopped

START TO FINISH:
15 minutes

MAKES:
8 to 10 servings

1 For dressing, in a small saucepan combine sugar, vinegar, and the water; heat and stir until sugar dissolves.

2 In a blender combine sugar mixture, oil, celery seeds, salt, and black pepper; cover and blend until well mixed. Add sour cream; cover and blend just until combined.

3 In a large bowl combine coleslaw mix and sweet pepper; add dressing. Toss to combine. Serve immediately.

MAKE-AHEAD TIP: Cover and chill salad for up to 4 hours. Stir before serving.

Nutrition Facts per serving: 122 cal., 9 g total fat (2 g sat. fat), 3 mg chol., 56 mg sodium, 12 g carbo., 2 g fiber, 1 g pro.

This simple slaw, dressed up with apple and cheddar cheese, is scrumptious with roasted or grilled beef or pork. Refrigerate any leftovers in an airtight container and use within a day or so.

CHEESY APPLE COLESLAW

START TO FINISH:

30 minutes

MAKES:

10 servings

4 cups finely shredded cabbage (12 ounces)

4 ounces cheddar cheese, cubed

2 medium carrots, shredded

1 large apple, cored and chopped

1 stalk celery, sliced

½ cup mayonnaise or salad dressing

1 tablespoon vinegar

1 teaspoon sugar

½ teaspoon salt

½ teaspoon black pepper

1 In a large bowl combine cabbage, cheese, carrots, apple, and celery. In a small bowl combine mayonnaise, vinegar, sugar, salt, and pepper. Pour mayonnaise mixture over the cabbage mixture; toss to combine.

MAKE-AHEAD TIP: Cover and chill salad for up to 4 hours. Stir before serving.

Nutrition Facts per serving: 149 cal., 13 g total fat (4 g sat. fat), 18 mg chol., 265 mg sodium, 6 g carbo., 2 g fiber, 4 g pro.

Maple syrup works magic here. It brings out the sweetness of the pecans and oranges and is a marvelous complement to the tangy spinach and savory bacon.

CITRUS SALAD WITH GLAZED PECANS

3	tablespoons red wine vinegar
3	tablespoons olive oil
2	tablespoons Dijon-style mustard
1	tablespoon pure maple syrup or maple-flavored syrup
1/3	cup coarsely chopped pecans
2	tablespoons pure maple syrup or maple-flavored syrup
2	slices bacon, cut up
1/2	of a medium red onion, cut into thin wedges
6	ounces fresh baby spinach, washed and stems removed
4	blood oranges or oranges, peeled, seeded, and thinly sliced

START TO FINISH:

30 minutes

MAKES:

4 servings

1 In a screw-top jar combine red wine vinegar, oil, Dijon-style mustard, and the 1 tablespoon maple syrup. Cover and shake well. Set aside.

2 In a medium skillet cook pecans in the 2 tablespoons maple syrup over medium heat for 3 to 4 minutes or until lightly toasted. Spread nuts on foil; cool. Break nuts into clusters.

3 Meanwhile, in a small saucepan cook bacon and red onion wedges until bacon is crisp, stirring occasionally. Remove from heat.

4 To serve, divide spinach and oranges among 4 salad plates. Top with bacon-onion mixture and pecans; drizzle with dressing.

Nutrition Facts per serving: 254 cal., 19 g total fat (3 g sat. fat), 3 mg chol., 142 mg sodium, 20 g carbo., 6 g fiber, 14 g pro.

This salad is almost too pretty to eat! It's sure to be a big hit with even the pickiest eater in your family.

MANDARIN-BERRY SALAD

START TO FINISH:

30 minutes

MAKES:

6 servings

6 cups torn mixed salad greens

1 cup fresh strawberries, hulled and quartered

4 green onions, sliced

½ cup canned rice noodles

¼ cup sliced almonds, toasted

1 11-ounce can mandarin orange sections, drained

¼ cup flaked coconut

2 teaspoons honey

2 teaspoons salad oil

2 teaspoons balsamic vinegar

½ teaspoon ground ginger

½ teaspoon salt

¼ teaspoon black pepper

2 ounces semisoft goat cheese, crumbled

1 In a large bowl combine greens, strawberries, green onions, rice noodles, and almonds. Set aside.

2 For dressing, in a food processor or blender combine ½ cup of the oranges, the coconut, honey, oil, vinegar, ginger, salt, and pepper. Cover; process or blend until combined.

3 Pour dressing over greens mixture; toss to coat. Top with remaining oranges and the cheese.

Nutrition Facts per serving: 153 cal., 9 g total fat (3 g sat. fat), 4 mg chol., 308 mg sodium, 16 g carbo., 3 g fiber, 4 g pro.

This fruity and fun dish makes a great kid-friendly snack or side dish.

PEANUT BUTTER FRUIT SALAD

1	8-ounce can pineapple tidbits (juice pack)
2	medium carrots, shredded
1	11-ounce can mandarin orange sections, drained
2/3	cup chopped apple
1/2	cup raisins and/or dried tart cherries
1/3	cup apple-cinnamon low-fat yogurt
2	tablespoons peanut butter
1	tablespoon shelled sunflower seeds

1 Drain the pineapple tidbits, reserving 1 tablespoon of the juice; set juice aside. If desired, set aside some of the shredded carrots for garnish. In a medium bowl stir together pineapple tidbits, the remaining carrots, oranges, apple, and raisins and/or cherries.

2 In a small bowl stir together yogurt, peanut butter, and reserved pineapple juice. Add to fruit mixture; stir to coat. Sprinkle with sunflower seeds and, if desired, reserved carrots.

Nutrition Facts per serving: 152 cal., 4 g total fat (1 g sat. fat), 1 mg chol., 44 mg sodium, 29 g carbo., 3 g fiber, 3 g pro.

START TO FINISH:
15 minutes
MAKES:
6 servings

A simple three-ingredient dressing livens up a bowl of fresh fruit. Try peaches, papaya, strawberries, and raspberries or create your own fruit combination.

SUMMER FRUIT WITH SESAME DRESSING

START TO FINISH:

25 minutes

MAKES:

6 servings

2   cups sliced peeled peaches or sliced nectarines

1   cup sliced peeled papaya or mango

1/2   cup sliced fresh strawberries

1/2   cup fresh raspberries

1/4   cup rice vinegar

1   teaspoon honey

1/2   teaspoon toasted sesame oil

6   cups fresh spinach leaves

2   tablespoons snipped fresh mint

1 In a large bowl combine peaches or nectarines, papaya or mango, strawberries, and raspberries. Set aside.

2 For vinaigrette, in a small bowl whisk together rice vinegar, honey, and sesame oil. Pour vinaigrette over fruit; toss gently to coat.

3 Serve fruit mixture over spinach. Sprinkle with fresh mint.

Nutrition Facts per serving: 80 cal., 1 g total fat (0 g sat. fat), 0 mg chol., 40 mg sodium, 18 g carbo., 7 g fiber, 2 g pro.

Combining orange yogurt with sweet mandarin orange sections and other fruits is a refreshing way to perk up a meal.

ORANGE DREAM FRUIT SALAD

START TO FINISH:

15 minutes

MAKES:

4 to 6 servings

1   cup chopped, peeled, seeded mango or papaya

1   11-ounce can mandarin orange sections, drained

1   cup seedless red and/or green grapes, halved

1/2   cup orange yogurt

1/4   teaspoon poppy seeds

1 In a medium bowl combine mango or papaya, mandarin oranges, and grapes. In a small bowl stir together yogurt and poppy seeds. Gently stir yogurt mixture into fruit mixture until combined.

Nutrition Facts per serving: 136 cal., 1 g total fat (0 g sat. fat), 2 mg chol., 26 mg sodium, 32 g carbo., 2 g fiber, 2 g pro.

This inventive salad is perfect for summer when you can find fresh raspberries in the store or pluck them from your backyard raspberry patch. Buttery-rich toasted pecans deliver some crunch to complement the soft textures of the fruit and mixed greens.

RASPBERRY PECAN SALAD

1/3	cup raspberry spreadable fruit
1/4	cup raspberry vinegar
1/4	cup salad oil
1	tablespoon honey
1	teaspoon poppy seeds
8	cups torn mixed salad greens
1	cup fresh raspberries
1	medium avocado, pitted, peeled, and sliced
1	cup sliced fresh mushrooms
1/2	cup pecans, toasted

START TO FINISH:

25 minutes

MAKES:

8 servings

1 For dressing, in a blender combine spreadable fruit, raspberry vinegar, oil, honey, and poppy seeds. Cover and blend until combined. (Or in a medium bowl whisk together the ingredients.) Set aside.

2 In a large salad bowl combine greens, raspberries, avocado, mushrooms, and pecans. Drizzle dressing over the salad. Toss to combine.

Nutrition Facts per serving: 201 cal., 16 g total fat (2 g sat. fat), 0 mg chol., 10 mg sodium, 16 g carbo., 4 g fiber, 2 g pro.

If you haven't tried edamame, the Japanese name for fresh green soybeans, here's a tasty way to sample them. The barley and edamame mixture spooned over spinach and tomatoes makes an enticing addition to a summer meal.

BEANS, BARLEY & TOMATOES

START TO FINISH:

30 minutes

MAKES:

6 servings

1   14-ounce can vegetable broth or chicken broth

1   teaspoon Greek seasoning or garam masala

1   cup loose-pack frozen green soybeans (shelled edamame)

¾   cup quick-cooking barley

1   medium carrot, shredded

4   cups fresh spinach leaves

4   small to medium tomatoes, sliced

1 In a medium saucepan combine broth and seasoning; bring to boiling. Add soybeans and barley. Return to boiling; reduce heat. Cover and simmer for 12 minutes. Stir carrot into barley mixture.

2 Meanwhile, divide spinach among 6 salad plates. Arrange tomato slices on spinach. Using a slotted spoon, spoon barley mixture over tomatoes. (Or drain barley mixture; spoon over tomatoes.)

MAKE-AHEAD DIRECTIONS: Prepare as directed through step 1. Cover and chill barley mixture for up to 24 hours. Arrange spinach and tomatoes as directed. Spoon chilled barley mixture over tomatoes.

Nutrition Facts per serving: 157 cal., 3 g total fat (0 g sat. fat), 0 mg chol., 314 mg sodium, 25 g carbo., 5 g fiber, 9 g pro.

Serve this vibrant rice, fruit, and vegetable salad with sourdough bread slices or breadsticks.

CONFETTI RICE SALAD

1   cup chilled cooked rice

1   cup shredded red or green cabbage

½   cup chopped tomato

¼   cup dried tart cherries

2   tablespoons chopped honey-roasted peanuts

1   tablespoon sliced green onion (optional)

¼   cup bottled sweet and spicy French salad dressing

1 In a medium bowl combine rice, cabbage, tomato, dried cherries, peanuts, and, if desired, green onion; toss to mix. Drizzle with salad dressing; gently stir to coat.

Nutrition Facts per serving: 171 cal., 8 g total fat (1 g sat. fat), 0 mg chol., 186 mg sodium, 23 g carbo., 1 g fiber, 3 g pro.

START TO FINISH:

15 minutes

MAKES:

4 servings

When unexpected summer guests stop by, whip up this four-ingredient special to serve with grilled burgers or hot dogs.

ITALIAN-STYLE MACARONI SALAD

1   7¼-ounce package macaroni and cheese dinner mix

1   cup loose-pack frozen pepper stir-fry vegetables (yellow, green, and red peppers and onions)

1   large tomato, seeded and chopped

⅓   cup bottled Italian salad dressing

1 Prepare dinner mix according to package directions. Transfer to a large bowl. Cover and chill in freezer for 10 minutes, stirring once.

2 Stir in stir-fry vegetables, tomato, and Italian dressing.

Nutrition Facts per serving: 399 cal., 17 g total fat (7 g sat. fat), 35 mg chol., 906 mg sodium, 49 g carbo., 2 g fiber, 11 g pro.

START TO FINISH:

30 minutes

MAKES:

4 servings

Mix and match the vegetables you use in this cheesy bow tie salad that's tossed with a creamy homemade French dressing.

BEST-DRESSED PASTA SALAD

START TO FINISH:

30 minutes

MAKES:

8 to 10 servings

12	ounces dried bow tie pasta (4 cups)
1/3	cup salad oil
1/4	cup ketchup
1/4	cup mayonnaise or salad dressing
3	tablespoons cider vinegar
1	teaspoon sugar
1/2	teaspoon paprika
1/4	teaspoon salt
1/4	teaspoon black pepper
2 1/2	cups sliced or chopped desired vegetables (such as carrots, sweet peppers, green onions, and/or celery)
6	ounces cheddar and/or mozzarella cheese, cubed (1 1/2 cups)

1 Cook pasta according to package directions; drain. Rinse with cold water; drain again.

2 Meanwhile, for dressing, in a screw-top jar combine oil, ketchup, mayonnaise, cider vinegar, sugar, paprika, salt, and black pepper. Cover and shake well. Set aside.

3 In a very large bowl combine cooked pasta, desired vegetables, and cheese. Pour dressing over pasta mixture; toss gently to coat.

MAKE-AHEAD TIP: Cover and chill salad for up to 4 hours. Stir before serving.

Nutrition Facts per serving: 403 cal., 23 g total fat (7 g sat. fat), 68 mg chol., 362 mg sodium, 37 g carbo., 2 g fiber, 12 g pro.

The beguiling combination of fruit and wild rice will have you hooked with the first bite. Fresh blueberries make a lovely substitute if raspberries aren't available.

FRUITED WILD RICE & SPINACH SALAD

6	cups torn fresh spinach
2	cups cooled, cooked wild rice
1	cup seedless green grapes, halved
¼	cup shelled sunflower seeds
¼	cup white balsamic vinegar or cider vinegar
¼	cup olive oil
1	tablespoon honey
2	teaspoons snipped fresh basil or ½ teaspoon dried basil, crushed
¼	teaspoon salt
¼	teaspoon freshly ground black pepper
1	cup fresh raspberries
2	oranges, peeled and sectioned

START TO FINISH:

30 minutes

MAKES:

6 servings

1 In a large salad bowl combine spinach, wild rice, grapes, and sunflower seeds. For dressing, in a screw-top jar combine vinegar, oil, honey, basil, salt, and pepper. Cover and shake well. Pour over spinach mixture; toss to coat.

2 Gently fold in raspberries and orange sections.

Nutrition Facts per serving: 235 cal., 13 g total fat (2 g sat. fat), 0 mg chol., 139 mg sodium, 28 g carbo., 7 g fiber, 5 g pro.

The ultimate in quick and delicious, this salad, loaded with ripe tomatoes and fragrant fresh basil leaves, screams summer goodness! With only 15 minutes of prep time, you can celebrate the fresh produce season whenever you like.

MOZZARELLA CAPRESE

START TO FINISH:

15 minutes

MAKES:

8 servings

4   medium tomatoes or 6 plum tomatoes

4   ounces fresh mozzarella cheese balls

2   tablespoons bottled balsamic vinaigrette salad dressing

½   cup loosely packed fresh basil leaves, thinly sliced

    Salt

    Cracked black pepper

1 Cut tomatoes into ½-inch slices. Cut mozzarella into ¼-inch slices. Arrange tomato and cheese slices on a platter. Drizzle with vinaigrette. Sprinkle basil shreds on top. Sprinkle with salt and pepper.

Nutrition Facts per serving: 64 cal., 4 g total fat (2 g sat. fat), 11 mg chol., 174 mg sodium, 4 g carbo., 1 g fiber, 3 g pro.

Even kids will love broccoli when it's teamed with some cheddar cheese, bacon, and a creamy dressing.

BROCCOLI-CHEDDAR SALAD

START TO FINISH:

20 minutes

MAKES:

6 servings

4   cups broccoli florets

1   small red onion, chopped or cut into thin wedges

1   cup cubed cheddar or smoked cheddar cheese

5   slices bacon, crisp-cooked, drained, and crumbled

½   cup mayonnaise or salad dressing

¼   cup bottled coleslaw or buttermilk ranch salad dressing

2   tablespoons vinegar

1   tablespoon sugar

1 In a large salad bowl combine broccoli, red onion, cheese, and bacon.

2 For dressing, in a small bowl stir together mayonnaise, coleslaw dressing, vinegar, and sugar. Pour over broccoli mixture; toss to coat.

MAKE-AHEAD TIP: Cover and chill salad for up to 2 hours. Stir salad before serving.

Nutrition Facts per serving: 330 cal., 30 g total fat (8 g sat. fat), 34 mg chol., 400 mg sodium, 8 g carbo., 2 g fiber, 9 g pro.

You can find avocado dip for this make-ahead salad in the dairy case.

EASY BEAN SALAD

1	15-ounce can three-bean salad, drained
1	15-ounce can pinto beans, rinsed and drained
1	small cucumber, chopped
1	medium tomato, seeded and chopped
½	cup refrigerated guacamole (avocado dip)
	Several dashes bottled hot pepper sauce

1 In a medium bowl combine drained three-bean salad, pinto beans, cucumber, and tomato. Add guacamole and hot pepper sauce. Toss until bean mixture is coated.

MAKE-AHEAD TIP: Cover and chill salad for up to 8 hours. Stir salad before serving.

Nutrition Facts per serving: 111 cal., 2 g total fat (0 g sat. fat), 0 mg chol., 426 mg sodium, 20 g carbo., 5 g fiber, 5 g pro.

START TO FINISH:
15 minutes
MAKES:
8 servings

Three-bean salad gets a delectable makeover when it's made with kidney, butter, and garbanzo beans and dressed with a mustard-tarragon vinaigrette.

TARRAGON BEAN SALAD

START TO FINISH:

20 minutes

MAKES:

8 to 10 servings

1	15-ounce can red kidney beans, rinsed and drained
1	15-ounce can butter beans, rinsed and drained
1	15-ounce can garbanzo beans (chickpeas), rinsed and drained
1½	cups chopped seeded tomatoes or halved cherry or grape tomatoes
1	medium carrot, cut into thin bite-size strips
2	tablespoons finely chopped red onion
3	tablespoons olive oil
2	tablespoons red wine vinegar
2	tablespoons Dijon-style mustard
1	tablespoon snipped fresh tarragon or ½ teaspoon dried tarragon, crushed
1	teaspoon sugar
¼	teaspoon salt
⅛	teaspoon black pepper

1 In a large bowl combine kidney beans, butter beans, garbanzo beans, tomatoes, carrot, and red onion.

2 For dressing, in a screw-top jar combine oil, vinegar, mustard, tarragon, sugar, salt, and pepper. Cover and shake well. Pour dressing over bean mixture; gently toss to coat.

Nutrition Facts per serving: 209 cal., 6 g total fat (1 g sat. fat), 0 mg chol., 628 mg sodium, 31 g carbo., 8 g fiber, 9 g pro.

Plump and deliciously sweet blueberries make these orange-accented muffins scrumptious. Serve them plain or with a dab of honey. For a special treat, combine honey with some light cream cheese and spread the mixture on the muffin tops.

BLUEBERRY GEMS

	Nonstick cooking spray
1½	cups all-purpose flour
¼	cup sugar
1½	teaspoons baking powder
2	egg whites
⅔	cup orange juice
2	tablespoons cooking oil
1	teaspoon vanilla
1	cup fresh or frozen blueberries

PREP:
10 minutes
BAKE:
15 minutes
COOL:
5 minutes
MAKES:
36 muffins

1 Lightly coat thirty-six 1¾-inch muffin cups with cooking spray. In a medium bowl stir together flour, sugar, baking powder, and ¼ teaspoon *salt*. Make a well in center of flour mixture; set aside. In bowl stir together egg whites, orange juice, oil, and vanilla. Add egg white mixture all at once to flour mixture; stir just until moistened. Fold in blueberries. Spoon into prepared muffin cups, filling each about ⅔ full.

2 Bake in a 400°F oven for 15 to 18 minutes or until toothpick inserted into centers comes out clean. Cool in pans on wire racks for 5 minutes.

Nutrition Facts per muffin: 35 cal., 1 g total fat (0 g sat. fat), 0 mg chol., 36 mg sodium, 6 g carbo., 0 g fiber, 1 g pro.

In only minutes you can transform plain corn muffins into a special treat that your family won't be able to resist. Chopped pecans add a rich nutty flavor while honey provides a touch of sweetness to complement the earthy cornmeal.

HONEY-NUT CORN MUFFINS

1	8½-ounce package corn muffin mix
½	cup chopped pecans
2	tablespoons honey

PREP:
10 minutes
BAKE:
15 minutes
MAKES:
6 to 8 muffins

1 Grease six to eight 2½-inch muffin cups; set aside.

2 Prepare corn muffin mix according to package directions, except stir in nuts and honey. Spoon batter into prepared muffin cups, filling each about ¾ full.

3 Bake in a 400°F oven about 15 minutes or until golden brown.

Nutrition Facts per muffin: 262 cal., 12 g total fat (1 g sat. fat), 36 mg chol., 298 mg sodium, 36 g carbo., 1 g fiber, 5 g pro.

Canned pumpkin and biscuit mix make these tender, flaky scones super easy. Stock the biscuit mix and extra cans of pumpkin in your pantry so you can enjoy these fruity scones year round.

PUMPKIN-RAISIN SCONES

PREP:

15 minutes

BAKE:

12 minutes

MAKES:

8 scones

2 cups packaged biscuit mix

$\frac{1}{3}$ cup raisins or dried cranberries

$\frac{1}{4}$ cup granulated sugar

2 teaspoons pumpkin pie spice

$\frac{1}{2}$ cup canned pumpkin

$\frac{1}{4}$ cup milk

1 tablespoon coarse or granulated sugar

1 tablespoon very finely snipped crystallized ginger

1 Grease a baking sheet; set aside. In a large bowl combine biscuit mix, raisins or dried cranberries, the $\frac{1}{4}$ cup granulated sugar, and the pumpkin pie spice. In a small bowl combine pumpkin and 3 tablespoons of the milk. Add pumpkin mixture all at once to dry mixture; stir until combined.

2 Turn out onto a lightly floured surface. Knead dough by folding and gently pressing dough for 10 to 12 strokes or until dough is nearly smooth.

3 Pat or lightly roll into a $\frac{1}{2}$-inch-thick circle. Cut into 8 wedges. Place wedges 1 inch apart on prepared baking sheet. In a small bowl combine the 1 tablespoon coarse or granulated sugar and the crystallized ginger. Brush dough wedges with remaining 1 tablespoon milk; sprinkle with crystallized ginger mixture.

4 Bake in a 375°F oven for 12 to 15 minutes or until a toothpick inserted near centers comes out clean. Cool slightly on wire rack. Serve warm.

Nutrition Facts per scone: 189 cal., 5 g total fat (1 g sat. fat), 1 mg chol., 377 mg sodium, 34 g carbo., 1 g fiber, 3 g pro.

Imagine the sweetness of sugar infused with the flavor of natural maple syrup. That wonderful flavor makes maple sugar worth the effort to track it down in specialty food stores or by mail order.

MAPLE SUGAR BISCUITS

1	8-ounce carton dairy sour cream
1	egg, beaten
1	cup granulated maple sugar or $\frac{3}{4}$ cup granulated sugar plus $\frac{1}{4}$ teaspoon maple flavoring
$\frac{1}{2}$	teaspoon ground allspice
$2\frac{1}{4}$	cups all-purpose flour
$\frac{3}{4}$	teaspoon baking soda
$\frac{1}{8}$	teaspoon salt

1 Grease a very large baking sheet; set aside.

2 In a large bowl combine sour cream, egg, maple sugar or granulated sugar plus maple flavoring, and allspice. In a medium bowl stir together flour, baking soda, and salt. Add the flour mixture all at once to the sour cream mixture. Stir just until combined.

3 Turn out onto a well-floured surface. Knead dough by folding and gently pressing dough for 10 to 12 strokes. Pat or lightly roll to a $\frac{1}{2}$-inch thickness. Cut dough with a floured $2\frac{1}{2}$-inch round cutter. Place biscuits on prepared baking sheet.

4 Bake in a 375°F oven for 12 to 15 minutes or until bottoms are brown. Cool slightly on wire rack. Serve warm.

Nutrition Facts per biscuit: 148 cal., 4 g total fat (2 g sat. fat), 22 mg chol., 102 mg sodium, 25 g carbo., 1 g fiber, 3 g pro.

PREP:

15 minutes

BAKE:

12 minutes

MAKES:

14 biscuits

Buttermilk, bacon, and chives make for delectable and savory biscuits that the whole family will love.

BACON & CHIVE BISCUITS

PREP:

10 minutes

BAKE:

8 minutes

MAKES:

6 to 8 biscuits

Nonstick cooking spray

1 7.75-ounce packet buttermilk or cheese-garlic biscuit mix

½ cup finely shredded sharp cheddar cheese (2 ounces)

4 slices packaged ready-to-serve cooked bacon, finely chopped

2 tablespoons snipped fresh chives or chopped green onion

1 Lightly coat a baking sheet with cooking spray; set aside.

2 Prepare biscuit mix according to package directions for rolled biscuits, except stir cheese, bacon, and chives into the dry mix before adding water. Drop batter into 6 to 8 mounds onto prepared baking sheet.

3 Bake in a 450°F oven for 8 to 10 minutes or until golden brown. Serve warm.

Nutrition Facts per biscuit: 211 cal., 10 g total fat (4 g sat. fat), 14 mg chol., 586 mg sodium, 23 g carbo., 1 g fiber, 6 g pro.

Cream-style cottage cheese, honey, and poppy seeds transform plain biscuits made from a mix into an irresistible treat.

HONEY & POPPY SEED BISCUITS

PREP:

15 minutes

BAKE:

10 minutes

MAKES:

10 to 12 biscuits

½ cup cream-style cottage cheese

¼ cup milk

2 tablespoons honey

2¼ cups packaged biscuit mix

1 tablespoon poppy seeds

1 In a food processor or blender combine cottage cheese, milk, and honey. Cover and process or blend until nearly smooth.

2 Prepare biscuit mix according to package directions for rolled biscuits, except substitute the pureed mixture and poppy seeds for the liquid called for on the package.

3 Bake in a 450°F oven about 10 minutes or until bottoms are lightly browned.

Nutrition Facts per biscuit: 148 cal., 5 g total fat (1 g sat. fat), 3 mg chol., 394 mg sodium, 21 g carbo., 1 g fiber, 4 g pro.

The next time you serve stew or chili, bake a pan of this down-home corn bread to use as scoopers and dippers. For those who don't scoop or dip, pass some honey to drizzle on top of the corn bread.

OLD-FASHIONED CORN BREAD

Nonstick cooking spray
1 cup yellow cornmeal
¾ cup all-purpose flour
2 tablespoons sugar
1½ teaspoons baking powder
¼ teaspoon baking soda
¼ teaspoon salt
¾ cup buttermilk or sour milk*
2 eggs, beaten
2 tablespoons cooking oil
Yellow cornmeal (optional)

PREP:
10 minutes
BAKE:
20 minutes
MAKES:
10 servings

1 Coat a 9×1½-inch round baking pan or ovenproof skillet with cooking spray. Set aside.

2 In a large bowl stir together the 1 cup cornmeal, the flour, sugar, baking powder, baking soda, and salt. In a medium bowl stir together buttermilk or sour milk, eggs, and oil.

3 Add buttermilk mixture all at once to flour mixture. Stir just until moistened. Spread into prepared pan or skillet. If desired, sprinkle with additional cornmeal.

4 Bake in a 425°F oven about 20 minutes or until golden brown. Serve warm.

*NOTE: To make ¾ cup sour milk, place 2¼ teaspoons lemon juice or vinegar in a glass measuring cup. Add enough milk to make ¾ cup total liquid; stir. Let mixture stand for 5 minutes before using.

Nutrition Facts per serving: 137 cal., 4 g total fat (1 g sat. fat), 43 mg chol., 159 mg sodium, 21 g carbo., 1 g fiber, 4 g pro.

Refrigerated crescent rolls take on a delicious new dimension when you dress them up with garlicky-herbed cheese and crisp toasted walnuts.

CHEESE-GARLIC CRESCENTS

PREP:

15 minutes

BAKE:

11 minutes

MAKES:

8 crescents

1   8-ounce package (8) refrigerated crescent rolls

¼   cup semisoft cheese with garlic and herb

2   tablespoons finely chopped walnuts, toasted

Nonstick cooking spray

Milk

1   tablespoon seasoned fine dry bread crumbs

1 Unroll crescent rolls; divide into 8 triangles. In a small bowl stir together cheese and walnuts. Place a rounded measuring teaspoon of the cheese mixture near the center of the wide end of each crescent roll. Roll up, starting at the wide end.

2 Lightly coat a baking sheet with cooking spray; place rolls, point sides down, on the prepared baking sheet. Brush tops lightly with milk; sprinkle with bread crumbs.

3 Bake in a 375°F oven about 11 minutes or until bottoms are browned. Serve warm.

Nutrition Facts per crescent: 141 cal., 10 g total fat (3 g sat. fat), 6 mg chol., 254 mg sodium, 12 g carbo., 0 g fiber, 3 g pro.

Let the kids help you with these simple swirls. No knives are involved, just brushing, sprinkling, and rolling—so even the youngest kitchen helpers can do their part.

PARMESAN CORN BREAD SWIRLS

PREP:

15 minutes

BAKE:

12 minutes

MAKES:

8 swirls

1   11.5-ounce package (8) refrigerated corn bread twists

2   tablespoons bottled Italian salad dressing

⅓   cup finely shredded Parmesan or Romano cheese

1 Grease a baking sheet; set aside.

2 Carefully unroll corn bread twist dough on a sheet of waxed paper. Brush lightly with Italian salad dressing; sprinkle with Parmesan or Romano cheese. Reroll dough. Separate along perforations to make 8 rolls. Place the rolls, cut sides down, on prepared baking sheet.

3 Bake in a 400°F oven about 12 minutes or until golden brown. Serve warm.

Nutrition Facts per swirl: 248 cal., 14 g total fat (6 g sat. fat), 16 mg chol., 730 mg sodium, 19 g carbo., 0 g fiber, 11 g pro.

Creamy, luscious lemon curd is a wonderfully versatile ingredient to have on hand. It brings a touch of the sun to these pinwheels with its cheerful yellow color and its rich and tangy flavor. Serve these pinwheels at holiday breakfasts, special brunches, and summer tea parties!

STICKY LEMON PINWHEELS

1/3   cup purchased lemon curd or orange curd

1/4   cup sliced almonds, toasted

1   11-ounce package (12) refrigerated breadsticks

1 Grease an 8×1½-inch round baking pan; set aside. In a small bowl stir together lemon curd and almonds. Spread mixture evenly into the bottom of the prepared baking pan.

2 Separate, but do not uncoil, the breadsticks. Arrange coiled dough over the lemon mixture in the baking pan.

3 Bake in a 375°F oven for 15 to 18 minutes or until golden brown. Immediately invert onto a platter. Spread any remaining lemon mixture in the pan over the pinwheels. Serve warm.

Nutrition Facts per pinwheel: 118 cal., 4 g total fat (1 g sat. fat), 7 mg chol., 200 mg sodium, 19 g carbo., 2 g fiber, 3 g pro.

PREP:
10 minutes
BAKE:
15 minutes
MAKES:
12 pinwheels

Asiago cheese has a rich, nutty flavor that complements the garlic in these easy dinner rolls. You might want to have copies of this recipe on hand as your guests are sure to ask for them.

GARLIC DINNER ROLLS

1   11-ounce package (12) refrigerated breadsticks

2   tablespoons purchased garlic butter spread, melted

1/2   cup shredded or grated Asiago or Romano cheese (2 ounces)

1   teaspoon dried parsley flakes

1/8   teaspoon cayenne pepper

1 Line a large baking sheet with foil; set aside.

2 On a lightly floured surface, separate and uncoil dough into 12 breadsticks. Cut each breadstick lengthwise into three strips, leaving ¾ inch uncut at one end. For each fleur-de-lis roll, coil strips from cut end down toward uncut base, coiling outside strips away from the center and coiling the center strip either direction. If necessary, pinch slightly to hold shape. Transfer to prepared baking sheet.

3 Brush rolls with melted garlic butter spread. In a small bowl combine Asiago or Romano cheese, parsley flakes, and cayenne pepper; sprinkle generously over rolls.

4 Bake in a 375°F oven for 13 to 15 minutes or until golden. Serve warm.

Nutrition Facts per roll: 112 cal., 5 g total fat (2 g sat. fat), 8 mg chol., 263 mg sodium, 12 g carbo., 0 g fiber, 3 g pro.

PREP:
15 minutes
BAKE:
13 minutes
MAKES:
12 rolls

Quick to prepare, these soft and tender delicacies are loaded with the intense flavors of dried tomatoes, fresh rosemary, and Romano cheese.

QUICK FOCACCIA BREADSTICKS

PREP:

15 minutes

BAKE:

12 minutes

MAKES:

10 breadsticks

¼   cup oil-packed dried tomatoes

¼   cup grated Romano cheese

2   teaspoons water

1½   teaspoons snipped fresh rosemary
     or ½ teaspoon dried rosemary, crushed

⅛   teaspoon cracked black pepper

1   10-ounce package refrigerated pizza dough

1 Lightly grease a baking sheet; set aside. Drain tomatoes, reserving 2 teaspoons of the oil. Finely snip tomatoes. In a small bowl combine tomatoes, the reserved oil, cheese, the water, rosemary, and pepper. Set aside.

2 Unroll pizza dough. On a lightly floured surface, roll the dough into a 10x8-inch rectangle. Spread the tomato mixture crosswise over half of the dough.

3 Fold plain half of dough over tomato mixture; press lightly to seal edges. Cut folded dough lengthwise into ten ½-inch-wide strips. Fold each strip in half and twist two or three times. Place 1 inch apart on the prepared baking sheet.

4 Bake in a 350°F oven for 12 to 15 minutes or until golden brown. Cool on a wire rack.

Nutrition Facts per breadstick: 113 cal., 3 g total fat (1 g sat. fat), 3 mg chol., 263 mg sodium, 18 g carbo., 1 g fiber, 5 g pro.

Spiff up plain white dinner rolls by giving them a coating of sesame, poppy, dill, and/or caraway seeds.

SEEDED DINNER ROLLS

PREP:

10 minutes

BAKE:

7 minutes

MAKES:

6 rolls

2   tablespoons butter, melted

1   to 2 tablespoons mixed seeds (such as sesame, poppy, dill, and caraway)

6   frozen baked soft white dinner rolls

1 Place melted butter in a small shallow dish. Place mixed seeds in another small shallow dish or spread on waxed paper. Dip tops of rolls into melted butter; dip into mixed seeds. Place rolls on a baking sheet.

2 Bake in a 375°F oven for 7 to 9 minutes or until hot. Serve warm.

Nutrition Facts per roll: 154 cal., 7 g total fat (2 g sat. fat), 11 mg chol., 299 mg sodium, 18 g carbo., 1 g fiber, 4 g pro.

DESSERTS

Biscuit mix is the key to this sunny cobbler that is ready in only minutes. Chances are it will take less than that for your happy diners to eat it up!

APRICOT-PEACH COBBLER

PREP:
10 minutes
BAKE:
per package directions
MAKES:
6 servings

1 15-ounce can unpeeled apricot halves in light syrup
1 7.75-ounce packet cinnamon swirl biscuit mix (Bisquick® complete)
1 21-ounce can peach pie filling
1 teaspoon vanilla
   Vanilla ice cream (optional)

1 Drain apricot halves, reserving syrup. Prepare biscuit mix according to package directions, except use ½ cup of the reserved apricot syrup in place of the water called for on the package. Bake according to package directions.

2 Meanwhile, in a medium saucepan combine pie filling, drained apricots, and any remaining apricot syrup. Heat through. Remove from heat; stir in vanilla. Spoon fruit mixture into bowls. Top with warm biscuits. If desired, serve with vanilla ice cream.

Nutrition Facts per serving: 284 cal., 4 g total fat (0 g sat. fat), 0 mg chol., 346 mg sodium, 59 g carbo., 2 g fiber, 3 g pro.

This simple version of an all-time favorite will appeal to busy home cooks who want to serve delicious desserts without a lot of preparation.

QUICK APPLE CRISP

START TO FINISH:
15 minutes
MAKES:
4 servings

1   21-ounce can apple pie filling
¼   cup dried cranberries
¼   teaspoon ground ginger or cinnamon
¼   teaspoon vanilla
1   cup granola
1   pint vanilla ice cream

1 In a medium saucepan combine pie filling, dried cranberries, and ginger; heat through, stirring occasionally. Remove from heat; stir in vanilla. Spoon into bowls. Top individual servings with granola. Serve with ice cream.

Nutrition Facts per serving: 507 cal., 15 g total fat (8 g sat. fat), 68 mg chol., 113 mg sodium, 88 g carbo., 6 g fiber, 9 g pro.

Refrigerated piecrust is a dessert lover's best friend. It's versatile, convenient, and best of all—it tastes wonderful, especially when paired with the sweet ingredients in this delectable recipe.

CARAMEL APPLE PASTRY

½ of a 15-ounce package (1 crust) rolled refrigerated unbaked piecrust

1 tablespoon butter

2 20-ounce cans sliced apples, well drained

½ cup packed brown sugar

1 tablespoon lemon juice

1 teaspoon apple pie spice or ground cinnamon

1 tablespoon purchased cinnamon-sugar*

Cinnamon or vanilla ice cream (optional)

Caramel ice cream topping (optional)

PREP:
15 minutes

BAKE:
15 minutes

COOL:
5 minutes

MAKES:
6 servings

1 Bring piecrust to room temperature in microwave oven according to package directions; set aside. In a large ovenproof skillet melt butter; stir in drained apple slices, brown sugar, lemon juice, and apple pie spice. Spread evenly in skillet. Cook over high heat until bubbly.

2 Meanwhile, on a lightly floured surface, unroll piecrust. Sprinkle piecrust with cinnamon-sugar; rub into piecrust with your fingers. Carefully place the piecrust over bubbly apple mixture in skillet, cinnamon-sugar side up. Tuck in piecrust around edge of skillet using a spatula to press edge down slightly.

3 Bake in a 450°F oven about 15 minutes or until piecrust is golden. Cool for 5 minutes. Carefully invert skillet onto a serving platter; remove skillet. Serve warm. If desired, serve with ice cream and caramel topping.

*TEST KITCHEN TIP: To make your own cinnamon-sugar, in a small bowl stir together 1 tablespoon granulated sugar and ¼ teaspoon ground cinnamon.

Nutrition Facts per serving: 381 cal., 12 g total fat (5 g sat. fat), 12 mg chol., 159 mg sodium, 69 g carbo., 3 g fiber, 1 g pro.

If you love caramel apples, you will adore this creative variation of the sweet fruit treat on a stick. It's also much easier to eat!

HOT TAFFY APPLE PITA PIZZA

PREP:

15 minutes

BAKE:

10 minutes

MAKES:

8 servings

2	pita bread rounds
½	cup purchased caramel dip for apples
¼	cup dairy sour cream
1	20-ounce can sliced apples, well drained
1	tablespoon butter, melted
2	tablespoons sugar
¼	teaspoon ground cinnamon
⅓	cup chopped pecans
	Vanilla or cinnamon ice cream (optional)

1 Place pita bread rounds on an ungreased baking sheet. In a small bowl combine ¼ cup of the caramel dip and the sour cream; spread over pitas. Top with drained apples. Drizzle with melted butter. In a small bowl combine sugar and cinnamon; sprinkle over apples. Drizzle with remaining ¼ cup caramel dip;* sprinkle with pecans.

2 Bake in a 400°F oven about 10 minutes or until heated through. Serve warm. If desired, serve with ice cream.

*TEST KITCHEN TIP: If the caramel dip is too thick to drizzle, heat it in a saucepan or microwave oven just until it thins slightly. An easy way to drizzle the dip is to spoon it into a plastic bag, snip off one corner, and squeeze the bag.

Nutrition Facts per serving: 233 cal., 10 g total fat (3 g sat. fat), 9 mg chol., 142 mg sodium, 36 g carbo., 2 g fiber, 3 g pro.

Nothing says "comfort food" better than warm and creamy rice pudding.

QUICK RICE PUDDING

1	4.1-ounce box French vanilla rice pudding mix
2	cups milk
½	teaspoon ground ginger
½	cup tropical dried fruit bits or dried fruit bits
¼	cup chopped macadamia nuts

PREP:
25 minutes
STAND:
5 minutes
MAKES:
4 servings

1 In a 2-quart saucepan stir together rice pudding mix with seasoning packet, milk, and ginger. Cook according to package directions. Remove from heat; stir in dried fruit. Cover; let stand for 5 minutes. Stir again. Divide among 4 dessert bowls; sprinkle with nuts.

Nutrition Facts per serving: 294 cal., 9 g total fat (3 g sat. fat), 10 mg chol., 181 mg sodium, 47 g carbo., 3 g fiber, 6 g pro.

A quick bake makes a crisp, melt-in-your-mouth brown sugar topping on these fruit-filled desserts.

FRUITED YOGURT BRÛLÉE

6	cups fresh fruit (such as blueberries and/or sliced strawberries, bananas, mangos, papayas, apricots, pears, peaches, or pineapple)
1	8-ounce carton vanilla low-fat yogurt
½	cup ricotta cheese
¼	cup packed brown sugar

PREP:
20 minutes
BAKE:
7 minutes
MAKES:
4 servings

1 Divide fruit among four 12- to 16-ounce au gratin dishes. Place dishes in a 15×10×1-inch baking pan. In a small bowl stir together yogurt and ricotta cheese. Spoon the yogurt mixture over fruit. Sprinkle with brown sugar.

2 Bake in a 450°F oven for 7 to 8 minutes or until brown sugar is melted. Serve immediately.

Nutrition Facts per serving: 279 cal., 6 g total fat (3 g sat. fat), 19 mg chol., 82 mg sodium, 54 g carbo., 6 g fiber, 8 g pro.

Although it's an awesome dessert, this warm cinnamon-spiced fruit makes a delightful side dish for breakfast or brunch too.

BAKED FRUIT AMBROSIA

PREP:

10 minutes

BAKE:

15 minutes

MAKES:

4 servings

2 medium oranges

1 8-ounce can pineapple tidbits (juice pack), drained

¼ teaspoon ground cinnamon

2 tablespoons shredded coconut

Fresh raspberries (optional)

1 Finely shred ½ teaspoon peel from one of the oranges; set peel aside. Peel and section oranges. Cut orange sections into bite-size pieces. Divide orange pieces and pineapple among four 6-ounce custard cups. Sprinkle with orange peel and cinnamon. Top with coconut.

2 Bake in a 350°F oven about 15 minutes or until fruit is heated through and coconut is golden brown. If desired, garnish with fresh raspberries. Serve warm.

Nutrition Facts per serving: 66 cal., 1 g total fat (1 g sat. fat), 0 mg chol., 12 mg sodium, 14 g carbo., 2 g fiber, 1 g pro.

When you're really in a hurry to savor these shortcakes, use purchased whipped cream that is available in a handy pressurized can.

QUICK STRAWBERRY SHORTCAKES

4   frozen unbaked buttermilk biscuits

⅓   cup strawberry jelly

1   pint fresh strawberries, sliced

½   cup whipping cream

⅓   cup purchased lemon curd or strawberry curd

PREP:
10 minutes
BAKE:
per package directions
MAKES:
4 servings

1 Bake biscuits according to package directions. Cool. Meanwhile, in a small saucepan heat the strawberry jelly just until melted. Place berries in a bowl; add jelly. Toss until mixed. Set aside. In a chilled medium bowl beat whipping cream with chilled beaters of an electric mixer on medium speed just until soft peaks form (tips curl).

2 Split biscuits horizontally. Spread bottoms with fruit curd; replace tops. Place biscuits on dessert plates. Spoon on berry mixture and whipped cream.

Nutrition Facts per serving: 472 cal., 22 g total fat (10 g sat. fat), 61 mg chol., 619 mg sodium, 48 g carbo., 5 g fiber, 5 g pro.

Shortcake isn't just for the summer anymore. With this inspired and easy recipe, you can enjoy it whenever you wish.

TROPICAL FRUIT SHORTCAKES

1   10.2-ounce package (5) refrigerated large homestyle buttermilk biscuits

     Milk

1   to 2 teaspoons coarse sugar or granulated sugar

1   8-ounce container low-fat vanilla yogurt

¼   cup coconut

¼   of an 8-ounce container frozen whipped dessert topping, thawed

1½   cups sliced or chopped fresh fruit (such as kiwifruit, bananas, and/or refrigerated mango or papaya)

PREP:
10 minutes
BAKE:
per package directions
MAKES:
5 servings

1 Place biscuits on an ungreased baking sheet. Brush tops with milk; sprinkle with sugar. Bake according to package directions. Meanwhile, in a small bowl stir together yogurt and coconut. Fold in whipped dessert topping. Split warm biscuits. Divide fruit among biscuit bottoms; top with some of the yogurt mixture. Replace biscuit tops. Top with remaining yogurt mixture.

Nutrition Facts per serving: 328 cal., 13 g total fat (6 g sat. fat), 2 mg chol., 689 mg sodium, 47 g carbo., 3 g fiber, 7 g pro.

A dazzling dessert doesn't get much easier—or more delicious—than this.

A BILLOW OF BERRIES 'N' BROWNIES

START TO FINISH:

15 minutes

MAKES:

12 servings

4	cups fresh red raspberries
4	to 5 tablespoons sugar
2	teaspoons finely shredded orange peel
2	cups whipping cream
1/4	cup raspberry liqueur (Chambord) (optional)
4	3-inch squares purchased unfrosted brownies (such as milk chocolate, blond, or marbled brownies), cut into irregular chunks

1 Set aside 8 to 10 of the raspberries. In a medium bowl combine the remaining berries, the sugar, and orange peel. Spoon berry mixture into a 1- to 1½-quart compote dish or serving bowl.

2 In a chilled bowl beat whipping cream and liqueur (if using) with chilled beaters of an electric mixer on medium speed until soft peaks form (tips curl). Spoon on top of raspberry mixture. Top whipped cream with brownie chunks and the reserved raspberries.

Nutrition Facts per serving: 263 cal., 19 g total fat (10 g sat. fat), 69 mg chol., 63 mg sodium, 23 g carbo., 5 g fiber, 3 g pro.

Toss together brownies, marshmallows, and peanut butter pieces into a to-die-for dessert.

GOOEY BROWNIE CUPS

4	purchased unfrosted chocolate brownies, cut into irregular-size chunks
1	cup tiny marshmallows
1/4	cup peanut butter flavored pieces and/or milk chocolate pieces
2	tablespoons chopped cocktail peanuts
	Chocolate or vanilla ice cream
	Chocolate-flavored syrup

PREP:
10 minutes
BAKE:
7 minutes
MAKES:
4 servings

1 In a large bowl toss together brownie chunks, marshmallows, peanut butter flavored pieces, and peanuts. Divide among 4 baking dishes.

2 Bake in a 350°F oven for 7 to 8 minutes or until warm and marshmallows are golden brown. Serve with ice cream and drizzle with chocolate syrup.

Nutrition Facts per serving: 581 cal., 28 g total fat (9 g sat. fat), 63 mg chol., 280 mg sodium, 78 g carbo., 3 g fiber, 9 g pro.

Chocolate, nuts, and toffee are a hard-to-resist combination—especially when they're teamed in a luscious brownie dessert.

CHOCOLATE BROWNIE PUDDING

1/3	cup whipping cream
2	purchased unfrosted chocolate brownies (each about 2×2½ inches)
2	3½- to 4-ounce containers chocolate pudding, chilled
1/4	cup English toffee pieces
1/4	cup chopped pecans, toasted

START TO FINISH:
15 minutes
MAKES:
3 servings

1 In a chilled medium bowl beat whipping cream with chilled beaters of an electric mixer on medium speed until soft peaks form (tips curl). Crumble one of the brownies; divide evenly among 3 dessert dishes. Divide one container of the pudding among the dessert dishes. Top with some of the whipped cream, toffee pieces, and pecans. Repeat layers.

MAKE-AHEAD DIRECTIONS: Prepare as directed. Cover and chill layered dessert for up to 1 hour before serving.

Nutrition Facts per serving: 441 cal., 30 g total fat (12 g sat. fat), 55 mg chol., 271 mg sodium, 41 g carbo., 1 g fiber, 5 g pro.

The "suzette" portion of this dessert refers to the classic combination of orange-butter sauce and orange liqueur. Here it gives bananas the royal treatment.

BANANAS SUZETTE OVER POUND CAKE

START TO FINISH:

15 minutes

MAKES:

4 servings

2	tablespoons butter or margarine
$\frac{1}{2}$	of a 10$\frac{3}{4}$-ounce package frozen pound cake, thawed and cut into 4 slices
2	medium ripe, yet firm, bananas
3	tablespoons sugar
2	tablespoons orange liqueur or orange juice
2	tablespoons orange juice
$\frac{1}{8}$	teaspoon ground nutmeg
1	cup vanilla ice cream

1 In a medium skillet melt 1 tablespoon of the butter over medium heat. Add pound cake slices; cook for 1 to 2 minutes or until browned, turning once. Remove from skillet; set aside.

2 Peel bananas; bias-slice each banana into 8 pieces. In the same skillet combine sugar, 2 tablespoons liqueur or orange juice, 2 tablespoons orange juice, and the remaining 1 tablespoon butter. Heat about 1 minute or until butter melts and sugar begins to dissolve. Add the bananas; heat for 2 to 4 minutes more or just until bananas are tender, stirring once. Stir in nutmeg.

3 To serve, place a small scoop of vanilla ice cream on each pound cake slice. Spoon bananas and sauce over ice cream and pound cake slices.

Nutrition Facts per serving: 394 cal., 18 g total fat (11 g sat. fat), 74 mg chol., 229 mg sodium, 53 g carbo., 2 g fiber, 4 g pro.

To make this appealing dessert, cinnamon-coated slices of pound cake are fried on a griddle until crisp and golden, then topped with strawberry puree and whipped cream.

CINNAMON-SEARED POUND CAKE

1   16-ounce carton frozen sliced strawberries in syrup, thawed

1/3   cup whipping cream

1   10¾-ounce package frozen pound cake, thawed

2   tablespoons butter or margarine, softened

½   teaspoon ground cinnamon

    Ground cinnamon

    Slivered almonds, toasted

START TO FINISH:

20 minutes

MAKES:

6 servings

1 Place undrained strawberries in a blender. Cover; blend until smooth. In a chilled bowl beat whipping cream with chilled beaters of an electric mixer on medium speed until soft peaks form (tips curl). Chill berries and whipped cream while preparing pound cake.

2 Cut a thin slice off each end of the pound cake. Cut remaining cake into 6 slices. In a small bowl stir together butter and the ½ teaspoon cinnamon. Spread butter-cinnamon mixture over a cut side of each cake slice.

3 Place cake slices, buttered sides down, on a griddle over medium heat; cook for 2 to 4 minutes or until golden brown, turning once.

4 To serve, divide strawberries among 6 dessert dishes. Top berries in each dish with a pound cake slice, buttered side up. Spoon on whipped cream and sprinkle with additional cinnamon. Top with almonds.

Nutrition Facts per serving: 360 cal., 20 g total fat (12 g sat. fat), 84 mg chol., 223 mg sodium, 44 g carbo., 2 g fiber, 3 g pro.

If you don't have parfait glasses, use clear glass dessert bowls or short drinking glasses to achieve the lovely layered effect.

COFFEE & ALMOND PARFAITS

START TO FINISH:

30 minutes

MAKES:

4 servings

½   of a 10¾-ounce package frozen pound cake,
    cut into ¾-inch cubes

2   8-ounce cartons vanilla low-fat yogurt

½   of an 8-ounce container frozen whipped dessert topping,
    thawed

2   tablespoons coffee liqueur or strong brewed coffee

4   amaretti cookies, coarsely crushed

1 In a shallow baking pan arrange cake cubes in an even layer. Bake in a 350°F oven about 15 minutes or until golden brown, stirring twice. Cool. Meanwhile, in a medium bowl stir together yogurt and whipped topping.

2 Layer ¼ cup of the cake cubes in each of four parfait glasses. Top with half of the yogurt mixture and remaining cake cubes. Stir liqueur or coffee into remaining yogurt mixture; spoon over cake cubes. Sprinkle with the coarsely crushed cookies. Serve immediately.

Nutrition Facts per serving: 368 cal., 14 g total fat (10 g sat. fat), 47 mg chol., 212 mg sodium, 46 g carbo., 0 g fiber, 8 g pro.

Buttery pound cake freezes well and is a versatile pantry staple. It is excellent served with fruit, ice cream, and any number of wonderful dessert sauces. Here broiled golden brown slices are paired with chocolate-hazelnut spread, mixed nuts, and caramel ice cream.

CRUNCHY POUND CAKE SLICES

4	½-inch-thick slices purchased pound cake
¼	cup chocolate-hazelnut spread
½	cup roasted mixed nuts, coarsely chopped
1	pint caramel or cinnamon ice cream

PREP:
15 minutes

BROIL:
2 minutes

MAKES:
4 servings

1 Place the pound cake slices on a cookie sheet. Broil 3 to 4 inches from heat about 2 minutes or until lightly browned, turning once. Cool slightly.

2 Spread one side of each slice with 1 tablespoon of the chocolate-hazelnut spread. Sprinkle with nuts; pat gently to form an even layer. Transfer each slice to a dessert plate and top with a scoop of ice cream. Serve at once.

Nutrition Facts per serving: 763 cal., 45 g total fat (22 g sat. fat), 206 mg chol., 421 mg sodium, 82 g carbo., 2 g fiber, 12 g pro.

This stunning all white dessert—angel food cake topped with whipped dessert topping, white chocolate, and coconut—is a heavenly treat.

SNOW ANGEL CAKE

1	purchased angel food cake
2	ounces white chocolate baking squares or ⅓ cup white baking pieces
1	8-ounce container frozen whipped dessert topping, thawed
¼	cup coconut

START TO FINISH:
15 minutes

MAKES:
12 servings

1 Place cake on a serving plate; set aside.

2 In a small saucepan melt white chocolate over low heat, stirring occasionally. Remove from heat.

3 Frost cake with whipped topping. Sprinkle with coconut. Drizzle with melted white chocolate.

Nutrition Facts per serving: 152 cal., 6 g total fat (5 g sat. fat), 1 mg chol., 190 mg sodium, 22 g carbo., 1 g fiber, 2 g pro.

Although you can make them in a flash, these cherry trifles also are a great make-ahead choice for days when you know you'll be pressed for time during the dinner hour.

CHERRY TRIFLES

START TO FINISH:

10 minutes

MAKES:

4 servings

1   8-ounce container plain low-fat yogurt

2   tablespoons cherry preserves

½   teaspoon vanilla

2   cups angel food cake cubes (about 4 ounces purchased cake)

1   15-ounce can pitted dark sweet cherries, drained

¼   cup purchased glazed walnuts, chopped

1 In a small bowl stir together yogurt, cherry preserves, and vanilla; set aside.

2 Divide half of the cake cubes among 4 parfait glasses or dessert dishes. Top cake cubes in parfait glasses or dessert dishes with half of the dark sweet cherries; spoon half of the yogurt mixture over cherries. Sprinkle with half of the nuts. Repeat layers.

MAKE-AHEAD TIP: Cover and chill for up to 4 hours before serving.

Nutrition Facts per serving: 280 cal., 7 g total fat (2 g sat. fat), 5 mg chol., 198 mg sodium, 51 g carbo., 2 g fiber, 7 g pro.

These cookies are the ultimate in convenience and taste great too. Another time, try the cookies with ground cinnamon or chocolate sprinkles in place of the pumpkin pie spice.

PIECRUST COOKIES

PREP:

15 minutes

BAKE:

8 minutes

MAKES:

about 25 cookies

½   of a 15-ounce package rolled refrigerated unbaked piecrust (1 crust)

1   tablespoon butter or margarine, melted

2   tablespoons packed brown sugar

½   to 1 teaspoon pumpkin pie spice or apple pie spice

1 Unroll piecrust according to package directions using the microwave method. Place on a lightly floured surface. Brush piecrust with melted butter. Sprinkle with brown sugar and pumpkin pie spice. Use a pastry wheel or pizza cutter to cut dough into 1½- to 2-inch square cookies (some of the edges may be smaller). Place on an ungreased large cookie sheet, leaving a small space between cookies.

2 Bake in a 400°F oven about 8 minutes or until golden brown. Serve warm or cooled.

Nutrition Facts per cookie: 47 cal., 3 g total fat (1 g sat. fat), 3 mg chol., 35 mg sodium, 5 g carbo., 0 g fiber, 0 g pro.

Refrigerated sugar cookie dough makes these chocolate morsels super easy. Put on a fresh pot of java while the cookies bake and you'll soon be ready for a relaxing afternoon coffee break.

MOCHA COOKIES

3	tablespoons sugar
2	tablespoons unsweetened cocoa powder
1	tablespoon instant espresso coffee powder or 2 tablespoons instant coffee crystals, crushed
1	18-ounce package refrigerated portioned sugar cookie dough
2	tablespoons milk

PREP:
10 minutes
BAKE:
10 minutes per batch
MAKES:
20 cookies

1 In a small bowl stir together sugar, cocoa powder, and espresso powder. Break cookie dough into portions. Roll each cookie dough portion in milk, then in the sugar mixture. Place cookie dough portions on an ungreased large cookie sheet.

2 Bake in a 350°F oven for 10 to 12 minutes or until edges are set. Transfer to a wire rack; cool.

Nutrition Facts per cookie: 123 cal., 5 g total fat (1 g sat. fat), 10 mg chol., 82 mg sodium, 18 g carbo., 1 g fiber, 1 g pro.

Pop these homemade snacks into lunch bags or knapsacks for lunchtime treats. Or leave some out on the kitchen counter alongside some fresh fruit for kids to enjoy as an afterschool pick-me-up.

CHEWY GRANOLA BARS

3	cups tiny marshmallows (½ of a 10-ounce bag)
2	tablespoons butter or margarine
2	cups granola with raisins
¾	cup crisp rice cereal
¼	cup sunflower nuts

PREP:
15 minutes
CHILL:
5 minutes
MAKES:
16 bars

1 Line a 9×9×2-inch baking pan with foil. Butter foil; set aside. In a medium saucepan combine marshmallows and butter. Cook and stir over medium heat until marshmallows are melted. Stir in granola, rice cereal, and sunflower nuts. Press mixture into prepared pan.

2 Cool in refrigerator about 5 minutes or until set. Lift by foil to remove from pan. Peel off foil and cut into bars.

Nutrition Facts per bar: 105 cal., 3 g total fat (1 g sat. fat), 4 mg chol., 75 mg sodium, 19 g carbo., 1 g fiber, 2 g pro.

Looking for a quick cure for between-meal hunger pangs? This chocolate and peanut butter spread on cookies or crackers is just the answer. Or stir in a little more yogurt and use it as a fruit dip.

PEANUTTY CHOCOLATE-FILLED COOKIES

START TO FINISH:

15 minutes

MAKES:

16 servings

½ cup chunky peanut butter

¼ cup plain low-fat yogurt

¼ cup chocolate-flavored syrup

½ teaspoon vanilla

32 vanilla wafers or 16 graham cracker squares

1 In a medium bowl stir together peanut butter, yogurt, chocolate syrup, and vanilla. Spread the chocolate mixture on flat sides of half of the vanilla wafers; top each with another wafer. (Or spread chocolate mixture on each graham cracker square.)

MAKE-AHEAD TIP: Tightly cover and chill the spread for up to 3 days before serving.

Nutrition Facts per serving: 117 cal., 6 g total fat (1 g sat. fat), 0 mg chol., 82 mg sodium, 13 g carbo., 1 g fiber, 3 g pro.

This is the best fast-fixin' chocolate dessert you'll ever taste!

FUDGE COOKIES IN CHOCOLATE CREAM

½   of an 8-ounce package cream cheese

¼   cup chocolate-flavored syrup

1   teaspoon vanilla

½   cup whipping cream

6   fudge-covered chocolate sandwich cookies, chopped

2   fudge-covered chocolate sandwich cookies, halved

1 In a medium bowl beat cream cheese with an electric mixer on medium to high speed for 30 seconds. Beat in chocolate syrup and vanilla until well mixed. Add whipping cream; beat until fluffy. Fold in chopped cookies. Spoon into dessert dishes. Top each serving with a half-cookie.

Nutrition Facts per serving: 426 cal., 31 g total fat (15 g sat. fat), 72 mg chol., 253 mg sodium, 39 g carbo., 2 g fiber, 5 g pro.

START TO FINISH:

10 minutes

MAKES:

4 servings

Three chocolate-flavored ingredients add up to a chocolate lover's delight.

CHOCOLATE-MINT SANDWICH COOKIES

⅓   cup canned whipped chocolate or vanilla frosting

8   layered chocolate-mint candies, chopped

8   purchased soft chocolate cookies

1 In a small bowl stir together frosting and chopped candies. Spread frosting mixture on the flat side of half of the cookies. Top with the remaining cookies, flat sides down.

Nutrition Facts per sandwich cookie: 420 cal., 23 g total fat (11 g sat. fat), 1 mg chol., 195 mg sodium, 56 g carbo., 2 g fiber, 3 g pro.

CHOCOLATE-PEANUT BUTTER SANDWICH COOKIES: Prepare as directed, except omit chocolate-mint candies and stir 2 tablespoons creamy peanut butter into frosting. Stir ¼ cup chopped cocktail peanuts or chocolate-covered peanuts into frosting mixture.

Nutrition Facts per sandwich cookie: 468 cal., 28 g total fat (11 g sat. fat), 0 mg chol., 258 mg sodium, 53 g carbo., 3 g fiber, 7 g pro.

START TO FINISH:

15 minutes

MAKES:

4 sandwich cookies

A little cream cheese and some strawberry preserves turn ordinary shortbread cookies into a scrumptious treat. Serve the sandwiches with afternoon tea or with a glass of milk.

STRAWBERRY SHORTBREAD SANDWICHES

START TO FINISH:

15 minutes

MAKES:

16 cookie sandwiches

2   ounces tub-style reduced-fat cream cheese
1   tablespoon strawberry preserves
    Red food coloring (optional)
32 plain and/or chocolate shortbread cookies

1 In a small bowl stir together cream cheese and preserves. If desired, stir in a drop of red food coloring. Spread cheese mixture on flat sides of half of the cookies. Top with the remaining cookies, flat sides down.

Nutrition Facts per cookie sandwich: 36 cal., 1 g total fat (1 g sat. fat), 2 mg chol., 38 mg sodium, 6 g carbo., 0 g fiber, 1 g pro.

A few minutes assembly time is all it takes to transform purchased cookies into a special dessert. Let the kids help you "decorate" the tarts with coconut and sliced fresh fruit.

MINIATURE FRUIT TARTS

START TO FINISH:

15 minutes

MAKES:

4 tarts

4   purchased large (3-inch) soft sugar or chocolate cookies
¼   cup tub-style cream cheese with strawberries, chocolate-hazelnut spread, or fudge ice cream topping
2   tablespoons coconut
1   cup sliced fresh fruit (such as kiwi fruit, bananas, and/or strawberries)

1 Spread flat side of each cookie with cream cheese, chocolate-hazelnut spread, or ice cream topping; sprinkle with coconut. Top with fruit.

Nutrition Facts per tart: 187 cal., 9 g total fat (5 g sat. fat), 23 mg chol., 116 mg sodium, 26 g carbo., 2 g fiber, 2 g pro.

Ooey, gooey, and delicious, s'mores get their unusual name from the fact that nibblers usually ask for more. With our super-speedy version, you can have "some more" in no time flat.

SUPER EASY S'MORES

8   chocolate or regular graham cracker squares

3   tablespoons chocolate-hazelnut spread

3   tablespoons marshmallow creme

1 Place graham cracker squares on a work surface; spread 4 squares with chocolate-hazelnut spread. Spread remaining graham cracker squares with marshmallow creme. Place graham crackers, marshmallow sides down, on top of chocolate-hazelnut spread. Place on a microwave-safe plate.

2 Microwave, uncovered, on 100% power (high) for 30 seconds. (If you want to heat the s'mores one or two at a time, microwave one s'more on 100% power [high] for 10 seconds or two s'mores for 20 seconds.) Serve at once.

MAKE-AHEAD TIP: Assemble up to 30 minutes before serving. Microwave just before serving.

Nutrition Facts per s'more: 129 cal., 4 g total fat (0 g sat. fat), 0 mg chol., 46 mg sodium, 21 g carbo., 0 g fiber, 1 g pro.

PEANUT BUTTER S'MORES: Prepare as directed, except use chocolate graham cracker squares and substitute peanut butter for the chocolate-hazelnut spread.

Nutrition Facts per s'more: 141 cal., 7 g total fat (1 g sat. fat), 0 mg chol., 95 mg sodium, 16 g carbo., 1 g fiber, 4 g pro.

PREP:
10 minutes
MICROWAVE:
30 seconds
MAKES:
4 s'mores

If no oatmeal cookies are available, use your favorite kind as long as they are soft enough to be cut with a fork.

COOKIES & CREAM

START TO FINISH:

15 minutes

MAKES:

6 to 8 servings

½ cup whipping cream

2 tablespoons honey

½ cup dairy sour cream

18 to 24 purchased large soft oatmeal cookies

Honey

1 In a small chilled bowl beat whipping cream and the 2 tablespoons honey with chilled beaters of an electric mixer on medium speed until soft peaks form (tips curl). Fold in sour cream.

2 To serve, lay 1 oatmeal cookie on each of 6 to 8 dessert plates. Top each with a spoonful of the whipped cream mixture. Top each with another cookie and another spoon of whipped cream mixture. Top each stack with a third cookie and more whipped cream mixture. Drizzle with additional honey.

MAKE-AHEAD TIP: Prepare whipped cream mixture; cover and chill for up to 1 hour before serving. Assemble individual desserts just before serving.

Nutrition Facts per serving: 456 cal., 21 g total fat (10 g sat. fat), 43 mg chol., 310 mg sodium, 61 g carbo., 2 g fiber, 5 g pro.

*Miniature phyllo dough shells are a real time saver for making desserts and appetizers.
Here they're filled with raspberries, chocolate syrup, and whipped cream for elegant bite-size mini tarts.*

RASPBERRY & CHOCOLATE TULIPS

½   cup frozen raspberries

2   tablespoons sugar

1   2.1-ounce package (15) miniature phyllo dough shells

4   teaspoons chocolate-flavored syrup

15   small squirts from a 7-ounce can pressurized whipped dessert topping

1½   tablespoons sliced almonds (optional)

START TO FINISH:

15 minutes

MAKES:

15 tulips

1 In a small saucepan combine raspberries and sugar. Cook over medium heat, stirring frequently, for 3 to 5 minutes or just until the sugar is melted and raspberries are completely thawed. Remove from heat; cool until slightly warm or room temperature.

2 To serve, place the phyllo dough shells on a platter. Spoon about ½ teaspoon of the raspberry mixture into the bottom of each shell. Top with about ¼ teaspoon of the chocolate-flavored syrup and a squirt of whipped dessert topping. If desired, sprinkle with almonds. Serve immediately.

Nutrition Facts per tulip: 46 cal., 2 g total fat (0 g sat. fat), 0 mg chol., 11 mg sodium, 6 g carbo., 0 g fiber, 0 g pro.

Refreshing lemon pudding is the easy base for these darling and delicious meringue tarts.

LEMON MERINGUE COOKIE TARTS

START TO FINISH:

20 minutes

MAKES:

6 tarts

2 3½- to 4-ounce containers lemon pudding (prepared pudding cups), chilled

1 teaspoon finely shredded lemon peel (optional)

¼ of an 8-ounce container frozen whipped dessert topping, thawed

12 vanilla-flavored bite-size meringue cookies

6 3½-inch graham cracker tart shells (one 4-ounce package)

1 Stir together chilled pudding and, if desired, lemon peel. Fold in whipped topping. Coarsely crush half of the cookies. Spoon half of the pudding mixture into tart shells; sprinkle with crushed cookies. Top with remaining pudding mixture and whole cookies.

Nutrition Facts per tart: 221 cal., 9 g total fat (3 g sat. fat), 0 mg chol., 176 mg sodium, 33 g carbo., 1 g fiber, 2 g pro.

Banana, strawberry, pineapple, and chocolate flavors meld to create a tantalizing filling for phyllo dough shells. They're perfect for a kid's birthday party or as a sweet ending to a summer meal.

FAST & FRUITY BANANA SPLIT TARTS

START TO FINISH:

10 minutes

MAKES:

15 tarts

1 8-ounce tub cream cheese with pineapple

¼ cup strawberry preserves

1 2.1-ounce package (15) miniature phyllo dough shells

1 banana, thinly sliced

⅓ cup chocolate ice cream topping

1 For filling, in a small bowl combine cream cheese and preserves; beat with an electric mixer on medium speed until light and fluffy. Spoon filling into phyllo shells.

2 To serve, divide banana slices among shells. Drizzle with ice cream topping. Serve immediately.

MAKE-AHEAD DIRECTIONS: Prepare and spoon filling into tarts as directed. Cover and refrigerate for up to 4 hours. Just before serving, add banana slices and drizzle with ice cream topping.

Nutrition Facts per tart: 115 cal., 6 g total fat (3 g sat. fat), 13 mg chol., 63 mg sodium, 14 g carbo., 0 g fiber, 1 g pro.

A drizzle of golden caramel adds a creamy richness to these irresistible miniature cream pies.

BANANA & CARAMEL CREAM PIES

1	medium banana, sliced
6	3¹/₂-inch graham cracker tart shells (one 4-ounce package)
2	tablespoons caramel ice cream topping
2	3¹/₂- to 4-ounce containers vanilla pudding (prepared pudding cups), chilled
¹/₄	of an 8-ounce container frozen whipped dessert topping, thawed

START TO FINISH:

15 minutes

MAKES:

6 servings

1 Divide banana slices among tart shells; drizzle with caramel topping. Spoon chilled pudding into tart shells. Top with whipped topping.

MAKE-AHEAD DIRECTIONS: Prepare as directed; cover and chill for up to 8 hours.

Nutrition Facts per serving: 229 cal., 9 g total fat (3 g sat. fat), 0 mg chol., 215 mg sodium, 34 g carbo., 1 g fiber, 2 g pro.

Blueberries and lemon always make a pretty pair. A little bit tangy and a little bit sweet, the combination never fails to refresh.

BLUEBERRY-LEMON TARTS

¹/₃	cup dairy sour cream
¹/₃	cup purchased lemon curd or orange curd
1	2.1-ounce package (15) miniature phyllo dough shells
¹/₄	cup fresh blueberries
	Sifted powdered sugar (optional)

START TO FINISH:

10 minutes

MAKES:

15 tarts

1 In a small bowl stir together sour cream and lemon or orange curd. Divide sour cream mixture among phyllo dough shells. Top with blueberries. If desired, sprinkle with powdered sugar.

Nutrition Facts per tart: 56 cal., 2 g total fat (1 g sat. fat), 7 mg chol., 18 mg sodium, 8 g carbo., 1 g fiber, 1 g pro.

These cones are a great way to get your kids to eat more fruit. Let them choose their favorite pudding flavor and their favorite fruits.

FRUIT-FILLED WAFFLE BOWLS

START TO FINISH:

15 minutes

MAKES:

4 servings

1	4-serving-size package instant lemon or white chocolate pudding mix
1⅓	cups milk
1	cup fresh fruit (such as blueberries, sliced kiwi fruit, sliced strawberries, sliced bananas, or raspberries)
4	waffle ice cream bowls or large waffle ice cream cones
	Fresh mint leaves (optional)

1 Prepare pudding according to package directions, except use the 1⅓ cups milk. Spoon fruit into waffle bowls or cones. Top with pudding. If desired, garnish with fresh mint. Serve immediately.

Nutrition Facts per serving: 196 cal., 3 g total fat (1 g sat. fat), 6 mg chol., 399 mg sodium, 40 g carbo., 1 g fiber, 3 g pro.

Tortillas aren't just great with meat, chiles, and cheese—fruit is just as nice piled on top of the crisp rounds. Think of these as quick-and-easy Mexican dessert pizzas!

BANANA TOSTADAS

1	cup sliced strawberries
½	cup cubed honeydew melon or cantaloupe
2	kiwifruit, peeled and sliced
2	tablespoons snipped fresh mint
2	teaspoons honey
2	teaspoons lime juice
2	7- to 8-inch whole wheat flour tortillas
2	tablespoons tub-style cream cheese with strawberries
1	medium banana, sliced
2	tablespoons crushed graham crackers
	Ground cinnamon
	Honey (optional)
	Vanilla yogurt (optional)

1 In a medium bowl combine strawberries, melon, and kiwifruit. Stir in mint, the 2 teaspoons honey, and the lime juice. Set aside.

2 In a large skillet heat each of the tortillas over medium heat for 2 to 4 minutes or until browned and crisp, turning once. Cool.

3 Spread each tortilla with 1 tablespoon of the cream cheese. Top each tortilla with half of the banana slices, half of the crushed graham crackers, and a dash cinnamon. Top with fruit mixture. If desired, drizzle with additional honey and/or yogurt. Cut into wedges to serve.

Nutrition Facts per serving: 189 cal., 4 g total fat (2 g sat. fat), 8 mg chol., 235 mg sodium, 36 g carbo., 4 g fiber, 4 g pro.

START TO FINISH:
20 minutes
MAKES:
4 servings

Dress up a purchased cheesecake in just minutes with some decadent fudge topping, crispy macaroon cookies, and toasted almonds. Your family or guests will think you've been busy all day in the kitchen!

CHOCOLATE-COCONUT CHEESECAKE

START TO FINISH:

10 minutes

MAKES:

12 servings

1   30-ounce package frozen New York-style cheesecake

1   12-ounce jar fudge ice cream topping

4   soft coconut macaroon cookies, crumbled

¼   cup sliced almonds, toasted

1 Thaw cheesecake following package directions for microwave thawing. Spread top of cheesecake with fudge topping, allowing some to drip down side of cheesecake. Sprinkle with crumbled cookies and almonds.

Nutrition Facts per serving: 371 cal., 17 g total fat (9 g sat. fat), 45 mg chol., 305 mg sodium, 48 g carbo., 0 g fiber, 6 g pro.

Rich ricotta cheese gives this traditional Italian pastry its distinctive and delicious flavor. Using purchased cannoli shells, you can easily make these treats for holiday buffets and dessert parties.

CANNOLI

START TO FINISH:

15 minutes

MAKES:

6 servings

¾   cup ricotta cheese

⅓   cup miniature semisweet chocolate pieces

3   tablespoons sugar

¾   teaspoon vanilla

¼   teaspoon ground cinnamon

¾   cup frozen whipped dessert topping, thawed

6   purchased cannoli shells

1 In a small bowl combine ricotta, chocolate pieces, sugar, vanilla, and cinnamon. Fold in whipped topping. Spoon mixture into a heavy plastic bag.

2 Snip off corner of bag; pipe filling into shells.

Nutrition Facts per serving: 263 cal., 16 g total fat (6 g sat. fat), 16 mg chol., 36 mg sodium, 26 g carbo., 2 g fiber, 6 g pro.

Sweet and tender slices of juicy pear simmered with maple syrup make a glorious filling for crepes. Toasted pecans sprinkled on top are a crunchy final touch.

CREPES WITH MAPLE-PEAR SAUCE

1	15¼-ounce can pear slices, drained
1	cup pure maple syrup or maple-flavored syrup
1	4- to 4.5-ounce package (10 crepes) ready-to-use crepes
½	cup chopped pecans, toasted

START TO FINISH:
10 minutes
MAKES:
5 servings

1 In a small saucepan combine pear slices and maple syrup; heat through.

2 Meanwhile, fold crepes into quarters; arrange on a serving platter. Pour hot pear mixture over crepes. Sprinkle with pecans.

Nutrition Facts per serving: 344 cal., 10 g total fat (1 g sat. fat), 36 mg chol., 77 mg sodium, 63 g carbo., 2 g fiber, 3 g pro.

Waffles are great for breakfast but they're even better for dessert. The crisp, honeycombed surface is perfect for holding generous dollops of this creamy sweet topping.

DESSERT WAFFLES

4	frozen waffles
1	8-ounce carton dairy sour cream
3	tablespoons packed brown sugar
1	teaspoon vanilla
1	cup sliced fresh strawberries
	Sifted powdered sugar

START TO FINISH:
15 minutes
MAKES:
4 servings

1 Heat waffles according to package directions.

2 Meanwhile, in a medium bowl stir together sour cream, brown sugar, and vanilla. Place waffles on individual plates. Top with sour cream mixture and strawberries. Sprinkle with powdered sugar.

MAKE-AHEAD DIRECTIONS: Prepare as directed. Cover and chill for up to 30 minutes before serving.

Nutrition Facts per serving: 266 cal., 15 g total fat (8 g sat. fat), 33 mg chol., 294 mg sodium, 30 g carbo., 1 g fiber, 4 g pro.

These nachos are sweet and simple reasons to keep flour tortillas on hand. They show off seasonal summer fruits to delicious advantage.

FRUIT-FILLED NACHOS

START TO FINISH:

30 minutes

MAKES:

4 servings

8	ounces fresh apricots (about 5)
¼	cup apricot nectar
2	teaspoons sugar
½	cup sliced fresh strawberries
½	teaspoon ground cinnamon
1	teaspoon butter or margarine, melted
2	6- to 8-inch flour tortillas
1	cup vanilla ice cream
¼	cup fresh golden or red raspberries

1 Halve apricots, discarding pits. In a medium skillet combine apricots, nectar, and 1 teaspoon of the sugar. Cook, uncovered, over low heat about 8 minutes or until apricots are cooked through. Stir in strawberries. Cover and set aside. Stir together remaining 1 teaspoon sugar and the cinnamon. Set aside.

2 Brush a clean skillet with some of the melted butter. Heat skillet over medium heat. Cook one of the tortillas for 1 to 1½ minutes or until lightly browned. Turn; sprinkle with half of the sugar-cinnamon mixture. Cook about 1 minute more or until lightly brown but still pliable (not crisp). Repeat with second tortilla.

3 Place a cooked tortilla, cinnamon-side down, on a clean cutting surface. Spoon apricot mixture onto the tortilla. Top with second tortilla, cinnamon-side up. Cut into 4 wedges.

4 To serve, scoop about ¼ cup of the ice cream into each of 4 dessert dishes. Place a tortilla wedge in each dish. Top with fresh raspberries. Serve immediately.

Nutrition Facts per serving: 339 cal., 12 g total fat (6 g sat. fat), 34 mg chol., 207 mg sodium, 55 g carbo., 7 g fiber, 6 g pro.

Raw sugar is usually available in the baking products aisle of supermarkets. There are two popular types—Demerara and Turbinado. Either one will be delicious with the fresh strawberries.

TRIPLE DIPSTER STRAWBERRIES

4	cups large strawberries with stems
1	8-ounce carton dairy sour cream
½	teaspoon ground cinnamon
½	cup coarsely chopped macadamia nuts, toasted
½	cup raw sugar or packed brown sugar
¼	cup chocolate-covered coffee beans, coarsely chopped

START TO FINISH:
20 minutes
MAKES:
4 servings

1 Wash strawberries; drain well on paper towels. Place in a serving bowl.

2 In a small bowl stir together sour cream and cinnamon. Place sour cream mixture, macadamia nuts, raw or brown sugar, and coffee beans in separate small serving dishes or bowls.

3 To serve, dip strawberries first in sour cream mixture, then in macadamia nuts, sugar, and/or coffee beans, as desired.

Nutrition Facts per serving: 415 cal., 27 g total fat (10 g sat. fat), 25 mg chol., 87 mg sodium, 45 g carbo., 5 g fiber, 4 g pro.

Dried tart cherries add a lovely burst of color and flavor to this decadent treat.

CHERRY-BANANAS FOSTER

START TO FINISH:

10 minutes

MAKES:

4 servings

¼ cup butter or margarine

⅓ cup packed brown sugar

3 ripe bananas, peeled and sliced (about 2 cups)

⅓ cup dried tart cherries

⅓ cup spiced rum or rum (optional)

Vanilla ice cream, pound cake, or angel food cake

1 In a large skillet melt butter over medium heat; stir in the brown sugar. Add bananas and cherries; cook and gently stir over medium heat for 1 to 2 minutes or until heated through. If using rum, in a small saucepan heat the rum until it almost simmers. Ignite rum with a long match. Pour over bananas and cherries. Serve immediately over ice cream, pound cake, or angel food cake.

Nutrition Facts per serving: 477 cal., 24 g total fat (14 g sat. fat), 100 mg chol., 140 mg sodium, 64 g carbo., 3 g fiber, 4 g pro.

Fresh mango and strawberries layered with yogurt and whipped dessert topping make terrific sundaes for youngsters and adults alike.

TROPICAL FRUIT CUPS

1   8-ounce carton piña colada yogurt or other flavor low-fat yogurt

¼   teaspoon vanilla

¼   cup frozen whipped dessert topping, thawed

1   cup cubed mango or papaya

½   cup sliced fresh strawberries

1   tablespoon coconut, toasted

1 In a small bowl stir together yogurt and vanilla. Fold in whipped topping.

2 Divide the mango or papaya between 2 parfait glasses. Top each with one-fourth of the yogurt mixture. Top with strawberries and remaining yogurt mixture. Sprinkle with coconut. Serve immediately.

Nutrition Facts per serving: 238 cal., 4 g total fat (4 g sat. fat), 5 mg chol., 79 mg sodium, 46 g carbo., 3 g fiber, 6 g pro.

START TO FINISH:
10 minutes
MAKES:
2 servings

Serve this fluffy dessert as a festive finish to holiday meals or whenever the craving for pumpkin hits you and there isn't time to bake a pie!

SPICED PUMPKIN CREAM

PREP:

20 minutes

CHILL:

10 minutes

MAKES:

8 servings

2	tablespoons butter or margarine
1/4	cup packed brown sugar
1	tablespoon dark-colored corn syrup
1 1/2	cups pecan halves
1	15-ounce can pumpkin
1	cup packed brown sugar
1 1/2	teaspoons finely shredded orange peel
1	tablespoon dark-colored rum or orange juice
2	teaspoons ground cinnamon
1/2	teaspoon ground cloves
2	cups whipping cream
	Sweetened whipped cream (optional)

1 For the candied pecans, line a baking sheet with foil. In a small saucepan melt butter over medium heat. Stir in the 1/4 cup brown sugar and the corn syrup. Cook and stir about 2 minutes or until sugar is dissolved. Cover saucepan and cook for 1 minute more. Uncover; add pecans. Cook and stir about 5 minutes or until fragrant and nuts are slightly darker. Immediately pour mixture onto the prepared baking sheet, spreading into a single layer. Cool completely. Break into pieces.

2 In a large bowl combine pumpkin, the 1 cup brown sugar, the orange peel, rum or orange juice, cinnamon, and cloves. Stir until sugar dissolves. In a chilled large bowl beat whipping cream with the chilled beaters of an electric mixer until soft peaks form (tips curl). Fold whipped cream into pumpkin mixture. Spoon into a serving bowl or into 8 stemmed glasses or dessert dishes. Chill for at least 10 minutes (or up to 3 hours) before serving.

3 To serve, if desired, top with sweetened whipped cream. Sprinkle with candied pecans.*

MAKE-AHEAD TIP: Prepare candied pecans up to 3 days ahead. Cool as directed. Store in a covered container at room temperature.

*****NOTE:** If any candied pecans are left over, store in a covered container at room temperature for up to 3 days. Sprinkle on puddings or other desserts.

Nutrition Facts per serving: 545 cal., 40 g total fat (17 g sat. fat), 90 mg chol., 66 mg sodium, 47 g carbo., 4 g fiber, 4 g pro.

This simple yet sumptuous mousse will be an instant hit with the coffee lovers in your clan.

MOCHA MOUSSE CUPS

2   teaspoons instant espresso powder
     or 1 tablespoon instant coffee crystals

1   tablespoon hot water

4   3½- to 4-ounce containers chocolate pudding
     (prepared pudding cups), chilled

½   of an 8-ounce container frozen whipped dessert topping,
     thawed

9   chocolate wafer cookies, coarsely crushed

1 In a medium bowl stir espresso powder into hot water until dissolved. Stir in chilled pudding. Fold in whipped topping. Divide half of the pudding mixture among 6 dessert dishes. Sprinkle with half of the coarsely crushed cookies. Repeat layers.

Nutrition Facts per serving: 187 cal., 7 g total fat (5 g sat. fat), 0 mg chol., 164 mg sodium, 27 g carbo., 0 g fiber, 2 g pro.

START TO FINISH:
15 minutes
MAKES:
6 servings

For a fancy presentation, layer the mousse with crushed gingersnaps in pretty parfait glasses.

LEMON CHEESECAKE MOUSSE

1   8-ounce package cream cheese, softened

½   cup frozen lemonade concentrate, thawed

½   teaspoon vanilla

1   8-ounce container frozen whipped dessert topping, thawed
     Purchased gingersnaps (optional)

1 In a medium bowl beat cream cheese with an electric mixer on medium to high speed for 30 seconds. Beat in lemonade concentrate and vanilla. Fold in whipped topping. Divide among 6 dessert dishes. If desired, serve with gingersnaps.

Nutrition Facts per serving: 282 cal., 20 g total fat (15 g sat. fat), 42 mg chol., 113 mg sodium, 21 g carbo., 0 g fiber, 3 g pro.

START TO FINISH:
10 minutes
MAKES:
6 servings

A traditional English fool is made with gooseberries, but this version showcases beautiful juicy strawberries or blueberries. Light, creamy, and simple-to-make, the fool highlights the fresh fruit.

FRESH STRAWBERRY FOOL

START TO FINISH:

15 minutes

MAKES:

4 servings

½ cup whipping cream

⅓ cup powdered sugar

½ teaspoon vanilla

1 8-ounce carton lemon yogurt

3 cups sliced fresh strawberries or 2 cups fresh blueberries

½ cup coarsely crumbled shortbread cookies (5 cookies)

1 In a chilled medium bowl combine whipping cream, powdered sugar, and vanilla. Beat with chilled beaters of an electric mixer on medium speed or a chilled rotary beater until soft peaks form (tips curl). By hand, fold in the yogurt and half of the berries.

2 Spoon some of the whipped cream mixture into the bottoms of four 10-ounce glasses. Top with half of the remaining berries and the remaining whipped cream mixture. Top with the remaining berries. Sprinkle with the crumbled cookies.

MAKE-AHEAD DIRECTIONS: Prepare as directed, except do not sprinkle with crumbled cookies. Cover and chill for up to 2 hours. To serve, sprinkle with crumbled cookies.

Nutrition Facts per serving: 272 cal., 15 g total fat (8 g sat. fat), 47 mg chol., 98 mg sodium, 32 g carbo., 3 g fiber, 4 g pro.

Incredibly juicy and exotically sweet and tart, mango makes this easy parfait a real winner.

MANGO PARFAIT

1	6-ounce carton vanilla low-fat yogurt
¼	of an 8-ounce container frozen whipped dessert topping, thawed
1½	cups chopped seeded and peeled mango, papaya, peaches, or apricots

START TO FINISH:
15 minutes
MAKES:
2 servings

1 Spoon yogurt into a small bowl. Fold in whipped topping. Spoon one-fourth of the yogurt mixture into each of 2 parfait glasses. Top with half of the mango. Repeat layers with remaining yogurt mixture and mango.

Nutrition Facts per serving: 231 cal., 6 g total fat (5 g sat. fat), 4 mg chol., 59 mg sodium, 39 g carbo., 2 g fiber, 5 g pro.

Serve these orange-kissed, indigo-hued blueberries with crisp, cigar-shaped pirouette cookies that can be found in most supermarkets.

BLUEBERRIES & ORANGE CREAM

2	cups fresh blueberries
1	8-ounce carton orange or lemon low-fat yogurt
¼	of an 8-ounce container frozen whipped dessert topping, thawed
1	tablespoon orange liqueur or orange juice
	Plain pirouette cookies (optional)

START TO FINISH:
10 minutes
MAKES:
4 servings

1 Divide blueberries among 4 dessert dishes. In a small bowl stir together yogurt, whipped dessert topping, and liqueur or juice. Spoon yogurt mixture over berries. If desired, serve with pirouette cookies.

MAKE-AHEAD DIRECTIONS: Prepare as directed; cover and chill for up to 4 hours.

Nutrition Facts per serving: 143 cal., 3 g total fat (3 g sat. fat), 2 mg chol., 34 mg sodium, 23 g carbo., 3 g fiber, 3 g pro.

Dip makes everything taste better to kids. Entice them to eat fresh fruit by letting them dip it twice—once in creamy caramel mixture and then in crunchy granola. They won't be able to resist!

DOUBLE DIPPIN' FRUIT

START TO FINISH:

15 minutes

MAKES:

6 servings

1   3½- to 4-ounce container vanilla pudding
    (prepared pudding cup)

3   tablespoons caramel ice cream topping

½   teaspoon vanilla

¼   of an 8-ounce container frozen whipped dessert topping,
    thawed

¾   cup granola

    Assorted fresh fruit (such as sliced apples, banana chunks,
    or strawberries)

1 For caramel dip, in a medium bowl stir together pudding, caramel topping, and vanilla until smooth. Fold in whipped topping.

2 To serve, spoon caramel dip into a serving bowl. Place granola in another serving bowl. Serve with fruit. Dip fruit into caramel dip, then into granola.

Nutrition Facts per serving: 131 cal., 3 g total fat (2 g sat. fat), 0 mg chol., 82 mg sodium, 23 g carbo., 1 g fiber, 1 g pro.

When strawberry season is over, serve this delectable dip with other fresh fruits, such as green grapes or pineapple chunks. Leftovers will store for up to a week in the refrigerator. Just stir before serving to fluff up the dip.

STRAWBERRY DIP

1   7-ounce jar marshmallow creme
1   8-ounce package cream cheese, softened
     Whole strawberries
     Finely chopped nuts, toasted coconut, and/or miniature semisweet chocolate pieces (optional)

START TO FINISH:
10 minutes
MAKES:
1¹/₂ cups

❶ In a medium bowl add marshmallow creme by spoonfuls to the cream cheese, beating with an electric mixer on low to medium speed until smooth. Transfer to a serving bowl. Use as a dip for strawberries. If desired, accompany with nuts, coconut, and/or chocolate pieces for rolling dipped berries in.

Nutrition Facts per 2 tablespoons dip: 120 cal., 6 g total fat (4 g sat. fat), 20 mg chol., 64 mg sodium, 14 g carbo., 0 g fiber, 2 g pro.

Busy chocolate lovers rejoice! Dessert fondues, such as this one, are super quick to prepare. Take your choice of any of the three flavor options.

CHOCOLATE-PEANUT BUTTER FONDUE

START TO FINISH:

15 minutes

MAKES:

5 (¹/₄-cup) servings

1   11½-ounce package milk chocolate pieces

¹/₄   cup milk

1   tablespoon crunchy peanut butter

   Milk

   Assorted fresh fruit dippers (such as star fruit [carambola] slices, orange sections, whole strawberries, pear slices, banana slices, and/or apple slices)

   Angel food cake or pound cake cubes

   Marshmallows

1 In a heavy small saucepan (or the top of a double boiler placed over gently simmering water) combine chocolate pieces and the ¹/₄ cup milk. Heat, stirring constantly, over low heat until chocolate is melted and smooth. Stir in peanut butter. Cook and stir until heated through. Stir in additional milk, 1 tablespoon at a time, until desired consistency.

2 Pour mixture into a fondue pot; place over a fondue burner set on low. With fondue forks or long skewers, dip fruit dippers, cake cubes, and/or marshmallows into chocolate mixture. (The fondue will hold for up to 1 hour on low. If mixture gets too thick, stir in milk, 1 tablespoon at a time.)

Nutrition Facts per ¹/₄-cup fondue: 360 cal., 23 g total fat (13 g sat. fat), 9 mg chol., 46 mg sodium, 43 g carbo., 3 g fiber, 4 g pro.

CHOCOLATE S'MORES FONDUE: Prepare as directed, except omit peanut butter. Pour mixture into a fondue pot; place over a fondue burner set on low. Add 1 tablespoon marshmallow creme to the center. Do not stir. Slowly pour 1 tablespoon rum into fondue pot. Ignite rum by touching lighted match to edge of pot. (Cooking or flambéing with an open flame should be done with great care. It will take about 1½ minutes for the flame to burn down.) After the flame burns down, carefully swirl the mixture. Sprinkle 1 tablespoon graham cracker crumbs over the top. Do not stir. With fondue forks or long skewers, dip fruit dippers, cake cubes, and/or marshmallows into mixture.

Nutrition Facts per ¹/₄-cup fondue: 360 cal., 21 g total fat (13 g sat. fat), 9 mg chol., 38 mg sodium, 45 g carbo., 3 g fiber, 4 g pro.

FLAMING CARAMEL-PECAN FONDUE: Prepare as directed, except omit peanut butter. Stir in 2 tablespoons caramel ice cream topping. Cook and stir until heated through. Pour mixture into a fondue pot; place over a fondue burner set on low. Slowly pour 1 tablespoon rum into fondue pot. Ignite rum by touching lighted match to edge of pot. (Cooking or flambéing with an open flame should be done with great care. It will take about 1½ minutes for the flame to burn down.) After the flame burns down, sprinkle 1 tablespoon finely chopped pecans over the top. Do not stir. With fondue forks or long skewers, dip fruit dippers, cake cubes, and/or marshmallows into mixture.

Nutrition Facts per ¹/₄-cup fondue: 381 cal., 22 g total fat (13 g sat. fat), 9 mg chol., 52 mg sodium, 48 g carbo., 4 g fiber, 4 g pro.

Take care to chop the chocolate into uniform pieces so it will melt evenly without burning. You won't want to waste a single drop of this sensational dip.

NO-DRIP CHOCOLATE DIP

8 ounces unsweetened chocolate, chopped

1 14-ounce can (1¼ cups) sweetened condensed milk

2 tablespoons light-colored corn syrup

½ cup milk

1 teaspoon vanilla

½ teaspoon ground cinnamon

Milk

Assorted cut-up fresh fruit (such as strawberries, pineapple cubes, banana slices, and/or kiwi fruit slices)

START TO FINISH:

15 minutes

MAKES:

2 cups

1 In a heavy medium saucepan melt chocolate over low heat, stirring constantly. Stir in the sweetened condensed milk and corn syrup until combined. Gradually stir in the ½ cup milk until combined. Stir in vanilla and cinnamon. Stir in additional milk as necessary to make dipping consistency.

2 Serve dip warm, using fruit as dippers.

MAKE-AHEAD DIRECTIONS: Prepare dip as directed; cool slightly. Cover and chill for up to 3 weeks. To reheat dip, transfer chocolate mixture to a medium saucepan. Cook and stir over low heat until smooth and heated through. (Or transfer to a microwave-safe dish. Microwave, uncovered, on 100% power [high] for 35 to 60 seconds or until smooth and heated through, stirring halfway through cooking.) Serve warm, stirring in additional milk as necessary to make dipping consistency.

Nutrition Facts per 2 tablespoons dip: 166 cal., 10 g total fat (6 g sat. fat), 8 mg chol., 40 mg sodium, 20 g carbo., 2 g fiber, 4 g pro.

This scrumptious ruby red sauce is wonderfully festive and is a must for the holidays—or anytime!

RASPBERRY-CRANBERRY SAUCE

START TO FINISH:

15 minutes

MAKES:

2 cups sauce

2   tablespoons sugar

1   tablespoon cornstarch

½   of a 16-ounce can whole cranberry sauce

1   10-ounce package frozen red raspberries (in syrup), thawed

2   tablespoons kirsch or brandy (optional)

Pound cake, unfrosted brownies, or vanilla ice cream

1 In a medium saucepan combine sugar and cornstarch. Stir in cranberry sauce and raspberries. Cook and stir over medium heat until thickened and bubbly. Cook and stir for 2 minutes more. Remove from heat. If desired, stir in kirsch or brandy.

2 Serve warm sauce over pound cake, brownies, or ice cream.

Nutrition Facts per 2 tablespoons sauce: 57 cal., 0 g total fat (0 g sat. fat), 0 mg chol., 8 mg sodium, 14 g carbo., 1 g fiber, 0 g pro.

Be sure to include this heavenly dessert sauce in your recipe repertoire. Spooned warm over pound cake or angel food cake, it makes a sunny finish to any meal.

GOLDEN CITRUS SAUCE

START TO FINISH:

15 minutes

MAKES:

about 1⅓ cups sauce

¾   cup orange marmalade

⅓   cup golden raisins

1   tablespoon water

1   4-ounce container mandarin orange sections, drained (about ⅓ cup)

1   tablespoon dry or cream sherry (optional)

Pound cake or angel food cake

1 In a small saucepan combine orange marmalade, golden raisins, and the water; heat and stir until marmalade is melted. Gently fold in orange sections and, if desired, sherry.

2 Serve warm sauce over pound or angel food cake slices.

Nutrition Facts per 2 tablespoons sauce: 79 cal., 0 g total fat (0 g sat. fat), 0 mg chol., 15 mg sodium, 21 g carbo., 0 g fiber, 0 g pro.

There's only one word to describe this rich, buttery sauce—divine!

BUTTER PECAN SAUCE

2 tablespoons butter or margarine

⅔ cup coarsely chopped pecans

1 10-ounce jar caramel ice cream topping

¼ cup half-and-half or light cream

Vanilla or butter pecan ice cream, pound cake, angel food cake, or apple pie

START TO FINISH:
10 minutes
MAKES:
1³/₄ cups sauce

1 In a small saucepan melt butter over medium heat; stir in nuts. Cook and stir about 3 minutes or until nuts are lightly toasted. Stir in caramel topping and half-and-half. Heat through.

2 Serve warm sauce over ice cream, cake slices, or wedges of pie.*

*****NOTE:** Store leftover sauce in the refrigerator for up to 1 week.

Nutrition Facts per 2 tablespoons sauce: 121 cal., 6 g total fat (2 g sat. fat), 6 mg chol., 68 mg sodium, 16 g carbo., 1 g fiber, 1 g pro.

BUTTER-RUM PECAN DESSERT SAUCE: Prepare as directed, except stir in 2 tablespoons dark rum.

Nutrition Facts per 2 tablespoons sauce: 117 cal., 6 g total fat (1 g sat. fat), 6 mg chol., 64 mg sodium, 15 g carbo., 1 g fiber, 1 g pro.

In an instant this lively sauce turns ordinary desserts into something special.

APRICOT-ORANGE SAUCE

START TO FINISH:

15 minutes

MAKES:

2 cups sauce

1   21-ounce can apricot pie filling
1   cup mixed dried fruit bits
¾ cup orange juice
½ cup chopped pecans, toasted
1   tablespoon orange liqueur (optional)
    Pound cake or vanilla ice cream

1 In a medium saucepan combine pie filling, fruit bits, and orange juice; cook and stir until warm. Stir in pecans and, if desired, liqueur.

2 Serve warm sauce over pound cake or ice cream.

Nutrition Facts per 2 tablespoons sauce: 93 cal., 2 g total fat (0 g sat. fat), 0 mg chol., 8 mg sodium, 17 g carbo., 1 g fiber, 1 g pro.

Chocolate and hazelnut is a classic dessert flavor combination. One bite of this simple yet luscious sauce and you'll know why. With only 10 minutes of prep time, you'll be tempted to make it often.

CHOCOLATE-HAZELNUT ICE CREAM SAUCE

START TO FINISH:

10 minutes

MAKES:

about ¾ cup sauce

½ cup chocolate-hazelnut spread
¼ cup half-and-half or light cream
1   teaspoon instant coffee crystals (optional)
¼ cup hazelnuts, toasted and coarsely chopped
    Vanilla, coffee-flavor, or other favorite ice cream

1 In a small saucepan combine chocolate-hazelnut spread, half-and-half, and, if desired, coffee crystals. Heat over low heat until spread is melted, whisking to make smooth. Stir in nuts. Serve warm over ice cream.

Nutrition Facts per 2 tablespoons sauce: 155 cal., 11 g total fat (1 g sat. fat), 4 mg chol., 24 mg sodium, 14 g carbo., 1 g fiber, 2 g pro.

Today's gourmet ice creams are a dessert unto themselves—but when you add this orange-caramel sauce, you really have something to celebrate.

ORANGE-PRALINE SUNDAES

1   12-ounce jar caramel ice cream topping

½   cup orange marmalade

⅔   cup coarsely chopped pecans, toasted

½   gallon cinnamon-, pumpkin-, or eggnog-flavor ice cream

1 In a small saucepan combine caramel ice cream topping and orange marmalade. Cook over medium-low heat until marmalade is melted, stirring occasionally. Stir in pecans; heat through.

2 Serve warm sauce over ice cream.

MAKE-AHEAD DIRECTIONS: Prepare sauce as directed; cover and chill for up to 24 hours. Just before serving, heat sauce in saucepan over low heat.

Nutrition Facts per serving: 482 cal., 24 g total fat (12 g sat. fat), 72 mg chol., 167 mg sodium, 64 g carbo., 2 g fiber, 5 g pro.

START TO FINISH:
15 minutes
MAKES:
10 servings

The robust flavor of the Cabernet Sauvignon gives this dessert an elegant touch.

PEACHES & CRANBERRIES WITH SORBET

PREP:

10 minutes

COOK:

5 minutes

STAND:

15 minutes

MAKES:

8 servings

1½ cups fresh cranberries

⅔ cup sugar

½ cup Cabernet Sauvignon or other dry red wine

1 teaspoon finely shredded orange peel

½ cup orange juice

1 3-inch piece stick cinnamon

1½ cups frozen unsweetened peach slices

1 quart raspberry sorbet

1 In a medium saucepan combine cranberries, sugar, wine, orange peel, orange juice, and stick cinnamon. Bring to boiling; reduce heat. Simmer, uncovered, about 5 minutes or until cranberries are tender.

2 Remove from heat; discard stick cinnamon. Stir in peaches. Let stand for 15 minutes before serving. Serve warm over raspberry sorbet.

Nutrition Facts per serving: 223 cal., 0 g total fat (0 g sat. fat), 0 mg chol., 11 mg sodium, 54 g carbo., 2 g fiber, 0 g pro.

In the summertime, this dessert is a perfect way to use an abundance of fresh peaches. In the winter, try it with frozen fruit.

AMARETTO PEACHES WITH VANILLA YOGURT

3	peaches, pitted, peeled, and sliced, or 2 cups frozen unsweetened peach slices, thawed and drained
1	tablespoon amaretto
2	teaspoons vanilla
2	8-ounce cartons plain low-fat yogurt
¼	cup sugar
⅓	cup coarsely chopped whole almonds, or slivered almonds, toasted

PREP:
20 minutes
STAND:
10 minutes
MAKES:
4 servings

1 In a medium bowl toss together peach slices, amaretto, and 1 teaspoon of the vanilla. Let stand for 10 minutes.

2 Meanwhile, in another bowl stir together yogurt, sugar, and the remaining 1 teaspoon vanilla. Spoon about half of the yogurt mixture into 4 dessert dishes or stemmed glasses; top with the flavored peaches and the remaining yogurt. Spoon any remaining liquid from peaches over the tops. Sprinkle with almonds.

Nutrition Facts per serving: 233 cal., 7 g total fat (2 g sat. fat), 7 mg chol., 80 mg sodium, 33 g carbo., 3 g fiber, 9 g pro.

It's important that the water and chocolate are together from the very beginning of cooking, otherwise they won't blend properly when heated.

ULTIMATE CHOCOLATE SUNDAES

START TO FINISH:

30 minutes

MAKES:

8 servings

8   ounces bittersweet chocolate, coarsely chopped

⅓   cup water

¼   cup sugar

¼   cup pear liqueur or pear nectar

4   small Forelle or Bosc pears (about 1 pound total)

3   tablespoons butter or margarine

2   tablespoons sugar

1   quart premium vanilla ice cream

1 For chocolate sauce, in a small saucepan combine chocolate, the water, and the ¼ cup sugar. Cook over low heat until melted, stirring slowly and constantly. Stir in pear liqueur or nectar. Set aside to cool slightly.

2 If desired, peel pears; cut into halves and remove cores.* If desired, leave stem on one portion. In a large skillet melt butter over medium heat. Add pear halves; cook about 12 minutes or until browned and tender, turning once. Add the 2 tablespoons sugar, stirring gently until sugar is dissolved and pears are glazed.

3 To assemble, place scoops of ice cream in 8 dessert bowls. Spoon a pear half and some of the butter mixture around the ice cream in each bowl. Top with chocolate sauce.

*NOTE: If pears are large, cut into sixths or eighths.

Nutrition Facts per serving: 466 cal., 27 g total fat (16 g sat. fat), 80 mg chol., 81 mg sodium, 56 g carbo., 5 g fiber, 5 g pro.

Summer fun goes on and on when you serve these show-stopping frozen yogurt parfaits.

FUN-DAY SUNDAE PARFAIT

1½   cups frozen vanilla or fruit-flavor yogurt or ice cream

½   cup coarsely crushed vanilla wafers or honey or cinnamon graham crackers

1   cup assorted fresh fruit (such as sliced bananas or strawberries; peeled, sliced kiwi fruit, peaches, or mangoes; cut-up pineapple; raspberries; and/or blueberries)

6   tablespoons strawberry ice cream topping

¼   cup frozen whipped dessert topping, thawed (optional)

2   maraschino cherries with stems (optional)

START TO FINISH:
15 minutes
MAKES:
2 servings

1 Place ¼ cup of the frozen yogurt in the bottom of each of 2 tall parfait glasses. Top each with 2 tablespoons of the crushed wafers, ¼ cup of the fruit, and 1 tablespoon of the strawberry topping. Repeat layers.

2 Top each with ¼ cup of the frozen yogurt. Drizzle each with remaining strawberry topping. If desired, top with whipped topping and garnish with maraschino cherries. Serve with long-handled spoons.

Nutrition Facts per serving: 375 cal., 9 g total fat (4 g sat. fat), 15 mg chol., 138 mg sodium, 70 g carbo., 2 g fiber, 4 g pro.

These healthful sundaes use chopped red and green apples instead of ice cream. Between the creamy caramel ice cream topping and the fluffy whipped dessert topping, you won't even miss it.

CARAMEL APPLE SUNDAES

START TO FINISH:

20 minutes

MAKES:

8 servings

2 medium red apples, cored and coarsely chopped

2 medium green apples, cored and coarsely chopped

1 tablespoon lemon juice

½ cup caramel ice cream topping

½ of an 8-ounce container frozen light whipped dessert topping, thawed

1 cup low-fat granola or toasted corn and wheat cereal flakes with oats

1 In a large bowl toss together red apples, green apples, and lemon juice.

2 Divide the apple mixture among 8 dessert dishes. Drizzle each with 1 tablespoon of the ice cream topping. Spoon whipped dessert topping on top. Sprinkle each with 2 tablespoons of the cereal. Serve immediately.

Nutrition Facts per serving: 180 cal., 3 g total fat (2 g sat. fat), 0 mg chol., 75 mg sodium, 38 g carbo., 3 g fiber, 2 g pro.

Despite their name, these chocolate peanut malts go down smoothly.

ROCKY ROAD MALTS

1	quart chocolate ice cream
1/3	cup milk
1/3	cup chocolate instant malted milk powder
1/4	cup creamy peanut butter
	Milk (optional)
	Marshmallow creme
	Coarsely chopped peanuts
	Miniature sandwich cookies
	Tiny marshmallows

1 In a blender combine half of the ice cream, the 1/3 cup milk, the malted milk powder, and peanut butter. Cover; blend until smooth, stopping and scraping down side, if necessary. Spoon in remaining ice cream; blend until smooth. If necessary, add additional milk to make desired consistency.

2 To serve, spoon into 4 glasses. Top with marshmallow creme, chopped peanuts, miniature sandwich cookies, and tiny marshmallows as desired.

Nutrition Facts per serving: 644 cal., 30 g total fat (12 g sat. fat), 47 mg chol., 340 mg sodium, 88 g carbo., 5 g fiber, 14 g pro.

START TO FINISH:
15 minutes
MAKES:
4 servings

Combat those soaring summer temperatures by shaking up a little action with your blender and some ice cream. You'll need a spoon to slurp these super-thick concoctions.

CHOOSE-A-FLAVOR SHAKE

START TO FINISH:

10 minutes

MAKES:

2 servings

1   pint vanilla or chocolate ice cream

¼   cup milk

1 In a blender combine ice cream and milk. Cover and blend until smooth. Continue as directed in the recipes below, stirring in desired ingredients.

GO-BANANAS CARAMEL SHAKE: Prepare as directed using vanilla ice cream. Stir in ½ cup coarsely chopped bananas, 2 tablespoons chopped pecans, 1 tablespoon chocolate-flavored syrup, and 1 tablespoon caramel ice-cream topping.

Nutrition Facts per serving: 285 cal., 13 g total fat (5 g sat. fat), 24 mg chol., 106 mg sodium, 43 g carbo., 2 g fiber, 5 g pro.

CHERRIES 'N' CHOCOLATE SHAKE: Prepare as directed using chocolate ice cream. Stir in ⅓ cup chopped drained maraschino cherries and ¼ teaspoon almond extract. To serve, spoon into two tall glasses. Drizzle each shake with 1 tablespoon chocolate-flavored syrup.

Nutrition Facts per serving: 246 cal., 8 g total fat (5 g sat. fat), 24 mg chol., 76 mg sodium, 43 g carbo., 1 g fiber, 4 g pro.

CONFETTI RAINBOW SHAKE: Prepare as directed using vanilla ice cream and adding 2 or 3 drops desired food coloring with the milk. Stir in 2 tablespoons candy-coated gum pieces. Because gum may pose a choking hazard, do not serve this shake to children under the age of 3.

Nutrition Facts per serving: 383 cal, 15 g total fat (9 g sat. fat), 60 mg chol., 124 mg sodium, 66 g carbo., 0 g fiber, 6 g pro.

Another time, try this silky, fruity shake with orange or pineapple sherbet.

STRAWBERRY-MANGO MILK SHAKE

2	cups halved fresh strawberries
1½	cups vanilla frozen yogurt
1	cup chopped mango
¼	cup milk
	Sliced fresh strawberries
	Sliced mango

START TO FINISH:
15 minutes
MAKES:
2 servings

1 In a blender combine the 2 cups berries, frozen yogurt, chopped mango, and milk. Cover and blend until smooth. Divide mixture between 2 tall glasses. Top each serving with strawberry slices and mango slices.

Nutrition Facts per serving: 262 cal., 5 g total fat (3 g sat. fat), 17 mg chol., 63 mg sodium, 50 g carbo., 5 g fiber, 5 g pro.

Cool and thirst-quenching, this quick and simple slush is impossible to resist on hot summer days.

CITRUS FREEZE

1	pint lemon, lime, or orange sorbet
½	cup lemonade, limeade, or orange juice
1	12-ounce can lemon-lime carbonated beverage, chilled

START TO FINISH:
10 minutes
MAKES:
4 servings

1 In a blender combine sorbet and lemonade. Cover and blend until smooth. Spoon into 4 glasses; top with lemon-lime beverage. Serve immediately.

Nutrition Facts per serving: 193 cal., 0 g total fat (0 g sat. fat), 0 mg chol., 28 mg sodium, 49 g carbo., 1 g fiber, 0 g pro.

All it takes are three simple ingredients to create this smooth sippin' soda fountain treat.

FIZZY MINT-CHOCOLATE SODA

START TO FINISH:

10 minutes

MAKES:

4 servings

¼ cup chocolate-flavored syrup

1 pint mint-chocolate chip ice cream

2 cups carbonated water or cream soda, chilled

1 Pour 1 teaspoon of the chocolate syrup into the bottom of each of 4 tall glasses. Add one scoop (¼ cup) of ice cream to each glass. Add 2 more teaspoons of the chocolate syrup to each glass. Top with another scoop of ice cream. Slowly pour ½ cup carbonated water or cream soda into each glass.

Nutrition Facts per serving: 245 cal., 11 g total fat (6 g sat. fat), 26 mg chol., 84 mg sodium, 33 g carbo., 0 g fiber, 4 g pro.

Cream cheese, ice cream, and cream soda make this fruity delight extra creamy.

RASPBERRY CHEESECAKE SHAKE

START TO FINISH:

10 minutes

MAKES:

6 servings

1 12-ounce package frozen unsweetened red raspberries, thawed

1 3-ounce package cream cheese, softened

¼ teaspoon almond extract

1 quart vanilla ice cream, softened

2 12-ounce cans or bottles cream soda

Fresh raspberries (optional)

1 In a blender combine thawed raspberries, cream cheese, and almond extract; add half of the ice cream and ½ cup of the cream soda. Cover and blend until smooth.

2 Divide blended mixture among six 16-ounce glasses. Add a scoop of the remaining ice cream to each glass. Top with remaining cream soda. If desired, garnish with fresh raspberries. Serve immediately.

Nutrition Facts per serving: 305 cal., 15 g total fat (9 g sat. fat), 54 mg chol., 130 mg sodium, 36 g carbo., 2 g fiber, 4 g pro.

PARTY FOODS

7

A coating of Cajun seasoning provides the peppery hotness for these broiled shrimp. Cajun seasoning varies from brand to brand, but most include onion, garlic, salt, and the classic Cajun trio of red, white, and black pepper. The mayonnaise dipping sauce is a cool counterpart to the spicy heat of the Cajun seasoning.

SPICY CAJUN SHRIMP

START TO FINISH:

30 minutes

MAKES:

8 appetizer servings

1	pound fresh or frozen large shrimp
½	cup mayonnaise or salad dressing
2	tablespoons tomato paste
1	tablespoon lemon juice
½	teaspoon bottled minced garlic (1 clove)
2	tablespoons butter or margarine, melted
4	teaspoons Cajun seasoning

1 Thaw shrimp, if frozen. Peel and devein shrimp, leaving tails intact. Rinse shrimp; pat dry with paper towels. In a small bowl stir together mayonnaise, tomato paste, lemon juice, and garlic. Cover and chill until ready to serve.

2 Thread shrimp onto skewers, leaving a ¼-inch space between shrimp. Brush both sides of each shrimp with melted butter. Sprinkle both sides of each shrimp with Cajun seasoning. Place skewers on the unheated rack of a broiler pan.

3 Broil 4 to 5 inches from the heat for 2 minutes. Turn skewers; broil for 1 to 2 minutes more or until shrimp are opaque. If desired, remove shrimp from skewers. Serve shrimp with mayonnaise mixture.

Nutrition Facts per serving: 181 cal., 15 g total fat (3 g sat. fat), 83 mg chol., 264 mg sodium, 2 g carbo., 0 g fiber, 9 g pro.

Beautiful peachy-hued apricots, fresh dark green chives, creamy flavorful cheese, and golden brown toasted pecan pieces add up to morsels that appeal to both the eyes and the taste buds.

BLUE CHEESE APRICOT BITES

1	4-ounce package blue cheese, at room temperature
¼	cup butter, at room temperature
1	7-ounce package dried apricot halves
¼	cup pecan or walnut pieces, toasted
	Fresh chives

START TO FINISH:

20 minutes

MAKES:

about 30 pieces (10 appetizer servings)

1 In a medium bowl stir together blue cheese and butter until smooth. Using a pastry bag fitted with a small star tip, pipe about 1 teaspoon of the cheese mixture onto each apricot half. Top each with a nut piece. Garnish with chives.

Nutrition Facts per piece: 150 cal., 10 g total fat (5 g sat. fat), 21 mg chol., 195 mg sodium, 13 g carbo., 2 g fiber, 3 g pro.

The flavors of lemon and dill bring out the taste of luscious smoked salmon in these easy canapés.

SMOKED SALMON-CUCUMBER ROUNDS

1	medium cucumber
6	to 8 ounces thinly sliced smoked salmon (lox-style)
⅓	cup mayonnaise or salad dressing
1	tablespoon snipped fresh dill
1	teaspoon finely shredded lemon peel
1	teaspoon lemon juice
	Fresh dill sprigs

START TO FINISH:

20 minutes

MAKES:

20 to 24 rounds

1 If desired, score cucumber by drawing the tip of a teaspoon or vegetable peeler lengthwise down cucumber at ½-inch intervals. Cut cucumber into ¼-inch slices. Arrange slices on a serving platter.

2 Cut salmon into pieces to fit cucumber slices. Place a piece of salmon on top of each cucumber slice.

3 In a small bowl combine mayonnaise, the snipped dill, lemon peel, and lemon juice. Spoon ½ teaspoon of the mayonnaise mixture onto each piece of salmon. Garnish with dill sprigs.

MAKE-AHEAD TIP: Cover and chill for up to 1 hour before serving.

Nutrition Facts per round: 39 cal., 3 g total fat (0 g sat. fat), 5 mg chol., 193 mg sodium, 1 g carbo., 0 g fiber, 2 g pro.

With a funky name and bright, trendy ingredients such as picante sauce, sweet peppers, corn, lettuce, and cheddar cheese, this festive fare will be the hit of any party.

FIESTA CHEESE TOSTADOS

START TO FINISH:

30 minutes

MAKES:

6 appetizer servings

6	6- to 7-inch corn tortillas
2	teaspoons cooking oil or olive oil
1	cup canned vegetarian refried beans
1/3	cup bottled picante sauce or salsa
1	medium red, yellow, or green sweet pepper, cut into thin bite-size strips
1/3	cup loose-pack frozen whole kernel corn, thawed and drained
3/4	cup shredded cheddar cheese (3 ounces)
1	cup shredded lettuce
	Dairy sour cream (optional)
	Chopped tomato (optional)

1 Place tortillas in a single layer on an ungreased extra large baking sheet. Brush top side of each tortilla with oil. Bake, uncovered, in 400°F oven for 5 minutes. Remove from oven.

2 Meanwhile, in a small bowl stir together beans and picante sauce or salsa. Spread bean mixture evenly over the tortillas. Top with sweet pepper strips and corn. Sprinkle with cheese.

3 Bake for 7 to 8 minutes more or until cheese is melted and filling is heated through. Top with lettuce and, if desired, sour cream and tomato.

Nutrition Facts per serving: 192 cal., 7 g total fat (3 g sat. fat), 15 mg chol., 365 mg sodium, 25 g carbo., 4 g fiber, 8 g pro.

TEST KITCHEN TIP: For lower-fat tostados, substitute reduced-fat cheddar cheese for the cheddar cheese and, if desired, light sour cream for the sour cream.

Nutrition Facts per serving: 168 cal., 6 g total fat (2 g sat. fat), 10 mg chol., 440 mg sodium, 22 g carbo., 4 g fiber, 8 g pro.

Meaty and deliciously earthy portobello mushrooms make an ideal base for salty feta cheese, pungent olives, and tangy dried tomatoes. If you like, you can remove the dark brown gills on the underside of the mushrooms by gently scraping them away with a small spoon.

FETA-STUFFED MUSHROOMS

4	fresh portobello mushrooms (5 to 6 ounces each)
1	tablespoon olive oil
1	4-ounce package crumbled feta cheese with garlic and herb or crumbled feta cheese
¼	cup chopped pitted ripe olives
2	tablespoons snipped oil-pack dried tomatoes

PREP:
20 minutes
BAKE:
10 minutes
MAKES:
16 appetizer servings

1 Remove and discard mushroom stems. Place mushroom caps, stemmed sides up, on a baking sheet. Brush with oil (if desired, use the oil from the tomatoes); set aside. In a small bowl stir together feta cheese, olives, and tomatoes. Divide mixture among the mushrooms.

2 Bake in a 425°F oven about 10 minutes or until heated through. To serve, cut each mushroom cap into 4 wedges.

Nutrition Facts per serving: 40 cal., 3 g total fat (1 g sat. fat), 6 mg chol., 102 mg sodium, 2 g carbo., 1 g fiber, 2 g pro.

Your guests will feel as though they've just arrived in Italy when they try these spectacular appetizers.

POLENTA & SALAMI SKEWERS

1	16-ounce tube refrigerated plain cooked polenta
2	tablespoons olive oil
1	teaspoon snipped fresh rosemary or sage or ½ teaspoon dried rosemary or sage, crushed
	Salt (optional)
1½	ounces thinly sliced Genoa salami or prosciutto, halved

START TO FINISH:
25 minutes
MAKES:
8 appetizer servings

1 Halve polenta lengthwise; cut each half lengthwise into quarters (you'll have a total of eight long wedge-shape pieces). Cut each wedge-shape piece crosswise into ½- to ¾-inch-long pieces. In a large nonstick skillet heat oil over medium-high heat. Add polenta and cook for 5 minutes, occasionally gently turning pieces with a pancake turner. Add rosemary. Cook for 7 to 10 minutes more or until browned and crisp, occasionally gently turning pieces with the turner. Transfer polenta pieces to a tray or platter lined with paper towels. If desired, sprinkle lightly with salt.

2 For skewers, fold the half slices of salami into quarters; place on skewers. Add a piece of polenta to the end of each skewer. (Or arrange polenta on a platter with salami.)

Nutrition Facts per serving: 100 cal., 5 g total fat (1 g sat. fat), 5 mg chol., 317 mg sodium, 11 g carbo., 2 g fiber, 2 g pro.

The creamy mild Brie cheese melts tantalizingly around the nuts and the pear mixture. Be warned though—these irresistible morsels may not make it out of the kitchen to the buffet table!

TOASTED MACADAMIA NUT PEAR SLICES

START TO FINISH:

25 minutes

MAKES:

24 appetizers

8 ounces sweet bread (such as Portuguese sweet bread, brioche, or Hawaiian king's bread)

2 tablespoons butter or margarine, melted

1 pear, peeled and finely chopped

1 tablespoon packed brown sugar

1 tablespoon lime juice

½ teaspoon ground cinnamon

¼ teaspoon ground allspice

3 ounces Brie cheese, cut into 24 pieces

⅓ cup finely chopped macadamia nuts

1 Cut bread into ½-inch slices. Trim crusts from bread slices. Brush both sides of each bread slice with melted butter. Cut bread into 2-inch squares. Place on a baking sheet. Bake in a 350°F oven about 10 minutes or until lightly toasted, turning once.

2 Meanwhile, in a small bowl combine pear, brown sugar, lime juice, cinnamon, and allspice.

3 Turn oven to broil. Top each bread square with a piece of cheese, a little of the pear mixture, and a few nuts; press lightly to secure nuts on top. Broil 4 to 5 inches from heat for 2 to 3 minutes or until cheese begins to melt and nuts are lightly toasted.

Nutrition Facts per appetizer: 70 cal., 4 g total fat (2 g sat. fat), 10 mg chol., 62 mg sodium, 7 g carbo., 1 g fiber, 2 g pro.

If you're lucky enough to have tiny red and yellow tomatoes growing in your garden, pick them when you pick the basil. No garden? Make a trip to your favorite supermarket or specialty food shop.

TOMATO, BASIL & MOZZARELLA CROSTINI

1	8-ounce loaf baguette-style French bread
2	to 3 tablespoons olive oil
$\frac{1}{8}$	teaspoon black pepper
4	ounces fresh mozzarella cheese, thinly sliced
12	red or yellow cherry tomatoes, halved
12	yellow or red pear-shaped tomatoes, halved
1	tablespoon snipped or shredded fresh basil
2	tablespoons olive oil
$\frac{1}{4}$	teaspoon salt

START TO FINISH:

20 minutes

MAKES:

16 appetizer servings

1 For crostini, cut French bread into $\frac{1}{2}$-inch slices. Lightly brush both sides of each bread slice with some of the 2 to 3 tablespoons oil; sprinkle with pepper. Place on a large baking sheet. Bake in a 425°F oven for 5 to 7 minutes or until crisp and light brown, turning once.

2 Top crostini with mozzarella slices, red and yellow tomato halves, and fresh basil. Drizzle with the 2 tablespoons oil; sprinkle with salt.

Nutrition Facts per serving: 95 cal., 5 g total fat (1 g sat. fat), 6 mg chol., 169 mg sodium, 9 g carbo., 1 g fiber, 3 g pro.

Oozing with cheese and studded with spinach, dried tomatoes, and nuts, these appetizer triangles are best served just out of the oven. Have sour cream on hand for dipping.

CHEESY SPINACH QUESADILLAS

PREP:

15 minutes

BAKE:

6 minutes

MAKES:

24 appetizers

½ of a 10-ounce package frozen chopped spinach, thawed and well drained

¼ cup purchased basil pesto

2 tablespoons seasoned fine dry bread crumbs

2 teaspoons snipped oil-pack dried tomatoes

1½ cups shredded Colby and Monterey Jack cheese or cheddar cheese (6 ounces)

⅓ cup finely chopped pine nuts or pecans, toasted

6 8-inch flour tortillas

1 In a small bowl stir together spinach, pesto, bread crumbs, and tomatoes. Stir in 1 cup of the cheese and half of the pine nuts or pecans.

2 Spread mixture evenly over 3 of the tortillas. Top with remaining tortillas. Place on an ungreased very large baking sheet. Sprinkle with remaining cheese and pine nuts. Bake in a 450°F oven for 6 to 8 minutes or until tortillas are lightly browned and crisp. Cut each into 8 wedges.

Nutrition Facts per appetizer: 78 cal., 5 g total fat (2 g sat. fat), 8 mg chol., 109 mg sodium, 5 g carbo., 0 g fiber, 3 g pro.

If you're a praline fan—and who isn't—you'll be swooning for this cheesy appetizer version of the sweet treat. In less than a half hour, you and your guests will be oohing and aahing in between delicious bites!

PRALINE-TOPPED BRIE

PREP:

10 minutes

BAKE:

15 minutes

MAKES:

10 to 12 appetizer servings

1 13- to 15-ounce round Brie or Camembert cheese

½ cup orange marmalade

2 tablespoons packed brown sugar

⅓ cup coarsely chopped pecans, toasted

Toasted baguette-style French bread slices and/or crackers

1 Place the round of cheese in a shallow ovenproof serving dish or pie plate. In a small bowl stir together orange marmalade and brown sugar. Spread on top of cheese. Sprinkle with toasted pecans.

2 Bake in a 350°F oven about 15 minutes for smaller round, about 20 minutes for larger round, or until cheese is slightly softened and topping is bubbly. Serve with bread slices and/or crackers.

Nutrition Facts per serving of cheese: 198 cal., 13 g total fat (7 g sat. fat), 37 mg chol., 242 mg sodium, 14 g carbo., 0 g fiber, 8 g pro.

Crabmeat is an absolute pantry must-have around the holidays or when you are planning to entertain. Sweet and succulent, the crab adds a touch of class to appetizers such as this.

HOT CRAB SPREAD

½	of an 8-ounce tub cream cheese with garden vegetables
1	6- to 6½-ounce can crabmeat, drained, flaked, and cartilage removed
1	green onion, sliced
1	teaspoon lemon juice
½	teaspoon dried dill
	Several dashes bottled hot pepper sauce
	Assorted crackers

START TO FINISH:
15 minutes
MAKES:
about 1 cup

1 In a small saucepan heat cream cheese over medium-low heat until softened, stirring occasionally. Stir in crabmeat, green onion, lemon juice, dill, and hot pepper sauce. Cook and stir for 3 to 4 minutes more or until heated through. Serve warm with crackers.

Nutrition Facts per 2 tablespoons spread: 72 cal., 5 g total fat (3 g sat. fat), 31 mg chol., 151 mg sodium, 1 g carbo., 0 g fiber, 5 g pro.

Blue cheese and walnuts are party favorites. Here the combo is used in a spread that takes just 10 minutes. You'll want to have this recipe in your "fast and festive" repertoire.

BLUE CHEESE WALNUT SPREAD

1	3-ounce package cream cheese, softened
2	ounces blue cheese, crumbled
¼	cup dairy sour cream
½	teaspoon Worcestershire sauce
¼	cup chopped walnuts, toasted
1	tablespoon snipped fresh chives
	Assorted crackers, apple slices, and/or pear slices

START TO FINISH:
10 minutes
MAKES:
1 cup

1 In a small bowl stir together cream cheese, blue cheese, sour cream, and Worcestershire sauce. Stir in toasted walnuts and chives. Serve with assorted crackers and/or fruit.

Nutrition Facts per 2 tablespoons spread: 100 cal., 9 g total fat (5 g sat. fat), 20 mg chol., 138 mg sodium, 1 g carbo., 0 g fiber, 3 g pro.

Get that fondue pot out of the closet and get dipping! Not only is fondue fun, the smoky chipotle peppers in this savory recipe make it unforgettable.

SMOKY CHIPOTLE FONDUE

START TO FINISH:

15 minutes

MAKES:

about 1 cup

8	ounces American cheese, cubed
2	tablespoons dry white wine
2	teaspoons Dijon-style mustard
½	teaspoon Worcestershire sauce
1	to 2 canned chipotle chile peppers in adobo sauce, chopped*
2	to 4 tablespoons milk
	Crusty French bread cubes or tortilla chips

1 In a heavy medium saucepan combine American cheese, white wine, mustard, Worcestershire sauce, and chipotle peppers. Cook and stir over medium-low heat until melted and smooth. Stir in enough of the milk to make desired consistency. Transfer to a small fondue pot; keep warm over a fondue burner. Serve fondue immediately with bread cubes or tortilla chips. If the fondue mixture thickens, stir in some additional milk.

*NOTE: Because chile peppers contain volatile oils that can burn your skin and eyes, avoid direct contact with them as much as possible. When working with chile peppers, wear plastic or rubber gloves. If your bare hands do touch the peppers, wash your hands and nails well with soap and warm water.

Nutrition Facts per 2 tablespoons fondue: 114 cal., 9 g total fat (6 g sat. fat), 27 mg chol., 427 mg sodium, 1 g carbo., 0 g fiber, 6 g pro.

Fruit salsa is the magic ingredient that adds a touch of sweetness to the rich cream cheese and roasted nuts. Could anything be simpler, yet so satisfying?

BAKED CHEESE

PREP:

5 minutes

BAKE:

20 minutes

MAKES:

16 appetizer servings

1	8-ounce package cream cheese
⅓	cup bottled fruit-flavor salsa (such as cherry, peach, or raspberry)
⅓	cup honey-roasted cashews, finely chopped
	Toasted pita wedges or assorted crackers
	Apple or pear slices

1 Place cream cheese in a 9-inch pie plate or au gratin dish. Spoon salsa over cheese. Sprinkle with cashews. Bake in a 350°F oven about 20 minutes or until cheese is softened and heated through. Serve warm with pita wedges or crackers and apple or pear slices.

Nutrition Facts per serving: 136 cal., 7 g total fat (3 g sat. fat), 16 mg chol., 136 mg sodium, 17 g carbo., 2 g fiber, 3 g pro.

This dip is a popular one at many restaurants. Now you can whip it up in your own kitchen whenever you like.

WARM ARTICHOKE & SALSA DIP

1	12-ounce jar or two 6-ounce jars marinated artichoke hearts
1/3	cup sliced green onions
2	tablespoons bottled green salsa
1/2	cup shredded Monterey Jack or white cheddar cheese (2 ounces)
1/4	cup dairy sour cream
1/4	cup snipped fresh cilantro
	Tortilla chips and/or assorted vegetable dippers

START TO FINISH:

15 minutes

MAKES:

1 1/2 cups

1 Drain artichokes; coarsely chop. In a small saucepan combine chopped artichokes, green onions, and salsa. Cook over medium heat until heated through, stirring frequently. Remove from heat. Stir in cheese, sour cream, and cilantro. Serve immediately with chips and/or vegetables.

Nutrition Facts per 1/4 cup dip: 144 cal., 13 g total fat (5 g sat. fat), 12 mg chol., 256 mg sodium, 5 g carbo., 0 g fiber, 3 g pro.

Kids will love this—especially when it's made just for them. Serve this smooth-as-silk peanut butter and honey dip with crunchy jicama sticks, carrots, apples, and pears.

PEANUT BUTTER DIP

1/2	of an 8-ounce package cream cheese, softened
1/2	cup creamy peanut butter
2	to 3 tablespoons milk
2	teaspoons honey
	Assorted dippers (such as celery sticks, peeled jicama sticks, carrot sticks, apple wedges, pear wedges, and/or graham cracker sticks)

START TO FINISH:

10 minutes

MAKES:

1 1/4 cups

1 For dip, in a small bowl beat cream cheese with an electric mixer on medium speed until smooth. Beat in peanut butter, milk, and honey until smooth. Serve with assorted dippers.

Nutrition Facts per 2 tablespoons dip: 122 cal., 11 g total fat (4 g sat. fat), 13 mg chol., 99 mg sodium, 4 g carbo., 1 g fiber, 4 g pro.

It used to be that the best time to make salsa was in the summer when fresh herbs are more readily available and produce is at its peak. But today you can find wonderful fresh herbs and delicious produce year-round, so it's easy to enjoy this sensational Greek-style salsa even on the coldest of winter days!

MEDITERRANEAN SALSA

START TO FINISH:

25 minutes

MAKES:

about 5 cups

2   2¼-ounce cans sliced pitted ripe olives, drained

2   medium cucumbers, peeled, seeded, and chopped (about 2 cups)

2   medium tomatoes, seeded and chopped (about 1 cup)

1   small red onion, chopped

½   cup snipped fresh basil

1   teaspoon snipped fresh oregano

1   teaspoon bottled minced garlic (2 cloves)

2   tablespoons olive oil

2   tablespoons balsamic vinegar

⅛   teaspoon black pepper

4   ounces feta cheese, crumbled (1 cup)

Toasted baguette-style French bread slices and/or pita bread wedges* or tortilla chips

1 In a medium bowl combine olives, cucumbers, tomatoes, red onion, basil, oregano, and garlic.

2 In a screw-top jar combine oil, balsamic vinegar, and pepper. Cover and shake well. Pour oil mixture over vegetable mixture; toss gently to combine. Transfer to a serving dish; sprinkle with feta cheese. Serve with toasted baguette slices.

*NOTE: To toast French bread slices, place slices on a baking sheet and toast in a 350°F oven for 10 to 15 minutes or until crisp and lightly golden brown. For pita wedges, cut each pita round in half horizontally so you have two rounds. Then cut each round into wedges. Toast as for the bread slices.

Nutrition Facts per 2 tablespoons salsa: 21 cal., 2 g total fat (1 g sat. fat), 2 mg chol., 60 mg sodium, 1 g carbo., 0 g fiber, 1 g pro.

A food processor makes quick work of this rich avocado-laced version of ever-popular spinach dip.

AVOCADO CHEESE DIP

1	large very ripe avocado, halved, pitted, peeled, and cut up
½	of a 10-ounce package frozen chopped spinach, thawed and well drained
¼	cup cottage cheese
2	teaspoons lemon juice
½	teaspoon bottled minced garlic (1 clove)
2	green onions, finely chopped
	Tortilla chips, assorted crackers, and/or assorted vegetable dippers

START TO FINISH:
15 minutes
MAKES:
about 1⅓ cups

1 In a food processor combine avocado, spinach, cottage cheese, lemon juice, garlic, ½ teaspoon *salt,* and ⅛ teaspoon *black pepper.* Cover and process until mixture is nearly smooth, scraping side as necessary. Stir in green onions. Serve with tortilla chips, crackers, and/or vegetable dippers.

Nutrition Facts per 2 tablespoons dip: 39 cal., 3 g total fat (1 g sat. fat), 1 mg chol., 159 mg sodium, 2 g carbo., 2 g fiber, 1 g pro.

Green chile peppers and picante sauce add a pleasant kick to this dip. If desired, transfer the mixture to a 3½- to 4-quart slow cooker; keep warm on the low-heat setting.

FAVORITE CHEESE DIP

1	large onion, chopped
2	tablespoons butter or margarine
1	10½-ounce can chili without beans
1	10-ounce can chopped tomatoes and green chile peppers
1	4-ounce can diced green chile peppers, undrained
¼	cup bottled picante sauce
½	teaspoon cumin seeds or ⅛ teaspoon ground cumin
1	pound process cheese spread, shredded
3	cups shredded cheddar cheese (12 ounces)
	Tortilla chips or large corn chips

START TO FINISH:
30 minutes
MAKES:
7 cups

1 In a large saucepan cook onion in butter about 5 minutes or until tender. Stir in chili, undrained tomatoes and green chile peppers, undrained chile peppers, picante sauce, and cumin. Add cheeses. Stir over medium-low heat until cheeses are melted. Serve with tortilla chips.

Nutrition Facts per ¼ cup dip: 124 cal., 9 g total fat (6 g sat. fat), 26 mg chol., 453 mg sodium, 3 g carbo., 1 g fiber, 7 g pro.

You can't have a party or get-together without serving a good salsa! This quick-to-fix version can be made up to 24 hours ahead.

EASY JALAPEÑO SALSA

START TO FINISH:

10 minutes

MAKES:

about 1 1/2 cups

1/4 cup coarsely chopped onion

1 to 2 fresh jalapeño chile peppers, seeded and coarsely chopped*

1/4 cup snipped fresh cilantro

1 14 1/2-ounce can Italian-style stewed tomatoes, drained

Tortilla chips

1 In a blender or food processor combine onion, jalapeño peppers, and cilantro. Cover and blend or process for 2 to 3 pulses. Add drained tomatoes and 1/4 teaspoon *salt*. Cover and blend or process for 1 to 2 pulses more or until salsa reaches desired consistency. Serve with tortilla chips.

***NOTE:** Because chile peppers contain volatile oils that can burn your skin and eyes, avoid direct contact with them as much as possible. When working with chile peppers, wear plastic or rubber gloves. If your bare hands do touch the peppers, wash your hands and nails well with soap and warm water.*

Nutrition Facts per 1/4 cup salsa: 24 cal., 0 g total fat (0 g sat. fat), 0 mg chol., 229 mg sodium, 5 g carbo., 1 g fiber, 1 g pro.

Garam masala—a traditional Indian mix of cumin, cardamom, cinnamon, and other spices— is available in many supermarket spice sections and at specialty food stores. Be sure to keep a close eye on the nuts when roasting them as they tend to burn easily.

GINGER CASHEWS

PREP:

10 minutes

ROAST:

20 minutes

MAKES:

2 cups

2 cups lightly salted cashews

1 tablespoon butter or margarine, melted

1 tablespoon minced or grated fresh ginger

2 teaspoons garam masala

1 Line a shallow baking pan with foil. In a bowl combine cashews, melted butter, ginger, and garam masala. Spread nuts in prepared baking pan. Roast nuts in a 300°F oven about 20 minutes or until golden brown and very fragrant, stirring occasionally. Serve warm or at room temperature.

MAKE-AHEAD DIRECTIONS: Prepare as directed. Store nuts in an airtight container at room temperature for 24 hours or in the refrigerator for 2 days. To rewarm nuts, bake in a 300°F oven about 5 minutes.

Nutrition Facts per 2 tablespoons nuts: 114 cal., 10 g total fat (2 g sat. fat), 2 mg chol., 42 mg sodium, 5 g carbo., 1 g fiber, 4 g pro.

Hot and crunchy—it's no wonder these spice-coated nuts disappear so quickly. Make a batch, mix some martinis, and kick back to the sounds of some cool jazz.

CAJUN PEANUTS

1	egg white
4	teaspoons salt-free Cajun seasoning
⅛	teaspoon cayenne pepper
2¼	cups honey-roasted peanuts (12 ounces)

1 Line a 15×10×1-inch baking pan with foil; grease foil. Set aside.

2 In a medium bowl beat egg white until frothy. Stir in Cajun seasoning and cayenne pepper. Add peanuts; toss to coat. Spread peanuts in a single layer on prepared baking pan.

3 Bake in a 350°F oven for 12 minutes, stirring once halfway through baking. Cool completely. Break up any large clusters of nuts.

Nutrition Facts per ¼ cup peanuts: 182 cal., 16 g total fat (3 g sat. fat), 0 mg chol., 142 mg sodium, 8 g carbo., 1 g fiber, 7 g pro.

PREP:
10 minutes
BAKE:
12 minutes
MAKES:
2¼ cups

Select the heat level you and your guests prefer by choosing regular or hot taco seasoning mix. Or make two batches—one regular and one with a little more heat. Be sure to label them to avoid any fiery surprises!

SOUTHWEST SNACK MIX

8	cups popped popcorn
	Nonstick cooking spray
1	tablespoon taco seasoning mix
2	cups peanuts
1½	cups corn chips
1	cup golden raisins
¾	to 1 cup toasted pumpkin seeds

1 Remove uncooked kernels from popped corn. Place popped corn in a very large bowl; lightly coat popcorn with cooking spray. Sprinkle popcorn with taco seasoning mix; stir lightly to coat. Stir in peanuts, corn chips, raisins, and pumpkin seeds.

Nutrition Facts per serving: 270 cal., 17 g total fat (3 g sat. fat), 0 mg chol., 187 mg sodium, 23 g carbo., 4 g fiber, 10 g pro.

START TO FINISH:
15 minutes
MAKES:
12 snack servings

A triple dose of fruit—pineapple juice, peach slices, and melon cubes—blends into a colorful slush that gets pizzazz from sparkling water. Make small cocktail skewers of fresh fruit to accompany this festive nonalcoholic beverage.

FIZZY FRUIT SLUSH

START TO FINISH:

20 minutes

MAKES:

12 (about 6-ounce) servings

1   12-ounce can frozen pineapple juice concentrate, thawed

1   15-ounce can peach slices (juice pack), chilled and drained

4   cups cubed, seeded watermelon or sliced fresh strawberries

1   1-liter bottle sparkling water with strawberry or peach flavor
      Crushed ice

1 In a blender or food processor combine pineapple juice concentrate, drained peaches, and watermelon or strawberries. Cover and blend or process until smooth. If using strawberries, you may want to strain the mixture through a fine-mesh sieve to remove seeds. Transfer fruit mixture to a large pitcher. Slowly stir sparkling water into fruit mixture. Serve immediately over crushed ice.

Nutrition Facts per serving: 98 cal., 0 g total fat (0 g sat. fat), 0 mg chol., 11 mg sodium, 24 g carbo., 1 g fiber, 1 g pro.

Your guests will be singing the songs of the islands after they sip this sweet and bubbly concoction. Serve the sipper in tiki glasses—if you can get your hands on a set. If there are small children at the party, bright and colorful plastic cups are just as much fun and safer, especially if they're around a pool or outside on a patio. Don't forget to garnish each glass with a paper umbrella.

HAWAIIAN LEMONADE

START TO FINISH:

15 minutes

MAKES:

6 (8-ounce) servings

$\frac{1}{2}$ of a 12-ounce can ($\frac{3}{4}$ cup) frozen lemonade concentrate, thawed

$\frac{3}{4}$ cup water

1   12-ounce can (1$\frac{1}{2}$ cups) apricot nectar, chilled

1   12-ounce can (1$\frac{1}{2}$ cups) unsweetened pineapple juice, chilled

2   cups ice cubes

1$\frac{1}{4}$ cups ginger ale, chilled

1 In a large punch bowl combine lemonade concentrate and the water; add apricot nectar, pineapple juice, and ice cubes. Slowly pour ginger ale down side of bowl; stir gently to mix.

Nutrition Facts per serving: 139 cal., 0 g total fat (0 g sat. fat), 0 mg chol., 8 mg sodium, 35 g carbo., 1 g fiber, 1 g pro.

Eggnog is available once a year, so make it extra special by transforming it into this heavenly punch.

EASY EGGNOG PUNCH

1	quart dairy eggnog, chilled
½	cup nondairy liquid hazelnut-flavored coffee creamer, chilled
2	tablespoons brandy or rum
	Grated fresh nutmeg

1 In a punch bowl combine eggnog, coffee creamer, and brandy or rum. Sprinkle with grated fresh nutmeg.

Nutrition Facts per serving: 274 cal., 13 g total fat (8 g sat. fat), 100 mg chol., 91 mg sodium, 30 g carbo., 0 g fiber, 6 g pro.

START TO FINISH:
10 minutes
MAKES:
about 6 (6-ounce) servings

This pretty punch is a lovely and refreshing alternative to traditional, rich holiday drinks. Offer it alongside eggnog so that your guests can choose the libation they prefer. When warmer weather rolls around, keep it in mind as it is equally delicious for summer get-togethers.

HOLIDAY PUNCH

1	12-ounce can frozen lemonade concentrate
1	10-ounce package frozen strawberries in syrup
1	8-ounce can crushed pineapple, undrained
3	1-liter bottles ginger ale, chilled
1	cup rum or vodka (optional)
	Ice ring (optional)

1 In a blender combine frozen lemonade concentrate, frozen strawberries with their syrup, and undrained pineapple. Cover and blend until smooth.

2 Pour strawberry mixture into a large punch bowl. Slowly pour ginger ale down side of bowl. If desired, stir in rum or vodka. If desired, add ice ring.

Nutrition Facts per serving: 68 cal., 0 g total fat (0 g sat. fat), 0 mg chol., 8 mg sodium, 17 g carbo., 0 g fiber, 0 g pro.

START TO FINISH:
10 minutes
MAKES:
about 30 (4-ounce) servings

Show off this colorful fruit-and-wine punch in a decorative clear glass pitcher. If you like, offer some fresh fruit, such as green grapes and pineapple chunks, alongside the punch for guests to add to their glasses.

PUNCHY SANGRIA

START TO FINISH:

15 minutes

MAKES:

about 10 (6-ounce) servings

4½ cups rose wine, chilled
1 12-ounce can frozen pink lemonade concentrate, thawed
⅓ cup lime juice
2 cups club soda, chilled
1 lemon, thinly sliced
1 orange, thinly sliced
   Ice cubes

1 In a very large pitcher stir together wine, lemonade concentrate, and lime juice. Slowly stir in the club soda. Add lemon and orange slices. Serve over ice.

Nutrition Facts per serving: 147 cal., 0 g total fat (0 g sat. fat), 0 mg chol., 17 mg sodium, 21 g carbo., 1 g fiber, 1 g pro.

Heating the cranberry juice with a combination of ginger, cardamom, black pepper, vanilla, and honey adds exquisite flavor. It also will fill your home with a tantalizing aroma that heralds the holidays!

MULLED CRANBERRY DRINK

START TO FINISH:

20 minutes

MAKES:

8 to 10 (4- to 5-ounce) servings

5 cups cranberry juice
1½ cups fresh cranberries
¼ cup chopped crystallized ginger
1 teaspoon cardamom pods
½ teaspoon whole black peppercorns, cracked
1 vanilla bean, split
⅓ cup honey

1 In a large saucepan stir together cranberry juice, cranberries, crystallized ginger, cardamom, cracked peppercorns, and vanilla bean. Stir in honey. Heat over medium heat until mixture boils and cranberry skins pop. Remove from heat. Cover and let stand for 5 minutes. Strain and discard solids. Serve warm.

TEST KITCHEN TIP: Cover and chill any leftovers. Reheat or, if desired, serve over ice.

Nutrition Facts per serving: 156 cal., 0 g total fat (0 g sat. fat), 0 mg chol., 5 mg sodium, 40 g carbo., 1 g fiber, 0 g pro.

Mulling spice mix transforms ordinary ingredients into an extraordinary beverage.

HOT GINGERED CIDER

2   cups ginger ale

2   cups apple cider or apple juice

1   tablespoon lemon juice

2   tablespoons mulling spices*

1   1-inch piece fresh ginger, sliced

1 In a medium saucepan combine ginger ale, apple cider, lemon juice, mulling spices, and fresh ginger. Cover and cook over medium-low heat for 5 to 10 minutes or until heated through (do not boil). Strain and discard the spices.

2 To serve, ladle mixture into heatproof glass mugs or cups.

***NOTE:** If purchased mulling spices are unavailable, use a mixture of 1 cinnamon stick, broken, and 1 tablespoon whole cloves.*

Nutrition Facts per serving: 101 cal., 0 g total fat (0 g sat. fat), 0 mg chol., 12 mg sodium, 26 g carbo., 0 g fiber, 0 g pro.

START TO FINISH:

15 minutes

MAKES:

4 (8-ounce) servings

By stirring in some caramel ice cream topping, this hot chocolate goes from tasty to tantalizing.

CARAMEL HOT CHOCOLATE

½   cup sugar

½   cup unsweetened cocoa powder

7   cups milk

½   cup caramel ice cream topping

1   teaspoon vanilla

     Marshmallows (optional)

1 In a large saucepan or Dutch oven stir together sugar and cocoa powder. Stir in ½ cup of the milk until a smooth paste is formed. Stir in remaining 6½ cups milk and the ice cream topping. Cook and stir over medium heat just until heated through (do not boil). Remove from heat; stir in vanilla. If desired, top individual servings with marshmallows.

Nutrition Facts per serving: 237 cal., 5 g total fat (3 g sat. fat), 16 mg chol., 152 mg sodium, 39 g carbo., 0 g fiber, 9 g pro.

START TO FINISH:

25 minutes

MAKES:

about 8 (8-ounce) servings

INDEX

Q – S

METRIC INFORMATION

The charts on this page provide a guide for converting measurements from the U.S. customary system, which is used throughout this book, to the metric system.

Product Differences

Most of the ingredients called for in the recipes in this book are available in most countries. However, some are known by different names. Here are some common American ingredients and their possible counterparts:

- **All-purpose flour** is enriched, bleached, or unbleached white household flour. When self-rising flour is used in place of all-purpose flour in a recipe that calls for leavening, omit the leavening agent (baking soda or baking powder) and salt.
- **Baking soda** is bicarbonate of soda.
- **Cornstarch** is cornflour.
- **Golden raisins** are sultanas.
- **Green, red, or yellow sweet peppers** are capsicums or bell peppers.
- **Light-colored corn syrup** is golden syrup.
- **Powdered sugar** is icing sugar.
- **Sugar** (white) is granulated, fine granulated, or castor sugar.
- **Vanilla** or vanilla extract is vanilla essence.

Volume and Weight

The United States traditionally uses cup measures for liquid and solid ingredients. The chart below shows the approximate imperial and metric equivalents. If you are accustomed to weighing solid ingredients, the following approximate equivalents will be helpful.

- 1 cup butter, castor sugar, or rice = 8 ounces = $\frac{1}{2}$ pound = 250 grams
- 1 cup flour = 4 ounces = $\frac{1}{4}$ pound = 125 grams
- 1 cup icing sugar = 5 ounces = 150 grams

Canadian and U.S. volume for a cup measure is 8 fluid ounces (237 ml), but the standard metric equivalent is 250 ml.

1 British imperial cup is 10 fluid ounces.

In Australia, 1 tablespoon equals 20 ml, and there are 4 teaspoons in the Australian tablespoon.

Spoon measures are used for smaller amounts of ingredients. Although the size of the tablespoon varies slightly in different countries, for practical purposes and for recipes in this book, a straight substitution is all that's necessary. Measurements made using cups or spoons always should be level unless stated otherwise.

Common Weight Range Replacements

Imperial / U.S.	Metric
$\frac{1}{2}$ ounce	15 g
1 ounce	25 g or 30 g
4 ounces ($\frac{1}{4}$ pound)	115 g or 125 g
8 ounces ($\frac{1}{2}$ pound)	225 g or 250 g
16 ounces (1 pound)	450 g or 500 g
$1\frac{1}{4}$ pounds	625 g
$1\frac{1}{2}$ pounds	750 g
2 pounds or $2\frac{1}{4}$ pounds	1,000 g or 1 Kg

Oven Temperature Equivalents

Fahrenheit Setting	Celsius Setting*	Gas Setting
300°F	150°C	Gas Mark 2 (very low)
325°F	160°C	Gas Mark 3 (low)
350°F	180°C	Gas Mark 4 (moderate)
375°F	190°C	Gas Mark 5 (moderate)
400°F	200°C	Gas Mark 6 (hot)
425°F	220°C	Gas Mark 7 (hot)
450°F	230°C	Gas Mark 8 (very hot)
475°F	240°C	Gas Mark 9 (very hot)
500°F	260°C	Gas Mark 10 (extremely hot)
Broil	Broil	Grill

*Electric and gas ovens may be calibrated using celsius. However, for an electric oven, increase celsius setting 10 to 20 degrees when cooking above 160°C. For convection or forced air ovens (gas or electric), lower the temperature setting 25°F/10°C when cooking at all heat levels.

Baking Pan Sizes

Imperial / U.S.	Metric
9×1½-inch round cake pan	22- or 23×4-cm (1.5 L)
9×1½-inch pie plate	22- or 23×4-cm (1 L)
8×8×2-inch square cake pan	20×5-cm (2 L)
9×9×2-inch square cake pan	22- or 23×4.5-cm (2.5 L)
11×7×1½-inch baking pan	28×17×4-cm (2 L)
2-quart rectangular baking pan	30×19×4.5-cm (3 L)
13×9×2-inch baking pan	34×22×4.5-cm (3.5 L)
15×10×1-inch jelly roll pan	40×25×2-cm
9×5×3-inch loaf pan	23×13×8-cm (2 L)
2-quart casserole	2 L

U.S. / Standard Metric Equivalents

$\frac{1}{8}$ teaspoon = 0.5 ml	
$\frac{1}{4}$ teaspoon = 1 ml	
$\frac{1}{2}$ teaspoon = 2 ml	
1 teaspoon = 5 ml	
1 tablespoon = 15 ml	
2 tablespoons = 25 ml	
$\frac{1}{4}$ cup = 2 fluid ounces = 50 ml	
$\frac{1}{3}$ cup = 3 fluid ounces = 75 ml	
$\frac{1}{2}$ cup = 4 fluid ounces = 125 ml	
$\frac{2}{3}$ cup = 5 fluid ounces = 150 ml	
$\frac{3}{4}$ cup = 6 fluid ounces = 175 ml	
1 cup = 8 fluid ounces = 250 ml	
2 cups = 1 pint = 500 ml	
1 quart = 1 litre	

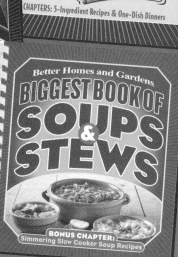

Better Homes and Gardens®
No-hassle meals for when you have to hustle!

Speed up meal prep and cook time—and add some ease to your already hectic day. This jumbo assortment of recipes includes the makings for three-course meals—main dish, side dish, and dessert—that are tableside in just 30 minutes! Imagine feasting on dinners like Quick Italian Pepper Steak and Cannoli with Garlic Cheese Bread. Revel in tasty side dishes such as Cheesy Apple Coleslaw and scrumptious Pumpkin-Raisin Scones. And leave room for dessert creations like luscious Banana Tostadas and creamy Rocky Road Malts.

✔ **The ultimate collection—more than 450 ready-in-a-flash recipes**

✔ Menus with every entrée for amazing 30-minute meals

✔ **Bonus section with more than 30 easy-does-it party food recipes**

✔ Savvy pantry-stocking tips to guarantee on-the-go cooking success

✔ **Time-saving hints to slice prep time in the kitchen**

Look for these titles in the *Biggest Book* series by Better Homes and Gardens®

Test Kitchen

Our seal guarantees that every recipe has been tested by our experts in the Better Homes and Gardens® Test Kitchen.

ISBN 978-0-696-22438-6

9 780696 224386   90000

$19.95
$21.95 in Canada
Visit us at bhgbooks.com